# Corporate Debt Restructuring in Emerging Markets

"What Richard and Tim have woven together is an enlightening and compelling read—using case studies to uniquely demonstrate the complex and challenging melting pot of personalities, situations and role players and then linking this with a structured navigation of phases and principles of restructuring."

—Stefan U. Smyth, *Partner/Principal, EYP-Turnaround & Restructuring Strategy, Ernst & Young Advisory Services (Pty) Ltd*

"With this book, Richard and Tim have managed to present a detailed look at how corporate debt restructuring really works by weaving together narratives that bring real deal stories to life by placing the reader inside the negotiation rooms. This practical approach gives the reader a better grasp of the competing perspectives, clashing personalities and legal and financial constraints across the main phases of a restructuring, with valuable insights. on how to overcome them. This book is a great read and an important contribution to the ongoing debate towards addressing the rising credit default risks in emerging markets, in a post-pandemic world."

—Wale Shonibare, *Director, Energy Financial Solutions, Policy & Regulations, Power, Energy, Climate & Green Growth Complex, African Development Bank (AfDB)*

"Richard and Tim's book focuses on principles first and provides a holistic view of tackling distressed situations. Furthermore, it discusses psychological, emotional and other 'soft' aspects and stakeholder dynamics—that are perhaps more important at the outset of a case than any technical details. It also usefully touches upon adapting common restructuring principles and approaches to countries with underdeveloped legal regimes and workout culture. Lastly, the book is very well written, talking about serious subjects in a light and entertaining manner, which makes it a useful and exciting reading to anyone who is planning to step into dealing with corporate stress and distress."

—Alexander Erofeev, *Chief Special Operations Officer, International Finance Corporation (IFC)*

"Richard and Tim center this book around their decades-long experience that restructuring negotiations can be as much about the personal and institutional context of the actors as the financial fundamentals of the case. Past mistakes are a burden for the present. Negotiating positions and decisions are not always rational. Emotions can play a central role. The book highlights the need to understand these factors and manage the process and the people accordingly."

—Martin Heimes, *Co-Head Financial Institutions Debt, responsAbility Investments AG*

Richard Marney · Timothy Stubbs

# Corporate Debt Restructuring in Emerging Markets

A Practical Post-Pandemic Guide

Richard Marney
Kuala Lumpur, Malaysia

Timothy Stubbs
Dentons Europe AO
Dentons
Moscow, Russia

ISBN 978-3-030-81305-5     ISBN 978-3-030-81306-2   (eBook)
https://doi.org/10.1007/978-3-030-81306-2

This Palgrave Macmillan imprint is published by the registered company Springer Nature Switzerland AG
The registered company address is: Gewerbestrasse 11, 6330 Cham, Switzerland

*To our families*

# Foreword

In the non-performing loan restructuring arena, if you were to ask a question to anyone involved—bankers, lawyers, company owners/entrepreneurs, consultants to name a few—on how they managed a successful restructuring, they will have a story to tell. Most of the time the story will be long, windy and "how the other side never understood." Perhaps if also comes with a happy ending (although not guaranteed…). The issues at hand when restructuring over-indebted companies are highly complex, sometimes painful as parties seek to ascertain and apportion losses in most cases, humanly difficult as egos collide, and legally complicated as the old balance sheet situation gives rise to a new challenge. Hence, when approached by the authors to consult their ideas and review their manuscript, I had uncertain expectations of how effectively a book would be able to cover such a wide array of topics and remain relevant.

The book now in the readers' hands, in my opinion as a directly involved party in this sector with 25 years of experience, does this with aplomb. It has managed just the right balance of detail without sounding boring, it interweaves theory and practice, it invites the reader to interact as well as reflect on the book's information and compare with their own experiences. All the key issues a loan restructuring officer in cross-border lending will face while seeking to preserve value and return an enterprise to health are covered in sufficient detail. This "mental" map created by the very experienced authors, Richard and Tim, does not force the issue but steadily draws the reader in by combining reality and fables to make their point.

The book's timing is also very important. The COVID 19 pandemic is wreaking havoc across the world's economies, with many companies unable to repay their debts. As we face a return to the new normal, there will be a serious need for well-executed restructurings which should return companies to health, allow them to continue to provide much needed employment and banks to amortize losses and continue to provide essential new capital to the economy to keep going. In such conditions, this book represents a useful toolkit for practitioners, a training guide for new participants in the sector and a good platform for even the more experienced participants in this sector to refresh and consolidate ideas.

In my day-to-day work, I have come to know the value of having well-informed counterparties, which is a cornerstone to a(ny) good solution. Perhaps in time, this book will become the standard by which other restructuring books are judged. Let's get to work.

Ilir Fani
Director—Corporate Recovery
European Bank for Reconstruction and Development[1]
London, UK

---

[1] The views expressed in this Foreword are those of Mr. Fani individually and do not necessarily represent the views of any entity with which he has been, is now, or will be affiliated, including the European Bank for Reconstruction and Development.

# Preface

*A smooth sea never made a skilled mariner*
*Anonymous*

This book was inspired by the first-time experience of teaching a course on corporate debt restructuring.

One of the authors greeted the class equipped with a syllabus heavy on theory, term sheets, and models; overall, a rigorous, technical approach to the topic. Two long days later, much of the thick course binder sat untouched. The class had waved off the slides, legal templates, and spread sheets, and instead asked to hear "war stories," as one participant described it. In the narratives of real-life deal stories that followed, the focus was predominantly on the context, the people, and the process—how the parties overcame conflicting objectives, clashing personalities, and financial and legal constraints to achieve the "least bad possible outcome."

As the course drew to a close, requests came for a summary of all the "stories." Little interest was shown in the corporate finance, credit analysis, and legal slides. As one student related, "I have dozens of books on these topics. I don't even need more business-school style case studies. What I would really like is a book of "lessons learned" from your decades in the industry. You know, like a mariner's rudder or a compass, so to speak."

The aim of this book is to provide such a set of "navigational aids" to present and future professionals involved in restructurings, whether as borrowers, lenders, lawyers, or other advisors. To achieve this aim, our book is part story, part textbook. Like a building with a steel frame, the book employs a set of *multiple narratives* (based on real-life professional experiences, albeit changed to "protect the innocent"[1]) as the central framework. Around these narratives we have constructed figures, technical analyses, and term sheets of the transactions—much as the glass and granite coverings encase an edifice.

We focus on cross-border, multi-creditor consensual restructurings (aka—workouts) of debt in the *private* (non-sovereign) sector of *emerging markets*, including debts of both *financial institution (FI)* borrowers and *corporate* borrowers. By emerging markets, we mean economies well on the path toward developed market status, as well as other less developed markets. The term is thus used broadly and not intended to follow any particular published institutional or academic list.[2]

Most importantly, we wish to convey the *actual practice and real world* of multi-creditor consensual restructuring transactions in emerging markets.[3]

We urge our readers to pay close attention to these narratives and to use them as educational tools for asking questions and applying the substantive and practical lessons we discuss in the more technical portions of the book (Parts II–V).

Our main opening narrative in Part I of the book charts the path of the Bank of Commerce and its cast of characters. Here, we present the story of a troubled bank in an export-dependent emerging market. Its US-based majority shareholder has benefited from it as a source of cash for pay-outs to investors and part of a greater, overly ambitious acquisition strategy in other markets. As the bank's local economy witnesses major commodity and currency shocks, we observe how individual representatives of the bank, its shareholders, and lenders respond. The interplay of personalities and the transaction process rests at the center of the action. The narrative is supplemented in Annex 3 with the financial statements, the pre-restructuring credit

---

[1] Each narrative is a kind of mosaic, where the multiple stones—the facts, situations and people—have been "mined" from the many transactions on which the authors have worked during their decades-long careers. Diverse pieces have been combined into a fictional depiction of the events and players involved in restructuring cases, designed to stress key challenges and lessons learned. No resemblance to actual persons, living or dead, or actual events, is intended.

[2] In researching this book, the authors have surveyed the insolvency and judicial systems of 46 jurisdictions. The results of such survey are reflected in the main text of the book as well as Annex 1. As highlighted throughout our discussion, countries identified as emerging markets *vary greatly* in terms of the extent of development of their financial markets, their observance of the rule of law and their legal systems (in particular their judicial and insolvency systems). We will try to avoid making sweeping generalizations but instead point out trends shared and differences identified in this broad group of countries.

[3] In this respect, we stress that our aim is not to teach readers how to profit on buying distressed debt or turning around failing businesses. Rather, we wish to assist current providers of debt and equity to preserve their investments (or "pick up the pieces") in a manner most consistent with their original objectives.

analysis, and a financial evaluation of the workout transaction. This Annex is optional, but it does provide technical details for the interested reader.

We present this narrative at the outset, as an opportunity for the reader to digest it on its face, before we move on to the more process-oriented chapters (which also include further narratives). How does the reader interpret what has happened? And will the reader view these events with a different lens, as we progress in laying out the methodology for understanding and approaching a restructuring? Throughout the opening narrative as a reading aid, we include footnotes, which highlight key questions and concepts.

Following the opening narrative, we move to Part II, where we present the *main phases and principles of a restructuring*. These are, namely:

(1) the pre-restructuring phase,
(2) the decision-making phase,
(3) the case set-up phase,
(4) the structuring and negotiation phase, and finally
(5) the implementation phase.

In Part II, we describe the main objectives and activities of each of the five phases. In each, we refer back to the action of the Bank of Commerce narrative to provide real-life context, and to identify and explain key learnings. We reinforce the lessons learned by introducing two further (albeit briefer) narratives: a second financial institution—Industrial Bank; and a manufacturing company—National Goods. These cases differ from the Bank of Commerce. They focus less on personalities (as in the Bank of Commerce), and more on process elements. In each, we compare and contrast differing institutional approaches to the same set of facts and challenges, classified (using the borrowed expression) as the "Good, the Bad and the Ugly."[4] The individual sections of these latter two narratives are interspersed to appear in the relevant chapters of Part II, to facilitate the reading.

The reader also has the option to test themselves by jumping to Annex 4, where we present a case study for a telecommunications company, Country Telecom (including suggested model answers).

We then supplement the discussion of these five main phases by addressing in Part III a key issue which often triggers the need to restructure (and indeed can bear heavily on the course chosen): an *Act of God* or other exogenous event. At the time of publication of this book, the global COVID 19 pandemic of 2020–2021 weighed heavily on the minds of many borrowers

---

[4] https://en.wikipedia.org/wiki/The_Good,_the_Bad_and_the_Ugly.

and lenders. How does lender leadership approach restructuring debt, in an atmosphere of uncertainty and unpredictability?

Together, the opening narrative of Bank of Commerce in Chapter 1 and the subsequent Chapters 2–9 (Parts I–III) form the core of this book.

Understanding that many readers will wish to delve into even greater detail on key technical issues bearing on emerging market workouts, we have added two final Chapters on these: the *macroeconomics and credit* issues on the one hand (in Chapter 10), and the *legal issues* on the other hand (in Chapter 11), in our so-called Reference Toolkit Part IV.

Having focused heavily on narratives, our intention is to allow the reader to "step into the shoes" of our various characters as they navigate the ups and downs of their respective transactions. The hope is not just to allow the reader to understand why characters act the way they do, but also to encourage critical, almost counter-factual thinking about *what the characters might have done differently* in each case. From this approach, readers should add their own insights to the lessons learned by the authors. Taken together, the readers should thus be able to create their own deal compasses for their future restructurings.

Penang, Malaysia                                          Richard Marney
Moscow, Russia                                           Timothy Stubbs

# Acknowledgments

The authors would like to thank many people who took time to read and comment on the various drafts of the book. In particular, we are grateful to Roman Borisovich, Lynn Exton, Ilir Fani, Johannes Feist, Martin Heimes, Stuart Lawson, and Josue Tanaka, all of whose honest and constructive criticism proved invaluable. We also thank the various practitioners for their input on legal, corporate finance, and macroeconomic issues, such as Mahmoud Abdel-Baky, Nafysa Adam Abdalla, Sam J. Alberts, Nadia Arriaga, Fernando Aued, Zain Azrin Zain Azahari, Priscilla Balgobin, Manuel Barrios, Roberto P. Bauzá, Jaroslaw Beldowski, Anna Booth, Keith Brandt, Catherine Bridge Zoller, Shalini R. Campbell, Maximo Capón, Bernardo Cardenas, Rocío Córdova, Tiberiu Csaki, Matthew Cumberpatch, Simon Dayes, Alexander Erofeev, Maw Shen Foo, Kurt Gerstner, Neil Griffiths, Alejandra Guevara, Kirith Haria, Lynn P. Harrison III, Roy de Jesus Herrera, Vanessa Jacklin-Levin, Joseph Alexander Jalasi, Koh Kia Jeng, Ghil-Won Jo, Zainal Azlan Abdul Kadir, Noor Kapdi, Adil Khawaja, Stephen Knight, Su Ann Kok, Tigran Kurdiyan, Soňa Kurillová, Jose Manuel Larrain, Frederique Leger, Ruben Eduardo Luján, Manfred Lum, Lauren Macksoud, Carolina Mansur de Grandis, Simona Marin, Katherine V. Marney, Stephen Massa, Patrick Maxcy, Tamsyn Mileham, Luci Mitchell-Fry, Claude Montgomery, Dennis Montgomery, Safwan Moubaydeen, David Mpanga, Cheah Chooi Mun, Pauline Ngiam, Gabriella Pataki, Dominic Pellew, Filipp Petyukov, Sandhya Pillai, Toh Gim Phaik, Anna Pukszto, Robert Richards, Benjamin Rodriguez, Semih Sander, Natalia Selyakova, Abai Shaikenov, Victoria Simonova, Alex

Skoblo, Stanislaw Soltysik, Bruno Steneri, Avto Svanidze, Aida Tleulina, Mateusz Toczyski, Jiří Tomola, Edgard Torres, Tomasz Trocki, Amanda Valdez, Stanislava Valientová, Dean Van Drasek, Chunyang Wang, Lee Whiden, Erwin K. Winenda, Michael Wingrave, Logan Wright, Shukhrat Yunusov, and Ulvia Zeynalova-Bockin and others. In addition to the above, we thank those Dentons lawyers who contributed to the survey for Annex 1 and named therein. And not least importantly, we are indebted to Marina Topal for her continued clerical support in the production of the manuscript.

In writing a book of this kind, the authors relied on their long and varied experiences in the financial services and legal professions. During their careers, each has benefited from the interaction with talented colleagues within their organizations and in the broader market. Whilst there are too many to mention all here, we would like to acknowledge Harvey W. Berman, Daniel de Lange, Nikolas Drude, Brian D. Fix, Milton R. Gleit, Jeffrey M. Hertzfeld, Mary Faith Higgins, Oleg Ivancychuk, George P. Macdonald, Theodore P. Matheny, Emmanuel Maurice, Philippe Max, Andrew McKnight, Stephen Petri, Enrico Pini, Christoph Sicking, Rob Ranocchia, Jerome Savelli, Silvia Spear, Robert Starr, James J. White, and Alireza Zavar.

# Contents

# About the Authors

**Richard Marney** is a senior advisor for risk management at responsAbility Investments AG, a Zurich-based development finance-focused asset management firm. He previously served as the firm's chief risk officer. Prior to responsAbility, Richard had a broad and varied 40-year career in emerging and frontier markets banking and principal investing, with senior-level business and corporate development, risk management, and operating roles, including with BNY-Mellon and JP Morgan. Richard currently sits on a number of boards of directors in the emerging markets, including the African Guarantee Fund, Trustco Group Holdings (Namibia), Mikro Kapital (Moldova, Belarus and Romania), and Finca (Armenia). He is a graduate of the Johns Hopkins University, Nitze School of Advanced International Studies.

**Timothy Stubbs** is a partner with the global law firm Dentons. He heads the firm's Russian Banking and Finance Group. Tim has worked on emerging markets transactions with Dentons (and its legacy firm Salans) since 1992, having previously practiced law in Chicago and New York. Tim also worked for two years in the Office of General Counsel of the European Bank for Reconstruction and Development (EBRD) in London on working sabbatical. Tim has led numerous debt restructurings as well as financings of all types, including bilateral and syndicated lending, real estate finance, and project finance. He is the author of the *Russia Country Chapter in Collier International Business Insolvency Guide*. Tim is a graduate of the University of Michigan Law School and Center for Russian, East European & Eurasian Studies.

# List of Figures

# List of Tables

# Part I

## Opening Narrative

# 1

# A Restructuring Tale: The Bank of Commerce

**Abstract** The case study, in the form of a narrative tale, depicts the Bank of Commerce, a troubled bank in a copper export-dependent emerging market. Its US-based majority shareholder has benefited from it as a source of cash for pay-outs to investors and part of a greater, overly ambitious acquisition strategy in other markets. As the local economy experiences major export revenue and currency shocks and the Bank's financial condition deteriorates, we follow the responses of individual representatives of the Bank, its shareholders, and lenders to deal with the spiraling crisis. Eventually, a debt restructuring becomes inevitable. Efforts to maintain the Bank as a going concern flounder as the shareholders are unable to recapitalize the institution, a sale or merger proves unviable, and the lenders cannot agree on a debt to equity conversion solution. As a result, an orderly wind-down must be engineered as an alternative to bankruptcy. The tale and discussion questions interspersed in the text provide a real-life context for the remainder of the book.

**Keywords** Bankruptcy · Basel III · Board of directors · Borrower ·
Confidentiality · Consensual restructuring · Coordinating committee ·
Corporate debt · Debt · Debtor · Debt to equity conversion · Deposits ·
Cash flow · Critical thinking · Currency peg · Devaluation · DFI
(development finance institution) · Distressed debt · Duration gap · Foreign
exchange · Emerging market · Exchange rate · Frontier market · INSOL II ·
INSOL principles · Insolvency · Lender leadership · Loan loss provision ·
New money · Non-performing loans · Pre-insolvency · Restructure ·

Restructuring · Restructuring plan · Shareholder(s · Standstill · Steering committee · Tier 1 Capital · Tier 2 Capital · Wind-down · Workout

# Preface

(1) The Market[1]

The Bank of Commerce operates in a middle income, emerging market economy. Buoyed by robust demand for its primary export product—copper—growth had averaged 5% in real terms per annum for much of the past decade. To encourage capital inflows, the Central Bank had maintained a peg for the local currency to the US Dollar at 1:1. This foreign capital propelled a rapid expansion not only in fixed investment in the mining sector, but also in a wide range of manufacturing activities. Local banks had intermediated a significant proportion of these investments. As a result, loan volumes and concentration levels reached historical highs, as had leverage throughout the corporate sector. Credit standards were relaxed, evidenced by looser financial covenants and lower collateral coverage ratios.

Beginning two years ago, global economic activity began to slow. Demand for copper declined, with predictable knock-on effects on the country's economy and financial sector. Growth fell. Lower export proceeds led to reduced foreign exchange (FX) reserves and more frequent market intervention to support the currency peg. The decline in export tax revenue necessitated higher levels of government borrowing at the very time that there was a discernible slackening in capital inflows. In local markets, liquidity tightened, and interest rates rose. These developments created stresses on the financial sector. Higher interest rates pressured lending margins. Asset quality began to show signs of deterioration.

The decline in global output accelerated, with notable reductions in demand for industrial metals. The adverse trends in the country intensified. Non-performing loans (NPLs) spiked, as the highly leveraged corporate sector confronted the various pressures of higher interest rates, depressed operating cash-flows, and ominously an incipient reversal in external capital flows. Over the next months, this reversal picked up steam. FX reserves fell, with Central Bank FX market intervention a significant contributor.

---

[1] In Chapter 10 (Macroeconomics and Credit Analysis) we present a discussion of the interaction between a country's economy and credit risk. Key terms and concepts are covered there and further referenced in the Glossary of Terms.

The Central Bank supplemented its reserves through swap facilities.[2] These actions encouraged the markets, and external pressures appeared to abate temporarily. However, soon thereafter, the Central Bank shocked markets by devaluing the currency by 25%. The action panicked the markets. Capital outflows rapidly accelerated. A few weeks later, the government was forced to act again. A number of measures to dampen capital outflows and stabilize exchange markets would have to be announced, including an abandonment of the peg.

The loss of value of the currency was a devastating blow to a financial sector heavily dependent upon foreign currency funding. The businesses had used cheap USD funding to support high-return local currency lending. After more than a decade of a secure peg, local lenders were unprepared. Open currency positions were the norm. The hits to profitability from FX exceeded those from the spike in NPLs. Together, they threatened systemic stability.

(2) The Bank

The Bank of Commerce was founded by a prominent local family as a consumer finance company in 1972, before converting to a full commercial banking license in 1983. Over time, the business model had evolved into a niche small and medium enterprise lender in the manufacturing sector. Under the original founders, the credit policy had been conservative. Lending primarily took the form of working capital financing and was subject to modest exposure ceilings, with strict collateralization requirements. The ALM aimed to limit duration and prohibited currency mismatches. Growth was modest, profitability moderate but with the institution exhibiting consistently strong liquidity and solvency metrics.

With the death of the family patriarch in 1999, the eldest son returned from London, where he had attended private school and university and worked for a large U.S. private equity firm in Mayfair. This event coincided with fundamental change in the local economy. With the objective

---

[2] A central bank liquidity swap is a type of currency swap used by a country's central bank to provide liquidity of its currency to another country's central bank. In a liquidity swap, the lending central bank uses its currency to buy the currency of another borrowing central bank at the market exchange rate, and agrees to sell the borrower's currency back at a rate that reflects the interest accrued on the loan. The borrower's currency serves as collateral. See https://en.wikipedia.org/wiki/Central_bank_liquidity_swap.

of diversifying the relatively closed economy away from its dependence on copper, the government undertook a series of measures to open the capital account, liberalize the financial system, and encourage foreign direct investment throughout the economy with tax incentives and streamlined approval processes.

Faced with the new opportunity, the son envisioned a more aggressive, diversified financial services strategy, patterned on the evolving American banking model, post-Glass-Steagall abolition. What he lacked was capital. To address this need, he invited a San Francisco-based publicly listed private equity fund, New West Investments, to invest in the Bank as a minority partner to support his growth plans. For almost a decade, the arrangement worked well. On a base of abundant, lower-cost, foreign currency funding a portfolio of high-yield, local currency-denominated business credits fueled spectacular growth and ever-rising profitability. The institution developed a reputation for its cadre of hard-nosed bankers.

Then came Lehman Brothers and the global financial crisis of 2008 (GFC).[3] The Bank confronted an existential liquidity crisis. When the dust settled, the son was a small minority shareholder in an institution now controlled by New West. Post-2008, the fundamental business model did not change, save that the new owners further ramped up leverage and recast the brand. The latter stroke of genius hijacked the reputation of a long-standing, local micro-enterprise lender by acquiring their operations and inviting the multi-lateral International Development Fund, a global leader in development of the sector, to invest. The legacy business was now clothed in the garb of respectability. It embarked on a period of unparalleled growth and profitability.

Then the country hit a wall.

Prior to the current episode, the summary financials and appeared as follows:

---

[3] See Annex 2—Bibliography for suggested readings. A brief summary of the GFC is available at https://en.wikipedia.org/wiki/Financial_crisis_of_2007–2008.

| Income Statement | | | Balance Sheet | |
|---|---|---|---|---|
| Grosa Interest Income | 400 | | Cash and Marketable Securities | 15 |
| Cost of Funds | 215 | | Gross Loan Portfolio | 2,000 |
| | | | Loan Loss Reserve | (75) |
| **Net Interest Margin** | **185** | | **Net Loan Portfolio** | 1,925 |
| *(%)* | *46%* | | **Total Assets** | **1,940** |
| | | | Deposits | 400 |
| Fees and Others | 90 | | Senior Debt | 1,200 |
| OPEX | 120 | | **Total Liabilities** | **1,600** |
| Provisions | 35 | | Sub Debt (Tier 2) | 190 |
| | | | Paid-in Capital | 100 |
| **Net Operating Income** | **120** | | Retained Earnings | 50 |
| *(%)* | *30%* | | **Total Equity** | **340** |
| | | | **Total Liabilities and Equity** | **1,940** |
| Taxes | 18 | | | |
| | | | **FX Position** | |
| **Net Income** | **102** | | **FX Assets** | **450** |
| *(%)* | *26%* | | **FX Liabilities:** | **1,290** |
| | | | Desposits | 200 |
| Dividends | 100 | | Senior Debt | 900 |
| *Dividend Payout Ratio* | *98%* | | Sub Debt | 190 |
| *ROA* | *5.3%* | | **Net Position** | **(840)** |
| *ROE* | *30.0%* | | **Net Open Position to Equity** | **-247%** |

(Millions - Local Currency)

Noteworthy were the headline credit metrics[4] of solvency (18%), comfortably in excess of the regulatory minimum (10%), with exceptional profitability (ROE 62% and ROA 11%). Asset quality was within reasonable bounds (Portfolio at Risk 2.1%), with adequate provisioning coverage (91%). With the long tradition of a secure currency peg and FX reserve coverage well above the IMF's minimum level, lenders gave scant attention to an open FX position equivalent to roughly 100% of equity.

### (3) The Players

*Ursula*: CEO of New West Investments (shareholder).

*JK*: Founder & Chairman of the Board of New West Investments (shareholder)

*Brian*: Vice Chairman of the Board of New West Investments (shareholder).

*Kristi*: Head of Strategy and Risk Management of Global Impact Funds (lender)

*Robert*: CEO of Global Impact Funds (lender).

*Reggie*: Chief Investment Officer of Global Impact Funds (lender).

---

[4] (i) Solvency denotes the level and can be interpreted as the adequacy of capitalization (net worth to total assets or risk assets). (ii) Regulatory Minimum is the solvency level set by the local financial regulator as the minimum for regulated institutions. (iii) ROE (return on equity) and ROA (return on assets) are measures of profitability. (iv) IMF Reserve Adequacy—a component of the IMF's analytic toolkit which evaluates the "adequacy" of a country's foreign exchange reserves.

*Maya*: Chief Restructuring Officer for Horizon Bank (lender).
*Todd*: Investment Officer of Edinburgh Partners (lender).
*Colin*: Managing Director of Edinburgh Partners (lender).
*Peter*: CEO and Chairman of Edinburgh Partners (lender).
*Stephen*: Managing Director of a Tifts (global restructuring firm).
*Martin*: Vice President of the International Development Fund (shareholder)
*Monique*: President of the International Development Fund (shareholder)

The three featured lenders to the Bank of Commerce are the Global Impact Funds (or GIF, the leading, global private impact sector asset manager), Horizon Bank (a social impact focused cooperative bank), and Edinburgh Partners (a multi-asset wealth manager). The three lenders are similarly sized institutions. For GIF (Kristi) and Horizon Bank (Maya), the two lead financiers are from the corporate restructuring, whilst for the third, Edinburgh Partners (Todd) is from the business development side of the house. As a percentage of assets or assets under management, as the case may be, Horizon Bank (Maya) is the most heavily exposed to the Bank of Commerce, followed by GIF (Kristi) and then Edinburgh Partners (Todd).

## The Tale

Kristi's London black cab lumbered into the hotel driveway. Two well-dressed figures stood by the hotel's revolving doors. One was arguing volubly, his arms gesturing wildly. The other stood immobile. She knew both well—they had all flown in for the same meeting to discuss the fate of the struggling Bank of Commerce.

Kristi had a very bad feeling about the day, and usually her hunches came true. There were a number of reasons this time around. And the first was just outside her taxi window.

To her friends and colleagues, Kristi was the "occasional economist." At sixty, she wore her grey hair as a medal of honor. Upon completing her Ph.D. at MIT, she had moved across town to teach for two years at that other school before being lured down to Manhattan to join a bank's newly founded macro-strategy group.[5] She quickly moved onto the trading floor where she stayed for a quarter of a century. Following her divorce, she had remarried, returned to Boston and moved into the "softer" side of finance, co-founding an emerging markets impact investment fund. The operation flourished and eventually attracted the interest of a large European insurance company. After the buy-out, Kristi was convinced to stay on as chief risk officer. In this role, she managed the firm's restructuring practice.

"I'm not going in! There's no point! The shareholders are not prepared to support the bank." Kristi heard the younger of the two say, as she tucked the taxi receipt into her purse, and approached the couple. He was Todd, an investment officer at the giant UK-based multi-asset manager, Edinburgh Partners. Kristi knew him well from their time together at her current firm. Smart and ambitious, he had jumped from the fairly staid world of Global Impact Funds to Edinburgh Partners for double the money, but at some risk. At 32, he had the opportunity to start a new investment line for Edinburgh Partners in the area of emerging market SME bank debt. His runway to show results was short. Kristi had warned him about Edinburgh Partners, "It's an unforgiving place. Miss your numbers even once, and you may be history. It's a very different world." Todd had laughed her off, even chiding her for having lost her drive. Now, Kristi could see the fear in his eyes—a $25 million loss staring him in the face.

"You've come all this way, Todd!" entreated the other, an attractive older woman. "For heaven's sake, at least hear them out." Maya was her name. She and Kristi had met in undergraduate school, and the two women had remained close friends since. Following a decade in government, divided between the Bank of England and the Treasury, Maya had moved into banking, rising to head the corporate restructuring group at Horizon Bank. A quarter of a century of attending restructuring kick-off meetings such as today's helped her understand Todd's desperation and empathize with him. "They'll change their tune if we all stand together."

They both turned to Kristi as she approached and nodded respectfully. Todd's expression evinced hope, desperate hope that perhaps Kristi brought good news. She was the de facto leader on this case. Kristi's many years of

---

[5] A global macro strategy is a hedge fund or mutual fund strategy that bases its holdings primarily on the overall economic and political views of various countries or their macroeconomic principles. See https://www.investopedia.com/terms/g/globalmacro.asp.

honing her skills in emerging markets restructurings had resulted in not only a few grey hairs but a solid network of friends and alliances—and a reputation for practical, effective leadership on steering committees. She always landed the plane.

"Have you heard?" Todd's words came out as a morbid, one-two-three. "They intend to tell us the problem is ours to fix. No support. Nothing." He wiped his brow with the back of his hand. "I went out on a limb to get this investment approved." His voice rose a full octave. "The shareholders have to make the situation good."

Kristi's eyes met Maya's. Both feared getting the shareholders to bail the lenders out would be very difficult. Ursula's messaging to that effect had been clear.

"I'll be finished. Finished!" Todd exhaled.

"Todd, look." Kristi said. Repeating Maya's counsel, "They may well start this way. But if we're firm and united, they'll come around. They stand to lose a lot if the bank collapses."

"That's what she says!" Todd countered, pointing his finger accusingly at Maya. "No, I believe they intend to stiff us."

"It's our job to ensure that doesn't happen." Smiling at the younger man, Kristi continued in her most reassuring voice, "Todd, why don't you take a walk for a few minutes, get some fresh air. We have almost an hour before the meeting starts. We'll need your help upstairs."

"Thanks, Kristi, I guess I do need to clear my head."

The two women watched him start to walk off.

"Maya, you know, he is in trouble if this goes badly. A 25 million loss could well end his career there. And, by the way." She continued. "His wife called me last week to announce she's due in two months. Their first child. No wonder he's so nervous."

"Good news at a bad time…but, you know, Kristi, he's not the only one with troubles if this case goes pear-shaped," Maya rued. "Heads will roll in my house."

"Maya, why don't you walk with him? We need him to be calm when the meeting starts."

> **Discussion Question Number 1**
> - What lies at the difference in temperament amongst our three financiers? Personalities or institutional pressures?
> - Edinburgh Partners is the least financially exposed, yet Todd is clearly the most agitated. Why? How does the answer affect how Kristi and Maya will approach managing Todd's house?
> - What is the significance of Kristi and Maya coming from the risk or restructuring versus Todd coming from the business origination side of the house? How might this influence how they operate on the deal? And Todd?
>   See Annex 5 for suggested answers to these questions.

Kristi walked into the conference room. Hotel staff were scurrying around, setting up the room.

She looked around for Ursula, the CEO of New West, the majority shareholder of the Bank of Commerce. They had agreed to talk before the full-lenders meeting began. Ursula was nowhere to be found.

Kristi checked her phone. There was a text from Ursula from 10 min ago. "Running late. I'll be down as soon as I can."

Kristi found a table, sat down, and waited. Fatigue washed over her. An overnight flight wasn't ideal preparation for the day. On top of this, she thought, today should never have been necessary. The signs had been obvious, to her at least, for quite some time—the link between the coming end of the commodity super-cycle and the financial sustainability of institutions like the Bank of Commerce.

Countries are best analyzed as companies, her doctoral supervisor, an ebullient and astonishingly brilliant Italian, had drilled into her. As China's historically unparalleled, growth drove an equally unprecedented expansion in the emerging and frontier markets, Kristi viewed with alarm the build-up of structural imbalances[6] in many countries. These reminded her of the excessively leveraged high-yield issuers whose debt she had traded. Like kites constructed of light paper, they could soar in the sunshine, but quickly melt and plunge to earth in a rainstorm. Capital inflows were generating well-needed local development but were also creating acute vulnerabilities to a sudden stop of external funding.

---

[6] Here, we employ a definition covering structural deficits in fiscal accounts (overall and primary balances) and the current account (trade balance ± income flows). The term "structural" is used to differentiate the situation from a cyclical episode. All things being equal, the higher the deficit in the fiscal balance and the current account, the greater the financing requirements of the country, and hence vulnerability to economic cycles and shocks.

When she undertook a systematic analysis of the fund's investee countries, she was shaken. In many and especially a number where despite her objections portfolio management had invested heavily, she observed widening current account deficits, de facto pegged exchange rate regimes contributing to overvalued exchange rates, high debt levels with precarious dependencies on short-duration, potentially very "hot money," and overheated local financial systems. Indeed, much of the so-called development finance into the country was little more than carry trade funds.[7] When the music stopped, there could well be carnage.

From this work, she had suggested caution to her underwriters. The reaction ranged from incredulity and scorn to Chuck Prince-like resignation,[8] but did little other than to make Kristi unpopular.

The Bank of Commerce represented one of her largest exposures. This prompted a deep dive into the numbers. Her conclusions were simple and straightforward. As she wrote to the Risk Committee, "Slowing growth will create severe asset quality problems, which could create pressures on solvency. However, if action is not taken to hedge the Bank's large open currency exposure, the inevitable breakdown of the peg will certainly bring the institution down, unless the majority shareholder rides to the rescue."

A few minutes later, Maya walked into the room with Todd.

"Sorry, Kristi," started Todd, "I should have controlled my temper before."

"No worries" Kristi consoled. "Tell me, Todd, what can we do to help you?"

"We need New West to step up and recapitalize the Bank. In my investment committee, I represented they would."

"But without an explicit guarantee?".

Todd looked intently at Kristi, "I reached out to Ursula. Later, she arranged a conference call, with JK on the line. I know what I heard. I relied on their assurances."

---

[7] In normal times, the interest rate yield curve is positively sloped. That is, the rate or yield for 6-months will be lower than for 10-years. Further, given market conditions, interest rates between countries will vary. In (theoretically) perfect markets, there is no possibility of profit or lower cost financing by borrowing in a cheaper interest rate country and investing in the higher interest rate country, as the depreciation in the former country's currency versus the latter's currency will wipe out the financial gain. In the case of the Bank of Commerce's country, the exchange rate is fixed (i.e., local currency pegged at 1:1 against the USD). Hence, the financial gain is not touched. Significant volumes of capital were borrowed at low rates for short-tenors in USD internationally and then invested at much higher rates for longer-tenors locally.

[8] *"When the music stops, in terms of liquidity, things will be complicated. But as long as the music is playing, you've got to get up and dance. We're still dancing."* See https://www.ft.com/content/80e2987a-2e50-11dc-821c-0000779fd2ac.

> **Discussion Question Number 2**
> - How practical is Kristi's macro-focused approach? Is she correct in believing that investors should have seen this coming?
> - On the question of shareholder support, who is at fault? New West or Todd? How should the lenders group play the angle of an implied support, if at all?
>
> See Annex 5 for suggested answers to these questions.

-&-

Floors above in the living room of the royal suite, Ursula put her phone away and turned back to the group. She struggled to control her temper. Then, she spoke, "These lenders are long-standing relationships.[9] They've stood by us over the years. Stephen, we can't just blindside them, especially in a large public meeting like this, to say, 'So sorry. It's your problem, not ours!' They'll go ballistic....".

The diminutive man, New West Board's mandated restructuring advisor, glowered back in return.

"Well?".

"Enough! JK, your chairman, and the rest of board have approved my approach. Why are we even discussing this now?"

"I repeat," Ursula shot back. "A one-sided rescue plan will not fly, and presenting a Hobson's choice - 'accept our plan or we'll throw the keys at you' – will only make a bad situation worse. And remember," She continued, pointing to the door, "even though the financial services segment is a small part of our overall business, what we do here will affect the market's view of us. Like I have said before, it's the 'character' issue. We have much bigger challenges in our group, and your approach won't help us there."

"To the contrary!" Sneered Stephen. "Weakness here will only embolden creditors in the future."

"This damn bank!" thought Ursula. She had never been comfortable with the investment. It had been another JK fait accompli. The son of the Bank of Commerce's founding family had been an associate working in New West

---

[9] Throughout the narrative, consider the important role that institutional and personal relationships must play. Why are relationships important? How do they manifest themselves? How does a more transactional attitude affect the restructuring process?

and had convinced him to buy the bank. The investment ran counter to the fundamental principle that had guided her during a meteoric twenty year rise in the private equity industry, which culminated in her being headhunted by JK several years before, "buy a compelling value creation story with a plausible exit strategy." For Ursula, neither applied for the Bank. When the dividend flow surpassed their expectations and JK had said, "I told you so!" her rebuttal was, "it won't last."

"With respect, Stephen, your approach carried by a slim majority of the board. I was in the dissenting minority. We have to reconsider."

Ursula looked over to the far corner of the room, where the tall, dark-haired man who had just spoken stood, leaning against the wall. His fitting suit on a slight frame and open-collar shirt set him off from the rest of the room. His name was Martin. A former investment banker, he now worked for the multilateral development finance institution (DFI), the International Development Fund, a co-investor in the bank, albeit holding only a minor stake.

Martin calmly walked over and pulled a chair over to place himself in the center of the group. His accent barely betrayed his French nationality. "I repeat: it is not too late to change course for today."

Ursula nodded in agreement. She had great confidence in Martin. He had acted as the investment banking advisor to her previous private equity firm on several acquisitions, before he stepped off the tread mill and joined the IDF. Soft spoken, patient, and unfailingly respectful, he won conference room battles by the strength of his preparation and the force of his arguments. She had brought the IDF into the shareholding group of the Bank of Commerce with the hope of marshaling these strengths. She had asked him to join this meeting as a counter-weight to Stephen and JK.

"We have a conference room of lenders downstairs," Stephen asked, "what are you suggesting we do now?"

"We need a consultative negotiating style aimed at a balanced solution."

Ursula joined in, "Global Impact Fund's senior representative, Kristi, is waiting for me downstairs. Let's have her join us, and we can strategize quickly."

Martin nodded in agreement.

Stephen interrupted, waving them off. "No, there is no need. The board has approved my recommended plan of action. There will be no changes."

There was a knock on the door. A dapper young man with a fresh haircut, sporting a blue suit and brown wingtip oxfords, stuck his head in. "We're ready to start." Turning to Stephen, "I've made your changes in the slides."

Stephen stood up. "Thanks, Connor." Glancing at Ursula and Martin. "Thank you for your thoughts, but I will follow the board's instructions."

"I hope you're right," Ursula sighed. "We can't continue to pay interest. The local operation is almost out of cash."

---

**Discussion Question Number 3**
- How would you characterize the board's approach?
- What are the underlying considerations driving Martin and Ursula's opposition?
- Who should be leading the New West contingent, Ursula or Stephen? Why?
- What might explain the absence of the management of the Bank in this pre-meeting?
  See Annex 5 for suggested answers to these questions.

---

-&-

The vast conference hall was overflowing. A long, elevated dais stretched across the front, reserved for the company, its shareholders, advisors, and even two lawyers. Raised presentation screens flanked the dais. Facing the platform were many circular tables, each with eight seats. All were taken. A number of participants milled by the entrance and against the wall, waiting for the hotel staff to deliver more chairs. Stephen led in the borrower's contingent. Their entrance silenced the room. The crisp, dark suits and thin ties contrasted discordantly with the audience's motley, informal attire.

Ursula scanned the room, making ticks on a lender list. Everyone was there, save for Edinburgh Partners. Several minutes passed. As Stephen finally called for order, she saw Todd skulk into the room. He stood rigidly against the wall, arms crossed and an angry expression on this face. "He doesn't look happy," she thought.

She began to speak. "Good morning, and thank you, everyone …".

Stephen cut her off. "I know everyone is busy so let's get right to it. We've all read the papers. The economy has gone off the rails," intoned the Stephen. "No one saw this economic crisis coming, so no need to finger point. The

Bank of Commerce needs to be recapitalized, and its current debt burden is unsustainable. It's time for you to step up. We are asking you to convert your debt into equity for a 49% shareholding in the bank."

Gasps filled the room.

-&-

Ursula tuned out the room and thought back to months before, when the whole situation had begun to unravel. She had just flown twelve hours from San Francisco to join a meeting of the Bank of Commerce's executive management. The group had been sitting around the conference table staring at the white board. A jumble of multi-colored boxes, circles, and lines reminiscent of a Cy Twombly painting crowded the surface, rendering the diagram almost unintelligible. The CEO shot a glance at the whiteboard, then laughed, admitting to Ursula and his senior team that his attempt to analyze the country's economic troubles was perhaps as inept as the government's efforts to deal with the burgeoning crisis.

Despite the botched presentation, the message was simple: the economy was tanking. Local businesses were suffering. Bad loans were mounting, but the true extent was being masked in part by the clever, if not under-handed, use of hidden restructurings. This couldn't last. Eventually, the deterioration in asset quality would become evident. Then the issue would be liquidity.

The CEO expressed the fear that his institutional funders—the bank had few retail depositors—would look at the trajectory of the economy and predict that non-performing loans would spike. Eventually, loan loss provisions would turn a long-profitable bank into one whose solvency could be questioned. Once this happened, *voila*: an illiquid bank in a country where the Central Bank's role as a lender of last resort, the liquidity backstop, was weak at best. Shareholder liquidity support? Some possibly, but not enough.

"How bad could it get?" Ursula asked.

The CEO asked his Chief Risk Officer to respond.

"Let me show you." He moved to the back of the room and turned on the projector. A table appeared on the screen. "This is our current 'duration gap analysis.'"

## Box 1. Duration Gap Analysis*

Liquidity - Duration Gap Analysis   (Millions - Local Currency)

| Contractual Maturity Gap (in mm) | O/N | ≤ 1 mo | > 1 mo ≤ 3 mo | > 3 mo ≤ 6 mo | > 6 mo ≤ 12 mo | > 1 yr ≤ 3 yrs | > 3 yrs | Perp | Total |
|---|---|---|---|---|---|---|---|---|---|
| Cash | 8 | 5 | - | - | - | - | - | - | 13 |
| Unrestricted at CB | 2 | - | - | - | - | - | - | - | 2 |
| Banks | - | - | - | - | - | - | - | - | - |
| Financial Investments | - | - | - | - | - | - | - | - | - |
| Net Loans | - | 50 | 150 | 100 | 300 | 900 | 425 | - | 1,925 |
| Fixed and Other assets | - | - | - | - | - | - | - | - | - |
| Total Assets | 10 | 55 | 150 | 100 | 300 | 900 | 425 | - | 1,940 |
| Deposits (retail) | - | - | - | - | - | - | - | - | - |
| Deposits (Wholesale) | - | 100 | 100 | 200 | - | - | - | - | 400 |
| Senior Secured Debts | - | - | 200 | 400 | 400 | 200 | - | - | 1,200 |
| Senior Unsecured Debts | - | - | - | - | - | - | - | - | - |
| Senior Bonds | - | - | - | - | - | - | - | - | - |
| Sub debts & bonds | - | - | - | - | - | 190 | - | - | 190 |
| Other Liabilities | - | - | - | - | - | - | - | - | - |
| Equity | - | - | - | - | - | - | - | 150 | 150 |
| Total Liabilities and Equity | - | 100 | 300 | 600 | 400 | 390 | - | 150 | 1,940 |
| Liquidity Gap | 10 | (45) | (150) | (500) | (100) | 510 | 425 | (150) | |
| Cumulative Gap | 10 | (35) | (185) | (685) | (785) | (275) | 150 | - | |

Banks perform the task of maturity transformation. This role can be described simply as *"banks invest in long-term assets, funded by short-term liabilities."*[10] Inherent in this role is a mismatch between the maturities of assets and liabilities. The tool used to quantify and evaluate the mismatch is the "Duration Gap Analysis" schedule, an example of which appears above and was prepared by the Bank of Commerce. In this case, the Bank has a "Liquidity Gap," that is, more liabilities due than assets maturing in the four "time buckets" over the next 12-months. The Bank did this intentionally to maximize its profits (borrow cheap short-term funds and lend expensive long-term funds). This strategy was a great success *when funds flowed freely*. When they ceased doing so, a serious problem arose. The Bank of Commerce has a "Cumulative Gap" equal to $785 million, that is, over the next 12-months the Bank owes $785 million more than their currently available liquidity.

The CEO interjected. "Ursula, the $400 mm in deposits are principally from a handful of large local companies and individuals, friends of the old ownership family. They'll flee at the first sign of trouble."

"And the foreign lenders?" asked Ursula.

"That's a tough question," said the CEO. "Hard to say how they'll react. Save for a blip after Lehman, the last decade and a half have been happy times of non-stop growth and high profits. I'm not sure all of them even have workout groups."

---

[10] See https://www.frbsf.org/economic-research/files/wp2020-07.pdf, p. 3.

"Beyond that," offered the Bank's chief legal counsel, "they are subordinated to the uninsured depositors. In a liquidation, the local parties will get paid first. Two lenders have contacted me just recently to confirm this treatment."[11]

"Which means they're concerned." Ursula sighed.

An assistant spoke up, his voice slightly quivering, "We are already in violation of our loan quality covenants with four lenders. I've requested waivers. No agreement yet from anyone. A couple of lenders want to meet first." He turned to Ursula, "They want to know what New West is going to do in case we need help, before they'll consider a waiver."

Ursula ignored the comment. She stood up and looked more closely at the numbers. Her jaw dropped. "Jesus, you've got over three quarters of a billion coming due over the next year, and most of that in under six months. What about our FX exposure?".

The CEO's frightened expression said it all.

"How bad, really?" asked Ursula.

"Bad. Let me explain. You can tell from our financial reporting that we are short dollars and hence will have a massive translation loss should the exchange rate peg break. More than that, the small, but not insignificant number of our borrowers who have dollar-denominated loans will be badly hit. And these are just the direct impacts." The CEO reached for a glass of water, drank, and then turned back to Ursula. "Simply stated, no currency peg, no bank!"

---

**Discussion Question Number 4**

• How would you critique the evaluation of the Bank's financial position, as discussed above?

• What steps could be taken at this time to address the inherent risks?

• Should this have been the point at which a discussion of restructuring alternatives began?

See Annex 5 for suggested answers to these questions.

---

[11] As a general matter, lenders will sit behind depositors in a financial institution's insolvency, including in emerging markets.

-&-

The next day Ursula had caught the first flight back to San Francisco. Images of exploding bad debts, plunging exchange rates, and vanishing capital had danced in her mind throughout the long journey home. She slept terribly on the flight. Even the wine had not helped. New West could write-off the Bank of Commerce and it would not have a material impact on their performance. Besides, the dividends were already more than the original investment. It was the reputational damage she feared. A failed investment is bad public relations, both for the firm and for her. Ultimately, the latter concerned her more, if truth be told.

Immediately upon touch down, she had convened her finance team.

"I have two questions. Number one: assume we need to step in and support the bank's liquidity," she asked, "How much can we raise at the holding-company level and how fast? Number two: do we have access to long-term capital if we have to downstream new equity? I want your answers by 5 pm today."

The feedback was sobering.

"For the first, assuming the dividend stream from the Bank continues," her finance director had responded, "we can manage 50 million for a short time, say 6-months. On the second, maybe 10 million or so, but that'll start a major fight with the board, with JK."

-&-

With this news in hand, Ursula had taken the elevator upstairs to see JK, or as she joked to her husband, "The Once and Always CEO." A septuagenarian, he had started in a clerical role on Wall Street before rising to the top of the private equity world. Formally, he had stepped down from the firm he had founded five years ago and handed the reins to Ursula. But in truth, he still ran the business. His handpicked board was unfailingly loyal to him, and Ursula took her orders with a smile.

The habitual long, dark cigar jutted from JK's mouth. The blue-white smoke snaked across the spacious, almost regal office. He looked over at Ursula, who stood in the doorway. "Come in," he motioned to the seating area off to the right, facing the grand windows with a spectacular view of San Francisco Bay.

"JK, we have a storm brewing with the Bank of Commerce," Ursula began. She walked him through the economics and the liquidity position. "My greatest fear is the exchange rate. They're pegged to the USD. Although it's been in place for several years, pressures are building. Our treasury strategy there has been not to hedge our open position."

"How big?".

"In excess of 100% of capital."

"Can we cover quickly?".

Ursula frowned. "They're making market soundings now. I have a call with the CEO tomorrow. Hedging costs have spiked." She pointed at the report her team had produced, for emphasis. "Can we tell him we're good for the $50 mm in stand-by liquidity support?".

"That's not going to happen."

"Eh?".

"We've had some bad news last night." JK picked up the phone and buzzed his secretary. "Get the Vice-Chair, Brian on the line and also the banker leading our refinancing."

Whilst the two waited, JK spoke, "You are aware we are planning investor meetings in New York and then London next week for the upcoming bond issue?".

"Yes." Of course, I am, she swore to herself. How could I not be? We're sitting on two and half billion of high-cost credit borrowed to fund a recent acquisition of New Perspectives Energy. The loan is coming due next month. The banks holding the paper were refusing to renew.

"New Perspectives Energy's numbers will be published at the end of this week." JK hesitated, his ruddy face paling, "Not a pretty picture."

"What's happened?".

"Long story. I'll just say our judgement may be questioned. More headwinds for our bond issue."

The spider phone buzzed, and the red lights pulsated.

"Your callers are on the line," chimed the secretary.

-&-

An hour later, Ursula sat at her desk starring at the computer screen, lost in her thoughts. They were not pleasant. There was no prospect of financial support for the Bank. JK had vetoed it for the moment. He had also overruled her suggestion to have the Bank of Commerce hold off on the quarterly dividend. They'd have to weather the coming storm on their own. The Bank, she reminded herself, was the least of our problems. The New Perspectives Energy's news had shocked her. They rushed, overly rich acquisition had been to beat out several other private equity firms. JK and his team's diligence had been sloppy. Now, their carelessness had bitten them back. The accountants were still arguing about whether a big write-off would be necessary. Even at the low end, the impact on the fundraising would be damaging. The senior partner at the book-runner had told JK and his deputy that they had to postpone the investor meetings. Instead, he suggested they talk discreetly with the acquisition finance lender and ask for an extension, noting there was really no alternative.

Ursula's mobile phone rang, jolting her out of her reverie. She answered.

"Hi, Kristi. I'm sorry I didn't return your calls. There's been a lot going on."

"Yes, I gather." Kristi cut to the point, "Your secretary told me you were in country seeing Bank of Commerce. I'd like to hear what you're doing to support them."

"I don't understand?".

"Ursula, I spoke to the bank's CEO just after you left."

"What he did he tell you?" Her voice tightened. She mouthed a voiceless obscenity.

"He updated the liquidity analysis that we receive periodically, as required under our loan agreements. He's got close to half his funding book turning over in the next 12 months."

"But this is normal," Ursula protested.

"Perhaps, but these times are not." There was some static on the line. "I'm checking to see if my secretary has emailed you…yes, she has. Please check your email."

Ursula found the email and noticed the subject, "Devaluation, Asset Quality and Solvency." Opening the attachment, she saw three tables. "Yes, I've opened the file now."

"Good. Your CEO confirmed his current capital adequacy ratio at 17.5%.[12]

---

[12] The capital adequacy ratio (CAR) is a measurement of a bank's available capital expressed as a percentage of a bank's risk-weighted credit exposures. https://www.investopedia.com/terms/c/capitalad equacyratio.asp. This means roughly a $100mm buffer on top of the regulatory minimum of 12.5%. The tables are rough, but they make the point. Have a look."

**Box 2**[13]

#### Impact of Loan Loss Provisioning

| NPL | Required LL Reserve (100% Coverage) | Incremental Provisions | Adjusted Net Income | Adjusted Total Equity |
|-----|-----|-----|-----|-----|
| 10% | 200 | 125 | (23) | 317 |
| 15% | 300 | 225 | (123) | 217 |
| 25% | 500 | 425 | (323) | 17 |

#### Impact of FX Translation Losses

| Devaluation | Pre-FX Capital | FX Loss | Adjusted Total Equity |
|-----|-----|-----|-----|
| 15% | 340 | (126) | 214 |
| 25% | 340 | (210) | 130 |
| 50% | 340 | (420) | (80) |

#### Combination

| NPL | Adj Net Income | Devaluation | FX Loss | Beginning Total Equity | Ending Total Equity |
|-----|-----|-----|-----|-----|-----|
| 10% | (23) | 15% | (126) | 340 | 191 |
| 15% | (123) | 25% | (210) | 340 | 7 |
| 25% | (323) | 50% | (420) | 340 | (403) |

*Figures in millions (Local Currency)*

Kristi broke in, "The reason I sent this is I believe a double-threat looms. First, the last quarter's GDP figure showed a 3.5% decline year-on-year after a 2% decline the previous quarter. The consensus view is this current quarter may be as low as 5%. Thereafter? No immediate recovery. Our model estimates this growth decline will drive a spike in NPLs. Let's assume worst case, 20%. This is similar to the '97 crisis, the last time the economy slowed down this much. Second, the country's currency peg cannot hold much longer. Capital outflows are accelerating. The Central Bank is intervening aggressively. The country's foreign reserves are not unlimited. They can't keep buying local currency indefinitely. One of two things will happen, and soon:

---

[13] For the non-financial institution specialist: (i) When repayment is in doubt, the lender makes a "provision" to constitute a "reserve" against possible loan losses. The amount of the provision is an expense in the year it is taken. The amount follows through the income statement to capital. When the impact of the provision exceeds net income (ex-the provision), then capital is reduced accordingly. (ii) FX Translation gains (losses) occur when the adjusted value of FX-denominated assets are greater (less) than FX-denominated liabilities. These flow directly to the balance sheet.

either they devalue and hope that does the trick, or they go to the IMF, which will likely mean they get support but at the price of allowing the currency to float freely. That is, break the peg….."

"What kind of numbers?" Ursula interjected.

"25 to 50%."

"That's impossible."

"Actually, very possible," responded Kristi. "And even in the short run, at the low-end. My model spits out a 45% depreciation."

"You know, Kristi, our contacts at the Central Bank have expressed calm about the situation. They think the worst is over."

"Don't count on that. Look, Ursula, I think you should prepare for the worst. Let's assume NPLs of 20% and a devaluation of 25%. At these levels, your capital declines to close to zero. You need to have a standby plan to recap the Bank. Otherwise, besides the local financial supervisor baying for your blood, your funders are going to rush the exit."

"Kristi, with respect, this is crazy! 20% bad loans? 25% devaluation? If I go to my board with this, I'll be laughed out of the room. Our portfolio is sound and can comfortably ride out this temporary economic slowdown. A devaluation? You're the only one talking that way. The currency peg has held for a decade. Our house economist is not worried."

"I stand by my view. You don't have the luxury of waiting."

---

**Discussion Question Number 5**
- How serious is the threat? Is Kristi overstating matters?
- How would you characterize the situation?
- If you were advising Ursula, what would you say to her?
- After Ursula's brush-off, what should Kristi have done?
  See Annex 5 for suggested answers to these questions.

---

-&-

But Ursula had waited. Two months later, she had been hunching over the Bloomberg machine in her office. Just as Kristi had predicted, the Central Bank announced that the currency peg had been removed, and they would now allow the currency to float freely. This news accompanied a press release indicating the government and the IMF had reached a support arrangement. Still, the currency had lost a third of its value before stabilizing for a day and then dropping another 10%.

Her secretary walked into the office, unannounced. "You have calls. Lots of calls".

The list was long. At the top was Bank of Commerce's CEO, followed by Kristi and half a dozen of the bank's lenders. There were even several news correspondents.

Her mobile phone rang. There were many missed calls. Three from Kristi alone. She knew she could not continue to ignore the call. She took a deep breath and answered the call.

"Hello, Kristi. Sorry, I was in a meeting."

"Ursula, you need to organize a creditors meeting. Fast. "

"Why?".

"Lenders have woken up. If you don't move quickly, they will foreclose."

Ursula looked again at the list of calls. "Alright, you win! What do you suggest we do now?".

"The two sides have to start talking."

---

**Discussion Question Number 6**

- What should be done before the two sides "start talking?"
- Who should be involved?

    See Annex 5 for suggested answers to these questions.

---

-&-

Ursula's flashback ended. She snapped out of her daydream and found herself back on the dais at the lenders' meeting.

Stephen had just finished a digression on some topic then returned to the kill. "Time to share the pain."

Todd stood up. He looked straight at Ursula, then at JK, his tone increasingly agitated. "So you're saying you'll do nothing? You promised me the shareholders would always be there. When you came to our officer, you looked me right in the eyes and said that. Don't tell me you forgot that. You know that's why we came in last year. I put myself on the line with my fund's board for you guys. Now, nothing?".

JK pulled out a cigar and slowly placed it in his mouth, staring past Todd.

The silence hung uncomfortably.

"Well?" Todd's voice cut the air like a knife. He looked around the room, desperately searching for an ally.

Ursula attempted to speak but was waved off by Stephen. "I have thirty years of restructuring experience," he continued, raising his hands in the direction of the lenders, "I recognize this is all new to most of you. The choice is simple, you recapitalize the bank by converting your debt into equity, for which you will get a 49% share of the common shares or," he melodramatically pulled a set of car keys from his pocket, "or we hand you the keys to the bank, and you fix it yourself."

Stephen attempted to continue, but the conversations that erupted throughout the room drowned out his words. Some lenders huddled across tables where they sat. Others moved across to congregate in groups. Kristi joined Maya and another lender, both of whom she had wanted to invite to "the planning session that never was."

Kristi rolled her eyes. "Let's ask for a recess." She jerked her head to towards the dais, "Get them the hell out of here!" Several people around her blanched. "And then see if we keep this group together for now."

In the meantime, Todd had stormed out of the room.

---

**Discussion Question Number 7**
- What could Ursula have done at this point?
- Did Kristi handle the situation correctly?
  See Annex 5 for suggested answers to these questions.

---

-&-

A planned 30-minute recess stretched for an hour, then two. Lunch came and went. Todd never returned. His all-caps SMS to Kristi was ominous: "LIQUIDATION IS THE ONLY COURSE." The atmosphere resembled the slow build-up to a summer thunderstorm, followed by a sudden explosion of sound and fury.

Finally, emotions spent, the group coalesced around a response. Kristi texted Ursula. "Can you and Martin meet us in the business center in 10 minute?".

-&-

Accompanied by Martin, Ursula was ushered into the small meeting room. Kristi and Maya sat at a table waiting. Ursula and Martin closed the door and joined them at the table.

"We need to lower the temperature," Kristi began. "That's why we asked just to see you."

Ursula nodded her head in understanding.

Kristi continued. "The lenders have asked me to communicate our response. We'll all pretend this morning didn't happen. We want you to come back to us within two weeks with a 'going concern' plan, based on a serious commitment from your shareholders. Everyone will sit still for the time being. Failing this, we'll need to pursue a wind-down, an orderly extra-judicial wind-down[14] with your full cooperation."

"Are Edinburgh Partners on board?" asked Ursula.

"We'll manage them. You realize, Todd really went out on a limb for you. Understandably, he's concerned about…frankly… his job now. Maya," Kristi motioned towards her, "knows his boss, Colin, very well."

"I'll travel up to Scotland and see them tomorrow," Maya affirmed. "I don't want to rub this in, Ursula, but I did warn you not to borrow from them. They're fair-weather friends. Their reputation in work-outs is troublesome, even before considering Todd's current temper."

Kristi frowned at Maya but then continued, addressing herself to Ursula. "In the meantime, I have a few suggestions."

"These are?".

"First, get Stephen out of the deal or failing that, at least hide him. Second, confirm to the lenders you are indeed working on the 'new' approach. Third, don't take any more money out of the bank."

"I can't commit on any of this by myself. You know that, Kristi. I have to go back to the board."

Martin spoke up. "Yes, I am sure Kristi understands that."

"Of course, but I need your promise you'll do whatever you can."

Ursula said, "I will, but Martin I will need your help."

"You'll have it." Turning to Kristi and Maya, Martin continued. "I suggest we take advantage of being together here this evening and take the time to work together on the restructuring plan. I actually think we can cover a lot of ground. Next week, Ursula and I will be on the New West board retreat. I'd like to use that occasion to secure board approval. We have allies. Is this ok with all of you?"

Ursula nodded.

"Good. How about we meet at my suite at the Hyatt Regency on Portman Square. Say, 4 pm?" asked Martin.

"You go, Kristi." Maya said. "I'd like to fly up to Edinburgh tonight."

Kristi nodded her head in agreement. "Okay. See you two then."

---

[14] See Chapter 11 for a discussion of this concept.

---

**Discussion Question Number 8**
- Critique the roles and interactions of Kristi, Martin, Maya, and Ursula.
- Is it realistic that Ursula can break with her board like this? If not at present, what does she have to do to neutralize Stephen and coax the board to adopt a more constructive posture?
- Look for examples of when and how a cooperative partnership amongst parties straddling the multiple sides of a transaction proves itself to be an essential element in a successful outcome.

  See Annex 5 for suggested answers to these questions.

---

-&-

The door to Suite 562 opened.

Ursula stood in the doorway, her mobile phone lodged between her ear and shoulder, an unopened bottle of wine in her free hand. She motioned towards the phone with the Chablis, as if to say to Kristi, "Sorry, bear with me." Martin sat at the table with his head perched over a laptop computer.

Kristi followed Ursula into the well-appointed suite.

"Look," Ursula continued into her headset. "I understand what you said, JK…" A grimace crossed her face. She dropped the bottle onto the seat cushion, grabbed a notepad and became even more absorbed into her call. Several minutes passed. "I'm not prepared to decide that now…not at all!" She flushed. "I will talk with you when I'm back." She clicked off the phone.

Kristi smiled encouragingly.

"You don't want to know." Ursula searched the minibar stand for a corkscrew and reached for the Chablis. "At least, not until we've made a dent in this," she smiled impishly, as she began to pour the wine.

"Are you sure you won't have a drink, Martin?"

He shook his head, without slowing his typing.

"Okay, look. Here's the deal, I feel like I'm sinking in quick sand," Ursula began, in a more somber tone. "My board is standing to one side, the lenders to the other. All are holding onto the rope, but instead of helping me out, everyone is shouting at each other. Before too long, I'll sink in over my head, and after I am gone, the real shouting will start."

"Is that a metaphor for you or for New West?"

She sighed. Then, faintly chuckling, she answered. "Both, I guess."

Kristi reached out and placed her hand softly on Ursula's wrist. "Please confide in me. You have many friends in the lender community. Truly. Ursula, you've earned our respect and trust over the years. Our interests are aligned.

We just need transparency and," she rolled her eyes and breathed out, "a lot less sophomoric displays of testosterone overdose."

"Where do you want me to start?"

"How did we get here?".

"As you know, our investment in the Bank of Commerce started as a whim. JK obliged the son of the old owners whom he knew from the past. He announced it as a fait accompli. Once done, we made the best of it. Actually, it turned out as a good PR move. SME lending was hot, good for our image. The 'aggressive Silicon Valley group helps the poor' story. It was great for investor relations." She gestured towards Martin. "Then, getting Martin's group to invest gave us credibility. What we hadn't realized was how profitable the operation could be. The up streamed funds have been an unexpected bonus, especially in these challenging times."

"What do you mean, challenging times?".

Ursula drained her glass. She looked over to Martin. Her eyes widened.

Martin prodded her, "You can't expect her help if she doesn't understand what's going on, Ursula."

Kristi looked from Martin to Ursula and back to Martin. "Understand what?".

Ursula hesitated.

"Tell her!".

"Martin, I know what you want me to say, but…"

"Ursula, I want you to tell the truth. If you don't," he nodded towards Kristi, "then she will logically think you can recap the Bank but just won't. That this is a deal, another trade, almost a game, where the high-flying group of private equity billionaires profit at the expense of the ignorant social investors."

A firm knocking sound resonated from the other side of the door.

Ursula froze momentarily, then looked warily toward the door.

"Room Service," called a male voice from outside the door. Ursula's body relaxed.

"I honestly thought it might be JK."

Everyone laughed.

-&-

The waiter rolled the trolley in, laden with dishes under polished cloches, crystal goblets, and a silver ice bucket.

Ursula motioned the waiter to the dining table near the large window which looked out on the green square down below. "Could you please set it up over there? Could you also please put this wine in that bucket?".

Once the waiter left, Kristi spoke out. Her tone was distinctly brass tacks and down to business. "Ursula, tell me now - what's going on? What did you mean by 'especially in those challenging times'?".

Ursula thought back to the last board meeting.

Her CFO had just completed the presentation on the group's debt and cash flow position, post the pulling of the bond issue. They had avoided an immediate catastrophe. The bank which had provided the two and half billion-bridge finance[15] for the New Perspectives Energy acquisition had no choice. At this level of exposure, the age-old adage of the problem no longer being the borrower's but the lender's was apt. The damage to the bank would have been material, and their chief executive had quietly approved a six-month extension. However, she was still cash constrained. Their sparse liquidity was committed multiple times. For the Bank, nothing was available, and, she shuddered at the thought, she needed the quarterly dividend to be paid. The "restructuring plan" to be pushed on the lenders was a 100% debt conversion for a 49% shareholding.

"Not to leave this room, Kristi," began Ursula, "and that includes Maya and your management, for now. Agreed?"

"Alright."

Ursula walked through the New Perspectives deal and the difficulty they were encountering refinancing the short-term acquisition debt.

When Ursula finished, Kristi said softly, "Wow."

"'Wow' it is indeed," agreed Martin.

"Ursula, will New West default?".

"For the moment, no. The bankers will roll our debt over. But it means any rescue for the Bank of Commerce will require their agreement. Our board will be hesitant to ask them."

---

**Discussion Question Number 9**
- Consider the significance of the shareholder situation in this case. Does it act for or against a constructive role in the Bank of Commerce Restructuring? Why might Ursula's view differ from that of JK and the majority of the board?
- What do you think is going through Kristi's mind? How might it affect her attitude and approach?

---

[15] "Bridge financing" is a form of temporary financing intended to cover a company's short-term costs until the moment when regular long-term financing is secured. https://corporatefinanceinstitute. com/resources/knowledge/credit/bridge-financing/.

> • Given the sensitive nature of the New Perspectives Energy information, how do the parties incorporate it into the discussions?
> See Annex 5 for suggested answers to these questions.

-&-

The blue digital desk clock faintly glowed at 2:15 a.m. The Chablis leaned in its bucket, almost-finished. The ice had melted hours earlier. The dinner plates sat, still nestled under their cloches, untouched. Kristi's laptop projector beam flashed a term sheet on the wall.

At that moment, Martin opened the door to the suite, arriving back from the hotel business center. He handed out three sets of papers. The three collaborators sat quietly for several minutes, proofing their work product. The crux of the deal was new equity capital from the shareholders, a conversion of 50% of existing senior debt into Tier 2 qualifying subordinated debt, and a medium-term refinancing of the other 50%.[16]

Kristi spoke first.

"Is this the best we can do?"

"Yes, Kristi, and even this is a stretch, you realize. We will have to tap outside money, and this is highly problematic in today's context." Ursula's voice was now heavy with fatigue. Smiling, "I'll probably get sacked for just suggesting it."

"And with your dismissal, any chance of our avoiding a court-administered liquidation?" Kristi added.

"My institution would not allow that to happen." Martin assured her. "I doubt JK would want to get a call from Monique, my President."

"Assuming I can deliver my side, can you convince the lenders?"

"I'd place even worse odds on success." Kristi started. "First, Todd will understandably have to play hardball in order to safeguard his job. So, Edinburgh Partners are a big question mark. Second, the rest are prepared to refinance, give you more time, but fundamentally they believe you have the capacity to recap the Bank. They will strongly resist the debt-to-equity

---

[16] Basel III (https://www.bis.org/bcbs/basel3.htm) represents a set of measures designed to strengthen micro- and macro-prudential regulation and oversight of the global financial system in the aftermath of the Global Financial Crisis of 2007–2009. The measures address: (i) quality and level of capital; (ii) methodologies to calculate credit, market, credit-valuation, and operational risks; (iii) leverage limits; (iv) liquidity standards; and (v) disclosure and supervision. Within the provision pertaining to capitalization, there are minimum levels for specified classes of capital, built around the concepts of Tier 1 (common equity and retained earnings) and Tier 2 capital (revaluation reserves, hybrid capital instruments and subordinated term debt, and certain reserves). In summary form, the minimum standards appear: (i) Tier 1 Common of 4.5% (of Risk Weighted Assets); (ii) Tier 1 of 6.0%; (iii) Tier 2 of 2.0%; and (iv) Total Equity (Tier 1 plus Tier 2) of 8.0%.

conversion. Thirdly, for some, their funds are debt vehicles and simply may not be able to take equity. And fourthly, those who can probably don't have the expertise or the institutional patience to stay in. I can't stress this enough."

"Then it's liquidation!" Ursula sighed. "In this country's local courts, you'll get nothing."

"No, there are alternatives."

"I know, but you know JK. Bringing in a new investor? Under the current circumstances, any external party would require a valuation that would dilute New West into a minority role. JK must always be in control. It's been his approach for decades. An outright sale? Out of pride, he won't transact at a fire-sale price. An orderly wind-down where he gets nothing? Never. He'd prefer to burn the house down and blame the lenders for starting the fire."

Martin spoke up. "I agree he will resist. But the rest of the New West board is less certain. I am not sure that his hold over all the board is as strong as it was in the past. JK's miscues are catching up with him. The Vice Chair, Brian, is ambitious. He could well use the current situation to challenge the old man."

"I agree," chimed in Kristi. "A messy liquidation coming on top of every-thing else," she glanced covertly at Martin, "would be a body-blow to New West's prestige, delivered by the press, the lenders, my investors, and Martin's government shareholders."

"So what's next?" asked Martin.

"Maya sees Todd tomorrow. I've arranged a call with some of the lenders, my chosen core group, once you give me the green light on the plan. There are four, including me. The others are Maya, and the next two largest creditors. The restructuring folks at these other two are very clever, so we are lucky in this case."

"Good." Martin said.

Kristi looked at her watch. "I'd better run. I'm on duty again at 8am." She pulled her papers together, stuffed them into her briefcase, said goodbye and walked from the room.

The door closed behind her.

Once they were alone, Martin asked Ursula, "Do you really think there is any chance you'll be able to find money for the equity?".

"Very challenging until the New Perspectives Energy refinancing is completed. The Board is focused on solving this problem first."

"As I feared."

Martin concluded, ruefully. "Kristi was very clear. For her part, she would support an even bigger contingent debt conversion, but she needs to see fresh money from the shareholders. Under the current circumstances, we can't fix the problem without the lenders,"

"I recognize that." Ursula's eyes glistened. "Getting this plan done is my challenge. She put down her now almost empty glass and picked up the sheath of papers. "A big challenge. But I will do my best."

"Our challenge." Martin assured her. "We will contribute our pro-rata share, but anymore will not fly."

---

**Discussion Question Number 9**

- Consider the significance of the shareholder situation in this case. Does it act for or against a constructive role in the Bank of Commerce Restructuring? Why might Ursula's view differ from JK and the majority of the board?
- What do you think is going through Kristi's mind? How might it affect her attitude and approach?
- Given the sensitive nature of the New Perspectives Energy information, how do the parties incorporate it into the discussions?
- Is there a deal here?

See Annex 5 for suggested answers to these questions.

---

-&-

Kristi sat up. She had slipped in and out of a fitful sleep, dreams with flashes of red ink on fund performance reports. "Damn, damn, damn!" A sleepless night after a tough yesterday was going to make her today a nightmare. "I give up," she sighed and rose from bed.

Moments later, fortified with caffeine, she sat down and began to type her memo to her investment committee.

She cut and pasted into the draft the term sheet which she had prepared with Ursula and Martin then turned her attention to the background section. Two hours later, she pushed back from the desk.

Her mobile phone buzzed. Picking up the handset, she saw the time. 7:30 a.m. Maya's name flashed on the screen.

"Hi Kristi, this is Maya."

"Hi, can you speak up? The background noise is bad."

"Sorry, I am on the street. I was on my way to meet with Todd."

"Was?".

"Yes, was! He's been side-lined."

"Fired?".

"I'm not sure. His personal assistant said he would be back in the office next week. She told me his manager, Colin, my ex-colleague, was on the case now and had replaced him."

"Will he see you?".

He's tied up until early afternoon. She'll try to fit me in.

Kristi sat down on the bed. The lack of sleep, Todd, and her upcoming call with the Executive Management Committee flooded her thoughts. Struggling for control, she took several deep breaths.

"Kristi? Are you still there, Kristi?".

"Good. By the way, we worked out a draft term sheet, which I'll send you as soon as we are off this call." She outlined the main points.

"That's going to be a very hard sell, for both sides."

"Yep. Trim the sails, we're heading into stormy weather."

-&-

Later that day, Kristi sat in an airport café, directly across from her gate. A cold coffee stared up at her from the table, as if to console her. The hour delay in service had not helped to cheer her up after a day of never-ending waves of bad news and heated discussions.

First, there had been her Executive Management Committee call.

"Kristi," the chief investment officer Reggie had started, before she could even begin to brief the committee, "Stephen from Tifts called me last night."

Kristi had forgotten Reggie once worked with him.

"He accused you of failing to control the lenders. Now, there is a risk of default or worse. He says we will be responsible."

Kristi tightened her lips into a narrow line, her eyes popping from her head, but she let the silence hang.

"Kristi, are you there?".

"I am. That accusation is false and outrageous."

Reggie sounded ready to erupt once again. But Robert, the CEO spoke up, "Both of you settle down now." His voice was kind. "Kristi, please tell us what happened."

Kristi summarized the events of the day before, from the conversation with Todd through the late-night session with Ursula and Martin. "The proposed package can stabilize the situation," she concluded. "Getting the various parties together will be a challenge. No doubt. I won't even try to handicap the odds until we have some feedback from New West. What I can say is that only two things are certain—without some new money from the borrower's side, the lenders will push to wind them down; number two, we risk losing everything if we slide into a court-administered bankruptcy that

Ursula fears JK would do simply out of spite. A trade sale or an outside equity infusion under the circumstances is unlikely to be accepted by JK."

"What do you think Stephen meant by 'pain'?"

"We convert all our debt for 49% of the Bank."

"And from their side? What would they do?"

"Nothing."

"Nothing? Truly?".

"*Nada. Rien. Nichego.* Clear enough?".

Robert's words were directed to Reggie. "When you spoke to Stephen last night, did he not tell you this?".

Reggie spluttered. "Well, yes, more or less..." Regaining his confidence, he continued, "He was furious the lenders were so aggressive and appeared unreasonable. We should have let them send their proposal in writing first. That was your mistake, Kristi."

Robert probed, "Kristi, why didn't you just wait for their proposal?".

"Of course, they are free to say whatever they want. I judged that under the circumstances, receiving such a proposal in writing would merely inflame passions. We need a solution with which both sides can live."

"You mean, like what you worked out earlier today with Ursula?" Robert asked.

"Yes, I hope so. But to repeat, getting this done will be a challenge."

"Why so, Kristi?".

"The new money is central. And I have my doubts that New West will deliver on it."

"And so," Robert doodled on his pad, "...when your efforts fail?"

"Then we confront the even bigger challenge of engineering an orderly wind-down with a potentially uncooperative counter-party in a country where this has never been done before, with one or more rogue lenders in the mix."

"One moment, Kristi, there's a call coming in," interjected Robert. "I'll put you on hold for a moment."

Kristi knew there was no call. The Executive Management Committee just wanted to talk it through, offline. She could even write the script. Reggie didn't like Kristi and would be tempted to take JK's side to wound her. On the other hand, Robert was dispassionate and calculating. Deep down he knew New West's "offer" was poor, and Kristi's plan, if successful, was a far better outcome for them. On top of all of it, he recognized presciently this would be the first of many similar emergencies to fix. The markets were turning. A bad precedent here could come back to haunt them. Robert and Kristi shared this view. By now, Kristi estimated Robert had overruled Reggie, and the rest of the committee, true to form, was ready to go along with Robert and her.

On schedule, Robert came back on the line. "Sorry about that, Kristi. Okay, please proceed as you suggest. And keep us informed. We will support you as much as we can."

"Before we close, may I ask your help?"

Robert cleared his throat. "How's that, Kristi?" he asked.

"Well, I sense this thing might get messy, since we already have one holdout. Could you please ask our general counsel Colleen to have one of her staff members pull the docs out from the legal department safe and do a quick legal audit? I want to be ready to file a claim, if need be. I also want to know if there are any weaknesses in our position. Just a precaution."

"Understood," Robert replied.

---

**Discussion Question Number 10**
- Interpret and critique Stephen's call to Reggie. What was the purpose? Did it help or hurt?
- Why did Kristi ask for a legal audit of their debt documents?
  See Annex 5 for suggested answers to these questions.

---

-&-

Hours later, Maya had called.

"You know, Kristi, Edinburgh are going to be a big problem."

"Why so?".

"I reckon there are a lot of very embarrassed people inside their building. They wrote a big ticket at a time when most everyone else was scrambling for the exit. Colin's definitely singing from the same hymnal as Todd."

"What's the story with Todd?".

"He's on very thin ice."

"That's bad. Colin is using Todd as the scapegoat."

"Sounds like him. So, what should we expect next?"

"He said they'll sit tight for two weeks max. No more. Then we'll see how really serious they are."

"We should give thought to how we mobilize political pressure, should that become necessary. They have vulnerabilities like everyone else."

"Kristi, at a high level, I'm fine with your term sheet. I'm prepared to negotiate on this basis, but ultimately I will have to go to our committee for approval of the final deal."

Immediately after hanging up with Maya, Kristi called Ursula's mobile. After ringing and then jumping to another calling area and ringing some more, the call finally went to voice mail. Kristi decided to leave a voice message.

"Hello, Ursula, Kristi here. Wednesday evening at 7pm my time. Maya and I both have approval to negotiate on the basis of the summary term sheet you and I drafted. Maya didn't see Todd but did talk with his boss, Colin. He's on the same page as Todd. We have two weeks before they act. Good luck at your board retreat."

---

**Discussion Question Number 11**

Note how Maya and Kristi have handled the preliminary "approval" of the term sheet. In each case, their institution has effectively delegated to them the authority to negotiate the best possible deal in their opinion without requiring a committee approval at this point.

- What are the pros and cons of such an approach?
- Should institutions allow even these experienced individuals to operate this way?

See Annex 5 for suggested answers to these questions.

---

-&-

Days later, Ursula needed that good luck.

JK's words ricocheted around the room. She sat quietly, but not frightened. This board retreat was not going well.

"So, you spilt the beans, undermining our strategy," he puffed, "to pursue a plan that is not in our interest…and…" His face reddened, "that is unlikely to be accepted by the lenders, leaving us with a Plan B is to wind-down the operation and likely realize nothing."

"May I say a word?" Martin intervened, knowing what might come next.

JK began to wave him off, but Brian, the Vice-Chair interjected, "Please, Martin. Go ahead."

Martin spoke, with his habitual, almost unearthly calmness. "Your original plan was never realistic. The Lenders would have responded with something like Ursula's alternative, or worse. You have a chance, slim in my opinion, to bring the Lenders on board with her solution. But failing this, unless you are prepared to recapitalize the Bank of Commerce, what other choice do you have but an orderly wind-down?".

"First, we fight them in court! Accuse them of complicity in the bank's problems," exploded JK.

"Enough!".

All eyes went to the end of the table where a slightly built, middle-aged man sat. He was a prominent Wall Street lawyer and had been on the board for just under a year.

"In the first instance, there are absolutely no grounds for such a reckless claim." He glanced around the room. "I am confident all here agree, JK. Second, that does nothing to help the Bank of Commerce."

"Then we'll declare insolvency and allow the Lenders to collect their pennies in the local court," JK jeered.

"No," Martin spoke out, "that's exactly what you cannot do. The recovery for the Lenders will be dramatically higher in an orderly wind-down than in a bankruptcy."

"And do I care?".

Brian spoke. "We must. At this fragile moment for us, we need to demonstrate seriousness and responsibility. Screaming "screw you" in this case will reverberate elsewhere. We need to stay focused on the New Perspectives refinancing".

"Exactly so," continued Martin, his voice becoming steely as he focused his eyes on JK. "My shareholder governments, including Washington, will not look favorably on such a reckless action."

"Not to mention, as Brian said, the public relations disaster you'd create," added the lawyer, "which will not help us in tackling our own financial problems."

There were murmurs of agreement around the room.

"Lastly," Martin concluded, "you must cooperate fully with the Lenders, should the orderly wind-down happen."

Brian stood up. "Martin, I agree with you." He turned to Ursula. "May I ask you and Martin to step aside? I would like to discuss all of this with my colleagues."

-&-

A few days later, the lenders assembled on a video conference call.

"So, all five of us lenders are here, plus Martin." Kristi said, completing the roll call.

Kristi had expanded this core lenders group to five for this early call in order to get a better sounding of the lenders' reaction to the plan. The fifth was a minor creditor, but one who would be an excellent barometer for the views of the smaller lenders.

"As you heard, I have asked Martin to join us. Just for the first few minutes. I'd like to have him update us on the Group reaction before we talk. Martin, over to you."

"All, briefly, let me summarize. The Board has asked JK to step away from his involvement in this particular transaction. Brian, the Vice Chair, has asked me to be the Board's interface with Ursula. Ursula and I have been asked to lead the negotiations with you. The advisor, Stephen, whom you all met at the recent meeting, will no longer be involved. The New West Board has accepted the proposal prepared by Ursula and Kristi as the basis for the negotiations, but with two caveats."

"And these are?" Maya interrupted.

"They relate to the new money. First, the New West Board needs a week or so to confirm they can raise it. Second, they want to leave the precise post-money/post-debt conversion shareholding percentages for the moment."

Kristi asked, "Questions?".

"What's happening behind the scenes, Martin?" Asked Maya. "Really happening?"

"Sorry, Maya, that's all I can say for now."

"That doesn't help me. How do I explain that a multibillion-dollar fund, constantly in the news about one acquisition or another, can't support a small investment?"

"Yes!" another chimed in, "why must I convert my debt into equity, when they appear to be rolling in money?"

Martin began, "All I can do is to repeat what I just said."

"Perhaps I can help," Kristi interjected. "I think it's fair to say that there are financial constraints. Agreeing to this plan is a blow to the Group, a grave blow. They wouldn't do this unless absolutely necessary."

"But why be so evasive with us?"

Kristi jumped in, "Think about it! New West is publicly listed. Many of their portfolio companies are listed. If there's a liquidity problem, they can't especially announce it in the meeting hall."

"I know that! But I can't sell this deal internally unless I can explain 'why'."

Kristi turned to Martin.

"My sense from Ursula - I spoke to her briefly before this call – is they'll disclose more later, once they've completed their regulatory filings and announcements. Do you think so?"

"I presume yes." Martin responded.

Maya spoke. "I think we all agree that the new money is a proxy for the shareholder's commitment to the future. Consider this question: for whatever reason, unwillingness or lack of capacity, are we the Lenders prepared to own and operate the Bank of Commerce alone? My house will not."

There was general agreement.

"I need to be frank," spoke one lender. "It is unlikely my management will go along with a debt–to-equity conversion. If the rest insist on doing that, then we will look to sell our exposure, or…"

"What?" Kristi asked.

"…failing that, accelerate and take our chances in court."

Martin spoke up. "You are getting into territory where you should be alone. If there are no other questions, I'll leave the call."

"Before you go, are there other questions?"

"We only have an hour. Let's talk amongst ourselves. We can send Martin a list of follow-up questions later."

-&-

The rest of the call did not go especially well.

The objective of the conversation was to have the lenders opine on the fundamental question: would they accept a debt-to-equity conversion as part of a deal? The rest of the summary term sheet would be negotiated later. To coax new money out of New West, the lenders had to appear to give something beyond a simple extension of repayments.

"Two likely no's and one tentative maybe" is the way Kristi described it to Martin when she called him afterward.

"One 'no' said they are not permitted to convert debt into equity under their fund's PPM, without special approval. In the past, such requests have been turned down. Instead they've demanded to be bought out. The second 'no' has had uniformly bad experiences in similar structures, and their executive management would unlikely approve such a step this time. Their fallback position? Who knows at this point? The 'maybe' said it depends on the deal, and they don't like what they see thus far from New West."

"That doesn't close the door," Martin suggested.

"No, true, but when thinking about the rest of the lenders, the odds become longer. Not impossible, but very challenging. The sense is that of the remaining lenders, most will be very hesitant to play along. We'll have to poll them, of course."

Chuckling, Martin said, "Getting them all in will be your job. Ursula and I will have our hands full with the Board."

---

**Discussion Question Number 12**

- Does Kristi's approach of polling a limited group in this way make sense to you?
- Why do you think she chose to do it in this way?

See Annex 5 for suggested answers to these questions.

---

-&-

Two weeks later, Kristi and Maya walked into the New West HQ board room.

The two had been very busy since the last all-lenders call. They had divided up the lenders into two groups, and each had applied enormous pressure on their assigned names to support the restructuring proposal. Martin and Kristi had modified the original proposal to address certain lender concerns. Most prominent were the timing and conditionality of the lenders' debt to equity conversion and, of course, the amount of New West's financial contribution. The shareholder new money would go in first, and the lenders' debt conversion would follow if and when necessary. Even two CEOs were contacted. Eventually, all but two agreed to cooperate: a US-based fund and Edinburgh Partners.

Then the focus had shifted to New West. Martin worked intensively inside the board and enlisted Kristi's CEO, Robert, to help. He called Ursula and then his university classmate, the New West board Vice Chair, Brian. Kristi was not aware of what precisely was said, but Robert assured her the New West folks understood the revised plan was the best the lenders could do. Still, the conversations between New West and its investors and bankers were not going well. Until the acquisition finance on the New Perspectives deal was refinanced, new money for the Bank of Commerce would prove elusive.

In the board room, Kristi saw Martin, deep in conversation with Ursula. Off to the side stood Brian, and another board member—the lawyer—talking, appearing to share a private joke. The other three figures sat rigidly at the table. Kristi recognized them as the Bank of Commerce's executive management.

Brian looked over and saw the new arrivals. "Ah, we can start now."

"We are here to attempt to fashion a 'going concern' solution for the Bank of Commerce." He began. "Each side, all of us, will have to sacrifice. New

West will attempt to mobilize funding. I must stress, however, that we expect significant concessions from you, the lenders."

At that moment, there was a knock on the door. A page walked in and delivered a note for the Bank of Commerce's CEO.

As he read it, his face fell.

"What's wrong?" asked Ursula.

"We've just been served with a demand notice."

"Edinburgh Partners," gasped Ursula.

"Yes," intoned the CEO. "They have called an event of default and accelerated their loan."

"Game over?" It was the lawyer.[17]

Martin lifted his hand to signal his intention to speak. "Not at all. I suggest all of you focus on the restructuring plan for the Bank. Leave Edinburgh to me. Let's continue and not get distracted. Unless both sides give a little..." sighed Martin, "This," pointing to the document lying on the conference table, "doesn't add up." His glance moved to the representatives of the two lenders, both US-based funds, who remained opposed to the debt conversion proposal, and then to the New West Vice Chair, Brian, whose recent communications had been unsettling. "We are still working on it, Martin" had been his last text. This morning, he was equally non-committal. As had been Ursula.

Martin's words were greeted with silence.

Kristi looked across the room, trying to make eye contact with Ursula, who stared aimlessly into space. The team from the Bank of Commerce sat to Ursula's right. The implications of a failure to reach an agreement were written across their faces. Jobs lost. Reputations damaged. Not happy thoughts. The rest of the lenders circled the table. None appeared engaged, not even Maya. Colin's empty seat glared.

At length, Kristi spoke. "Let's start with the lenders. Are all on board?".

All nodded their heads in agreement. Even the holdout.

"And New West?" she continued.

Ursula turned to the Vice Chair, who signaled with his hand for her to speak.

---

[17] In multi-lender situations, a single (holdout) lender's service of a demand notice (i.e., the calling an event of default and acceleration of rights to payment under the loan agreement) can trigger a domino effect of cross-defaults, which then ordinarily triggers a formal insolvency proceeding.

"We have tried, but failed, to secure the full commitment of our share-holders to fund our new equity contribution to the Bank," Ursula began. "The alternative approach of tapping the debt markets has been foiled by the warning from our bankers that such a move is not viable at this time. We can only manage 10 to 15 million, which I realize is only a fraction of what you were expecting."

She had sucked in her breath, clearly pained, before concluding.

"Therefore, regretfully, I have to inform you, the lenders, that we are unable to fulfil our side of the deal."

The news hit Maya like a brick in the head. "So, what are you suggesting we do now, Ursula?".

Kristi was equally shocked, but she maintained her poker face whilst quickly regaining her wits. "Yes, Ursula, please help us understand where we go from here?".

"Our thinking is that you the lenders will convert enough debt into equity to stabilize the capital base and commit to maintaining the rest of your financing."

"Post-conversion," Maya shot out, a scornful look on her face, "what do you expect to have in the Bank?"

Ursula checked her papers. "Our ask is for 40%."

At this point the room needed no further leads from either Maya or Kristi. This was JK redux. The lenders spontaneously convulsed with anger. Shouted questions, and even threats, ricocheted off the walls. This was not going well, to say the least.

A pen rapped against a water glass. "Please, everyone." Someone was trying to restore order to the unruly group. It was Martin. He tapped again, then waited several seconds until the room had quieted down. Whispers of indignation continued amongst one or two lenders, but at least it was now quiet enough for him to speak. He did not want to lose this chance.

"My suggestion is the two sides meet separately and consider how we can bridge the gap."

Before anyone could object, he stood up and signaled to Ursula and the Bank of Commerce management to leave the room with him.

Once alone with the lenders, Kristi tried to steer the conversation. But she lost control. Maya was the most vocal. Kristi knew why. Inside her house, there had been unexpected pushback on the original deal. She had used a lot of political capital to get the deal across the line. Now, she would have to go back with a far less attractive alternative. Maya was now on the warpath. Job be damned, she would not be cowed. She would show Ursula no quarter. Two hours in, Kristi had succeeded in cooling Maya off.

---

**Discussion Question Number 13**

- What are the possible explanations for Kristi and Maya having applied pressure on the lenders for the rest of the deal before knowing whether the new money was forthcoming?
- Martin undoubtedly knew of the difficulty in advance. What should he have done?
- Where do they go from here?
  See Annex 5 for suggested answers to these questions.

---

-&-

Prior to the meeting reconvening, Kristi asked to see Martin alone. The two spoke for a few minutes before calling in Ursula.

An hour later, the three joined the rest of the group.

"So, what have you been cooking up?" Maya snapped.

Kristi began. "We have…" but stopped and turned to Martin "Perhaps it's better that you do this."

Martin said, "Happy to." He stood up and looked around the room. His stare rested on Maya for a long moment. He knew they needed her on side and regretted now not having also called her into the meeting. "We have all come into this sector for a higher purpose. We operate with a double-bottom line—return for our investor or in my case our government sponsor and support for economic and social development in our investee markets. Key to continuing our business, this mission of ours is the confidence of multiple stakeholders. If we allow the Bank of Commerce to crash and burn, then we weaken this confidence. Now, it is clear that we lack the financial means to keep the Bank alive long-term. New West can't provide new money in the necessary quantity. The lenders, all of you, were prepared to agree to a contingent debt to equity conversion, but not to be the primary source of the recapitalization. Hence our original deal is not feasible. What do we do now? Do we have an alternative to bankruptcy? Yes. We will look into a trade sale. There are several banks who might be interested. However, we must be prepared for the eventuality that there is no buyer. In such a case, we must engineer an orderly wind-down of the institution. With this, we can fashion a smooth landing for the borrowers and the employees of the Bank. But we will do even more. We will show the market that even in adversity we are able to act responsibly."

He reached for his water bottle and then resumed.

"Now, for a back-up plan for the eventuality of no trade sale - the shareholders commit to support an orderly wind-down of the Bank of Commerce. For our part, New West and my institution will provide up to twenty million dollars to support liquidity and capital adequacy during the process. Should additional recapitalization be necessary, you the lenders will be expected to forgive sufficient debt from time to time to maintain minimum regulatory capital."

Bank of Commerce's CEO spoke, his voice shrill. "To protect ourselves, the management and directors, we would need to declare bankruptcy. A wind-down when we are technically insolvent will never be allowed by local authorities. Indeed, the minute the deposit insurance corporation hears of the breakdown of these discussions, I foresee immediate intervention."

"Which means," Martin intoned, "we have to tread carefully."

---

**Discussion Question Number 14**
- Why the resistance to a bankruptcy procedure?
- For an orderly wind-down, why would the shareholders committing a modest amount of capital be helpful? Why do you think they are prepared to consider it in this case?
- What underlies the concerns of the Bank of Commerce CEO?
  See Annex 5 for suggested answers to these questions.

---

-&-

Martin walked into the restaurant at the Heathrow Airport hotel. Across the room, he saw Colin and his CEO, Peter Baines. The two were settling their bill. They saw Martin at the same time and waved him over.

As Martin sat down, he apologized for his tardiness, "Hello Peter. Sorry, Colin, the traffic was jammed."

"No worries, Martin. But we have only a few minutes before having to leave for our flight, so let's get right to it."

Martin quickly summarized the discussion from yesterday's meeting. In a nutshell, the parties had decided to work confidentially with the local regulator to engineer an orderly, out-of-court wind-down of the Bank of Commerce. The shareholders and the lenders would undertake to keep the Bank solvent throughout the process and would ensure depositors are protected in full. The idea is to transfer good quality assets and deposits to local bank.

"Will there be anything left for us?" asked Colin.

"Yes," responded Martin. "The quality of the loan book is actually not bad. Not 100 cents on the dollar, but something in the 60% range is quite possible. Maybe higher."

"The equity is wiped out and we start at a 40% loss?"

Martin nodded in agreement. "But we need the agreement of the local supervisor and will have to be sure the public is kept in the dark. Once word gets out, we run the risk of borrowers' refusing to repay."

"Fair points."

"We have some ideas on how to handle this, assuming the government and the party to which we transfer the deposits play along."

Colin questioned, "Why not just a court-administered liquidation?".

"Local sources have argued against this as the worst possible option. Long, complex, expensive. And you know how the courts work there. We're not in Kansas, as they say."

"Kansas?".

Chuckling, Martin explained. "From a classic American film, the Wizard of Oz." He continued, "Going into court there is foolish. We will not have the same protections as in a more developed legal system. In the end, we could all count on pennies on the dollar at best."

Peter spoke up at last. "I've worked with this government in another context. Are you sure you can trust them? There's a lot of money to be made by the locals, should the bank collapse. Are you not concerned that they'll prioritize their wallets over systemic stability? One slip in secrecy, and they'll be forced to intervene to 'protect the public."

Martin lowered his eyes and fell into silence for several minutes. Looking up, he said, "You have a point, Peter. The local CEO is the advocate of a more open and transparent approach."

Peter smiled wryly. "Give it some thought."

Martin nodded.

"What are the shareholders doing?" Colin asked.

Martin sighed. "Not as much as the lenders want. At my insistence, some funds and we will maintain the management and the board in place. There will be full cooperation with the lenders and the process." He handed Colin a sheet of paper. "This is the crux of the deal."

---

**Box 3. Key Elements**

1. The lenders maintain all their principal exposure and capitalize the past and future accrued interest
2. The shareholders inject funding in the form of Tier 2 qualifying junior capital to ensure liquidity up to an agreed maximum of USD 20 million
3. As necessary to maintain regulatory solvency through the process, the lenders will forgive portions of their loans from time to time according to a quarterly review and conversion schedule
4. During the process, the loan book will be slowly run down under the guise of a strategic reorientation of the business, paying off the depositors first, the lenders second, and the shareholders last
5. As a parallel exercise, a sale or merger will be explored

---

Colin shook his head. "This is embittering. We feel let down, Martin. No worse than that, tricked and betrayed."

"I know. All the lenders feel the same. But we are where we are, and we need to move forward."

"Why are you so involved?".

"Bad luck, maybe?".

The three chuckled.

"But seriously," Martin continued. "We've discussed this topic at great length. We recognize we made a mistake hooking up with JK and his cut-throats. I know this was not your fault personally, but still. Now, we feel the equity, including ourselves, should pay the price. For the lenders and the broader market, we want to limit losses and the negative spill overs to this vital investment space."

"Punish the money but protect systemic stability, then?"

"Yes."

Peter looked at his watch. "We have to run."

"Where do you stand?".

"I'll have to consult with my colleagues. As you know, we have held off taking the next step, after our payment claim, waiting for your news today. I personally agree that we should avoid the courts, if possible. There are differing views inside my house. Leave me a couple days. I'll be back in touch on the weekend."

-&-

Martin dropped the headset back onto the cradle.

"Not good." He said to the empty room. He considered waiting to call Kristi and deliver the news on Monday but, hell, he thought, if Colin can ruin my weekend, I should be able to do the same to Kristi…

He hit the speed dial, and within seconds Kristi was on the line.

"Oh, Martin! Thanks for calling me. You saw my email then?"

"No, what was it about?".

"The question of transparency with the local regulator?"

"And?" Queried Martin.

"Through a trusted, well-connected local 'friend" we've validated Peter's concern. One whiff of our plan within the government and they'll move in. Game over."

"What do you and Ursula suggest?".

"Well, Martin I think we create the illusion of business as usual. We sustain this until we can sell off the parts and/or run down the loan book and slowly pay off, first the depositors and then the lenders. Until then, we must ensure we are strictly in conformity with regulatory liquidity and solvency minima."

"Will the local CEO play along?".

"If paid enough. I'll convince the lenders to agree a hefty success bonus for him and the team."

Martin asked, "Yes, but before we get there, have all your lenders obtained their internal approvals?".

"I am waiting on several. One was delayed going to committee. One was unexpectedly turned down but has appealed."

"Odds are?".

My CEO, Robert is talking to the top brass there. If he can't do it, no one can. But tell me, why did you call?".

"I spoke to Colin." His voice tightened.

"Why not Peter?".

"I think for the moment, Colin is running with the ball."

"What did Colin say? Bad?".

"Could be. The issue is they need to avoid classifying their loan to the Bank of Commerce as non-performing."

"Ever?".

"For now. They are in the midst of a fundraising effort apparently. They will refrain from any action against the Bank of Commerce as long as their loan is serviced normally." said Martin. "They will not acknowledge our process in any way."

"Eventually, their principal starts coming due. That's in under 3 months," interjected Kristi.

"It means we have just under three months to fix our Bank of Commerce problem."

"The wind-down process will take a minimum of two years. There's no prospect of anyone getting 100 cents on the dollar... under any scenario. At some point, they'll have to face a loss," warned Kristi. "The rest of the lenders may agree to keep them current on interest for now, but on the assumption that what they get paid now comes out of their eventual recovery. One question that will come up is whether they will recall their declaration of default and payment demand."

"Once interest is brought up to date, yes, I understand they will."

"Oh, dear!" sighed Kristi. This was going to be hard before. Now? "The best we can do is try," she concluded. This would be an even more arduous path."

"Check with the other lenders. Hopefully we can have something sorted by the time we meet in Oxford next week."

---

**Discussion Question Number 15**

- What are the issues with the local financial authorities? Why the need for secrecy?
- What should the lenders be thinking about around the problem of Edinburgh Partners?

See Annex 5 for suggested answers to these questions.

---

-&-

The four weary travelers approached the reception desk at the conference center at Oxford University's Keble College.

"We are the International Capital meeting."

"Ah, yes, we have been expecting you. A number of the attendees have already checked-in."

"Who?" asked Martin.

The attendant handed him a list. Of the Bank of Commerce lenders, Martin saw that all but three had already arrived. Along with Kristi and Maya, who stood at his side, that meant only Colin was missing. He had not been expected. His messages had been increasingly threatening over the past days.

Martin turned to Ursula. "When do your lawyers arrive?".

"In the morning. They plan to drive up early from London."

"The same with ours." Added Kristi. "And the operational consultants flew in to Heathrow a few hours ago and will come in here later tonight."

Martin turned to the attendant. "The full group starts at 10am tomorrow morning. For tonight, as I wrote, we'd like a conference room and dinner so this smaller group can work."

"Why certainly, sir. You may leave your luggage here, and I will show you to the conference room."

-&-

Near midnight, Kristi ran her eyes up and down the list, one last time.

"I think that does it." She sighed. "Are we missing anything?"

The other three pondered the question and one by one shook their heads. "That does it," concluded Ursula.

On the white board was a list below the heading, "Challenges." The list read:

1. Prioritization of depositors over the lenders
2. Neutralization or Co-option of Edinburgh Partners
3. Allowance for Early Exits
4. Recapitalization mechanism given (2) and (3)
5. Determination of cash pay-out shares given (2), (3), and (4)
6. Wind-down operations: division of role/responsibilities
7. Legal Documentation

Martin walked to the white board and picked up a red marker.

He circled (1) to (5) and wrote "Working Group #1 – Lenders", then (6), "Working Group #2 – Operational Consultants and Bank of Commerce Management," and finally (7) "Working Group #3 – Legal Counsel."

"I've arranged for a plenary room and four breakout rooms. We'll meet first as a full group, then break into the working groups. Ok?"

-&-

Kristi let her warm brow slip into her hands, covering her painfully tired eyes.

The bickering had been going on all day.

The lenders had broken into two factions. One of two lenders opposed any concessions to Colin. "There is one deal or no deal." The rest, including Kristi and Maya, did not like the idea of a side accommodation, but were not prepared to risk blowing up the deal as a matter of principle, should Colin play hard ball. That said, their tactic was initially to call his bluff and see where the things fell out.

Maya spoke up. "Let's focus on net recovery levels."

A voice bellowed out, "Timing is also important. Your idea of deducting anything Colin gets from future shares of cash pay outs assumes we get to the end of a successful wind-down. What happens if we don't? They walk away, better off for having put a gun to our heads than the rest of us who acted responsibly. I can't accept this."

Kristi joined in. This would be her last try. "How about this?" She turned to Ursula, who had joined the group. "Can we manage to pay pro-rata shares to all the lenders to coincide with EP's interest instalments? He calls it interest. We deduct this from his remaining principle, as we will do for the rest of us. This would buy us enough time to close the overall wind-down, and then we confront him. If we have a deal and some estimate of expected, net proceeds, then he has to decide."

Martin added, "This could work. He needs to delay an admission of his screw up to his board for now. This could buy him enough time."

"So, for the time being," another lender asked, "What do we tell him?"

"My suggestion," voiced Kristi, "first, is that we… actually, you, Martin, reach out to him and send the message they will risk your institution's goodwill if they take any action risks destabilizing our process. They'll be kept current on interest in the meantime. Second, assuming there's sufficient liquidity we distribute just enough to keep their interest current and the rest of us even. Ursula and the local management will have to guide us there. Third, we work like hell to get a deal in place. Lastly, once this is done, Martin talks to Peter again as necessary. When there is a deal at hand and the right pressure applied."

-&-

Two mornings later, at dawn Kristi and Martin trudged through the University Parks and approached the side of the River Cherwell. Oxford still slept. As did the rest of the group. The meeting had broken up yesterday at around 8 p.m. Many had rewarded themselves for a surprisingly successful second day with a trip to a local pub. Kristi and Martin had slipped out after a symbolic ale to return to the conference center to meet the two side's attorneys. The two sets of lawyers would be leaving the next morning after a brief closing meeting to return to London to begin the drafting. There was likely a late night and a huge bar tab. In this case, well deserved.

Martin espied a bench along the riverside. "Let's sit there."

"Good idea," Kristi huffed. "We should agree the agenda for this morning, and…"

Chucking, Martin finished her sentence for her, "…And how I am to plan my attack on our rogue lender!".

"Yes, Martin." Kristi smiled. "And?".

"You know Kristi, were it not for the threat that the local supervisor could step in and shut us down to protect the depositors, then I'd work on Colin directly, one-on-one. However, that way we may prolong the uncertainty and give Colin more time to mouth off. He's the security risk. So…"

"What do you plan to do?".

"I plan to fly to headquarters in Paris and meet our MD to enlist her help." Kristi frowned. "For something so minor?".

"She's a classmate of Peter Baines. Their families are close. She has also been the driving force behind our support for the micro-enterprise lending sector. Like you and me, she realizes a messy ending to the Bank of Commerce would be black eye to the industry."

"But not enough to bail-out the bank?"

"No, Kristi. The rest of the managing committee would never go there. She was able to get them to support our contribution to the wind-down plan, but nothing more."

"So what will you ask her to do?"

"Ensure that our friend Colin agrees to our plan."

Kristi pursed her lips. "With that kind of pressure, Martin, why should we cut them the "different" deal we are?".

"Colin is a very proud man. We have to let him keep face. If ordered to back-down entirely, he's just the kind of person that could explode and jeopardize everything."

Kristi looked at her watch. It read 06:18. "We'd better head back to Keble. Our meeting starts at 7:30."

-&-

Samuel Worthington III, the head of restructuring at Maybank and Johnson, stood at the end of the conference room. He gestured to Kristi, his long-time client and to his counterpart counsel for the borrower, Jade Martinez.

"I think we can begin."

The room grew silent.

"I have distributed the skeletal draft heads of terms for the wind-down agreement. Jade and I, along with our teams, completed this overnight based on yesterday's discussions. The text is still unfinished, and it has a lot of blanks. But that's why we are all here, right? Let's get to work." Turning to his colleague, he continued "Dennis, could you please put the first page up on the screen?"

**Box 4. Term Sheet**
**Bank of Commerce**
  **Wind-Down Agreements**

| | |
|---|---|
| Parties | Company, Parent, Affiliates, Liquidation Monitor, Lenders |
| Representations and warranties | Standard capacity, authority, enforceability etc. for all parties |
| Undertakings of lenders | No enforcement measures or changes in relative positions |
| Undertakings of company | No leakage / adverse steps etc |
| Undertakings/confirmations parent and affiliates | Mirror above |
| Wind-down milestones | Initiation of voluntary wind-down by [], cessation of loan collections by [], completion of voluntary liquidation by [], if requested by lenders Parent to sell Company by [] |
| Early termination | If a termination event occurs, majority of lenders may terminate wind down / standstill (subject to consultation period and final termination notice) |
| Restrictive covenants | To be discussed |
| Reduction of services | Parent and Affiliate to reduce services [level to be discussed] but undertake continued support at FMV, subject to cap |
| Share retention | During wind-down Parent to retain full ownership and control of Company |
| Role of liquidation monitor | Liquidation Monitor to act as independent monitor and advisor to Lenders [list rights, including full information access]; no voting or decision-making within Company and no consent required for corporate action. [Further disclaimers to be provided]. Compensation |
| Regulatory requirements | Regulatory capital requirements to be reflected; reporting; periodic principal adjustments (certification by Liquidation Monitor) |
| Releases | By Company, Lenders, Liquidation Monitor, of Liquidation Monitor—to discuss timing |
| Indemnity | To be discussed (must cover Liquidation Monitor) subject to usual carve outs |

(continued)

(continued)

| Parties | Company, Parent, Affiliates, Liquidation Monitor, Lenders |
|---|---|
| Lump sum payment | To be discussed—to be made within [] days of effective date |
| Establishment/funding escrow/indemnity reserve | To be discussed—foreign bank account to be funded through special distribution for indemnity reserve. Amount to be discussed. Escrowee to be discussed |
| Periodic distributions | Subject to regulatory capital requirements, periodic distributions of available cash to be made pro-rata to Lenders—Liquidation Monitor to certify |
| Currency conversion | All loans to be redenominated into USD on [] |
| Early Exit | To be discussed (including haircut and other terms) |
| Management incentives/severance | Senior and middle management incentive and severance to be discussed |
| Obligations of company | Budget, reporting, new policies subject to Lender approval, customer messaging |
| Liquidation | Cessation of loan monetization / sale of remaining portfolio |
| Standstill during Wind-down | Usual standstill subject to termination events |
| Full and final satisfaction and settlement | Upon final settlement date/completion of wind down |
| Company's restructuring advisors | Cap on Company counsel fees to be discussed |
| Lender group counsel | Company to reimburse |
| Costs and expenses | General reimbursement of all costs; cap on Lender counsel fees to be discussed |
| Disclosure of information | Standard non-disclosure / no announcements |
| Accession mechanism | For selling lenders – usual deed of accession for transferees |
| Boilerplate | Standard including English law, LCIA |

Martin's taxi from Charles de Gaulle airport had made record time. A good day for that! He could not be late for his meeting.

The conference in Oxford had ended well. The lenders had agreed on the term sheet. The lawyers were working away. All that remained was Edinburgh Partners.

He gazed ahead and saw the modernistic glass tower, prominent in the La Defense area. This was the headquarters of the International Capital Fund. He picked up his smartphone and dialed ahead to let the office know he was moments away.

"*Allo*, the office of the President," chirped the secretary.

"This is Martin Baudelaire."

"Ah, very good. We see you in 15 minutes, *oui?*"

-&-

Martin stepped out of the elevator into the thickly carpeted reception area of the President of the ICF.

"I am here to see President Du Bellay."

"Yes, we are expecting you, Monsieur Baudelaire."

The receptionist escorted Martin into the president's office.

Monique Du Bellay stood at the end of the spacious office, reading at an antique standing desk. She was framed by a floor to ceiling window with a spectacular view of central Paris. She looked up, and her face brightened.

"Martin, you are early. Please sit down." Motioning to the conference table. "I will be with you presently."

Martin took a seat and pulled out his papers.

He snuck a glance at Monique. She was engrossed in the memo, to which she was making dramatic corrections with a red pen. In her early sixties, Monique displayed the same frenetic energy now that Martin had experienced twenty years before when they had first met.

She put the pen down and hit the intercom button. "Sophie, I have a redraft for you."

As she walked over to Martin, a secretary came in.

"Have this prepared for my signature. And in 10 minutes, Sophie, initiate my call with Peter Baines at Edinburgh Partners."

The secretary acknowledged the instructions, with a slight bow to her head. As she turned to leave, "Your car to the airport for the flight to Washington leaves in one hour."

"Washington?" queried Martin.

Monique smiled. "Long story." She sighed. "Now, let's get to the Bank of Commerce case. I read your note. Simple and clear. As you just heard, I have set up a call with your Colin's boss, Peter Baines. Any last minute news?".

"I touched base with the team in London on my way in from the airport. Despite the deal's complexity and a road forward littered with potholes, we are in surprisingly good shape."

"Still want us to bail them out?"

Laughing, "No, Monique. That was never in the cards. A bank dependent on wholesale, cross-border funding is no longer viable in the country. When China was buying up every space ounce of copper, the business model made sense. Now that we've returned to a more normal world, *ca ne va plus.*"

"Your early thinking was to merge them with a local bank, *non*? What happened there?"

"Would never have happened with terms any of us could have accepted. The indicative haircuts to the debt the potential buyers that we contacted were demanding were excessive. The lenders are better off going the wind-down route."

"Understood, Martin." Monique walked over to her desk. Sitting down, she opened a leather portfolio and laid a pen to the side. She centered the spider phone. She checked her watch. "To battle!"

-&-

Martin closed the door to Monique's limousine. As the car pulled away, he smiled and waved. He pulled out his phone and hit the speed dial button.

"Hello, Kristi!".

Her voice jumped out the handset, "So, how did it go?".

Martin allowed a weary smile to spread across his face. "*Je touche du bois*, I think we're there. Monique was masterly. Barnes was evasive at first, claiming he would need to talk internally. She pressed him, and eventually he indicated they'd be cooperative."

"So, good, eh?".

"Yes." Martin hesitated. "He wouldn't commit on the transaction structure… that's fair, they haven't seen the details."

"That gives them a lot of wiggle room."

"Peter Barnes committed to Monique that Colin would cooperate. Under no circumstances, he promised on several occasions, would Edinburgh Partners be the reason the deal fails. Remember, that house cannot risk Monique's 'displeasure'."

"Still, I suspect Colin will go kicking and screaming."

"Possibly… likely, I guess, but in the end I'm confident we'll get there. Monique."

"Hold for one moment." Kristi said. "Another call coming in." A few minutes passed before Kristi returned. "You'll never guess who just called!"

"Colin?".

"Yes."

"How did he sound?" Asked Martin.

"Sullen."

"So, what happened?" asked Martin.

"Yes. We've agreed on a call tomorrow. I'll have counsel send him the term sheet and make himself available for Q&A."

"Do you want me on the call?"

"No, let's keep you in reserve."

-&-

The Zoom window appeared on the screen in the conference room to the side of Kristi's office.

Colin came on. He looked careworn. Maya joined moments later.

Kristi started, "Is anyone else joining?".

"No!" Colin barked.

"Understood," Kristi assured him. He's unusually nervous, she thought to herself. Something is up. "I take it you've read the term sheet?"

"Yes, I have."

"Questions?".

"No, your counsel called earlier today and went over the document, page by page."

"Excellent. Do you have comments?".

"Yes, of course we do."

"Will we also get this in writing?"

"Of course!" Again the bark. "As soon as this call is over!"

Kristi took a deep breath. "Ok, shoot."

Colin picked up a single sheet of paper and read, "We will sign a separate, bi-lateral parallel agreement with the Bank of Commerce and the shareholders. It will conform to your deal, save for one element."

"And this is?" Asked Maya.

"We will structure the language to ensure we achieve a minimum recovery of 65%.

Kristi raised her finger to pre-empt the explosion she knew was coming from Maya. "Two immediate questions. First, why the separate agreement? Second, if the wind-down can't generate this, what then?".

"We don't wish to be part of the group. Policy reasons."

"These are?" Maya interjected.

"None of your business!".

"Of course, we need to understand why! You can't expect us to…"

"Maya," Kristi jumped in, "Let's leave this for now. Colin, we will discuss with counsel the practical implications of two parallel agreements and revert to you."

Colin countered. "This is not open to discussion, Kristi!".

Kristi ignored his response and moved on to the second point. "You realize of course, Colin, there is no certainty about the recovery level. The Bank of Commerce can't commit to this level, so we have to conclude you're effectively telling the shareholders and the lenders to underwrite the 65%."

"I'm glad you understand." Colin sneered.

-&-

"Of course the 65 is mad, Kristi," agreed Martin, "and totally inconsistent with being 'cooperative'."

"So, what's up?".

"Two possibilities. One, Colin is trying to be cute and see if they can sweeten the deal somewhat. Not get an underwritten recovery, but something, say a premium of a few points, something to show they did better than the rest of us."

"That makes sense," Kristi acknowledged. "His demand is ludicrous. A joke. What's the second?"

Maya interrupted, "Colin's actually doing this on his own!".

"What?" Martin and Kristi exclaimed together.

"Think about it! Who made the loan? Todd! Who's Todd's boss? Colin. Edinburgh Partners is notorious for the "one strike and you're out" approach to mistakes. Todd's already a goner. Colin could well be next. So, he's desperate for a "success." His survival may depend on it. To be criticized for embarrassing Peter Baines in front of Monique may be forgiven, if he secures a much better deal."

Several moments passed.

"I'll call Peter," concluded Martin. "He knows I'm close to Monique, and she's not the kind to cross on something like this."

-&-

A month later, Kristi turned off Wadsworth Street and headed toward the MIT Department of Economics building. Her gait was animated on this sunny, warm spring morning. She was enjoying her first week off in over a year. Before driving out to the Cape, she had arranged to meet her former doctoral supervisor to talk about her future.

Her work on the Bank of Commerce had ended well, just a few days ago. The last negotiating "bump," the "65% demand," had in fact been Colin's futile last move. Whether Peter had actually been aware of Colin's gambit Kristi still did not know for certain. Martin's call to Peter Baines had been short, spiced with choice expletives, and ended with Peter's promise, "We'll do your deal!".

Hours later, the lenders convened a call to review the term sheet. Edinburgh Partners was represented by an attorney and a risk officer. The business side had finally stepped aside. Colin had disappeared. Less than two hours later, there was agreement. A follow-on call with Ursula, Martin, and their lawyers ensued and ended with equal success.

"What's the catch?" Kristi had joked to the group.

After weeks of acrimony and near-disasters, the deal was set.

Much remained to be done. Many risks loomed. Final documentation, setting up the operational team in country, and above all, executing the wind-down. But like Martin, Kristi's role as an architect of the process was now at an end. Lawyers would argue about commas, but the documentation would be signed. Managing the Bank of Commerce through the wind-down would be the responsibility of the external consultants and the staff of the bank. Periodic updates and the occasional course correction, hopefully minor, would be considered by a lenders' steering committee. She had agreed to advise a colleague, whom she had designated to take over her role. The day-to-day work would no longer be her worry. The question of success or failure was shifting from negotiations in airport hotels and scattered office conference rooms to the capacities of the Bank of Commerce, its staff and customers. The hope was that when the dust settled, local borrowers would have repaid their loans to the Bank of Commerce and found new lenders to support their businesses, and the bank staff, new jobs. A successful conclusion for all. For the lenders and the shareholders, there would of course be losses. A successful wind-down should minimize them, but nonetheless all would lose money. On the positive side, there would be many valuable lessons learned for all.

For the moment, Kristi put this all aside as she entered the building. She checked in with the security guard.

"I'm here to see Dr. Romano."

"Ah, yes. Here is your name. Please wait."

Moments later, the white haired, diminutive figure ambled down the corridor. He embraced Kristi, "Welcome home!".

-&-

# Epilogue

As with most multi-creditor consensual restructurings, the rest of our tale of the Bank of Commerce was not straightforward. The law firms battled it out over the minutiae of the wind-down agreement, going into overtime, triggering an extension of the original standstill.

Edinburgh Partners ultimately then became a positive force in the group. Peter Baines' promise to Monique proved as good as gold. But where one glowed, others dimmed. One small lender in particular cooled on the deal, demanding an immediate pay-out well above the expected recovery rate. When the rest of the group balked, the lender threatened to accelerate. Weeks were lost. At last, the bank's own threat of an imminent US Chapter 11 proceeding helped to bring this prodigal child back into the fold of the main body of lenders.

Unfortunately for Kristi, she would have to rejoin her colleague to help negotiate key strategic points. A number of issues between the lenders and the borrower side raised temperatures, even in a few cases to the point of talk of a breakdown in the process. Many of these revolved around the local staff of the bank.

*First,* whilst Ursula delivered on her financial promises without delay, she was uncompromising, on protecting the bank's staff and board members against any potential personal liability which might arise from the wind-down. These protections carried a price tag, which could dilute the lender's recovery. In the end, funds would be added to the offshore escrow account established for a variety of potential liabilities and costs, including local taxes.

*Second,* conflicts arose between the Bank of Commerce executive management and the team placed in the bank by the lenders to oversee the wind-down (the liquidation monitor). Key to success was maintaining the impression of a going concern. This would necessitate some new lending. Disagreements on control over how much and to whom arose and required a compromise between the two sides.

*Third*, as the wind-down progressed, the number and type of staff would have to change. Who would make the decision to reduce staff numbers? What would be the severance payment arrangements? A myriad of questions arose. Again, compromises were reached. In both main issues (second and third in this paragraph), the local management would make a recommendation, the liquidation monitor would opine, and then Ursula would consult with the lenders. The understanding was the lenders would be guided by the liquidation monitor, and Ursula would overrule them only in the most extreme cases. Ultimately, local management remained on board, and the deal was signed.

With the successful closure, out of excess cash the bank made an initial lump sum payment to the lenders and funded the escrow indemnity reserve. The liquidation monitor worked well on the whole with local management. Minor disagreements arose but were quickly and amicably resolved. Three months into the process, the Bank of Commerce reached an agreement with another local bank to divest their operations in the capital city. Under the transaction, the Bank of Commerce assigned to the other bank the relevant assets and all of the deposits. In addition, the Bank of Commerce received a moderate cash payment. Over the next year, the liquidation monitor administered regular periodic payments to the lenders. Several lenders had chosen to cash out early (at a steep discount), leaving a potentially much high return on the loan book's monetization to be shared by those remaining.

Toward the end of wind-down period, the market ultimately caught on to the end-game for the Bank of Commerce. The foreign shareholders had decided to exit the business (a strategic rethink) ran the story-line. Ursula was approached thereafter by a local investor group, interested in acquiring the banking license, the physical network, and the remaining assets. The lenders had made provision for such an event, with the requirement they have the right to approve such a step and be the ultimate beneficiary of proceeds. The sale generated an unexpected windfall. Further, the risk of an adverse tax audit and other residual costs were eliminated.

The central importance of the Bank of Commerce's local management cannot be stressed enough. First, without their support, the critical mass of legacy staffing could not have been retained (from the executive management down to key junior staff). In such case, the process would have been still-born. Second, their maintenance of the public face of a "going concern" until very late in the process was an essential ingredient in the performance of the recovery program. Third, their contacts and market knowledge underlay the divestiture of the capital city operations and the sale of the rump operations. The lenders had to agree to generous bonuses to retain the local management, but their investment paid rich dividends.

In the end, the remaining lenders were handsomely rewarded for their perseverance. All realized a gross recovery of almost 90 cents on the dollar. The shareholders lost everything, including the liquidity capital invested to cement the deal. For Ursula, as she would quip later, New West came out alright, when the dividends received over the years were considered. Further, besides the acknowledgment by her shareholders of her mature leadership in cleaning up JK's mess, there would be the benefit of the market's recognition of her firm's responsible behavior for future fundraisings. Everyone makes mistakes. Owning up to them measures your worth. Ursula came out smelling sweet as a rose.

For Martin and his DFI stakeholders, the financial loss was balanced against the intangible value of maintaining market stability. Many would argue Martin's intervention was unwarranted. Lenders lose money on a Monday and forget the loss by Friday. Martin saw the situation differently. He believed the Bank of Commerce episode contributed to the maturation of the market. The successful orderly wind-down demonstrated that a diverse collection of parties working in a challenging market and legal environment could cooperate to achieve a "least bad" outcome. He remained convinced that this example would prove invaluable for the future.

**Discussion Question Number 16**

Recall the moment at the New West HQ, when the "go-ahead" was given to pursue the orderly wind-down, Martin commented:

*Do we have an alternative to bankruptcy? Yes. We will look into a trade sale. There are several banks who might be interested. However, we must be prepared for the eventuality that there is no buyer.*

The original reason cited for not pursuing a trade sale at the outset was JK's unwillingness to dispose of the Bank of Commerce at a fire-sale price, where the valuation might just cover the cost of the debt, leaving New West empty-handed.

- Is it realistic that the lenders did not consider acting earlier to force a sale of the Bank of Commerce with the limited goal of maximizing their debt recovery? Why or why not?
- At this later date, has this answer changed?
- What might such a deal have looked like?
- What would likely be the reaction of the local financial supervisory authority to such a solution to the Bank of Commerce case?

See Annex 5 for suggested answers to these questions.

# Part II

## The Restructuring Process

# 2

# Purpose and Structure of the Book

**Abstract** The chapter represents a segue from the opening tale of the Bank of Commerce to an introduction of the book's central purpose—a presentation and analysis of the restructuring process and the various conflicting institutional and personal currents present in such transactions. The lessons learned from the tale and other "war stories" in the book are aimed at aiding the parties involved in future deals to navigate the deal and relationship challenges present in restructurings. The text opens with a summary of the tale and the major issues and questions arising from the action. This is followed by an exposition of the purpose of the book, complemented by a discussion of what the book does not pretend to be, and of the central structure of the five phases of a restructuring process, namely: (i) Pre-Restructuring (i.e., analysis and monitoring); (ii) Decision to Restructure; (iii) Decision to Restructure; (iv) Case Set-up; and (iv) Structuring and Negotiation. The latter is done in a highly summarized form in order to create a road map of the core of the book that follows.

**Keywords** Bankruptcy · Borrower · Consensual restructuring · Coordinating committee · Corporate debt · Debt · Debtor · Credit analysis · Credit monitoring · Credit checks · Distressed debt · Emerging market · Frontier market · INSOL II · INSOL principles · Insolvency · Lender leadership · Non-performing loans · Pre-insolvency · Restructure · Restructuring · Restructuring plan · Standstill · Steering committee · Workout

© The Author(s), under exclusive license to Springer Nature Switzerland AG 2021
R. Marney and T. Stubbs, *Corporate Debt Restructuring in Emerging Markets*,
https://doi.org/10.1007/978-3-030-81306-2_2

Let's look back at our opening narrative of the Bank of Commerce. What happened? What observations can we make, what lessons can we draw?

*First*, we faced a potentially insolvent counter-party. Prior to the first restructuring meeting, it would have been hard to find a single lender who would have questioned the financial capacity of the shareholder, New West Investments, to undertake the necessary recapitalization of the Bank of Commerce. Lenders appeared to have been in the dark about the high leverage JK had used to support an aggressive acquisition strategy. The lenders asked—could JK not just raise new equity, divest investments to generate cash? "They could if they want to" undoubtedly figured in lender thinking.

The problem (in the lenders' minds) was not capacity but willingness to support the Bank of Commerce. Todd and a number of the other lenders certainly believed New West had the capacity to rescue the Bank. Lender skepticism hardened. From the inside, Ursula knew better. New West did not have surplus funds. Indeed, they had big problems of their own brewing. The failed refinancing of the New Perspectives Energy acquisition represented a grave threat to their future. A new equity raise? Given the bad press around New Perspectives Energy, this was impossible. Their bankers made that painfully clear. Sell an investment? A fire sale would have ensued.

Kristi did not have Ursula's intimate knowledge of the group's inner workings but had concluded for other reasons there was no money coming. Even in the good times, New West had "milked" the Bank for dividends. Ninety-percent plus of net income is up-streamed every year. The Bank of Commerce had become an important source of cash for the group. She knew there was no board-level support for taking value from New West's core "new economy" strategy to rescue a small enterprise lender in some underdeveloped economy most of their investors couldn't even find on a map. Damaging contagion to the rest of the business? Here it was nuanced.

The board was not worried about the impact of the Bank failing for the same reason they would not commit new money. Their core investor group didn't care and might have even liked the idea of eliminating a distraction. The Bank had been bought for a pittance, and they had gotten their money back multiple times over.

However, Martin's threat about the reaction of his government shareholders had resonated with the board; hence the agreement to support an orderly wind-down. Any doubts Kristi had were eliminated when Ursula and Martin spilt the beans that evening at the Hyatt Regency.

Kristi knew that Maya got it, but the rest of the lenders, most notably Edinburgh Partners, were still not "true-believers." Most could never accept

New West's claims of penury. Emotions were raw, and *debilitating conflict* lied just under the surface.

*Second*, despite warning signs, no one acted until the crisis arrived. Why was this? Justified ignorance or willful prevarication? Bits of both, depending on where people sit. The borrower-side knew the full extent of the pressures on liquidity and solvency, whilst the lenders operated with less complete and delayed information. Understandably, the borrowers downplayed the negative financial prospects and gave a positive spin to or even discounted the bad economic news. The lenders also played a role in the delay to act.

In lending, business proposes, credit analysis evaluates, and a committee (or a chain) of credit officers approves. When loans go bad, orthodox risk management theory calls for a recusal by the parties who made the loan (including the credit analysis crew). The case should be handed to a separate, independent group ("restructuring" or "special situations"). This team needs to be "clean," that is, free from bias due not having been involved in the underwriting function and, importantly, with a reporting line insulated from this underwriting function. Like the borrower-side, elements of the lender-side who are professionally invested in the credit may be naturally disposed to err on the side of hope.

In Kristi's case, she sat above the business and, judging from her meeting with the CEO months before, was independent and empowered. Despite her firm having some internal conflict (the Chief Investment Officer), the critical mass of the executive management did indeed support her. Had the power dynamics been different, who knows? The failure to act earlier and with resolve reflected borrower inertia. Time was lost. Action waited until it was too late.

This playing out of events highlighted the importance of *institutional characteristics and culture*. The crucial influence of the *personalities* of the involved parties cannot be stressed enough at each phase of the process.

*Third*, people negotiate with people. How two sides *communicate*, how each player treats the others, whether ultimately there is trust and respect are as, if not more, important than the actual content of the case. How often in daily life do we observe this? Too often, one suspects. Achievable outcomes are blown up when parties become overly emotional and cease dealing with each other and the situation with poise and calmness.

Consider Stephen's behavior at the kick-off meeting. Could Todd have been managed better with "sugar," rather than the dollops of "vinegar" actually served up?

To be sure, no two restructuring cases will ever be exactly the same. This is a simple, ever-present truth about restructurings: they are *bespoke* transactions and play out on the background of their own factual circumstances. In an emerging market workout, the situation is often made even more complex by the still-developing and often nascent legal infrastructure required to protect stakeholder rights—rule of law, a balanced and well-drafted insolvency system, an independent judiciary which will mete out justice in a practical, commercial, and predictable manner. Given this, how does one approach the task of writing a restructuring guide, and in particular on managing such complex, bespoke transactions in an emerging market?

To answer this question, let's start with what this book is not.

*First*, it's certainly not a dry textbook on accounting, credit analysis and law, although the discussion relies importantly on these subject areas. There are enough of these on bookshelves already, written by far wiser authors. *Second*, it's not an Ikea-like manual, those "how to do it," step-by-step instructional pamphlets used to assemble your child's chest of drawers. It is not enough to know "what to do." Instead, we need to understand the "why" underlying the design. *Lastly*, we avoid the route of compiling a voluminous library of case studies with explicative notes in the hope of furnishing a useful analogue and guide for any conceivable case on which the reader might work. We shun creating the kind of map ridiculed by Jorge Luis Borges in his novel On Exactitude and Science[1] (and quoted in Richard Bookstaber's The End of Theory)[2]:

> *In that Empire, the Art of Cartography attained such Perfection that a map of a single Province occupied the entirety of a City, and the map of that Empire, the entirety of a Province. In time, those Unconscionable Maps no longer satisfied, and the Cartographers Guilds struck a Map of the Empire whose size was that of the Empire, and which coincided point for point with it.*

As in Borges' novel, too detailed a restructuring guide would be useless and quickly discarded. Too much detail is no detail at all. Instead, our objective is to equip the reader with a few basic "navigational tools and principles" to permit sailing successfully through uncharted seas, unpredictable storms, and hidden shoals.

So, how have we approached the book?

---

[1] J.L. Borges, Collected Fictions, Translated by A. Hurley, Penguin Press, New York, 1998.
[2] R. Bookstaber, The End of Theory: Financial Crisis, the Failure of Economics, and the Sweep of Human Interaction, Princeton University Press (2017).

*First*, we asked ourselves, "If we had just a day to mentor a group of restructuring professionals early in their careers on emerging markets restructurings, what would we tell them?" Our response focused primarily on the *lessons we've learned* from our various successes and failures in the field. The accounting and law books would be left for later. To catalogue these observations, we considered transactional narratives derived from actual cases in diverse emerging and frontier market geographies, commercial and financial sectors, and company-types since the early 1980s. From these narratives, we distilled a set of key observations that became principles to shape solutions and guide decision-making in diverse and unique restructuring cases, the aforementioned "uncharted seas."

*Second*, from this cataloguing work, a consistent process structure emerged. From monitoring company health and engaging in preventative medicine as an alternative to restructuring through the stages of setting up and executing when a workout could not be avoided, we constructed an architecture of *five main phases*. We have thus organized our discussion around these five phases.

*Third*, we recognized that *emotions* arguably play a greater role in the field of restructuring than in most other financial service transactional areas. Kahneman's "Endowment Effect"[3]—the avoidance of loss taking on greater value than the achievement of gain—manifests itself with financiers fighting for economic recoveries and structural advantage with much greater vehemence in a workout case than might be present when the original investment was made.

As a result, the capacity to balance the prerequisites of the business transaction with the need to *manage around the human foibles* that inevitably plague the transaction parties is essential for success. In our study, we explored the personality traits and transaction management skills of effective restructuring professionals, especially those who step into leadership roles in workouts. Common characteristics included good listening skills, empathy, humor, self-deprecation, patience, and perseverance. These trumped the hard charging, dominating, and loud arrogance of the stereotypical financial services stars, the so-called "alpha male" personalities (actually both men and women). To exploit an overused comparison, General Omar Bradley would have made a better restructuring professional than General George Patton.

Through the rest of the book, we will look back on and analyze Kristi's leadership of her emerging market restructuring case. We will also introduce the reader to several shorter narratives of restructuring cases in different

---

[3] https://www.behavioraleconomics.com/resources/mini-encyclopedia-of-be/endowment-effect/.

emerging markets, with different facts and players. These various case narratives will adhere to the five-phase framework. Along the way, we will step back to analyze what has happened, why and how their handling of the challenges might translate into "lessons learned." These form the principles from which a navigational toolkit can be assembled and the knowledge to use it effectively gained.

Let's now take a high-level look at these five phases in Chapter 3. We will then analyze them in more depth in Chapters 4–8.

# 3

# Main Phases and Principles of a Restructuring

**Abstract** This chapter takes a birds-eye look at the aforementioned five main phases of the restructuring process. The summary introductory discussion of each of the phases is intended to set up the reader for the subsequent Chapters 4–7 that follow, where the main elements on which the authors believe the reader should focus are analyzed in much greater detail. As the reader completes the chapter, there should be the growing realization that whilst each transaction has its own unique set of circumstances and layers of human dynamics, there are similarities across cases, and an overarching approach will serve the transaction parties well. The content of this chapter figures as a useful reference guide to which the reader can return to keep the overall process structure and key issues or challenges well in mind.

**Keywords** Bankruptcy · Borrower · Consensual restructuring · Coordinating committee · Corporate debt · Debt · Debtor · Credit checks · Credit evaluation · Credit monitoring · DFI (development finance institution) · Distressed debt · Emerging market · Frontier market · INSOL II · INSOL principles · Insolvency · Lender leadership · Non-performing loans · Pre-insolvency · Restructure · Restructuring · Restructuring plan · Standstill · Steering committee · Workout

© The Author(s), under exclusive license to Springer Nature Switzerland AG 2021
R. Marney and T. Stubbs, *Corporate Debt Restructuring in Emerging Markets*,
https://doi.org/10.1007/978-3-030-81306-2_3

# Introduction

As we recall in our opening narrative of the Bank of Commerce, Kristi and her colleagues faced a deepening economic crisis in a commodity-dependent emerging market that threatened the survival of a major, local bank borrower. The price of copper, the country's predominant export product, had collapsed. The economy was battered by the multiple negative waves of slowing growth, a sudden stop of capital flows, and a rapidly depreciating currency.

In the immediate term, the institution confronted an immediate liquidity squeeze and, ultimately, insolvency. The bank was controlled by a Silicon Valley-based investment group, which had branched out into emerging-markets micro-enterprise lending. Despite the existential threat, the parent maintained its aggressive business strategy to permit the continued upstreaming of cash, on which the highly leveraged shareholder group had become increasingly dependent.

The tale depicted further a swirling pool of complex personal dynamics between shareholders and their management, borrowers, advisors, and lenders, with inter-departmental dynamics within the lenders' own organizations. In play were not only business considerations, but also cultural differences and personality traits. The challenge of bridging the gap between two understandably opposing sets of objectives was made all the more difficult as a result.

As with all restructurings, this tale had its own unique set of circumstances and layers of human dynamics. Yet, there are similarities across cases. In evaluating these shared characteristics, we have observed that almost all cases go through a series of *five identifiable main phases*. It is through the lens of these five main phases that one may make sense of how the case developed, how our friends arrived where they landed at the end of negotiations and how they ultimately brought their restructuring to a successful close, in the form of an orderly wind-down.

These five main phases are:

- **Phase 1: Pre-Restructuring,**
- **Phase 2: Restructuring Decision,**
- **Phase 3: Case Set-up,**
- **Phase 4: Structuring and Negotiation, and**
- **Phase 5: Implementation.**

In this Chapter, we will now take a birds-eye look at these five main phases. In the chapters that follow we will dig more deeply into them, outlining in more detail the main elements on which the authors believe the reader should focus. Through our discussion, we will analyze Kristi and her colleagues' work and the "lessons learned," to elaborate in more detail the principles of a successful strategy for each such phase. We will also include in these chapters several shorter narrative restructuring cases, to help reinforce the learnings.

# Phase 1—Pre-Restructuring

*An Ounce of Prevention is Worth a Pound of Cure.*
Benjamin Franklin, 1735

After three centuries, Benjamin Franklin's advocacy mobilizing the citizens of Philadelphia to create a city fire department has become a meme for the wisdom of averting disaster before it strikes.[1]

A lender in emerging markets will ordinarily have established its own paradigm for monitoring of the performance and risk levels of portfolios and individual borrowers, to maintain credit portfolio quality and minimize the accumulation of sub-standard and/or non-performing loans (NPLs). This not only enhances the lender's profitability but also reduces its own capital needs. An individual borrower will, from the moment of loan origination, have been introduced into the monitoring process and become an ever-moving dot on the lender's radar screen.

Even the most well-developed economies can and regularly do experience instability. But emerging markets have an even greater level of volatility in economic and financial performance. Their institutional environments are still under development. Local business customs and cultural norms, combined with nascent contract-enforcing mechanisms and what some have called the great "institutional voids" and lack of "soft infrastructure," can make them even more challenging.[2] They are typically far more susceptible to macro-economic events (e.g., greater inflation, changes in commodity prices, currency collapses, etc.). There is often less liquidity and far greater difficulties

---

[1] The Pennsylvania Gazette, 4 February 1735.

[2] T. Khanna, K. G. Palepu, J. Sinha, Strategies That Fit Emerging Markets, Harvard Business Review (June 2005).

in raising capital. There are likely to be poorer corporate governance systems for business. There may be weaker auditing or regulatory systems. Only a small number of them have developed secondary debt markets. And whilst less inclined toward outright expropriation than in prior decades, regulatory and governmental actors may nonetheless be opaque, unpredictable, or even confiscatory in their actions, thus creating "policy risk."[3]

At the same time, emerging markets present a wealth of investment opportunities given their pace of growth in goods and services. Growth rates still generally dwarf those of developed economies. The return on investment can often be far greater than in developed economies, driving competitive advantage and shareholder returns. Like our friends JK and Ursula in Bank of Commerce, investors from global financial capitals have found that in good times their emerging markets investments can provide a veritable cash cow.

To be sure, the balance of risk and reward in a particular industry or with an individual borrower in an emerging market will be much starker than that encountered in more developed markets. This enhanced level of risk and reward places an even greater premium on lenders' credit monitoring and pro-active risk mitigation. Once a problem arises, it can often be too late.

Larger, more institutional lenders in such markets (e.g., multilateral development finance institutions (DFIs) and international commercial banks and their local subsidiaries) ordinarily will have established state-of-the-art infrastructure and fine-tuned policy directives for monitoring assets. Smaller international lenders in emerging markets (e.g., impact investment funds) may apply a less institutional approach, given their more modest internal resources. That said, even amongst institutional lenders, the level of effectiveness in credit monitoring (hence losses) may vary.[4]

Today, a wealth of general know-how on the science (or, some might say, the art) of credit monitoring has been amassed. The authors will not endeavor to repeat or summarize such knowledge here.[5]

Still, the authors believe certain key aspects of credit monitoring and related activities during the Pre-Restructuring Phase merit lenders' highest attention in the context of emerging markets.

---

[3] W. J. Henisz and B. A. Zelner, The Hidden Risks in Emerging Markets, Harvard Business Review (April 2010).

[4] First-mover matters: Building credit monitoring for competitive advantage, McKinsey Working Papers on Risk, No. 37 (October 2012).

[5] The authors re-emphasize that an in-depth look at some macroeconomic issues in emerging markets, as these are relevant to credit monitoring, is fully justified. Accordingly, Chapter 10 is devoted to macroeconomic issues.

These may be summarized as:

- Establishment of an effective *credit monitoring* framework, tailored to account for the individual borrower profiles and industry and customized to account for the specifics of the particular emerging market;
- Ensuring that the credit monitoring framework includes an *early warning system* to cover the threats to macro-economic and financial system stability;
- Holding of ordinary and extraordinary internal *credit evaluation* discussions with borrowers;
- Where borrowers are in a regulated industry (e.g., banks, microfinance organizations, insurers, etc.), establishment of an *independent relationship* with and *consulting* on an ad hoc basis *with regulators*; and
- Maintenance of a practice of making *credit checks with other lenders* to the same borrowers/borrower groups/ultimate beneficial owners (UBOs).[6]

We will discuss these key aspects as well as their application in practice in Chapter 4.

# Phase 2—Decision to Restructure

> *Only a Fool Learns from His Mistakes. The*
> *Wise Man Learns from the Mistakes of Others.*
> Otto von Bismarck, 1872

When an individual borrower's "credit light" changes from amber to red during the Pre-Restructuring Phase, each lending institution faces a crucial decision. As our nineteenth-century German statesman and mastermind observed, clearly it is far preferable to base one's decisions on lessons learned from the experiences of others, than to engage in the slow, painful process of one's own trial and error.

In this respect, how a lender decides the course forward when its credit red light flashes will be critical in determining the extent of the lender's recovery—from possibly zero to something hopefully closer to 100%.

---

[6] An Ultimate Beneficial Owner (UBO) is the person who ultimately owns a legal entity or legal person during a transaction. This can include anyone that has direct/indirect control. *See* https://complyadvantage.com/knowledgebase/ultimate-beneficial-owner/.

The lender's decision will be informed by various factors, including to name a few:

- the institution's *general vision* on how distressed-loan situations are best approached;
- the practice it has put in place for how best to ensure that the *right talent* deals with a given situation (including inter-departmental hand-overs of responsibility);
- the taking of a *clear decision* it becomes when evident that the status quo can no longer be tolerated;
- the assessment in making such decision of the *likelihood of success* of various possible courses of action given the entirety of facts, including in particular input from *other lenders*;
- the *inclusion (or recruitment)* in such decision of the borrower and its major shareholders; and
- the lenders' and borrower's commitment to ensure that the chosen course will *be quickly and effectively implemented*.

The "how" and the "when" of the approach to the borrower (and at times, the shareholders) must be handled carefully, given relationship considerations and differing interpretations of the facts.

Lenders may differ considerably in their approaches to distress. For some, a quick exit is important. Where an emerging market's secondary market has developed, a sale of the position at a discount offers a solution.[7]

As will be discussed in Chapter 5, where no quick exit is available, the authors believe a *restructuring (judicial or consensual)* is most likely to give all parties (lenders and shareholders alike) the highest recoveries. Because in many emerging markets the judicial and insolvency systems are still lagging in their development, the ability to structure and execute consensual restructurings can be critical for a successful (i.e., least bad) recovery.

---

[7] Emerging markets vary in their stages of development of their financial markets and legal systems, from some who have risen to high levels of developmet (such as the new economies of the EU, who have undergone considerable development as a result of EU integration), to others with a more frontier profile.

# Phase 3—Case Set-Up

*Before Anything Else, Preparation is the Key to Success.*
Alexander Graham Bell (1847–1922)

*The Best-Laid Schemes O' Mice an' Men Gang Aft Agley,*
*An' Lea'e Us Nought but Grief an' Pain, for Promis'd Joy!*
Robert Burns, 1785

Making the move from the Decision to Restructure Phase to the Case Set-up Phase is a critical moment. Transaction leadership must mobilize parties toward a shared understanding of the need to restructure and how to achieve it.

The most careful advance planning must be made of the how, what, where, when, why, and whom of the messaging to other participants. At the same time, it must be recognized that things will almost never go as planned. So contingency planning is essential. In short, the lender must balance the wisdom of both Messrs. Bell and Burns.

If possible, a first *all-lenders and borrower ("kick-off") meeting* should be convened. The kick-off meeting acts as a catalyst to effective collective action and sets the overall tone for the ensuing restructuring process. The value of a well-designed and successful first meeting cannot be overstated. A shared positive attitude, spirit of openness, and good faith can go a long way in pushing a restructuring transaction to successful close. The opposite—a poorly planned and managed kick-off meeting—can complicate, or even derail an otherwise achievable restructuring process.

The meeting's objectives, roster, roles and responsibilities, and key issues must be clearly outlined and agreed between the borrower/shareholders and an unofficial core group of lenders *beforehand*. The parties must strive to *adhere to the agenda* encompassing these key issues.[8] The atmosphere of the meeting and the quality of the presentation are as important as the content. There is only one chance to make a first impression on the larger group of lenders. The attending representatives will in turn report back to their headquarters, whose senior management will develop expectations and biases through the lens of their representatives.

---

[8] The authors have witnessed more than once when multi-lender kick-off meetings became chaotic when transaction leadership did not force the parties to stick to the agenda. Although some 'venting' at the outset will be necessary from a purely tactical standpoint, nonetheless, the agenda must drive the meeting.

It will be highly desirable to ensure that the attending representatives are restructuring specialists, that they are empowered to represent their respective organizations (even if they may not yet be in a position to bind their organizations to formal amendments to their loan agreements) and that previous possible sources of bias have been neutralized.

Of course, it will not always be the case that all lenders are represented by restructuring specialists in this initial phase. Lingering bias in the larger lender group is often unavoidable. Indeed, there needs to be a recognition that emotions may (to varying degrees) be frayed on the lenders' side, due to the perception of feckless management, the perceived failure of shareholders to support the borrower adequately and/or other unmet expectations. It may also arise out of sheer embarrassment and/or fear on the part of the representative (witness the case with our friend Todd, a principal promoter of his institution's recent significant disbursement and now in fear of imminent dismissal). Time must be budgeted to allow for "venting."

The borrower and its shareholder(s) must also create the strong, genuine impression that they are *prepared to listen with an open mind*. They must try to understand concerns, without negative or other unconstructive comments reflecting defensiveness or derision of lenders' concerns (whether held rightly or wrongly).

Helpfully, this part of the first meeting can also be informative in understanding the greater group dynamics, potential allies, and threats, and whether a sufficient "critical mass of like-minded lenders" required for a successful restructuring is achievable. Thus, in addition to cathartic qualities, some free discussion will present an excellent opportunity for useful intelligence gathering and planning.

Following the initial discussion, the parties should move to deal with the reality of the situation and seek a constructive path forward, however daunting this may seem.

Lenders need not attempt at this stage to assess definitively whether a restructuring can be achieved or what its substantive commercial and legal parameters will be. Usually, the first meeting will be too early for such conclusions to be made. Significant financial diligence and analysis will drive such conclusions, and this will usually only come later. To be sure, potential restructuring alternatives may be explored in the spirit of an open, transparent brainstorming session. Such a session may prove fruitful for the longer term and may certainly be on the agenda. But it is not the main goal.

Rather, other main goals should drive the agenda and ideally be achieved at (or as a result of) the meeting. At a minimum, the parties should strive to agree certain key elements at the meeting. We will refer to these as the *"case set-up"* elements:

- the *governance* of the lender-side group,
- the *work plan and timetable*,
- the engagement of *professional advisors*,
- the establishment of *standstill* arrangements, and
- the assignment of *initial financial and analytics.*

In more complex restructuring cases the parties (often at the borrower's initiative) endeavor to proceed based on multiple ongoing parallel bilateral discussions between the borrower and its individual lenders, in lieu of a group meeting. This might reflect a (misguided) "divide and conquer" tactic by the borrower, its shareholder(s), or their advisors. Or it might merely be unavoidable given the circumstances (the practical inability to convene a meeting of all lenders).

Such approach can sometimes work. But in the authors' experience it can risk complications. These include the lack of collective spirit amongst lenders, suspicion arising from the lack of transparency, ineffective communications, disorder amongst lenders and more frequently delay, inefficiency and higher cost. As in social relationships, once trust is damaged or lost amongst the parties in a restructuring process, effective collaboration and the achievement of a successful outcome becomes more challenging.

Thus, it is highly preferable from the lenders' perspective (and the authors would argue from the borrower's perspective) for the process to take place as a *transparent all-lenders' meeting* with the borrower and its main shareholder(s) (or series of such meetings). Clearly, confidential discussions of a breakout nature will be required. It may be that the initial "meeting" will be a series of meetings close in time. Given the heightened importance which individual personalities can play and more complete information to be gained from face-to-face interaction, the preference will be for either in-person meetings or video-conferencing platforms. Lastly, to the extent practical, pre-meeting analytics and other materials should be shared amongst the core participants in advance,[9] to ensure that all are operating with a common fact set. An imbalance of information can easily lead to misunderstandings or conflicting ideas on the best way forward.

We will discuss these issues and their application in practice in Chapter 6.

---

[9] Ideally materials should be circulated no less than 24 hours before the meeting; a late circulation will reflect poorly on lender leadership and can waste valuable time (if parties do not have time to read and prepare).

# Phase 4—Structuring and Negotiation

*Effective Cat Herders Who Can Bring Business Enemies Together and Turn Them, at Least Temporarily, Into Colleagues, Perform an Invaluable Service.*
Victor Lipman, 2013

Restructuring transactions present some of the most challenging, yet also most interesting, transactions in the financial services industry. They involve a number of disappointed (and often embarrassed) parties with conflicting objectives in a stressful situation. They must find a common solution with very little to work with, within a very short period, before disaster strikes them all. Parties invariably articulate unrealistic, intractable positions, often contrary to their own interests, for largely subjective reasons ("They can't do that to me! I'll show them!"). The knee-jerk inclination to find or to deflect fault frequently interferes with constructive discussion. Parties normally used to viewing each other as competitors are thrown into the position of having to collaborate.

Leadership in a workout thus faces a task which might indeed be aptly labeled "cat herding." Or for parents, it might be reminiscent of dealing with tired, young children or recalcitrant teenagers.

This divergence of interests requires unwavering focus on the primary objectives, a high level of organization and tenacity and the ability to communicate effectively to ensure all participants (borrower, shareholder(s) and other lenders) fully understand and support a common objective—and with it the inevitable sacrifices to be made as compared with the expected results of their earlier financial contributions.

In the authors' view, therefore, the main elements of a successful structuring and negotiation will be:

- firstly, re-enforcing the clear, shared consensus between all stakeholders (lenders, the borrower and its shareholders) of the *main goals*,
- performing a *cost–benefit analysis* as to whether a workout is most appropriate in the circumstances,
- taking into consideration the *particular emerging market* in question and how this affects the above,
- analyzing the financial, commercial, and legal due diligence performed to date, to agree the specific *building blocks of the restructuring* and how these will be implemented in the given case (i.e., business restructuring and/or balance sheet restructuring), and

- continual *pro-active leadership* of the transaction on all sides (or to quote a phrase used earlier, effective cat-herding).

We will discuss these issues and their application in practice in Chapter 7.

# Phase 5—Implementation

*The action of conducting is connecting with the musicians. The conductor is not only the person that is in front of the orchestra and shows the tempo or the dynamics. He is a person that has to guide and inspire.*
Gustavo Dudamel, Conductor, Los Angeles Philharmonic

From the basis laid during the Structuring and Negotiation Phase of a multi-lender workout, the parties move into the Implementation Phase. The deal agreed is now brought to life and taken to its designed conclusion.

This phase has its own special dynamics. It is often the most challenging of the entire process. On the positive side, from an atmosphere of chaos and dissonance, the parties have made at least an initial harmonious step forward. At the same time, the amount and complexity of financial, legal, and organizational work required to close the deal is formidable. Many actions by various parties will need to be carefully coordinated.

The best way to think about the Implementation Phase is to indeed compare the work to conducting a symphony orchestra. Missed or misplayed notes or chords can threaten the harmony of the performance. The job of the conductor is to ensure this does not happen in the same way that Kristi strives to keep the lenders working toward the common goal, or as Maestro Dudamel has described it, by "guiding and inspiring."

In emerging markets, this can be a formidable challenge: the stakeholders may not yet have fully embraced developed nations' time-tested approaches to restructuring. Some markets may have "their own way" of dealing with distress (often regrettably involving the courts and insolvency).

Transaction leadership will by now have successfully crossed the initial milestones of holding a kick-off meeting. Hopefully the parties will have agreed the rough parameters for a possible workout amongst providers of funding (assembling the critical mass of lenders ready to forbear; investigating possible business and balance sheet restructuring measures to achieve the main restructuring objectives; assembling a work plan and timetable; engaging external legal and financial advisors).

It is at this point that the implementation work begins in earnest. This will include:

- identifying the *main steps* which need to be taken and executing on these,
- coordinating the actions of all *main actors* and the roles they will play in this process, and
- agreeing, preparing, and executing the *final text(s)* of the main restructuring agreement(s), and other ancillary steps (e.g., regulatory steps).

Naturally, lender leadership will play the driving role in this process. However, external counsel and technical advisors, including liquidation monitors, will be integral parts of the process.

-&-

In the ensuing five Chapters, we will delve into more details on these main elements of each phase and apply them in practice to Bank of Commerce and several new narratives.

# 4

# Pre-Restructuring

**Abstract** The chapter begins the fable of the "Stork and the Fox" which will open and flow through the next four chapters as a means of highlighting in simple terms the major theme(s) of the respective chapters. In this chapter, the hungry stork (the lender) must cooperate with the wily fox in order to find a meal (a risky, but profitable credit opportunity). Sound credit analysis, transaction structuring, and monitoring are the financier's protective tools, as open-eyes, a safe distance, and a healthy dollop of cautious skepticism are the stork's. The chapter outlines the main elements of the analysis and monitoring activities and then reinforces the learnings through (i) two new case studies (a bank and manufacturing company); (ii) a digression on the topic of critical thinking and credit analysis; and (iii) a concluding section, which applies the learnings to this phase from the opening Bank of Commerce Tale.

**Keywords** Bank secrecy · Bankruptcy · Borrower · Confidentiality · Consensual restructuring · Coordinating committee · Corporate debt · Debt · Debtor · Cash flow · COVID-19 · Credit analysis · Credit evaluation · Credit monitoring · Critical thinking · Currency peg · Devaluation · Distressed debt · Exogenous shock · Financial statements · Emerging market · Exchange rate · Frontier market · Hybrid restructuring · INSOL II · INSOL principles · Insolvency · Lender leadership · Non-performing loans · Pre-insolvency · Restructure · Restructuring · Restructuring plan · Standstill · Steering committee · Supervisory authorities · Workout

### Preface: The Stork and the Fox—Part I (A Fable)

*The wily fox always prided himself on thinking ahead. No sooner would he finish his breakfast than he'd be thinking about lunch. He almost never went hungry.*

*One morning, he was reposing under an apple tree, his paws resting contentedly on his full stomach, when a stork landed across the field, near a small creek. "Aha!" he thought. "That will make a tasty meal." The fox stood up. He reached a low tree limb and pulled down a red apple. He ambled across the field in the general direction of the stork, who was poking around the edge of the creek" in search of food.*

*"Good morning!" exclaimed the fox.*

*The stork stepped back into the water, wary of the wily fox.*

*The fox took a bite of the apple and frowned. "Sour." He shook his head. "Too early in the summer for apples."*

*"Yes," agreed the Stork.*

*"A better time for spring berries." He turned to leave. "I will have to walk to Thompson's Farm. There is a wonderful berry patch there." Looking over his shoulder, he pointed into the distance. "It's over there just across the way, on the other side of river."*

*"Are they tasty berries?" asked the stork.*

*"Oh, yes. I would be happy to show you the way" offered the fox.*

*The stork hesitated but then felt her stomach murmur. She was hungry.*

*The two started out.*

*The fox devised a plan. They would go to the Brandywine Bridge and cross the river there. The water was much too deep to wade across, and the fox was not a good swimmer. Once across and in the secluded forest, he would have his lunch.*

*As they walked, the stork asked the fox about how far was Farmer Thompson's berry patch.*

*"Not far and it's very easy to find." The fox answered. "Just across the river. Then a short walk through the forest, at the base of White Mountain."*

*As they approached the river, the fox could hear the sound of the water, dancing down the rapids just above the bridge. "We are almost there," said the fox. "Can you hear the water?"*

*"Yes, I can. I flew over the river just this morning, but further up. The winter snow melt is heavy this year. And the spring rains are heavier than usual. Many bridges have been damaged."*

*"Oh?" The fox became concerned. His stomach growled noticeably, and he looked longingly at the stork. "Let's look for another way across. I can even try to carry you on my back...."*

*"No, let me fly and check first." Said the stork.*

*Before the fox could react, the stork had spread its wings and rose up into the sky. Minutes passed, and the stork did not return. The fox came to the river's edge. The river was well above its banks. Brandywine Bridge had been carried off by the current. There was no way across.*

*Just then, the stork circled above the fox and called down. "I have found Thompson's Farm. I am sorry you cannot join me." Then smiling wily, the stork added, "I am sure you can find lunch somewhere else."*

-&-

Was the stork smart or lucky? Had the bridge not washed away, would the fox have enjoyed his tasty lunch? When the fox suggested they look for another way or even try to swim across, why did the stork not agree? Counterfactuals aside, we can conclude that fortunately for the stork, she reacted decisively and fled from what likely would have been a ghastly end. Like the stork agreeing to accompany the fox, credit and lending officers have to examine a business opportunity and make a decision. Careful diligence does not end there. The stork kept her eyes on the fox and her surroundings throughout the journey. With the bridge out, she observed the fox's apprehension and perhaps even heard his stomach growl. This appeared to drive her decision to flee.

Likewise, credit analysts must keep focused on their financial partners. Their personal early warning systems need to be constantly attuned to when potential, previously identified risks crystalize or facts change and new threats arise. When they fail to monitor the economy, the market, and the counterparty, they are negligent. Even when they do their jobs well, they may miss things. To err is human. Most frustrating is when they rigorously monitor all, successively decipher the meaning of complex and dynamic change, but then are blocked by commercial arguments, bureaucratic rigidities, or biases on both sides.

Think about Kristi's case with Bank of Commerce. Sometimes, fortunately rarely, it takes more than just industry and smarts. Saying no to the bread winners of the firm, either on an initial approval or later to a covenant waiver or refinancing request, requires courage. Careers have been hurt this way. The organizational structure and institutional culture must foster an open, balanced credit debate, without fear of reprisal.

In this first part of this chapter, we explore the thought and execution processes of successful credit analysis and monitoring. To be clear, the nuts and bolts of financial statement analysis and corporate finance are referenced but not covered in detail here. The reader can consult the Bibliography in the Annexes for suggested readings on the topic.

We start with a discussion of the key aspects of credit monitoring and related activities mentioned in Chapter 3 above. Again, these primary aspects are credit monitoring, credit checks with other lenders, credit evaluation discussions and building relationships with local authorities.

We then follow with two brief cases, where for each we evaluate the performance of three hypothetical analysts, the "Good, the Bad and the Ugly," to borrow the title from the classic Clint Eastwood movie. We ask, what distinguishes the good from the bad and the ugly? From this discussion, we suggest an overlay of critical thinking concepts (levels, if you will) to the process of credit analysis and monitoring as a means of sharpening the profile of the effective credit officer as a forward looking, speculative thinker. Seeing what's present but not obvious, anticipating what is not yet there, being the chess master thinking multiple moves ahead; these are the attributes of the successful credit professional.

We will first focus on the initial credit analysis and then on the monitoring activity. Like the stork, we will look to refine our approach to the initial decision—hers being whether to accept the fox's invitation to visit the berry patch, ours being whether to make the loan—and subsequently, how better to watch the action play out and react appropriately to preserve our capital, hopefully as well as the stork safeguarded her life.

# Main Elements of the Pre-Restructuring Phase

## Effective Credit Monitoring

The most essential element of the Pre-Restructuring Phase for every portfolio loan will be the development, implementation, and (critically) constant evolution/re-invention of a framework of effective credit monitoring.

One might say, the objective of monitoring is to *see problems before they become problems*. As such, effective credit monitoring is not simply historical analysis; it is informed, forward-looking speculation. The loan and credit teams in their collaboration must move beyond simple financial reporting templates, to a rigorous process of identifying and evaluating risk elements and, based on scenario analysis, classifying the residual risks to inform credit management strategy.

An effective strategy furthermore requires effective *recruitment*—that is, winning the heart and the mind—of the borrower. The borrower's genuine understanding of, voluntary enrolment in and active participation in this process will be essential. Its survival depends on establishing a transparent, collaborative relationship with its lender. Information covenants in the loan documentation, whilst important for the performance of legal obligations (to avoid a formal default and acceleration) are indispensable elements of a broader *"fire-prevention" system*. This system should be designed to assist the lender and borrower together as a team to overcome external and internal risks and safeguard all stakeholders' interests in the continued survival—indeed growth and prospering—of the borrower's business.

Given the *statutory creditor priorities* of insolvency systems generally, including those of emerging markets, shareholders invariably suffer the greatest loss in an insolvency. Absent more malign intentions (e.g., fraud or self-dealing), this fact alone should serve as ample motivation for borrower/shareholder collaboration in making this fire alarm system work continuously and effectively for all parties.[1]

The lender and the borrower must therefore work together to integrate the borrower into the credit monitoring system and to ensure the constant, real-time flow of reliable, meaningful data for achieving this goal. Real-time data input will be based not only on loan covenants, monitoring templates, financial statements, reports, and risk matrices, but also regular and ad hoc consultations, credit evaluation meetings with the borrower's management and (as appropriate) majority shareholders/ultimate beneficial owners, and frank assessments and re-assessments of risk-mitigation strategies and tactics.

A system for spotting so-called early warning signals (an *EWS*), quantitative and qualitative, is an integral element of this process. *This cannot just be at portfolio level but critically must be at the single-borrower level.* It must work in real time and not rely solely on late-emerging information (post-factum financials, ratings changes, etc.).

The *linkage between macroeconomic and business performance* is intuitive and indisputable. The nature, speed of transmission, and distribution of shocks vary, as does the strength of their feedback loops. For each country, sector and individual enterprise, the credit analyst should create a macroeconomic and market risk matrix. This tool facilitates the monitoring of the build-up of these risks and allows the anticipation of any credit negative spillovers before they metastasize into serious threats. In Chapter 10, we discuss useful elements of macroeconomic analysis and a monitoring toolkit.

Moreover, the smart lender will conceive of and implement both: (1) a regular practice of pre-defined actions as well as (2) conscious ex-post-facto

---

[1] Take our Bank of Commerce example. Imagine how the outcome would have been different had JK, Ursula, Kristi and others maintained a monitoring dialogue, by which the rising threat could have been identified and an effective response agreed in time.

analysis of its success and continued fine-tuning of its system.[2] As Albert Einstein reportedly said, "Once you stop learning, you start dying."

## Credit Evaluation Discussions

Preparing for and executing frank and effective credit evaluation discussions with borrowers can present a daunting task for any lender. This is particularly where the lender has multiple relationships with the borrower's shareholders (e.g., as its own funding source and/or both a lender to, and shareholder in the organization) and hence a greater potential commercial knock-effect. However, it is these initial discussions which test the mettle of the effective lender and its ability to help its borrower avoid running over the cliff of insolvency. The keys to effective communication in these cases will be having built a solid relationship with the borrower as well as *careful advance preparation* before the discussion.

Once the warning light turns from green to amber, the lender will benefit from a previously established, "trusted financial advisor" relationship to ensure a link into the financial news flow of the borrower. The lender's representative will wish to position himself or herself as a person of confidence to the borrower's and its shareholders' management.[3]

A successful strategy will depend on persistent *relationship-building efforts* which will have been made by the lender's representatives (loan officer(s)) during the life of the loan, including during any earlier watch-list events in which credit officers or restructuring team members may have participated. The message of genuine desire to *collaborate* must have gotten through, loud and clear, to the borrower and its shareholder, to avoid an "us versus them"/zero-sum mentality.

The process of advance preparation will include a careful analysis of the borrower and its situation, including from the perspective of shareholders

---

[2] First-mover matters: Building credit monitoring for competitive advantage, McKinsey Working Papers on Risk, No. 37 (October 2012).

[3] The authors do not have in mind any actual or implied financial regulatory relationship or other legal duty of care here, e.g., as might be the case with a regulated financial advisor. Any implication of a relationship which might create vicarious (shadow director) liability in an insolvency under the local bankruptcy regime must similarly be avoided. Rather, the authors have in mind a strong, informal level of personal trust and comfort. Lending documentation and correspondence should naturally always confirm non-reliance and independence of decision-making by the borrower. The lender's actions must always be consistent with this position. That said, many legal systems will not impose a fiduciary obligation on the lender where it has not expressly and unequivocally assumed such a role, and lending documentation will often include disclaimers of such a relationship. *See* P. R. Wood, *Principles of International Insolvency*, Thomson Sweet and Maxwell (2nd ed., 2007), Chapter 22.

and managers (not just of the lender), identifying missing critical information to be obtained, evaluating proposed actions against the test of realism, and practicality and preparation of a discussion guide which acts as a "road map" toward a realistic set of actions to neutralize threats before a liquidity or solvency crisis arrives.

Additionally, the willingness and capacity of the shareholders to provide liquidity and/or equity support must be accurately understood in real time throughout the life of the credit relationship (and not merely assumed, e.g., due to perceived or actual reputation). The lender must remain flexible, as the borrower or other stakeholders may well suggest alternatives which (sometimes with adjustment) can assist in achieving this objective.

The meeting itself (sometimes, multiple meetings) will ideally be in a *face-to-face* format (though during a pandemic and/or due to inability to travel may need to occur via a video-conferencing platform). Personalities and human interactions play a huge role in restructurings. A video platform is thus highly preferred over an audio-only platform.[4] The written discussion guide should be provided in advance and define the agenda and content of the meeting. The outcome, actions, roles, and responsibilities must all be well-defined as a result of the meeting(s), and diligent and effective follow-up immediately implemented and repeated. Detailed notes should be prepared, distributed, and agreed amongst the participants.

Notably, a formal request to restructure should unequivocally come from the borrower (not the lender) in order to mitigate against the risk to the lender later on of having imposed some solution on the borrower. Recall that Kristi "suggested," but never "demanded," that Ursula engage with the lenders.

## Relationships with Local Supervisory Authorities

Local supervisors play a central role in regulated markets. They are a clearing house for data to monitor performance and financial condition. They set and enforce rules. In extremis, they intervene to safeguard markets, investors,

---

[4] A multitude of reasons support the pro-active use of video platforms (and the preference over audio-only platforms) for sensitive discussions like credit evaluations. For example, they are generally considered to minimize 'tuning out,' to minimize miscommunications, to allow participants to process key visual information, to process and retain information better, to read counterparties' body language and facial expressions, to break down barriers and to create a greater sense of collaboration. The global 2020–2021 COVID-19 pandemic, resultant office closures and remote working resulted in their widespread use, with the range of available options having grown considerably. Although many people in corporate and financial workplaces have experienced some 'burn out' with over-usage of video conference platforms during the pandemic, the authors continue to believe the video platform is the preferred approach for sensitive discussions in the workout context.

and consumers (depositors), even to the degree of forcing enterprise liquidation. In these activities, supervisors usually will adhere to a strict standard of confidentiality.

Nevertheless, direct discussions with these authorities can provide, within these limitations, *real-time, valuable, and actionable intelligence* on borrowers who are regulated institutions. Not only does this concern the local market generally, but it can also be directly relevant to individual borrowers' financial condition.

The nature of the interaction will vary. Typically it takes the form of confirming public but not necessarily widely known information and providing helpful interpretation of events and pronouncements.

Establishing and maintaining a personal relationship with individuals within the local supervisory authority over time can greatly assist monitoring and managing credit risks.

The attitudes of authorities will of course vary considerably, depending on the respective emerging market, and functionaries' attitudes toward transparency. But the authors have observed that on the whole, authorities in many emerging markets display a willingness to meet and to try to be helpful to international lenders.

## Credit Checks with Other Lenders

Commercial and legal considerations can reinforce the predisposition for a lender's loan officers to avoid entering into too detailed discussions on individual borrowers with competing lending institutions or through a lending syndicate.

At the same time, a nuanced approach to such interaction warrants serious consideration and application. This is especially true in emerging markets. With appropriate precautions, the establishment of cordial relations and candid discussions can often be an invaluable source of information critical for an effective EWS and loss-prevention strategy. It will be essential for this information-gathering exercise to produce clear and understandable information which can then in turn be input into the EWS.

Prudent lenders will keep well-informed on who a borrower's, its main shareholders' and UBOs' other lenders are. They will maintain a regular (if cordial and highly discreet) dialogue with these parties. This can ensure *access to market intelligence and lay the groundwork for future cooperation* in the event of a need for restructuring. It can be especially helpful for credit officers and restructuring heads to build strong relationships with their counterparts in co-lender institutions. These strong relationships will also undoubtedly help at later phases if a restructuring becomes necessary.

At the same time, relevant *legal, commercial and reputational considerations* must be borne in mind and an effective policy established and followed by lender personnel to ensure legal compliance.

*Legal* issues will include bank secrecy (the rules of which may arise in various jurisdictions for a given case, including at least the borrower's and lender's own respective jurisdictions) and confidentiality (which may be contractually imposed by the terms of the loan document) and possibly also competition-law issues (which may arise if lenders are seen as coordinating commercial lending terms or otherwise engaging in anti-competitive behavior). Discretion should be strictly followed in written and/or electronic communications with third parties. In the era of social media and smart phones, the parties must also exercise prudence. Not only could claims of breach of confidentiality be triggered, but possibly also claims for defamation. In Chapter 11, as part of our reference toolkit dealing with legal issues in restructurings, we discuss these issues in greater detail.

From the *commercial* standpoint, it must be remembered that discussions can be a two-edged sword. In today's financial markets, lenders' outlook on their relationships with borrowers may be changing daily. Adverse information volunteered to another lender may well trigger an action on its part prejudicing the lender's position and/or complicating the smooth resolution of a distress situation (e.g., where another lender is secured and obtains adverse information, this may make it more inclined to enforce on security).

Finally, from the *reputational* standpoint, even if discussions of the borrower and/or its UBO with another lender do not trigger legal or commercial concerns, borrowers can be sensitive to their being discussed "behind their backs." It must be understood that any discussions remain off the record.

The savvy lender will ensure (after taking account of the advice of its in-house legal team) that the *maximum appropriate level of dialogue* is maintained with other lenders in the most effective and discreet manner, consistent with applicable law, contractual obligations, commercial and reputational objectives.

-&-

Now let's move on with two new case studies to re-enforce the importance of these concepts and how they are applied in practice.

# Application in Practice: Case Studies

# The Good, the Bad, and the Ugly—Two Cases

## Case 1 (Industrial Bank)

### Background

Our borrower, Industrial Bank, is a large domestically owned bank in an oil-exporting emerging market. For much of the last decade, the oil prices have been generally range-bound, with an upward bias. The overall economic performance has been solid—growth has been robust, inflation moderate, the current account in a low deficit, and foreign reserves above minimum adequacy levels. External investors have placed significant funds into the local economy, including into the banking sector.

During this period, the exchange rate regime has been a managed float. The real effective exchange rate (REER)[5] has been on an appreciating trajectory and is approximately 20% above fair market value. The institution's financial and operating metrics have been consistently strong. The treasury function has run a limited open FX position (slightly short). However, a significant portion of the FX-denominated loans, representing about half of the total, has gone to borrowers with a limited natural hedge and no access to financial hedges. Asset quality is currently strong, supported by moderately high collateralization levels.

### Approach to Credit Analysis

1. **The "Good"**
   The analyst focuses on the nexus of: (i) the oil price; (ii) the exchange rate; and (iii) the capacity of the end-borrowers whose operating cash flows are in local currency to service FX-denominated loans should oil prices decline to a point where foreign investors lose confidence in the economy, driving down the value of the local currency, and straining debt service capacity of the end-borrowers. Recent developments in the oil sector—a major producing country threatening to increase output in order to drive

---

[5] REER: The real effective exchange rate is the weighted average of a country's currency in relation to an index or basket of other major currencies. The weights are determined by comparing the relative trade balance of a country's currency against each country within the index. See: https://www.investopedia.com/terms/r/reer.asp.

higher cost shale and oil-sands based producers out of the market—have been heard within the energy industry but have not surfaced yet in the global financial press. A weekly monitoring of short-long positions in the futures market had begun to show that smart money saw a downturn in prices as being highly likely.

As a result, the solvency of the bank is stressed for a series of increasingly down-sided cases, consisting of the two-major linkages: (i) oil prices-capital flows-exchange rates; and (ii) NPLs and solvency. The first relies on econometric-based analysis of the country/peer group's experience in similar episodes, adjusting for country-level characteristics. The second uses a combination of such system-level analytics and in-depth conversations with the bank's risk management team in order to understand the prospective asset quality in the downside scenarios. The questions probed center on the adequacy of current capital buffers and, were it to become relevant, the capability and willingness of the shareholders to increase capital.

The result is a recommendation to the lender's credit committee to: (i) lower the exposure amount significantly (a complete exit would not be feasible); (ii) reduce the duration through a combination of a shortened final maturity and more frequent amortizations; (iii) increase the capital adequacy ratio to widen significantly the buffer between the current solvency level and the regulatory minimum; and (iv) place limitations on dividends and other fund upstreaming from the bank to the shareholders.

2. **The "Bad"**

The analyst's macroeconomic analysis assumes no change in the oil market fundamentals. He depends on more non-specialist sources and has had no credible indication that the price level may change. Hence the rigorous, forward-looking projections, even the downside case, results in the conclusion that no material change in the credit rating is necessary. The bank's surprising announcement that they are prepared to increase the level of the solvency ratio is seen as credit enhancement. When the bank asks for a moderate increase in the level of exposure, the lender agrees.

3. **And the "Ugly"**

The third lender is new to the relationship, having been recently approached by the bank and invited into their historically tightly knit funders' group. The bank's investor relations team's information package and financial projections are thorough but do paint an optimistic picture of the future. The lender's analyst relies heavily on these materials and predicates the conclusions on the long, positive historical record of the bank. Consistent with the bank's view, no change in oil market fundamentals is assumed. No rigorous financial projections are undertaken. Further comfort is taken from the broad support the bank enjoys in the lender community. A large-amount, long-duration loan is approved.

## Summary

As history would show, a subsequent collapse in oil prices did result in the abandonment of the managed float, producing a severe depreciation of the currency, heightened NPLs and the rest. How did the credit analysts do?

1. The "Good" hit the bullseye—accurate inputs supporting relevant projections leading to a conclusion that limited the damage for the lender. The focus was not on yesterday repeating itself tomorrow. Instead, the analyst had previously determined the most likely credit threat (oil) and transmission channels and made it her business to gain insider's access to industry numbers, market scuttlebutt, and other non-public information to anticipate adverse developments. She had also worked on the more technical aspects to estimate the impact on the exchange rate under various scenarios. This prepared her for when the long-bull market in oil ended. By the time the crisis hit, the lender's exposure had fallen to a very low level.
2. The "Bad" may have had the technical elements of an effective projection capability in place. However, for whatever reason, he missed the signals about future oil prices. In fairness, there is a tendency for analysts to emulate some economists and predict ten out of the last two financial crises. The failure to call the oil price collapse is perhaps understandable and forgivable. Notwithstanding, rather than following the first lender to reduce exposure, the analyst contributed to the opposite occurring.
3. To mix movie metaphors, the "Ugly" read the travel brochure for the Titanic and boarded the ship last minute. Name lending, herd lending, what have you, describes the approach. The analysis was based excessively on the bank's historical narrative, the view that it would continue, and the bank's impressive cohort of long-standing lenders.

# Case 2 (National Goods Company)

## Background

The National Goods Company had just celebrated its twenty-fifth year as the dominant manufacturer of household appliances in the emerging market. Its market leading role, buttressed by high standards of product quality, had made its name synonymous with the products it manufactured. One didn't put clothing into a washer or dryer, but rather into a machine known by the National Goods' name. With the passing of the company's founder, the next generation decided to abandon the pure wholesale model and undertake a vertical integration into the retail sector. An intensive, debt-supported program of building the brick and mortar of a national network of retail sales outlets and acquiring several of the pre-existing consumer appliance chains ensued. The original debt was sourced locally. The financing was for short tenors and required significant collateral support and tight financial covenants.

The management decided to tap the external markets where it would be possible to borrow for longer tenors, with more relaxed terms. A well-known global investment bank was hired to advise on and ultimately lead a USD syndicated loan facility to refinance the local debt. The issue was oversubscribed. The company made the decision to use the unplanned liquidity to fund the expansion of their new vertically integrated model into neighboring countries. The world was their oyster....

## Approach to Credit Analysis

1. **The "Good"**
   The lead analyst had read the information memorandum for National Goods and had recommended the proposal be declined. His initial focus was on the local retail market. Were the expected results credible? Previously, the company had sold merchandise to retailers on a cash and carry basis. As a result, they lacked clarity on the asset conversion cycle. When talking to retailers, the analyst saw that the company had materially underestimated the inventory days on hand. Additionally, as product penetration in the market had reached into lower-income groups, extended credit terms (12–36 months) became necessary to close sales. Additionally, on these receivables, payment defaults were material and had shown a decidedly upward trend. The company had shockingly not assumed these longer-duration receivables, nor their cost of risk in the financial projections.

Secondly, he asked the question of whether the company's predominant position (close to 90% in certain product categories) would continue—and therefore were the top line revenue and gross margin assumptions credible. His findings were unsettling. Several new entrants had developed more energy-efficient products. These were getting traction in the market, especially with younger, environmentally conscious buyers. Sales data for the past year and market-soundings had belied the company's claim that these eco-friendly machines were a novelty that would soon fade. When retailers were questioned, their feedback had further raised red flags for the company. There were waiting lists for the eco-friendly products, whilst the company's legacy merchandise was not moving. Conversations with the new entrants confirmed much of the retailers' inputs. When asked, the company had confirmed a "minor" slowing in sales but denied any change in market demand. Just the combination of these two factors, when incorporated into a new base case, changed markedly the financial outlook and called into question the company's strategy.

Lastly, he had consulted with his in-house economist and asked for a view on the company's macroeconomic and financial outlook. The bankers had gotten it wrong. After years of low-interest rates, easy credit and frothy asset markets, the weather was changing. He did not predict a full-blown crisis, but he did believe central bankers in the G-3 would have to raise interest rates in order to cool markets down. This would dampen capital flows and exert pressure on the company's home currency and hence increase debt service costs. In the credit committee presentation, the analyst focused on the best reasonable future scenario and concluded that the expansion was ill-conceived. Even if economic conditions held steady, the business prospects were problematic. The projections showed operating cash flow would be insufficient to cover debt service, due to a spike in the working capital required to support the sales effort. New borrowings would be necessary. However, as he described to his colleagues, should the competing products do even better than expected, this cash flow deficit would increase markedly and would certainly spook even the local banks. In concluding his comments, he noted that on top of all of this, should their respected economist's forecast come true, the company would be in serious jeopardy.

2. **The "Bad"**

The risk function faced a challenge. The lender had been mandated to co-lead the first (and would have a similar role in the follow-on) issue. The engagement had been based on a precursory analysis, prepared by the other co-lead, and who would be responsible for the final analysis to be included in the information memorandum. The bank's chief credit officer requested a more in-depth, independent review to determine the final retention amount. The designated credit team traveled to see the company. Their review did raise the concern about the sales projections, but based on the view that the possibility of interest rate hikes could result in slowing economic activity and hence dampen sales. The new entrants' competitive threat was mentioned and figured prominently in their downside case. No conversations were held with local retailers or the new entrants.

Market soundings were based on local brokerage houses and think-tanks, whose output was highly generalized (and rosy, in retrospect). These commentaries underplayed the threat of the new entrants, variously referring to their products as fads or arguing that the company could always move into the space and dominate given their strong brand. The business side would seize on this view.

Despite all, credit still recommended the bank to do the deal, albeit at a slightly reduced retention level. In the end, the business side won out, with the original hold maintained. It was too late to change.

3. **And the "Ugly"**

The business side pushed hard to participate in the syndication. Their motivation was asset building for revenue purposes, with no real relationship focus. They argued successfully that the credit team should rely on the information memorandum prepared by the co-leads. An in-country diligence was vetoed as being "uneconomic." The credit team's document was more of a sales pitch to participate in the deal than a true credit analysis. The relevant sections of the document provided a descriptive background, consisting of historical financial statements, a narrative of the company's history, structure, and business, a pro-forma discussion of risk considerations.

The credit analyst used the content to populate the first draft of his write-up. He asked for a call with the company. This was arranged. The analyst reviewed a list of questions over a period of approximately two hours. The next day, the company provided answers to a number of pending questions. Later that day, the analyst competed the evaluation of the company and the transaction, recommending approval.

## Summary

1. The "Good" analyst was prescient on the whole. The breadth and depth of the analysis permitted the identification of the major vulnerabilities in the company's expansion project. The use of primary in-country sources,

such as retail competitors, allowed him to challenge the overly optimistic financial projections. Within 18 months, the company did hit the strong headwinds which the analyst had projected. The full roll out of the retail network was delayed by construction and licensing issues, something which had not been expected. And for those that did open, the retail sales performance disappointed, as feared. The company failed to recognize the need for deferred payment terms to juice retail sales. This pushed buyers to competing retail shops. When there, buyers found that these merchants were reacting to the company as a serious, new competitor by pushing the new entrants' products as a way of striking back. This translated into a fall in the company's wholesale revenue. Reacting to these developments, the company undertook a more aggressive retail strategy, which combined discounts and more generous deferred payment terms ranging up to two years. With these steps, revenue and gross margin declined at the same time as working capital funding requirements increased, straining oper-ating cash flow. As feared, higher interest rates in the major advanced economies resulted in a moderate outflow of portfolio capital in the country, but sufficiently strong to cause the currency to depreciate by roughly 15%.

2. The "Bad" analyst's work failed to dig deeply and broadly enough to uncover the same fact set as the "Good." The commercial pressures of the lender's role as a co-lead on the syndication undoubtedly could have played a significant role in the approach to the analysis. The chief risk officer's initial intervention was helpful but was not enough to counter the business side's pre-existing commitment to the deal. Whether and how the analyst felt this pressure is a mystery. Did he limit the scope of work inten-tionally, work hard but fail to uncover all the facts, or did he discover the truth but hide the results in order to avoid a firefight with powerful senior executives on the business side of the house? What is clear is that the credit evaluation lacked rigor and hence was too favorable to the company. On this faulty foundation was built the lender's approval.

3. The "Ugly" analyst followed the road of the "stuffee" that syndicate desks love, the less sophisticated lender who is wooed into a deal by the effective sales pitch of the bulge bracket firm, private or public, that they don't fully understand. The credit department was not positioned to undertake an independent, critical analysis of the company. The submission was little more than repackaging of the information memorandum. The lender had effectively outsourced its credit process. It would now pay the price.

# Critical Thinking

What inferences can we draw from the above analysts' performances?
Most are fairly obvious. To cite a few:

*First*, a holistic, dynamic, and forward-looking evaluation of the critical risks and mitigants derived from the forgoing (and other considerations) and their ranking in order of probability and severity of impact lie at the heart of a good credit analysis.

*Second*, the macroeconomic and market context can weigh heavily on credit quality in an emerging market and therefore needs to be understood, as shocks to terms of trade, capital flows, and exchange rates can set in motion forces that may overwhelm even financially strong borrowers over time;

*Third*, rigorous diligence should be characterized by: (i) contacts with a wide range of relevant stakeholders (suppliers/funders, customers/borrowers, government, et al.); and (ii) a focus on the commercial, financial, regulatory and other linkages of these parties to the borrower, and not be limited solely to: (a) an analysis of the borrower; and (b) company or potentially conflicted sources of secondary market research (e.g., brokerage houses, industry groups, etc.);

*Fourth*, as shown in Case 1 (Industrial Bank) within the financial institution space, the characteristics and vulnerabilities of a bank's end-borrowers may well matter more than the initial profitability, solvency and liquidity of the institution;

*Fifth*, as shown in Case 2 (National Goods Company), an evaluation of a borrower's business prospects is not possible without a thorough grasp of the structure and competitive dynamics of their market context, especially new business areas—retail white goods in our case—even if it appears the borrower should know what they are doing (i.e., they know better than I can ever know, they are rational, so why worry…);

This last one requires further explanation and will act as bridge to the ensuing discussion.

Let's start by asking a simple, yet nonetheless core question which should be present first and foremost in any credit analysis. "Can the borrower repay the loan?".

After the reader has stopped laughing at the seeming absurd naivety of the query, consider that it is indeed the very essence of what we must ask ourselves. Given all the background facts, figures, and analytics filling many pages, answering this question is the objective. Full stop. Getting there and being confident, or at least as confident in a fundamentally uncertain future outcome as one can be, is after all the "why" of credit analysis.

Let's explore the word "uncertain."

Uncertainty (to be uncertain) in the Knightian sense is "*a lack of any quantifiable knowledge about some possible occurrence, as opposed to the presence of quantifiable risk. The concept acknowledges some fundamental degree of ignorance, a limit to knowledge, and an essential unpredictability of future events.*"[6] Will I find true love? Will there be a war in the world in 2036? What is the next pandemic? What will sea level be in 2050? None of these can be answered with certainty, much less be associated with a reasonably predictable level of probability. In a credit context, uncertainty would mean that we cannot really know the odds of repayment. Analysts would object to this statement, citing empirical, rating agency default data for similar borrowers or presenting financial projections demonstrating sufficient cash flow to service the debt. Whilst there may be hesitation to offer a precise percentage to describe the repayment prospects, analysts are happy to make statements such as "we are highly confident" or "the evidence clearly shows."

How do analysts get to their conclusions? In the above cases, our three analysts reached quite different views on the same credits. Why was this? It is arguable that institutional biases (e.g., the business team pushing for a revenue-generating or even employment-security ensuring transaction) may have influenced the analysts' conclusions, even driving an *ex ante* decision to limit the scope and rigor of the work ("the deal will get approved anyway, so why stick my neck out."). However, on the whole, institutional safeguards and personal integrity act as effective guardrails.

What we have experienced is that *methodology*, the approach to the credit analysis, contributes to the difference in conclusions, as much do honest, well-reasoned, and documented disagreement on the *risk profile* and ultimate creditworthiness of the proposal. The relative weights of these two factors vary over time, but a central argument of the book is that the "how to" of credit analysis plays an important role. Think about the above cases in this chapter-the "Good" asked, "What happens if the price of oil collapses," or "What happens if the new entrants' products take market share from the company, or to counter competitive pressures, deferred payment terms become necessary?" The others failed to ask these questions at all.

The difference can be framed by considering four levels of critical thinking:

1. Description:   What?
2. Analysis:      Why and how?
3. Evaluation:    Known or reasonably predicted implications?

---

6 F. Knight, Risk, Uncertainty and Profit, Boston, Hart Schaffner & Marx; Houghton Mifflin Company (1921).

4. Speculation:    Alternative outcomes and possible implications?

Using the example of the Spanish Armada, a historical event:

1. Description:    Dates, number of ships, names of commanders, etc.?
2. Analysis:       Weather, tactics, key moments, ship & armament performance, etc.?
3. Evaluation:     Political, military, economic significance of the outcome?
4. Speculation:    The future of Europe in the event of a Spanish victory?

Or a current event, the COVID-19 Pandemic:

1. Description:    Nature of the virus, data?
2. Analysis:       Drivers and impact—health, economics, and socio-political factors?
3. Evaluation:     Near-term outlook, based on current information and trend?
4. Speculation:    Alternative scenarios based on multiple assumptions—factors such as population behavior, vaccine development, public health policies, mutation of new, more resistant, and/or transferable strains, etc.

How do we apply this approach to the credit analysis process? Let's consider the generic example (Fig. 4.1):

Using this framework to think back to the two cases in this chapter, what do we find?

*First*, we might expect Level 1—Background should be the same for all analysts. This is not true in all cases, unfortunately. The analyst should not rely on reporting templates prepared by borrowers or credit departments, but instead use primary reporting sources. These include, most notably, audited financial statements with complete explicative notes (spoiler alert: this is where the real juicy stuff is), management letters, etc., when available or for interim dates, copies of the same reports the management or the boards use. The portfolio of background materials should also include macroeconomic, market and competitor data and intelligence.

As in Case 1 (Industrial Bank), where the "Good" focused intensively on the oil market outlook, the pool of background data and intelligence to be used in the credit analysis should extend to economic and relevant financial sector and commodity market areas. The "Bad" did this, but far less rigorously than necessary, with the result that the risk of an oil price collapse

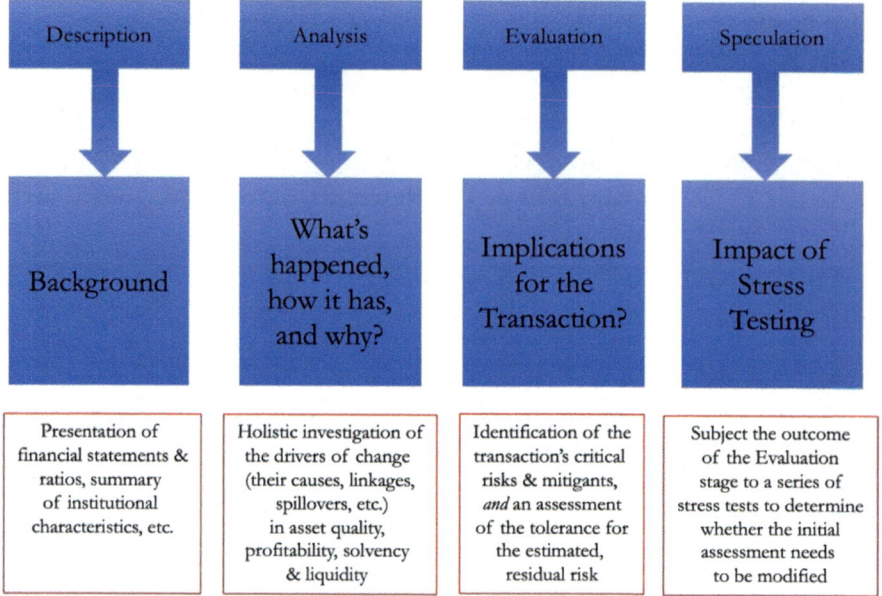

**Fig. 4.1** Critical analysis and credit analysis

and the follow-on effects were minimized. The "Ugly" failed completely. For the borrower's context, the scope of the portfolio of background data and information should be broad enough to permit subsequent analysis and evaluation of all material drivers of the financial and operating performance of the borrower, and hence the risks or threats to this performance, not just the financial statements of the borrower. Choosing the appropriate scope is an essential step. The failure to do so will impair the subsequent analysis.

*Second*, the key cause of success or failure of Level 2—Analysis is not how well an analyst explains why or how yesterday's events happened, although this is important. Instead, does the analyst succeed in drawing out from this historical record or backward-looking view the key risk considerations for the subsequent (Evaluation and Speculation) levels? For example, in Case 2 (National Goods Company), the "Good" questioned the company's thinking about the vertical integration strategy by examining the existing white-goods retail sector. From this work, two facts became evident: (i) new entrants' more eco-friendly units were increasing displacing the company's legacy product lines in customer preferences; and (ii) to move the company's products off the floor, deferred payment terms had become necessary. These factors would be central contributors to the subsequent, correct view of the company's future. The "Bad" and the "Ugly" missed these, and, well, we know what happened.

*Third*, many analysts stop at Level 2 and do not get to Level 3. The "Ugly" did in Case 2 (National Goods Company). The credit work was a simple description of the historical record, with a perfunctory extension of the past performance into the future despite the transformational impact of the move into retail sector. The "Bad" moved on to Level 3, but failures on Level 1 (background intelligence—Oil markets in Case 1, retail sector in Case 2) meant that the situational analysis on Level 2 was flawed. As a result, the Level 3—Evaluation could not arrive at a correct estimation of the severity of the risks confronting the borrower in each case. The "Good" arrived at Level 3 equipped with well-targeted and, in the end, accurate analysis, which permitted the evaluation to identify, define, and measure the risks to non-payment. Using this form of "risk matrix," a projected base case is constructed. This may be enough to make a negative decision, but it should never be enough to support a positive one. Level 4 is necessary for a positive decision.

*Fourth*, the "Bad" and the "Ugly" have closed up and gone home by the time we arrive at Level 4—Speculation. In contrast, the "Good" was just rolling up her sleeves and starting to work in earnest. The borrower and transactional risk matrices begun in Level 3 were used to construct alternative scenarios for Level 4. The mechanical preparation of upside and downside projections does not constitute this activity. All who have read lending or investment proposals know that scenario analysis is a standard element of credit packages. They were undoubtedly present in the work of the "Bad" and the "Ugly."

The key is *what underlies the assumptions*. One can only imagine the projections prepared by the "Ugly" would have shown a upside case of an x% increase of sales, or a downside case of a y% decline in sales, etc. Numbers plucked out of the air, with no linkage to the facts. In comparison, the "Good" had identified specific risk elements with a degree of precision that allowed measurement, and hence the introduction of quantification. For example, in Case 1, the analyst employs data and analytics to form assumptions concerning the impact of a collapse of oil prices on the exchange rate, NPLs and eventually solvency. In Case 2, the focus was on a number of factors, retail sale competition, credit terms, and interest and exchange rates. In both, the quality test is not how precisely accurate the numbers are, but rather, does the output identify risks sufficiently to permit a well-reasoned credit decision? Had the risks been of a different nature or less severe, the analysts' insights could have been used to introduce structural mitigants to the transaction. However, in our two cases, this was not possible.

-&-

Let's turn now to the monitoring process—the most essential element of the Pre-Restructuring Phase.

One of the authors recalls walking from a conference room, in which an investment committee had just approved an especially complex and challenging transaction, toward the elevator bank and hearing the young credit analyst on the case quip, "I am relieved I won't have to dig into this one again!" The author, working on the business development side of the house at the time, retorted, "Your job is just starting!" The analyst looked perplexed. "Of course, I'll have to watch for covenant breaches, but assuming no problems, I won't have to analyze like this again," he claimed, waving the folder holding his credit work on the loan in question. The elevator opened, and the conversation ended. The rest of the conversation never happened, as the analyst left the bank soon thereafter to join a hedge fund that (perhaps coincidentally?) did not navigate the 2008 turbulence particularly well.

The young analyst's comments are a good example of the fundamental misconception, and hence mistake, around the monitoring function. Monitoring is not a simple exercise of tracking financial performance until a problem crystalizes. In fact, using the term monitoring itself may well be an indication that the activity is being approached the wrong way. "Monitoring and Credit Management" or just "Credit Management" far better denotes the appropriate role.

Suggesting these alternative labels is more than just a cute, semantic play to name a department or credit group activity. Rather, the words are meant to denote a *pro-active role* whose mandate is to *prevent, when possible, market and idiosyncratic stresses from transforming into credit problems.* The activity has a far wider scope and responsibility than being a kind of blinking amber light, warning that another workout is looming. Effective credit management monitors and evaluates developing credit stresses and, from this diagnostic exercise, identifies mitigating actions. These responses vary between (i) suggesting or, where possible due to covenant violation or new money pressures, imposing on the borrower remedial actions (e.g., slowing dividends, deleveraging, limits on new investments or acquisitions) and/or (ii) portfolio re-weighting to reduce exposure over time.

Sometimes in credit training classes, monitoring is compared to the annual, factory-floor like medical check-ups our insurance company allows us. In these, a white-uniformed nurse first takes our blood pressure and runs a battery of tests (which can be likened to covenant checks). Unless there is something seriously wrong, the brief concluding interview with the doctor will typically end with, at worst, a few platitudes about lowering your cholesterol and losing a few pounds. But this analogy is at best incomplete, worst misconstrued.

The best comparison is to your family doctor (remember these?). The analyst should understand the case—business model, market and competitive environment, stakeholders, etc.—as well as your GP knows you—medical history, lifestyle, etc. When these characteristics or facts change, the analyst should plug the new "stuff" into the analytics and ask what the effects will be over time, in a manner similar to your doctor, who comments on your new recent daily whisky and cigar routine. The obvious, pertinent questions follow. In the case of the credit manager, "What could the macroeconomic shock mean to the bank's solvency over time? Should I suggest to the business they discuss the bank's thinking about this and whether, should the worst happen, they have contingent capital plans?" That is, the same preventative medicine in which a careful doctor engages when confronted with the new lover of Macallan and Villiger La Vencedora Churchills, and the beginning of a bulge in the midriff. He starts by suggesting a healthier lifestyle.

In a similar vein, credit management's intervention should aim at identifying a *future problem* (macro shock—slowing growth—reduced revenue and operating cash flow—increased problem loans and provisioning—net losses and capital destruction) when the dynamics are still in the early stages and there is time to mount a response *before the crises ensues*. The good doctor endeavors to convince the patient to deemphasize his trips to his study in the early evenings for a wee dram and a smoke, in favor of a walk around the neighborhood with his wife, long before clinical examinations would display danger signals.

Neither author here is a trained medical professional. However, as lifelong patients, we have experienced the sobering words from our doctor, "We have a situation here," or its equivalent. Accepting that in the real world not all problems, medical or credit in nature, are preventable is not an argument for not trying. Most of the time in credit work, short of fraud or an unanticipated exogenous shock, the unpleasant words, "We have a situation here" presage a workout which should have been expected, if not prevented.

As a digression before continuing the discussion, we must admit: when sharing the foregoing thoughts with colleagues in the past, the reaction has often ranged from skeptical to dismissive. "Of course, we just don't wait for a covenant breach to occur before reacting." More recently, during the COVID-19 pandemic, "Look what we're doing now, stress testing every name!" Acknowledging that a once-in-a-century, global public health has sharpened the preventative credit management focus is not the same as concluding this crisis-era practice should be the norm and should continue once the world returns to "normal." One can hope, but we shouldn't assume too much.

To reinforce this distinction between a reactive/remedial and a pro-active/preventative approach, let's return to our cases. We will focus on the second—our eager white-goods wholesaler the National Goods Company, who has cost its fate with a move into retail sales.

Loan agreements customarily will specify a reporting regime, say, quarterly financials using a pre-agreed template and, as may be required, a covenant compliance certification. Annually, the audited financial statements must also be provided. There may be a periodic credit call to discuss the financials. In the absence of a covenant violation or a readily identifiable prospective adverse change in the financial condition of the borrower, the monitoring review requirement is ticked and the file put away until the next time. That's what we can assume the "Ugly" and maybe even the "Bad" would do. Their operative principle—no problem until there is a problem.

How does this contrast with the Good? As we recall, our analyst there identified three, critical risks: (i) the competition from more eco-friendly products; (ii) a growing requirement to provide credit terms to support sales; and (iii) the prospect of higher debt service due to a rise in interest rates and a depreciating local currency. At the time of the original approval, these were analyzed in a form of a risk matrix, which estimated/evaluated for each the severity of impact, likelihood of occurrence, possible/actual mitigants, and the residual risk. The financial projections and scenario analysis in the credit package incorporated these risk elements. The "Good" analyst will have shared this thinking (and ideally the actual risk matrix itself) with his counterpart at the company. Customized reporting requirements covering these risk elements would have been designed and agreed. Over the life of the loan, their impact (and others that may have arisen) would be subjected to new scenario analysis.

Let's assume we are a year into the loan. Sales appear to be slowing as consumer preferences opt increasingly for the eco-friendly washers and dryers. The marketing team has suggested addressing this trend by capping price increases, despite a moderate level of domestic inflation, and offering 24–36-month credit terms. Overall working capital requirements will have to increase, especially as these credit receivables are booked. As predicted, monetary policy tightening in the major economies has led to an increase in global interest rates, with the knock-on effect of capital outflows and a defensive rise in the local central bank policy rate. Despite this action and periodic intervention in the exchange market, the local currency has come under selling pressure. Nothing big yet, but the capacity of the government to engage in counter-measures is not unlimited. The financial reporting shows a slight reduction in sales growth, a moderate tightening in gross margin, but no material weakening elsewhere. All covenants are met. An evaluation based on historical data gives a clean bill of health. In the absence of a re-run of the scenario analysis, the story would end there until the next quarter or more likely the end of the next fiscal year.

Fortunately, the "Good" analyst plugs in the critical risk updates into the analytics and then activates the amber warning light. Since the company is in compliance with all explicit financial covenants, there is nothing that can be done for the moment (invoking a material adverse change clause is legally tenuous[7]). Five months thereafter and well before the end of the next fiscal year, as predicted operating cash flow turns negative due to the increase in credit receivables. A patchwork of small foreign and local currency unsecured lines of credit is assembled to fund the deficit in anticipation of a more formal fundraising effort. Hence, the company is forced into the credit markets again. At this time, exchange market pressures are heightening the likelihood of a depreciation, and the debt service coverage ratio is on the brink of a violation.

The Good's lending institution is contacted and asked to talk about new money. Armed with an updated set of analytics, the Good's relationship and credit teams meet with the company and have a "come to pray" meeting. The damage of the ill-designed foray into retail sales cannot be fixed immediately, but the company has engaged an external consulting team to reassess their strategy, including the question of product redesign. On the financial side, the "Good" recommends immediate hedging of the foreign currency exposure and a program consisting of: (i) a refinancing of the USD facility into a combination of USD (hedged) and local currency term loans; and (ii) a local currency receivables securitization. National Goods' management listens carefully, but takes no action for the time being. It is only a matter of time.

## Conclusions

Let's summarize quickly what happened in our opening narrative of Kristi and the Bank of Commerce, up to the point where the decision to restructure was taken.

---

[7] *See* more detailed discussion of MAE clauses in Chapter 11.

- A shock (copper price collapse) to the country's terms of trade put in motion forces that threatened the Bank's future. Kristi had carefully monitored and seen this. The other lenders did not.
- Kristi was the only lender who had approached Ursula. Either New West was not convinced, or Ursula accepted Kristi was right but realized JK would never support a decisions to stop dividends or, even worse, provide new equity funding. As a result, Kristi's warnings went unheeded. The "car continued to speed toward the cliff."
- After the first devaluation, Kristi tried again to convince Ursula to act but was rebuffed.
- Only with the breaking of the currency peg (which exacerbated already deteriorating conditions in the financial system) did lenders wake up. The Bank of Commerce was put under the credit microscope. The diagnosis was frightening. But by this time, the patient's condition was dire.
- Then and only then was the decision taken to start restructuring discussions.

What are the "takeaways" or "lessons learned" from our narrative?

- **The role of sound credit analysis—"Prevention is 99% of the Cure."** Lending always carries the risk of default, and ultimately loss. This is the old "dogs have fleas" adage. Ultimately, lenders are paid for assuming this risk. *Ex ante*, the greater the expected risk, the higher should be the return (interest spread and fees). The trick for lenders is to evaluate accurately this expected risk. The correct risk concept to be employed is a defined residual or adjusted risk after taking into consideration elements such as external support and the transaction structure. External support typically takes the form of a guarantee (or other security), rated according to the capacity and willingness of the guarantor to fulfill their obligation (or liquidity and speed/ease of enforcement against collateral provided). The structural considerations are varied and complex. These range from the *de jure* nature of the debt (e.g., senior v. junior capital, unsecured v. secured, etc.) to elements such as control of cash flow, limits on debt, negative pledges, and the like.

  The lenders missed or underestimated several significant risks in the case of the Bank of Commerce.

  *First*, JK was dependent on the up-streamed dividends from the Bank, a need that became more acute as New West's liquidity tightened. He prioritized his cash-flow need over the building up of pro-cyclical capital buffers at the Bank of Commerce level. On his orders, Ursula continued upstreaming cash, even when it became clear that market conditions were driving the bank toward operating losses and a serious threat to its solvency.

*Second*, to maximize profitability, the bank borrowed in cheap dollars and leant in expensive local currency. This strategy resulted in a large open-currency position at the bank level and a currency mismatch at the borrower level. This worked well whilst the currency peg held. The balance of payments pressures that built up in the aftermath of the collapse of copper prices forced the government to abandon the peg. Disaster ensued. In both cases, the lenders appeared to have missed these risks, judging from the absence of suitable preventative measures built into the structure. No financial covenant was present to limit dividends, and the capital adequacy covenant was set just above the regulatory minimum. The financial covenant addressing the open currency position was set at a multiple of capitalization, adequate for a limited degree of depreciation, but potentially fatal at higher degrees of currency weakness.

- **Credit's job is just beginning at disbursement—"Keep your Eye on the Ball."** In the Bank of Commerce case, lender monitoring of the local institution and credit management were inadequate—the lenders for the most part missed the significance of the copper market shock for the macro-economy and the borrower's operations and financial condition. As the numbers worsened, most assumed that the problems were merely temporary. In hindsight, elementary economics students and novice credit analysts should have been able to see the problem coming. But years of market stability and counter-party growth clouded the analytic screen. This was not only true for the lenders (save for Kristi) but also for Ursula and JK in our opening narrative.

- **Don't assume shareholder support—"Nothing is Written."** Relying on the conventional wisdom that well-moneyed shareholders would never let their investments go sour is risky. In the case of Bank of Commerce, many lenders believed the presence of a strong shareholder was tantamount to a guarantee. When market conditions turned, not only were lenders surprisingly nonchalant, but certain of them actually increased their exposure to compensate for business lost elsewhere in a collapsing economy. This expectation remained until very late in the game, as evidenced by Edinburgh Partners' late entry into the mix. Todd's subsequent shock and anger were not feigned. These lenders' credit approval assumed something that was never there—that JK had money and would eagerly use it to succor the Bank of Commerce. We all can cite many examples where such blind reliance on shareholder support turned out badly. If it is not written down properly and legally binding, do not assume anything.[8]

- **Accept hard realities—"The Emperor Has No Clothes."** Earlier than the rest of the Bank of Commerce lenders, Kristi saw the bank's future, clear as day. As soon as the market shock hit, she confronted local management and then Ursula. There was a clash in views. Non-performing loans were up marginally, but they should have been rising even faster given market conditions, Kristi felt. She pointed out that restructured loans were increasing to a historically high level. She also knew the trick. Many could well be disguised as bad loans. Provisions should be hiked, Kristi adduced. Management dismissed her worries, claiming these were just performing loans being re-calibrated to adjust to a moderately weaker economic environment. No increase in provisions was necessary. There was a clash in views. Kristi feared that the bank could be technically insolvent if the loan book were provisioned accurately. Management demurred. Was the emperor clothed in finery, as management contended, or was he stark naked, as Kristi suspected (and probably knew)? The future would validate Kristi's evaluation. At this early stage when remedial alternatives were more numerous, however, she failed to convince management and shareholders. Subsequent conversations with lenders were equally futile. Business as usual would continue, with precious capital continuing to be up-streamed until the crisis actually engulfed the bank, its shareholders, and the lenders.

---

[8] The authors are only too aware of a number of cases where bankers unwisely relied on verbal support from parent companies—sometimes accompanied by so-called 'comfort letters.' Issuers clearly hedge their bets in such comfort letters and ordinarily will issue them only after the most meticulous review by their counsel. The letters are intentionally vaguely drafted, to avoid a legally-enforceable obligation. Indeed, the argument may be made that comfort letters serve the sole purpose of confusing, more than anything else.

# 5

# Decision to Restructure

**Abstract** Torrential rains (a negative credit shock) have caused flooding that threatens the fox's life (a pending payment default). In flight, the stork is able to espy a path to refuge and points this out (the need to undertake remedial action, possibly including a debt restructuring). There is resistance. The fox's predicament becomes more precarious as did that of the Bank of Commerce in the opening Tale. The chapter continues with an exposition of general topics of: (i) precedents and types of restructurings; (ii) differences across markets; and (iii) the distinction between judicial versus nonjudicial restructuring (aka workouts) and the conceptual framework and rationale for the latter. The question of the right "talent" is debated, before moving on to the circumstances and decision-making criteria leading to the choice to proceed to a restructuring. To reinforce these concepts, the chapter returns to the two case studies introduced in Chapter 3. The chapter ends with a set of key learnings, using again the opening Bank of Commerce tale.

**Keywords** Act of God · Balance sheet · Bankruptcy · Borrower · Confidentiality · Consensual restructuring · Coordinating committee · Corporate debt · Debt · Debtor · Cash flow · COVID-19 · Credit analysis · Credit monitoring · Currency peg · DFI (development finance institution) · Distressed debt · Exogenous shock · Foreign exchange · Emerging market · Exchange rate · Frontier market · INSOL II · INSOL principles · Insolvency · Lender leadership · Loan loss provision · Non-performing loans · Pre-insolvency · Restructure · Restructuring · Restructuring plan · Standstill · Steering committee · Workout

### Preface: The Stork and the Fox—Part II

*The fox returned to his den that evening, uncharacteristically hungry.*

*The rains resumed that night and continued into the next day. The fox stayed under shelter; the weather was too inclement to venture outside. Night fell, and the rains continued. By morning, the land around his den had become spotted with puddles. Still, the rain fell.*

*The next morning, he looked outside. Dark, grey clouds filled the sky. The rain had subsided for an hour, and only a few drops of rain fell.*

*"Hello," a voice called from above.*

*The fox looked up and saw the stork, circling above.*

*"The river has breached its shores and is flooding the low lands. Soon, the waters will be here." The stork said. "You'd best move into the foothills for safety."*

*The fox's den was still dry and comfortable. He had supplies to last a couple of weeks. "No, I will stay here. The river has never overflowed its banks or threatened these parts."*

*The stork flew closer to the fox. "I am not so sure. My kind have never seen such rains before. You should flee whilst there is still time."*

*The fox shook his head stubbornly and went back inside. A few hours later, his neighbors, a family of three foxes stopped by. "We are moving to higher ground. Would you like to join us?"*

*"No, there is no need. I am safe here."*

*Later that night, the fox went to sleep but was soon awakened by the sound of the rain battering the outside of his den. The storm had begun again, this time more forcefully than before. The fox dozed off again. But in the morning, he awoke to find his den awash. He struggled to the entrance. What he saw amazed him. The fields were underwater. Still, the rains fell.*

*The fox now realized he could tarry no longer. He hurriedly packed a small bundle and ventured outside. The water was almost to his shoulders.*

*He trudged across the lowlands, looking for a way to higher ground. He entered the thick forest, shrouded in fog. He feared he was lost. Still, the rains fell.*

*The water kept rising. His incredulity finally transformed into a deep sense of regret. "How I wish I had left with my neighbors yesterday!" The fox moaned, now fearful for his life.*

*Later, he came upon a small clearing. Under the low clouds, he espied the stork gliding above.*

*The stork motioned to the left before flying off into the distance. "Go in this direction," she called.*

*The fox kept walking, but now at a faster pace. Soon, through the rain, he saw the beginnings of a pathway into the foothills. Still, the rains came.*

-&-

The fox may not reach dry land. Why did he not react when he saw that the bridge had been washed out in Part I of the fable? Or when the rains started again? Not responding perhaps made sense. The area had never been flooded in recent memory. Leave home? A big and unprecedented step. A more cautious and curious fox might have thought about what might be coming. Our fox didn't. But when the rains intensified?

When first the stork, then his fox neighbors warned him, his failure to consider his growing danger with an open mind morphed into recklessness. Still, he stayed put. Only when the waters rose to a level that actually threatened his life did he move. Once his flight to safety began, he came to appreciate the neighbors, ruing his failure to listen. Later, when he feared all was lost, the stork pointed a way forward. We will have to wait to see whether he makes it to higher ground. What we can assume with a high degree of certainty is that if there is a next time, he will heed the warning signs and listen more closely to others.

For Kristi in our opening narrative, the storm clouds took the form of a changing macroeconomic environment. Slowing global growth lowered fixed capital investment. The rains were the knock-on effect of the decline in copper prices as demand for the industrial metal fell. In the same way that the river lowlands near the river where our fox lived were vulnerable to flooding, the home country of Kristi's borrower was acutely exposed to the debilitating cycle started by a term of trade price and export proceeds shock. The government had maintained a peg against the US dollar. As a result, the currency was overvalued. During this time, significant volumes of foreign portfolio capital had flowed into the country. The financial system became highly dependent on these dollarized funds.

To address the notional, open currency risk, US dollar-denominated lending had become the norm, despite the general lack of foreign currency cash flow on the part of the banking system's end-borrowers. As macro-financial theory predicted, the end result was a spike in the cost of risk threatening systemic solvency. Kristi put the pieces together very early, much as we might expect the stork to have done when she saw the bridge washed away by the rising waters. By and large, the rest only recognized the danger when the government abandoned the peg.

Let's now examine in greater depth the questions that lenders like Kristi must ask and answer well when the proverbial "credit risk warning light" starts flashing amber.

To do this, we will first return to the main elements of the Decision to Restructure Phase outlined in Chapter 3. We will then return to some of the case studies we started in our previous chapters to reenforce these elements.

# Main Elements of the Decision to Restructure Phase

## A General Vision

Bankers and policymakers have devoted considerable attention to the multitude of financial crises and their impact upon national, regional, and global economies over centuries, not least the twentieth and twenty-first centuries. From the Great Depression of 1932 to the 1970s Energy Crisis; the Lost Decade in Latin America to the US Savings and Loan Crisis of the 1980s–1990s; the Russian Financial Crisis of 1998 to the Lehman-Brothers Global Economic Crisis of 2008–2009; the "double whammy" Ukrainian Crisis of 2014/Oil Crash of 2015 to the global 2020–2021 COVID-19 pandemic, history is replete with crises, big and small, global and regional—and lessons learned.

Globalization has amplified the effect of financial crises and the speed and extent to which these can snowball.

Out of the ashes from each of these crises' blazes, a veritable phoenix of financial and legislative reform has taken shape, informing an approach to risk allocation and enhancement of national insolvency systems aimed at creating clearer, fairer rules for the providers of capital. And again, the process of globalization and the mobility of international capital has taught local governments that these rules are critical to competition for the capital resources they need in order to develop their economies.

In developed countries, the legislative toolboxes for distressed situations thankfully include transparent and (critically) predictable rules of the game, in the form of relatively well-drafted bankruptcy laws and transparent and efficient court practice. The governments of many emerging-market economies, often with the help of global or regional DFIs and higher educational institutions, have tried to emulate more developed economies to offer lenders more refined, harmonious systems of insolvency law.[1]

---

[1] For an excellent summary of core insolvency system principles, *see* EBRD Core Principles of an Effective Insolvency System, published by the European Bank for Reconstruction and Development's Law in Transition Program, at www.ebrd.com (September 2020).

Nonetheless, despite the strong understanding local policymakers may have, and indeed despite their best efforts to reform their nascent judicial and insolvency systems, from the practical standpoint many such systems continue to pose major risks for international lenders. Even larger emerging-markets which in recent decades have become attractive to international lenders, law, and practice can seem murky. Formal insolvency proceedings in some of these countries are seen as a venue of last resort, with the initiation of such proceedings often being in the first step toward an inevitable liquidation.[2] At the same time, *not all emerging markets are alike*—a number have made extraordinary steps forward in advancing their insolvency systems.[3]

Where lenders are secured by sufficient liquid collateral or other credit support, they may well take the view (other considerations aside, e.g., mandate, reputation, customer relationships, etc.) that opportunistic acceleration/foreclosure presents the most effective solution.[4]

To be sure, offshore credit-support structures (where support is either recourse to deep-pocket international sponsors or where the security structure allows speedy, easy assumption of control over the operational asset such as via an offshore special purpose vehicle (SPV) structure can present a reliable step forward swift, attractive exit. Real estate, ship, aircraft, and other single-asset type secured financings may lend themselves well to foreclosure and sale of the asset (usually with the assistance of industry intermediaries).[5] Similarly, in those cases where credit default insurance or swaps with reliable counterparties have been put in place, there is a clear and sunny path forward.

But where these luxuries are not extant (e.g., uninsured senior unsecured loans, subordinated loans, etc.), the decision becomes more complex. The

---

[2] *See* T. Stubbs and M.F. Higgins, "Creditors' Rights: The Russian Revolution," Law in Transition 2010, European Bank for Reconstruction and Development, pp. 76–81. *See also* more detailed discussion in Chapter 11.

[3] *See*, e.g., EBRD Insolvency Assessment on Reorganisation Procedures: Preliminary Assessment Report, April 2021, https://www.ebrd-restructuring.com/storage/uploads/documents/94228029cc1b 26d88b75222c6a9d0df0.pdf. The report reflects an accelerated review of national insolvency frameworks in the 38 emerging markets economies where the EBRD operates. *See also* more detailed discussion in Chapter 11 as well as Annex 1.

[4] That said, insolvency systems will often include automatic stays which suspend foreclosure on local security and require that foreclosure take place in the context of the insolvency proceedings and subject to its rules.

[5] The topic of collateral—its structuring, valuation, perfection of security interests, monitoring, and enforcement—would in fairness require its own chapter. We note here only that the lenders: (a) must take care to ensure the perfection of their claim and to provide for workable enforcement arrangements should this become necessary; (b) be realistic in their understanding of the certainty, ease, and speed of enforcement of security, and (c) ensure that their valuations are made in real-time post-distress. Many loan documents will provide for margin calls (i.e., topping up security), regular revaluations of security and the like. However, intervening events like an Act of God (e.g., the COVID-19 pandemic) can impact severely on the value of collateral and the ability quickly to monetize it. *See* more detailed discussion of security in Chapter 11.

lender faces calling default/acceleration (risking cross default and insolvency) versus "cutting a deal" on a unilateral or multilateral basis between the borrower and other stakeholders. Even if the loan documentation is clear on remedies, will acceleration really achieve the objective of a clear exit with no (or modest) losses? Lastly, there are reputational and relationship considerations, which may influence the timing of the decision to accelerate. Does a lender want to be identified in history as the "one who pulled the plug," especially when the action is taken alone?

Even in developed economies with advanced insolvency systems, after decades of crisis management, international lending institutions have come to a more or less shared general conclusion that *where appropriate/achievable, a collaborative preventative restructuring can (and often does) provide a better return* for the lender, the borrower, and its shareholders, than a formal insolvency.

Restructurings may generally be broken down into two separate and distinct categories:

- **Judicial** restructurings (sometimes referred to as rescue proceedings), in which some court intervention is used—this category may be broken down further into (i) *hybrid* proceedings (which involve only limited court interaction, e.g., approval of a pre-agreed plan) or (ii) *full* restructuring proceedings (which involve ongoing interaction with courts); and
- **Nonjudicial** restructurings (also known as *consensual restructurings or workouts*[6]), in which *no* court intervention is sought. Instead, the stakeholders "work out" the terms of the restructuring on a purely *contractual* basis, amongst themselves.[7]

Developed economies such as the United States, the United Kingdom, and members of the European Union (EU) have developed quite effective hybrid restructurings procedures. In the United States, this will include "pre-negotiated" and/or so-called "pre-packaged" US Chapter 11 bankruptcies,

---

[6] We use the terms "consensual restructurings" and "workouts" synonymously throughout this book.

[7] Note that in some emerging markets there a more formalized workout is increasingly becoming popular whereby a legislative framework for a workout is established but without court oversight. A number of the countries surveyed in Annex 1 have insolvency legislation which expressly envisages that parties may enter into pre-insolvency workouts and even provides general guidelines for such workouts (e.g., Uzbekistan). This may be useful in countries where local entrepreneurs and lenders culturally prefer to have some acknowledgment or "steer" from the authorities as to the acceptability of pursuing a private workout. *See also* R. Olivares-Caminal, C. Bridge-Coller, H. Volchak, D. D'Alvia, N. Goglidze and N. Pagkou, *Corporate Restructuring in Times of COVID-19: A New Insolvency Law Assessment to Facilitate Corporate Rescue*, pp. 460–464, International Corporate Rescue (Chase Cambria) 2020.

whilst in the United Kingdom this will include schemes of arrangement and (more recently, following 2020 reforms) restructuring plans.[8] In EU member states this will include national insolvency systems which now enjoy the overlay of, and are in the process of implementing, the recent 2019 EU Directive on preventative restructuring.[9]

A number of emerging markets have made considerable progress in creating insolvency systems with effective hybrid restructuring rules, importing the concepts of US Chapter 11, UK schemes of arrangement, etc.[10] Regrettably, many other emerging markets have lagged in this respect. *A distinct lack of homogeneity amongst emerging markets is thus evident.* So generalizations (e.g., "All emerging markets have bad insolvency systems") are difficult.

What are the practical implications of this? *Lender leadership must always make a case-by-case assessment* (with assistance of local and transaction counsel) on the extent to which the borrower's respective local insolvency system supports (or does not support) the use of a *judicial restructuring versus a consensual restructuring.* Other key factors may also come into play in determining whether the courts and the insolvency infrastructure may be relied on.[11]

Where the local insolvency system has no effective judicial restructuring regime (or where other factors make it unattractive or unworkable), the authors believe that *consensual restructurings present the most viable alternatives for maximizing lender recoveries* (and giving shareholder equity the best possible chance of survival).

These alternatives will be either on an ad hoc, bilateral or multilateral party basis, often enhanced by reference to a *common set of behavioral norms* shared by the relevant lenders, the borrower, and its shareholders.

---

[8] 11 US Code Title 11 (Sections 1101–1195); Part 26 of the UK Companies Act 2006; Part 26A UK Companies Act 2006. The jurisdictional hurdles to using the US and UK courts for judicial restructurings of emerging markets borrowers are outlined in Chapter 11.

[9] Directive (EU) 2019/1023 of the European Parliament and of the Council of June 20, 2019.

[10] Notably this includes Singapore, whose insolvency system has even started to operate as a *regional hub* providing both judicial management and schemes of arrangement for non-Singaporean countries from the region, under the Insolvency Restructuring and Dissolution Act 2018. *See* Chapter 11 for a discussion of jurisdictional issues in considering Singaporean courts for this purpose. A number of other emerging markets have similarly endeavored to improve their insolvency systems to harmonize them with best global practice, some quite recently, and now include judicial restructuring procedures. Although these countries may not play the same regional hub role as Singapore, nonetheless their improved systems are of great benefit on a domestic level and for international lenders active in these countries. *See* more generally Annex 1.

[11] *See* more detailed discussions in Chapters 7 (sections "Cost-Benefit Analysis" and "Impact of the Emerging Market Environment") and 11, as well as Annex 1.

In this latter respect, during the 1980s–1990s the so-called *"London Approach"* reflected an understanding that when lenders share such a set of voluntary behavioral norms, this often produces higher returns—the proverbial win–win result. The London Approach has been defined as a "non statutory and informal framework introduced with the support of the Bank of England for dealing with temporary support operations mounted by banks and other lenders to a company or group in financial difficulties, pending a possible restructuring."[12] It gained considerable traction in the London marketplace, which quickly grew as one of Europe's (indeed, one of the world's) most prominent and successful financial centers.

The four main principles of the London Approach are: (1) voluntary standstill; (2) confidential sharing of reliable information; (3) negotiation and decision on viability; and (4) business plan and new money.

These principles inspired the adoption in 2000 by INSOL International (the international insolvency/turnaround professional organization) of a set of principles based on the London Approach, entitled the *Statement of Principles for a Global Approach to Multi-Creditor Workouts (INSOL I)*. These latter principles expanded the London Approach into a broader set of eight principles. Subsequently, in 2016–2017, INSOL International updated INSOL I and entitled the resultant updated eight principles the *Insol International Statement of Principles for a Global Approach to Multi-Creditor Workouts II (INSOL II)*.[13]

INSOL II provide a clear and well-balanced conceptual framework for consensual restructurings.

Given the enhanced risks of insolvency in many emerging markets and the frequent absence of effective hybrid alternatives, lenders, and equity investors alike in these markets are well-advised to pay close attention to INSOL II as an indispensable game plan in their playbooks for approaching distressed loan situations. The prudent lender's institution will have made considerable use of, and ensure that its team of talent is well-versed in the practical application of, the INSOL II Principles.

For their part, borrowers' management and shareholders will be pleased to know that their interests are well-accounted for in INSOL II, and having a balanced framework for discussions with lenders (to allow resuscitation of a distressed business) is well worth its weight in gold. Indeed, the authors

---

[12] Dr. J. Garrido, Out-of-Court Debt Restructuring, A World Bank Study, The World Bank (2012).

[13] Chapter 11 includes the full text of the eight main INSOL II Principles. A detailed commentary by the working group on the principles may be found at: www.insol.org/_files/Publications/StatementOfPrinciples/Statement%20of%20Principles%20II%2018%20April%202017%20BML.pdf.

believe the INSOL II Principles are designed as much to protect equity positions as they are debt claims.

The authors therefore postulate that INSOL II Principles should drive consideration of alternative courses of action and preparatory measures (e.g., early preliminary discussions amongst all lenders, the borrower, and its shareholders) toward such courses.

That said, as with the extent of development of judicial restructuring regimes, *emerging markets are not all alike in their exposure to or regular reliance on INSOL II Principles.* The authors observe that the financial communities in only a relatively small handful of emerging markets (including banks, borrowers, legal and financial consultants) have enjoyed meaningful exposure to INSOL II Principles and the concepts embedded in them.[14,15] Whilst individual members of the financial or academic communities in other emerging markets may have had the occasional exposure to them, largely the INSOL II Principles are not used as a game plan. Accordingly, depending on the particular country, the identities of the lenders (international versus local, DFI versus commercial, etc.), and similar factors there may (or may not) be some *learning curve* in getting parties to subscribe to these.

That said, the name which one gives these concepts is ultimately secondary. Paramount is that the stakeholders *understand the concepts* behind INSOL II and be prepared to try applying these concepts in the given situation. The concepts support the preservation of value and fact-based assessment of the best way to preserve and enhance debt and equity recoveries.

For this purpose, lender leadership must itself understand their essential elements and be prepared to *communicate these and enlist all stakeholders in accepting them.*

## The Right Talent

As noted above, at the Decision to Restructure Phase, credit management of the borrower relationship should sit with (or at least be in a process of an orderly transfer over to) a *specialized restructuring team.* This transfer of responsibility is essential, in order to free the institutional response from so-called "backside-covering," past or present relationship biases, and/or expedient delays by the business in loss crystallization in defiance of a reasonable view of long-term expected losses. In addition, the restructuring team should

---

[14] *See* more generally Annex 1.

[15] Emerging market governments (including legislators and regulators) vary in the extent to which they have actively promoted the Principles themselves and/or their main elements. *See* more generally Annex 1.

have a reporting line to executive management *outside of the business* to avoid indirect pressures on their work.

In the absence of fraud or a sudden, traumatic exogenous event (e.g., war, pandemic, sanctions, etc.), a lender should never be surprised by the need to restructure. Given the natural tendency of borrowers to delay a move to restructuring until or beyond the last point of safety where prospects are less favorable, the failure to anticipate the need to restructure—and to ensure well in advance a future transfer of responsibility to an appropriately experienced, non-biased team—borders on the edge of professional negligence. Again, whilst larger institutions (DFIs, international banks) will have established clear departmental boundaries and rules for transfers, smaller lenders (such as impact investment funds) may have greyer boundary lines. Whatever the case, the result should be the same: *the team must be specialized, non-biased, well-equipped, and independent.*

As also noted above, the lender's actions must be based on a rigorous data-based approach, open to a balanced outcome for all stakeholders as best possible, without which the odds of success are diminished. The active application of tried and tested principles such as INSOL II and the team's unbiased, unemotional examination of the borrower's situation and other variables (micro and macro) will take on a premium.

It is of course axiomatic that the lender's restructuring team must work closely with its in-house and/or external *legal advisors*. The two teams must share a common understanding of vision as well as appropriate expertise and experience. Counsel must have a very deep understanding of transactional issues in banking and finance, corporate law, private international law, insolvency, and litigation. The role of effective external legal advisors for Phases 3, 4, and 5 cannot be understated.

## The Decision

Trigger events leading to a restructuring decision will vary in nature. As broad as the painter's color palate and as various as her media may be, there will be a core set of "primary tints and solubles." Risks also may be broken down to a primary taxonomy articulating the main categories of trigger events.

One possible taxonomy might divide distress factors into three main categories (some or all of which might be evident in a given case): *(1) idiosyncratic build-up; (2) systemic build-up; and (3) exogenous shocks*:

| Idiosyncratic build-up | • **Definition**: institution-level policy and operational management decisions and their aftermath, leading to financial impairment<br>• **Example**: rapid portfolio growth by an FI borrower into a new sector for which the institution's credit management is ill-equipped, leading to a spike in NPLs |
|---|---|
| Systemic build-up | • **Definition**: macroeconomic and market developments creating systemic imbalances and pressures, whose impact will vary at the institutional level, but are generally credit negative<br>• **Example**: After a build-up of short duration, foreign-currency-denominated external capital funding on the books of local financial FI borrowers, the country's exchange rate enters a period of progressive depreciation |
| Exogenous shocks | • **Definition**: a necessary distinction is between: (i) reoccurring, definable, and/or measurable, but severe market events (Market Based); and (ii) an unexpected, sudden, indeterminate, and /or nonmeasurable event (an Act of God or human-made event such as war, etc.)<br>• **Examples**: (i) Market Based—an oil price shock due to the breakdown in discussions between oil-exporting countries or an attempt by one major exporter to force higher cost producers out of the market; (ii) Act of God—the global 2020–21 COVID-19 pandemic |

Prior to forming a solution, the restructuring team must *accurately identify the problem* in the above or some other taxonomy. They must identify which of these factors is has triggered the current distress, are they continuing, and what is being done or must be done to eliminate them or mitigate against the ongoing effect.

What solutions need to be taken, from the standpoint of the borrower's business? Are problems of a balance sheet nature or a business nature? Or both? Will money alone solve the problem (if so, capital or debt, and is the problem a temporary shortage of liquidity or a longer term, structural solvency problem), or are there deeper problems with the borrower's business? Most fundamentally, is the borrower's business (or can it be made) viable? No restructuring can occur without a deep analysis of these and related questions.

At the same time, the lender's legal rights will also drive the extent to which it can achieve a successful restructuring. The lender must ensure it has a *clear understanding of its legal rights*. An internal legal review (legal audit) of the transaction structure, documentation, and security documents/arrangements and borrower's and other obligor's status is indispensable.[16] Whilst many

---

[16] *See* more detailed discussion in Chapter 11.

lenders' in-house legal departments will have the resources for this, others may need to outsource the exercise to a trusted external legal advisor. (It will be recalled from our Bank of Commerce narrative that this was one of the first steps Kristi took.)

It is also worth mention that as issues of bias can drive banking and credit decisions and thus must be addressed, similar issues of bias may arise with transaction counsel from the loan origination stage. As may be practical, the same separation between the business and restructuring teams should be considered in the case of in-house counsel and/or external counsel. The restructuring and legal functions must work hand in hand in approaching the problem and crafting solutions, free from preexisting bias.

A clear understanding of *how the relevant local insolvency regime works* is absolutely essential (including an understanding of the lender's position in the priorities of creditors as well as other relevant issues, e.g., shadow director issues, antecedent transactions, and the like).[17]

*Overt actual defaults* under loan documentation must be considered for potential formal reservations of rights vis-à-vis the borrower. This will entail at the least informal electronic communications of short reservation notices and possibly longer, more formal notices. A more detailed analysis of legal issues relevant to Phase 2 (and later phases) may be found in Chapter 11.

Separate from the issue of ascertaining whether an actual event of default has occurred and what to do about it (e.g., to accelerate or not), the lender must consider the impact on any commitment to fund further loans or draw downs (e.g., in the case of multi-tranche loans, lines of credit, demand loans, overdrafts, etc.). This must be carefully considered with counsel (ordinarily in-house) in conjunction with a careful reading of the text of the loan document and applicable law (which may vary considerably). A lender's *refusal to lend* under the terms of the contract may well constitute a breach of contract, and the lender may become liable to the borrower for damages.

Before any cancellation or refusal to lend under an existing commitment, the lender must ascertain: (1) that there is a clear right to decline to lend further (e.g., conditions precedent not met, potential or actual event of default, etc.), (2) what any relevant notice requirements are (in some jurisdictions notice plays an important role), and (3) that this is not capable of being characterized by the borrower as subjective or arbitrary. Some jurisdictions scrutinize such actions and imply a covenant of "good faith," which could be deemed breached in the event of a sudden or unexpected termination of a line of credit without notice.[18]

---

[17] *See* discussion in Chapter 11.

[18] P. R. Wood, *Op. cit.*

A *comprehensive understanding of all potential claims* against the borrower (tort, employment, taxation, trade, financial, and otherwise) must inform any decision. The possibility of restructuring will ultimately be driven by achieving a bulk of like-minded claimants (ordinarily the lender and other financial creditors) who are able to implement a contractual restructuring. The origination, credit, restructuring, and legal teams should work together to formulate a "play-book" for how they see the loan restructuring process working as between the lender and these other financial institutions. The process will include initial preparatory discussions with these other lenders and ultimately also with the borrower.

At this stage, the aim will not yet be to assemble a formal lenders' coordinating (or steering) committee. Instead, the ideal will be to engage in *a limited set of discreet discussions* with key lenders (e.g., by size of exposure and/or influence) to lay the groundwork for an eventual process for Phases 3, 4, and 5.

Ideally, the borrower will verbally agree to allow its lenders generally to discuss its situation and possible solutions.[19,20] Under all circumstances, the lender will wish to avoid any actions which risk creating panic by other lenders or the borrower. The lender will benefit from diverse views on the borrower's case and will hopefully gain a better understanding of the objectives, preferences, and constraints of each lender with whom it speaks. The discussions will also help to scope out who may ultimately form the core leadership group of candidates for the coordinating (steering) committee and, by contrast, who may be inadvertently or intentionally disruptive.

Just as discussions by medical professionals of a critical patient's condition may lead to a greater and more holistic understanding of appropriate forms of medical treatment, so too can early multi-lender discussions also assist in agreeing a diagnosis of the borrower and its financial situation and agree a preliminary remediation approach to be discussed with the borrower. The discussions must be fact- and data-based, and participants must be prepared to speak truth to power.

---

[19] If the borrower verbally agrees to allow a lender to discuss its distress situation on a discreet basis (e.g., with one or more other key lenders), then this could mitigate against a future claim by the borrower for breach of confidentiality. The relevant banker/restructuring officer in such case should record that this discussion with the borrower took place.

[20] See discussion on bank secrecy and confidentiality in Chapter 11.

## Borrower Inclusion

The preliminary discussions amongst lenders should agree the steps which will culminate in an "intervention" of sorts, or the "come to pray" moment with the borrower. Although lender discussions may be less formal or a series of individual discussions (face-to-face or audio format), ideally the meeting with the borrower which follows should be in person. Depending on circumstances (e.g., logistical or other limitations) a video-conferencing platform may be an unavoidable "second best" alternative to an in-person meeting.[21] Lenders will be well advised to have had a preliminary "dress rehearsal," scripting the meetings, preparing for the sharing and validation of their collective diagnosis, and aiming to agree on next steps. Of crucial importance is to anticipate potential "shoals" (legal, financial, institutional relationships, etc.) around which the process will have to navigate. Critically, this first meeting with the borrower (and often its major shareholders) will inevitably set the tone for further discussions. As noted earlier, it is important to have notes documenting the proceedings and to confirm[22] all participants' agreement with their content.

-&-

Let's move on again, to see how these concepts work in practice.

## Application in Practice: Case Studies

When the amber warning light goes off, lenders face crucial decisions—whether and how to act. What considerations are typically at play? What should be done? And how can we apply the main elements discussed above in practice in a given situation? Let's reiterate these main elements in slightly different terms for practical purposes.

*First,* define the problem. This consists of an attempt to posit the: (i) nature (liquidity v. solvency); (ii) drivers (macro, market, idiosyncratic, or a combination); (iii) severity (quantification); and (iv) expected duration (short-run v. open-ended) of the credit threat. The analytic work in the monitoring phase will have laid the groundwork. These definitions inform the rest.

---

[21] *See* discussion in Chapter 4 above on videoconferencing platforms.

[22] In this respect, appropriate legal disclaimers should be on the face of all correspondence and documents circulated between participants. This would include language characterizing discussions as without prejudice and non-legally binding.

*Second*, identify the broad parameters of possible solutions. When liquidity is the issue, determine whether the problem is short term (cyclical, temporary mismatch, etc.) or structural (current level and nature of funding requirements are not sustainable long term). Alternatively, when capital adequacy is the problem, can the size of the recapitalization requirement be handled by existing shareholders? Can they, and will they, pitch in? If not, are external options available, and will the existing shareholders accept the dilution, even loss of control, that might ensue?[23]

*Third*, organize the lenders' efforts. Ultimately, as many as possible should be included in order to achieve the required critical mass. However, in this phase, it may not be necessary or even possible. If the challenge is to convince the borrower to act, then a signal from a unified lenders group can be compelling. However, conflicting objectives of the broad stakeholder group, emotional sensitivities, logistical challenges, etc., argue for a smaller group (at least at first) to evaluate the situation and agree strategy to move the ball forward. Even when the borrower signals first to the lenders the need to restructure, initial smaller-scale conversations are preferable to frame the issues and agree next steps. These will often involve the lenders with the highest exposure levels.

*Fourth,* frame the rules of engagement for the process to come. Again, the authors propose that the main conceptual framework to which all stakeholders should subscribe (to the fullest possible extent) will be INSOL II, subject to the various caveats and observations we have discussed in this book and adapting them to the local landscape. The prospective returns for all parties from a consensual restructuring is likely to be far greater than merely letting the borrower fall into an insolvency (assuming no effective judicial restructuring procedure is available and there are no other factors which favor insolvency, such as having an untrustworthy borrower/shareholder, etc.).[24]

---

[23] By the time a shareholder or lender group must consider external capital support, the situation is fraught and their negotiating leverage likely to be weak. On the assumption there is a credible, albeit risky, pathway forward, the price of the money will be dear. This fact reflects a combination of the financial risk present in the troubled borrower, the potential for reputational damage for the new investor(s) should the borrower still fail, and the capacity of the capital providers to extract high returns. Even when funding is offered, not all rescues happen. Timing, dilution, structural complexity, and regulatory process and approval issues can stand in the way. Additionally, as in the specific case of the Bank of Commerce, where the lenders felt that their recovery would likely be higher in an orderly wind-down than in a transaction where a recapitalization or a merger would figure, lenders may choose to decline the support. Lastly, there is the interplay of personalities and emotions. The authors introduced the admittedly melodramatic character of JK to highlight how pride can play a pivotal role in these negotiations and threaten to "clutch defeat from the jaws of victory."

[24] *See* discussion of INSOL II principles in Chapter 11, as well as earlier discussions of pros and cons of workouts vs. insolvency in Chapter 7.

*Fifth*, recognize that in many markets, "We're not in Kansas anymore." Dorothy's classic line from the Wizard of Oz is well worth remembering. Local regulations, local stakeholders (government and otherwise), local customs and culture will influence or even in some cases determine the outcome. Reality-check all thinking against what's actually happening on the ground.

*Sixth*, within the lender organizations, empower the right team. The restructuring skill set is very different from the business side—experience does count. Once it becomes apparent that a restructuring is (or will soon become) in play, ensure that the appropriate talent deals with the situation. This includes undertaking swift, effective interdepartmental handovers of responsibility where necessary. Once working, the team must have the independence to do their jobs suitably. An essential principle is that the team tasked with fixing the problem must be different from the one that created it. The analytic exercise leading to a decision to restructure must be taken outside of the reporting line of the business, but subject to executive management oversight.

*Lastly*, show courage. When necessary, take the hard decision. And take it in a timely manner. You may be tempted for more and/or better information. But remember, the "perfect is the enemy of the good." Delay may be comfortable for one of many reasons. But it can (and often does) lead ultimately to even bigger problems, probably avoidable problems.[25] As the fox struggles to safety, unsure of whether he will escape the floodwaters, he has surely learned this lesson.

-&-

To reinforce these considerations, we will now turn back briefly to the "Good, the Bad and the Ugly" narratives we started in Chapter 4.

---

[25] One leading theory of leadership, promoted by the former head of US military forces and former US Secretary of State Colin Powell, posits that a leader should take significant decisions when they have 40–70% of the information required to take the decision. The preference of course is to achieve at least 70% after deep study, but this may not be possible. By implication, a significant amount (30–60%) of decision-making by successful leaders should be based on intuition.

# Continuation of Two Cases: The Decision to Restructure

## Case 1—Industrial Bank

### Background

Recall that Industrial Bank is located in an oil-exporting country with a highly dollarized financial system. As with the Bank of Commerce in Kristi's case (copper, in her case), an exogenous shock occurs leading to reduced export proceeds and fiscal revenue, with a negative knock-on effect to aggregate demand. Orthodox risk management theory warns of a double whammy in such a case: (i) illiquidity—capital outflows; and (ii) insolvency—flow through to asset quality through the exchange rate and the aggregate demand.

The signals of the impending collapse of oil prices were well known within the industry, via developments in stock levels, new shale permits, futures, etc. The front pages of the financial news alerted readers only once prices had begun to fall. Even then, the cable television pundits remained divided on the length and depth of the "bear market in oil." In the opinion of one popular conservative cable network, the dour market forecasts were "hoaxes, meant to undermine the global economy."

The government in our oil-exporting country starts with adequate foreign exchange reserves, in the 100 to 150% range of the IMF reserve adequacy metric adjusted for the oil buffer. Their aggressive intervention succeeds initially in stabilizing the currency peg in light of reduced export proceeds and whispers of capital flight. "Crisis avoided" headlines populate the media at first.

But prices slide further. The government approaches their minimum, precautionary foreign exchange level, even after drawing down on external swap lines. The subsequent decision to abandon the peg and let the currency float freely shocks many. Most lenders wake up to the reality of translation losses on the books of local banks due to open currency positions and pressures on funding. A smaller number recognize the threat of heightened loan loss provisions resulting from the absence of natural hedges on the part of the local borrowers.

As oil market conditions continue to deteriorate, local economic activity weakens further, and the exchange rate depreciates more. The government's capacity to support the financial system is assumed to be strong. Insiders realize the ruling party will force foreign creditors to shoulder much of the burden should recapitalizations be necessary. Outside of a core group of systemically important banks, the rest are on their own. One by one, the calls come—covenant waiver requests, bilateral payment extensions, and eventually payment defaults.

## Making the Decision

### 1. The "Good"

Our first lender's early warning system employed for monitoring macro-conditions has well-developed linkages into the oil market specialist world. Therefore, the prospect of the oil price decline is recognized. Our lender's conversations with the bank's (initially skeptical) management do have a constructive result. The borrower recognizes the threat and, as market conditions worsen, accepts the need for action. The borrower invites a small group of creditors for a business update where the intention is to exchange views on a way forward. Our lender encourages the parties to agree to a follow-on confidential two-day workshop with an enlarged, but still "core" group of key creditors to outline: (i) a series of measures to be taken by the bank and its shareholders to lessen the impact on the financial condition of the borrower (slow the loan growth, strengthen the hedging, de-dollarize the funding and loan books where possible, arrange contingent Tier-II funding from shareholders and certain external parties, etc.) and (ii) informal stand-by arrangements with the broader lenders group (a "handshake," if you will) to activate an orderly restructuring process should this become necessary. The gist of the plan is communicated to the local supervisory authority.

When the full-blown currency and banking crisis occurs, the impact on the borrower is significant, but more limited than elsewhere in the sector. The handshake arrangements are transformed into a formal standstill, with the core group enlisting the support of the remaining lenders.

From this base, a remedial plan is agreed, under which: (i) the shareholders agree to convert Tier 2 capital into common shares and provide a subordinated, convertible shareholder loan to address the immediate solvency problem and to ensure a buffer above the regulatory minimum in a reasonable downside case; and (ii) the lenders refinance the next 24 months' installments for another 24 months each. With this package in place, depositors are placated. The bank actually experiences a moderate increase in deposit levels.

## 2. The "Bad"

For our next lender, the amber warning light only begins to flash on the eve of the breaking of the currency peg. Scattered, "concerned" calls with the bank take place. The local management understands the risk implications and had taken some remedial measures to mitigate the impact of a "downside" scenario of a depreciating currency and slowing economic activity. The bank's shareholders are hesitant to start a dialogue amongst the stakeholders for fear of creating a panic, when it is not certain that the worst will happen. Certain lenders "compare notes" but take no action.

The day the currency is allowed to float freely, the bank recognizes the need to act. Separate meetings with the shareholders and telephone conversations with the more active lenders begin. Progress is slow, given the continued unwillingness of the bank to subject itself to the unpredictability of an all-lenders forum. The two largest lenders communicate to the bank that the "storm is coming" and imply no covenant waivers in the absence of a more constructive response. That is, a plan in which all creditors are engaged and whereunder the shareholders ensure a going concern. There is no consensus. When polled, the remaining lenders fail to support a restructuring until there are outright payment defaults.

The shareholders are prepared to consider shoring up total equity, but they want to wait until there is greater clarity concerning the size and what the lenders will themselves do to help. Despite this, the two aforementioned lenders visit the bank. They work with the management and a shareholder representative to frame a restructuring concept. Time runs out before further progress is possible. A payment default occurs with a lender who is prepared to accelerate. Cross defaults will follow. With this development, the parties are forced to act with urgency. The news, worse each day, combined with the threat of liquidation raises the emotional temperature in the discussions and risks to collapse even before the formal restructuring negotiations can begin.

## 3. And the "Ugly"

With our third lender, the attitude is best described as "a problem is not a problem until it is a problem."

In this case, until there was a payment default, there was zero action by either the borrower or the lenders. For the shareholders and management, the failure to act was just to play for time and hope. Hope that something would change for the better and the problem would go away prevailed. Should the worst happen, the shareholder's management expected that the lenders might be more malleable in a crisis resolution mode than in a prevention mode. For the lenders, the reasons for inaction were various. For some, since the last quarterly covenant compliance check was clean, the file was put away until next time. For others, the relationship team was aware of the nature of the problem but resisted taking action, which would have resulted in the asset being transferred to the workout team. Bad optics, but good politics.

When the payment default finally occurs and the real prospect of escalating cross defaults cannot be ignored, all the parties are forced to act. The time to find a solution and forestall supervisory intervention is very limited, perhaps too short.

## Case 2—National Goods Company

### Background

Our second case relates to National Goods Company, the dominant white goods manufacturer who decided to move into retail at what would turn out to be a questionable time.

Recall that: *First*, their antiquated product line was under threat from more energy efficient models. *Second*, due to this consideration, the existing third-party retail stores were having to offer discounts and credit terms to move our company's merchandise, squeezing margins, and creating a significant requirement for receivables financing. *Third*, the global economy faced the prospect of monetary tightening in the major, advanced economies, which would mean increased borrowing costs and depreciating pressures on the local currency. The first two were missed by the company (and the "Bad" and the "Ugly" analysts), with the result that revenue projections and working capital needs were far off the mark. Whilst interest rate and currency hedging could mitigate the third, finance would become more costly going forward (again, our analysts did not earn gold stars for this). *Fourth*, with the oversubscription of the international fundraising, the company used the additional resources to invest in retail outlets in neighboring countries.

As noted in Chapter 4, sales underperformed, margins were squeezed, and working capital requirements spiked. Global markets did evolve as feared, with higher interest rates and a depreciating local currency. Increased debt service costs ensued. Together with the hit to the operating cash flow, events pushed National Goods into a breach of the debt service coverage ratio.

## Making the Decision

### 1. The "Good"

With our first lender, as described in Chapter 4 in the Monitoring discussion, the action played out much as the "Good" analyst had forecasted in the downside case. Following disbursement, the credit monitoring team had established with the company a reporting template that focused on this case's key, most vulnerable elements (sales, gross margin, receivables, inventory. etc.). The frequency was monthly, and a local consultant was engaged to work with the company to ensure timeliness and reliability of the data. As a result, as the company's operating and financial performance suffered, the analyst was able to project the credit trajectory. The credit warning light began to flash for this lender well in advance of an actual covenant breach. The team had attempted to work with the company to fix matters early, but the company pushed back.

When the waiver request arrives, the lender is ready with a restructuring proposal. The remedial action plan requires more drastic measures than would have been necessary had the company responded earlier (a more detailed plan is described in Chapter 6). At the lender's strong recommendation, the company agrees to engage immediately an external restructuring advisor to refine the lender's proposal and run the process. The intention is to call an immediate lender meeting, where a standstill will be requested.

The lender's proactive approach has positioned the company well to begin the restructuring work. The challenge now is to bring the other lenders along.

### 2. The "Bad"

With our second lender, credit monitoring had noted the tepid operating performance. Questions arose as to the "why," and increasingly the company's answers had left the lender suspicious that there were bigger problems. Nothing more is done for the moment. When results continued to disappoint, a team was sent to undertake on-site diligence. This visit resulted in the realization that the expansion program had misfired significantly. Conversations ensued about possible solutions, but these failed to produce concrete progress.

Later, when the covenant breach did occur and the invitation to the lenders meeting followed, the internal debate was acrimonious. The risk side of the house had felt pressured to do the deal by the business area. Risk blamed the business for railroading the approval. The business arguably had done just that. Their stance was that the problem confronting the borrower was being overblown. A simple, incremental "course correction" was all that was necessary, nothing more. Indeed, instead of a meeting of restructuring staff, the company should assemble the business-side relationship executives. In the end, approval is given to attend the first meeting. However, the business side will lead a group in which risk will be represented. The institution has no formal workout group at the time.

## 3. And the "Ugly"

With our third lender, credit monitoring had not followed the situation closely. Recall, this was a deal done with a non-relationship borrower purely to generate revenue. The executive behind the transaction left the bank soon after the closing. The lax attitude reflected therefore the lack of ownership of the transaction within the lending institution. When the covenant breach occurred and the invitation to the lenders meeting followed, no one stepped forward. The transaction was referred to the lender's chief risk officer, who ordered the staff "to get the hell out of the trade, as fast as possible." The lender declined to participate at the lenders' meeting. Furthermore, they indicated to the company they were planning to call a default.

## Summary

1. A pattern is emerging. In the Good, *first*, we saw that the better the credit analysis, the more focused and therefore effective is the monitoring. This rigor is a product of the internal credit culture. *Second*, the difficult discussions about the borrower and the transaction will have already taken place during the approval process. Best is when there is a well-developed view on the credit, with downside risks identified and well-understood before disbursement. In such a case, the more a lender understands the critical risks and evaluates accurately their implications for the borrower's financial and operational sustainability going in, the more realistic can be the assessment of the way forward when trouble arises. Further, the likelihood of finger pointing and infighting that might complicate the response is reduced. *Third*, the greater this degree of realism, a shared view of the situation between lender and borrower, the better the cooperation will be in a workout. In the "Bad," these "links in the chain" are incomplete and flimsy. The company's financial situation was not a complete

surprise. However, the depth of understanding seen in the "Good" case is clearly lacking. The failure to grasp the degree of the threat and the internal "political" context (business versus risk) translates into a half-hearted response to the meeting invitation. The willingness to prescribe tough medicine will be a challenge as long as the business side is calling the shots. In the case of the "Ugly," all went wrong. The now impaired credit is like a long-lost lover you really never wanted to see again. The romantic night had been enjoyed at the time but was quickly forgotten. When he shows up again, unannounced and unexpected, the reaction is simply to slam the door and hope the problem disappears.

2. The nature of the relationship between the lender and the borrower contributes significantly to the attitudes adopted in restructurings. Lenders who have longer term commitments to the borrower (or even just to the industry) are more likely to act in a responsible manner. This does not mean they are push-overs, just that they realize serious lenders accept there is an obligation to work with borrowers in good times and in bad. In contrast, we have all seen lenders whose first reaction is to say, "Take me out" (often initially at par or close to it). Like the "Ugly," they will be a disruptive force and must be neutralized one way or the other. Similarly, the attitude of borrowers can be influenced by the value they see in the future relationship with lenders. This outlook is predicated in part on the history between the parties. Recall how Ursula argued with JK that a number of the lenders he was planning to jilt were long-standing supporters of New West.

3. The foregoing highlights a discovery made by both borrowers and lenders only through painful experience. For the borrower, the answer to the question, from whom you borrow, should always be as, if not more, important than at what terms you borrow. When things go wrong, lenders like the "Ugly" can be threats not only to the successful execution of a restructuring, but, *in extremis*, to the very survival of the borrower. Will the "Ugly" trigger a cascade of cross defaults? This is all too possible. Better to pay a bit more or operate within tighter credit parameters with a responsible and supportive relationship. The premium pays dividends many times over when times are tough.

# Once the Decision Should Be Clear

In the narratives we have presented, the time arrives for each lender where the need to start or join a workout becomes inescapable: their so-called "Road to Damascus" moment. There are times when a traumatic event on the borrower side, such as a payment default outright dictates the decision. Other times, a technical default (e.g., covenant breach) is responsible. This decision is not so simple. Is the breach material? Can it be cured easily? Most borrowers will predictably argue for a waiver. Sometimes this is founded on good grounds (and part of a larger intention to take corrective measures), whilst other times it is more of a ruse to buy time, rather than addressing the structural problems. Lastly, as we have discussed above, in some cases the decision to restructure is preventative. With the passage of time, unchecked, a payment default and/or a technical default will happen, but it has not happened yet.

As the saying goes, "prevention is better than cure." A smart borrower and/or lender anticipates the problem. When the borrower acts of its own initiative first, lender opposition is typically less strong, especially when a coherent and balanced remedial plan is simultaneously proposed. Alternatively, when the lender-side initiates the conversations, delay or even conflict may arise. Think about the Good's initial approach to the borrower in Case 2, above in this chapter, or Kristi's conversations with Ursula in our opening narrative.

What happens and why? How do the parties respond to ensure appropriate action is taken?

To answer these questions, let us consider again the two cases of Industrial Bank and National Goods. Each presents a different approach and allows us to examine the questions from different angles. In Industrial Bank, we depict the three scenarios where the labels borrowed above from Clint Eastwood's classic film are employed to describe the overall process—are the lenders' collective responses to the looming crisis "Good," "Bad," or "Ugly"? In National Goods, we focus on the individual lenders' reactions.

## Case 1—Industrial Bank

### The "Good"

The initiation of the process benefited from: (i) one lender's intensive monitoring and proactive approach to managing the credit relationship; and (ii) the realism of the borrower. From this base, a coalition of lenders quickly coalesced around a solution.

### The "Bad"

The parties acted only as the crisis erupted. The views on the nature of the problem were disparate, and this complicated the lender response. The borrower was not initially cooperative. As a result, the parties were still discussing the way forward, when events overtook them. A payment default occurred, and the subsequent cross defaults jeopardized the bank's survival.

### And the "Ugly"

Before the payment default, nothing was done. Enough said.

## Case 2—The National Goods Company

We recall that in this case, the "Good" convinces an initially unwilling borrower to commence a restructuring process. This case highlights several important observations. *First*, a party like our "Good" lender can act as catalyst to convince such a reticent (or blissfully ignorant or willfully denying) borrower to act. But the lender needs to come well equipped. The talented analyst at the "Good" lender arguably understood the challenges to the company's business as well as the management themselves did. *Second*, whilst getting the borrower on side should be the more formidable challenge, at times getting the lenders themselves onside may be more difficult. *Third*, following this observation, to avoid the potentially damaging reactions we see in this case—the one where the business (and not the restructuring team) is leading, the other where the immediate reaction is to threaten to blow up the deal if not taken out—it is helpful at times for either the restructuring advisor and/or a cooperative lender to reach out to other lenders to discuss the plans informally first.

This is not to negotiate bilaterally. Instead, the aim is three-fold: (i) to cushion the blow; (ii) to incorporate their thinking into the solution as possible; and (iii) to co-opt them into the process. Overall, the takeaways are—come armed with the facts and recognize that both the borrower and the other lenders must be convinced to cooperate.

# Conclusions

Let's now consider the main learnings in light of the above. First, we will recap our opening narrative of Kristi and her work with restructuring the Bank of Commerce.

Recall that the bank's problems arose from a price collapse in the global copper markets, which set off a vicious macro-financial cycle, including slowing exports and overall economic activity, capital outflows, and a severe depreciation in the local currency. FX translation losses and exploding NPLs in a portfolio of FX-denominated credits to borrowers lacking a natural hedge threatened insolvency and the continued support of the bank's funders. At the local level within the bank, the CRO understood the threat.

At first, Ursula, sitting half a world away overlooking San Francisco Bay did not and furthermore dismissed Kristi's warnings. In a meeting with the bank's executive management, Ursula "got gospel." She grasped finally the existential threats of illiquidity, and should the illiquidity survive for too long, of insolvency. Her attempts to mobilize her board in support of an urgent remedial plan are rebuffed. Pride, arrogance, and desperate reliance on dividends from the bank underlay JK's refusal to countenance any reaction to the "temporarily difficult" conditions in global markets.

Precious time is lost. The borrower side's inaction was abetted by laxness on the part of the greater lender community. Most did not wake up until the macroeconomic headwinds were already howling and financial damage to the bank had become inevitable. The combination of their unwillingness to renew funding lines and the heightened likelihood of covenant defaults pushed lenders to signal a red alert. Finally, Ursula broke the bad news to her board that they had to engage with lenders immediately or risk default and local central bank intervention. Thereafter, Ursula gave Kristi the news—"We have to restructure."

What are the "lessons learned" for this phase? There are many, but some of the more important ones might be summarized as:

- **Don't delay—"The Boiling Frog."** The failure to recognize the true nature of a borrower's "problem" and hesitance to act boldly even when the problem is clear can lead both the borrower and lender down a path that resembles the sad fate of the frog in the fable. All practitioners recognize the sequence of events: extension of maturities, reductions in interest rates, new money, haircuts, debt to equity conversion, ending with wind-downs or bankruptcy. There are occasions when bold action (e.g., threatening to accelerate the indebtedness, or to force the existing shareholders to sell the borrower in a lender-administered sales process) is successfully advocated as an alternative to allowing the "water be brought to a slow boil" (e.g., a series of borrower-friendly, piecemeal measures, whilst the financial condition deteriorates). In the Bank of Commerce case, Kristi and Martin identified the minimum requirements for a going concern approach. When it became evident that this was not feasible, they moved resolutely toward an orderly wind-down. They were the frogs who jumped out of the water!

- **What seems harsh may well be appropriate—"Tough Medicine May Be the Only Medicine."** With the Bank of Commerce and, indeed in the other cases, when the threat of a potential bankruptcy became apparent, there was resistance on both sides to take difficult decisions. Procrastination, half-measures, asymmetric burden sharing, etc., were bandied about. Problems become bigger when the parties delay, doggedly maintaining that "such medicine would be too tough."

- **Avoid overestimating potential relationship damage—"Business is Business."** Lenders can often fear damaging long-standing relationships by taking obvious, precautionary credit actions, such as cutting back or even zeroing out exposure, on the basis of the logic that the counterparty may react badly and blacklist the lender. If the exit is well-explained and orderly, then this is not necessarily true much of the time. Even when there are bad feelings, the price may not be too much to pay. In any event, eventually borrowers often do come back, as money is money. JK's ace of spades for so long was this threat of irreparable relationship damage, should lenders ever cross him. People like Kristi's Chief Investment Officer can be extremely dangerous, as their fealty to the relationship blinds them to growing threats and sometimes lands them in opposition to their own firm's better interests.

- **Risk bankruptcy, sometimes—"Draw the Red Line."** Lenders usually enter into restructuring negotiations resigned to achieving some voluntary resolution. This is especially true for those with large exposures. In the face of unreasonable positions by lenders, borrowers, and/or guarantors, there is a tendency to say, "It's not alright, but we can't risk going to court."[26]

---

[26] As discussed in Chapter 7 and outlined in more detail in Chapter 11, the risks of a formal insolvency proceeding in an emerging market can often be significant for a lender, e.g., if the country's insolvency system is not well-developed, if its judiciary or its rule of law is weak, etc.. This must be analyzed on a *case-by-case basis*, since emerging markets *vary widely in their levels of development*. Lenders must know the reality of the relevant insolvency system going into discussions with the borrower and its shareholders. Even where the insolvency system is weak, due to the waterfall in claims priority under the insolvency system (which will usually put shareholders last in line, behind lenders), they often recognize they have more to gain by collaboration lenders in finding a solution. Moreover, in certain cases an alternative insolvency venue may be available (*see* discussion in Chapter 11 on international and regional insolvency hubs). To negotiate, lenders should be prepared to seek solutions promoting residual value of shareholder equity. The carrot-and-stick combination of prospective 100% equity loss versus some residual equity maintenance is often effective.

Opportunistic parties recognize this vulnerability and act to exploit it, by demanding more favorable terms than warranted or even demanding to be bought out. Sometimes, a line needs to be drawn in the sand. For financial, reputational, or other reasons, these parties will often back down, once they realize other lenders are genuinely prepared to go the bankruptcy path. Kristi and Martin have risked losing everything by their decision to stand up to JK's pressure. They appear to have drawn a line between an extra-judicial and a court-administered resolution, but the stakes are high in either case.

# 6

# Case Set-Up

**Abstract** The fox has finally been convinced to flee to a mountain-side refuge, where all the remaining animals of the forest, large and small, have fled. Before he is allowed to join the rest, the fox must agree to respect the others. In the same way, once the decision to begin the restructuring has been taken, an orderly process requires a shared vision of the objectives and the process. This chapter discusses the consideration around: (i) the establishment and governance of the lenders' group; (ii) work plan and timetable; (iii) engagement of professional advisors; (iv) standstill and other pre-negotiation letters; and (v) group assignments. To reinforce the learnings, the discussion returns to just the manufacturing case study. The chapter ends with a set of key learnings, using again the opening Bank of Commerce tale.

**Keywords** Bankruptcy · Borrower · Confidentiality · Consensual restructuring · Coordinating committee · Corporate debt · Debt · Debtor · Credit monitoring · DFI (development finance institution) · Distressed debt · Financial statements · Emerging market · Frontier market · INSOL II · INSOL principles · Insolvency · Lender leadership · Non-performing loans · Pre-insolvency · Restructure · Restructuring · Restructuring plan · Standstill · Steering committee · Workout

© The Author(s), under exclusive license to Springer Nature
Switzerland AG 2021
R. Marney and T. Stubbs, *Corporate Debt Restructuring in Emerging Markets*,
https://doi.org/10.1007/978-3-030-81306-2_6

## *Preface: The Stork and the Fox—Part III*

*The rains were finally slackening. To the east, a sliver of sunshine illuminated the dark landscape.*

*The stork glanced back over her wing as she flew away towards the high ground and saw the fox.*

*The water was up to his shoulders now. But she was confident he would be safe. The fields just in front were already beginning to slope upwards. Within a few miles, he would be on dry land.*

*She turned her gaze towards the copse of trees near the top of the hill that loomed in front. As she flew closer, she saw many animals and birds resting and feeding on the fruits and nuts from the surrounding land. One family of foxes was there—the group who had offered to help our fox—she knew them to be trustworthy. They would not disturb the others in the common refuge that had saved all their lives.*

*She landed in the center of the animals.*

*"How are the waters?" several chimed.*

*"Still rising, but the skies are starting to clear. The rains should cease soon."*

*"Oh good," offered a young rabbit. "Perhaps in the morning we will be able to return home?"*

*"It will be days," warned an ancient elk. "Still, we are safe for now. Let us. Night will fall soon."*

*The others nodded in agreement.*

*The mother fox spoke to the stork. "Did you see our neighbor, the fox?"*

*"Ah, yes," replied the stork. "I did. He left just in time. I have shown him the way here."*

*"Oh, no!" cried several of the smaller animals. "He will be trouble. He always is!"*

*"I could not just leave him to drown."*

*"You should have," replied another. There was general agreement.*

*A strong voice resonated through the clearing. It was the elk. "You were right to help him. Still, we need to protect the weak amongst us."*

*Others murmured.*

*The father fox looked around the group, silencing the group. He then turned to his wife. "We will go down and meet him. He must understand," He motioned to the land around them. "This is a place of refuge for all. He must respect everyone's safety."*

*"But will he?" questioned several. "We all know him to be wily."*

*"He must be made to," resolved the father fox.*

*The ancient elk agreed, "Yes. My brothers and sisters will come with you."*

*The stork spoke up. "I will guide you to him."*
-&-

Safety for the group already on the hilltop, or pity for the wily fox? Safeguard the interests of the many, or help the loner, however much perhaps he deserves his fate? Beyond more abstract concepts of right and wrong, is there not some sense of self-interest? Someday, any one of the animals having sought refuge from the flood might need the other members of the group to help them. The sacrifice for the broader group now, by accepting the wily fox into their midst, will pose a risk today. It will require effort and diligence. Does this balance out against the longer term benefit for all the animals and a deepened sense of community?

Many of the animals thought not. Leave the wily fox to his well-deserved fate, they argued. Don't bring him into our midst and threaten our welfare, even our lives, they pleaded. In contrast, the stork, the mother fox, and the father fox felt differently. In their own ways, these three had already made the decision to save the wily fox's life. The fox family—by inviting him to flee. The stork—by pointing the way to safety.

However, now the bigger challenge lay in front. How to safeguard the safety of the group in the face of the threat of the wily fox? The wise father fox knew how. They would talk to him. He would agree to behave, or he would not be allowed to join the group well beyond the danger of the floodwaters.

As the three made their way down the hill, undoubtedly the wise father fox said to himself that he and others would have to be diligent and be ready, just in case the wily fox agreed to behave but then subsequently failed to keep his word.

-&-

For our purposes, the decision to guide the wily fox and his "agreement" to follow the others to safety is, of course, comparable to the agreement of the varying sides to engage in a restructuring exercise. To allow the wily fox freely into the midst of the other animals may have helped him with his dinner plans, but it could easily prove a disaster for the rest. The two sides needed to talk first to see if there is a safe way to allow the wily fox in.

In the same way, for the parties to agree to an all-lenders/borrower restructuring meeting without preparation can be equally reckless. Think back to Kristi, Ursula, JK, and Todd in our case of the Bank of Commerce. This didn't happen.

Recall that before the kick-off meeting, Kristi suggested conversations between the two sides to frame the debate. Ursula ignored the suggestion, knowing JK did not intend to negotiate, but rather to impose a solution. Predictably, the opening meeting was a disaster. People left the room with frayed nerves or worse. Putting aside emotions, closing the gap between the two sides then becomes a gargantuan task, even after JK's expulsion. Meanwhile, Edinburgh Partners were arming their bomb.

The failure to see and to act preemptively to neutralize their threat may prove fatal. First Todd and now Colin are much like the hungry fox allowed into the sanctuary without "being talked to." At this point, it appeared highly doubtful that Kristi could rescue the situation.

In this chapter, we walk through the initialization stage—or Case Set-up Phase—of a restructuring process. We begin with the preparation for the kick-off meeting and continue through the analytic and legal work that lays the foundations for the negotiation of the restructuring solution. Like the animals on the hilltop facing off against the wily fox, the parties are confronted with the task of laying a foundation, however unstable, for a lasting outcome, despite significant differences in interests.

In restructurings, the most obvious and common conflict is between the lenders and the borrowers. But frequently fights arise amongst the lenders themselves, which can be material threats to closure. For the rest of this chapter, we explore how to navigate this opening phase, by finding enough common ground and a shared vision amongst the lenders and between the lenders and the borrower to achieve what may be often little more the "least bad outcome," the common ending to restructurings. Often there are no smooth roads, just bumpy ones and torturous journeys.

Let's begin by outlining the main elements of the Case Set-up Phase we outlined in Chapter 3. We will then return once again to our "Good, Bad and Ugly" narrative of the National Goods Company.

## Main Elements of the Case Set-Up Phase

### Establishment and Governance of the Lenders' Group

Based on their previous discussions, the lenders must agree on the circle of relevant creditors who will participate in the restructuring and which of them will play a leadership role. Notably, lender leadership is not granted authority to make commercial decisions for lenders (who retain full independence), but rather to interface and maintain dialogue with the borrower and other parties (e.g., the group's professional advisors) and to act as a conduit of information to the lenders throughout the restructuring process.

Selection criteria will vary, but the size of exposure (for both choices—participation and leadership) figures importantly. It is essential to obtain a

bulk of the debt representing the main financial claims against the borrower. The less numerous the creditors, the better (this will speed and ease of decision-making). But still, together they must account for a "critical mass" (bulk) of the borrower's debt. The nature of the creditors' businesses will also be critical. Their homogeneity will determine the extent to which they can form and share a common vision on how to deal with distress. This will usually be financial creditors.[1] Some creditors may be unfamiliar with the exigencies of a restructuring (e.g., local banks in emerging markets may be unfamiliar with the London Approach/INSOL II Principles), whilst others (e.g., local tax authorities) will not have proper authority or capacity to participate even if they are willing.

Creditor aggregation, therefore, obtaining a *critical mass of homogenous creditors with the bulk of debt who share similar/parallel interests,* is critical.[2]

A decision must be made on whether to separate different classes of creditors (e.g., secured vs. unsecured, senior vs. junior, international vs local) or to deal with their differences within a single group under the same leadership. It is essential that conflicts of interest be discussed openly and early. For example, to name a few:

- some lenders may have provisioned loans as NPLs, whilst others may not;
- some lenders may have credit insurance, security, or other risk-mitigation measures in place, while others may not;
- some lenders may have recently acquired the claims at a discount from their face value while others may be the original lenders.

An array of potential conflicts may arise and should be disclosed in good faith. These conflicts and the sheer size and complexity of the borrower's financial arrangements may well drive the creation of more than one coordinating committee, with separate sets of external professional advisors.

Whatever the number of committees, it is axiomatic that *equity creditors* as such (i.e., parties with debt claims against the borrower but who are nevertheless related to it, such as its parent and/or group companies) *should ordinarily be excluded* from the core lender group, as their claims against the borrower are likely to be viewed quite differently by arms-length financial creditors. At the same time, this rule is not an absolute one. Where a *bona fide* lending institution is both a creditor and a shareholder, then this party should agree to

---

[1] Hence, throughout this book we will refer to 'lenders," though in certain cases other creditors may also participate.

[2] Garrido, *Op. cit.*

establish an independent "debt" team to act with the lenders. (This situation can arise fairly frequently with DFIs in emerging markets.)

Within each respective lender group, the lenders should agree on an appropriately sized core leadership: either a single lead lender (in a smaller group) or a small group of lenders to act as coordinating (or steering) committee. The lenders should decide on *governance and process* amongst themselves and who will act as such lead lender and/or coordinating committee. It is not always possible or even necessary that a group of lenders lead; often where the total number of lenders is not large a single lender (e.g., a DFI) will act as de facto lead for the group. (A DFI will often be seen by commercial lenders as fair, neutral, and competent in its leadership approach.) Alternatively, a private-sector lender can act in this role, when the institution and the individual have the trust of the remaining lenders.

In addition to the *size of exposure* of the leader(s), the importance of both *experience and availability* of leaders' individual representatives cannot be overstated. It is no good merely to have a heavily exposed lender on the committee if its individual representative is either inexperienced or unavailable due to his or her other personal or professional commitments. A less exposed, but more experienced and proactive representative may be more preferable. And again, the individual's experience (or "grey hair") as a restructuring specialist and unbiased attitude is essential.

The degree of *autonomy of the representatives* is an important question. Whilst strictly adhering to their respective institutional governance (i.e., approval) regulations, these individuals should be empowered to negotiate an acceptable solution and not be required to consult their head office on each and every element of the term sheet. Is the "chicken soup delicious and nutritious" is what head office should consider, not do they approve of "what herbs and spices were used." If the representatives are not empowered to negotiate, that is, to engage in a form of horse trading with their fellow lenders within the context of the committee, then the process becomes potentially unworkable. Lengthy, external consultations whose real decision-makers risk not seeing the necessary "give and take" amongst the competing interests of the wider cohort is not only time-consuming but may well render the negotiations unviable. (Again, remember that it is essential that the process be as speedy as possible.) The tendency of some lenders, even significant creditors, to place less experienced "messengers" (back to the real decision-makers at head office) on committees rather than seasoned "negotiators" has exercised a highly negative role in past restructuring transactions. This situation reflects an underinvestment in restructuring resources due to the (hoped-for) tempo-rary need for the activity and, in some cases, the belief that the activity is a professional dead-end.

The level of legal formality with which the coordinating committee is appointed can vary considerably. This will depend, e.g., on the total size and complexity of the finance structure, the general make up of the lender group and their history of working together in distress situations (including prior workouts), the lead lenders' general practice and expectations of lenders. This can range from an informal "hand-shake" approach (sometimes used in smaller deals where the lenders know each other and the borrower) to a much more formal set of appointment documentation negotiated and executed with the borrower.

The London-based Loan Market Association (*LMA*)[3] has developed for its members a recommended set of precedents, comprising both: (1) a letter of appointment from the borrower to the committee, and (2) a separate (inter-creditor) letter from the committee to lenders (the two-step process is intended to permit formation of the lender leadership early on, without having to wait for the entire lender group to form; this can be useful in larger restructurings).

The LMA precedents include inter alia general principles and functions of the committee, its role, its authority to act as a point of contact for the lenders, its authority to appoint professional advisors, exculpatory language, exclusions of liability (including disclaimer of fiduciary duty) and no reliance, indemnities for committee members and their individual representatives, provisions on disclosure and confidentiality of information as well as publicity and announcements. Not least importantly, the borrower-committee letter includes the borrower's obligation to reimburse the committee for all costs incurred for professional advisors to the lenders group. In some cases a single combined appointment letter between the borrower, committee members, and all lenders (to which late lenders then accede) may also be used.

The LMA precedents are generally intended for use in connection with existing LMA syndicated facilities but nonetheless may be used as a starting point and adapted for use with groups of bilateral loans.

As a less "legalistic" approach, in lieu of the LMA (rather document-heavy) approach, the governance and cost-coverage arrangements may instead be included into the external legal engagement itself (and countersigned by the borrower). In a number of deals, the authors have used external counsel engagement letters to reflect committee governance arrangements including

---

[3] The LMA is the leading trade body for the Europe, Middle East, and Africa (EMEA) syndicated loan market (founded in December 1996). *See* www.lma.eu.com.

communications, cost coverage, and other key issues. As it is essential to bring lenders' external counsel early into the restructuring process (see below), such an approach may prove quicker for smaller workouts and help minimize legal documentation and costs. But it also presupposes that the main group of lenders will have already swiftly congealed.

Whatever level of formality is applied in forming the committee, ultimately the objective will be to agree on *governance protocols and communications procedures* and ensure that *costs* of lenders related to the restructuring effort are ultimately borne by the borrower.

## Work Plan and Timetable

If not at the initial meeting, then certainly immediately thereafter the two sides should elaborate a work plan and timetable for the restructuring. This requires full sign-on by all parties and a commitment to keep the process on track with meaningful milestones.

One effective way of doing this can be to agree on a nonbinding protocol or heads of terms (i.e., *term sheet*) reflecting one or more possible restructuring directions and the expected work plan and timetable.[4] Of course, it may be impossible to reflect a clear, definable restructuring at this stage. More likely, the parties will not yet be able to define the parameters of the restructuring. They will need further information from the borrower and to consider various alternatives (usually only with the assistance of an outside financial advisor). As the lenders and the borrower already have formal legal arrangements in place (in the form of their loan documentation), absent special circumstances there is no genuine need for the operative/commercial provisions of the term sheet itself to have binding effect.[5] Indeed, it is likely that the lenders will wish to express the contrary. The term sheet is likely to be accompanied or quickly followed by more formal legal documentation, including the standstill where appropriate (see Part IV below).

The plan/timetable of work may also need to be updated and communicated to the larger group throughout the process. The lead lender or coordinating committee (as the case may be) will be expected to do this. But in the spirit of Robert Burns' timeless observation, the parties must anticipate some flexibility for market changes and other external events.

---

[4] As discussed at more length in Chapter 11, the term sheet can play a critical role.
[5] That said, it will be highly desirable for certain elements of the term sheet, such as applicable law and dispute resolution, to be binding. *See* discussion on term sheets in Chapter 11.

# Engagement of Professional Advisors

The efficient identification, selection, and engagement of competent professional advisors (i.e., an external legal counsel, a financial advisor, a transaction monitor, etc.) assumes a critical role in a restructuring transaction.

Restructurings are not "standardized" finance transactions—indeed, they are usually quite bespoke legal and financial arrangements which bring together a multitude of parties with complex financial relationships under the shadow of an imminent insolvency. A single external legal advisor whose mandate is to represent all lenders zealously and impartially is indispensable. An external financial advisor will be required to diligence the borrower's financial condition, provide a uniform set of financial data to all lenders, and formulate (or check) the viability of the restructuring proposal(s). And a transaction monitor may be required if the restructuring is ongoing (e.g., in the case of an orderly wind-down) over an extended period of time following execution of the main restructuring agreement.[6]

It is critical that all lenders feel that they have impartial expert advisors representing their collective interests. It is highly unlikely that they will see an individual banker, restructuring specialist, or internal counsel from a single lender organization as representing their collective interests.

The identification and selection process will usually depend upon the experience and established procurement practices of the lead lender and/or coordinating committee. Less formal lender organizations may proceed in an ad hoc manner, based upon referrals and/or prior successful existing relationships. Other institutions (e.g., DFIs) are likely to have more formal procurement rules, possibly including panels of candidate advisors. They may also have to engage through a competitive selection process.

Whatever the case, it is critical that the right outside advisors be chosen who have demonstrated successful and established practices in their field of expertise and have strong track records in the particular emerging market (or the type of emerging market) involved.

When considering external legal advisors, the client-lender institutions must ensure that their external legal team has both experienced *main transaction counsel as well as local counsel from the borrower's jurisdiction*. To be avoided is the trap of hiring a "big name" external law firm, only to find that the partner hands over the case to an associate on a day-to-day basis. More than, for example, in a debt capital markets transaction (where deals follow a more or less standard pattern and legal documentation is often

---

[6] In larger, more complex cases a set of external advisors may be appointed for each class of creditors.

highly standardized), a restructuring requires the experienced hands to be there throughout. The system of law to govern the restructuring agreement is likely to be one of the more widely recognized systems of law (e.g., English or New York law). And a deep understanding of the local insolvency system, regulations and other relevant laws of the borrower are indispensable. Accordingly, the legal team must have a strong offering in both of these areas. Where a single law firm does not have a local office in the particular market, it must team up with a solid local firm.

The role of financial advisors and/or transaction monitors is often played in larger deals by international accounting firms (big four or mid-tier), and in smaller or more specialized deals by specialized turnaround houses. The importance of reliable, independent financial diligence cannot be overstated. The supporting arguments for the engagement of such an advisor include: (i) multiple lenders require an independent party; (ii) individual lenders may not have the specialized technical and transactional experience or have the time; (iii) the borrower side may give greater credibility to the work of an independent party. Typically, the actual mandate is given by the borrower side, but working according to terms of reference drafted by the lenders.

These professional advisor relationships may be structured either bilaterally with the lead lender and/or with a member of the coordinating committee (with reliance rights of group lenders), or in smaller deals multilaterally with all lenders under a multi-lender engagement.[7]

Documentation should be structured to mitigate against potential claims of shadow directorship (vicarious liability and agency) of advisors or transaction monitors, by appropriate disclaimers and actions consistent with such disclaimers.[8]

---

[7] Although there are differing opinions on the issue, in the authors' view an appropriate professional duty of care should be established in respect of all lenders in the group of lenders being advised, subject to balancing the interests of the external advisor in negotiating an appropriate liability cap. The engagement should expressly stipulate that the legal advisor representing the lenders group shall not advise any one of them individually against the others (including in respect of any insolvency claim filed against the borrower should it go into insolvency proceedings). The whole point is that the lenders must feel secure that counsel represents their interests collectively. The engagement should also lay out mechanics for dealing with conflicts as these arise during the course of the workout.

[8] *See* discussion in Chapter 11.

# Legal Standstill Agreements/Pre-negotiation Letters

The essence of a standstill is encapsulated in the first three Principles of INSOL II.[9] It will ordinarily be needed to stabilize the discussions and create a "breathing space," free from the threat of acceleration by creditors or value leakage by the borrower, in order to obtain and evaluate information on the borrower and allow sufficient time to formulate and assess whether a restructuring is viable.

During the standstill, the relevant creditors agree to refrain from enforcement steps or other exposure reduction measures. In return for their forbearance, for its part the borrower agrees *inter alia* to refrain from taking actions adversely affecting the creditors' prospective returns, including value leakage.[10] During the standstill, critical diligence will usually take place by the lenders' financial advisor and formulate the basis for proposals and ultimately the restructuring agreement.

Of course, a standstill need not be executed where no formal event of default has yet occurred (or is yet imminent). However, when an event of default has occurred (or is imminent), it is desirable that the standstill be put in place as quickly as possible.

Whilst the duration of a standstill can vary as appropriate (ordinarily it will be several months[11]), it must be put in place quickly. This will usually be done by the lenders' external counsel. The standstill should not be conflated with the definitive restructuring agreement, which will usually come later only after the initial investigatory period.

Where a standstill is not required (e.g., no events of default have occurred or are imminent), a pre-negotiation letter setting out the parameters for the parties' discussions may be used instead, if some formal legal document confirming the negotiations is deemed appropriate.

An informal standstill understanding (or "handshake") amongst the parties can serve initially before legal drafting starts, but a firm (well-drafted, signed) standstill agreement (or pre-negotiation letter) will usually be the preferred alternative and ideally should quickly replace any such informal arrangement. Lenders should in any event pending the formal standstill (or pre-negotiation letter) remember to have reserved rights (by way of individual reservation of

---

[9] *See* discussion in Chapter 11.

[10] Ideally any 100% shareholder (and arguably majority shareholder) should also be a party and undertake procural obligations toward ensuring no leakage.

[11] Ideally the parties should aim for a period sufficient to achieve completion of due diligence and negotiation and execution of the restructuring plan. Ideally, they should avoid having to extend the standstill, though sometimes this is unavoidable.

rights emails or letters, which can usually be done by lenders' own in-house counsel based on their standard precedents).

More detail on these issues may be found in Chapter 11.

## Assignments—Financial and Other Analytics

Overall, as the work progresses, the committee should manage the preparation of requisite analytics to ensure there is a sound basis to the larger lenders' group decision-making, remembering, "Facts and data win arguments."

A necessary first step is to agree on a working model between the two sides. A small group of lenders (sometimes, a subset of lenders on the coordinating committee) should be chosen to work with a designated set of executives from the borrower side. Where leadership is in the form of a committee (as opposed to a single lead lender) the committee members may divide tasks up between them. The model is a dynamic depiction of the borrower and the terms of the restructuring. The inputs must be updated throughout the process to reflect the evolving financial condition of the borrower and the negotiations. Both sides must understand and agree to its changing content to ensure discussions are predicated on a common fact base.

Critically, the lenders should not rely blindly on financial information provided solely by the borrower or shareholder(s) or their advisors. The lenders must always rely on the verification of accuracy of financial data by their own external financial advisor. For this purpose, it is essential for their advisor to be given full, unfettered access to financial information and records of the borrower.

By the same token it is critical that the borrower authorizes its management and external financial advisor to engage openly and transparently with the lenders and their external financial advisor. The format of a reporting template should be agreed and a completion/update timetable established. Through the process, changes should be made to adapt to the evolving requirements of the process.

-&-

Now let's return to our case studies, to apply these concepts in practice.

# Application in Practice: Case Studies

## Continuation of National Goods Case: Case Set-Up

We will now describe two initialization "process" scenarios for the National Goods Company: one "Good" and one "Bad" or "Ugly" (depending on one's point of view), stemming from different starting points for both the lenders and the borrower.

### Background

Recall that in Chapter 5, National Goods has just sent a waiver request. The company is in violation of a debt service coverage covenant. The "cat is out of the bag." Time is limited. And the possibility now exists that one or more lenders could be prompted to declare an event of default and accelerate the indebtedness.

### 1. The "Good"

Let's go back in time. As described for the "Good" in Chapter 5, one lender's analyst projections had predicted a covenant breach much earlier. Their relationship team had met with the company's management to share the results and suggest an operating and financial remedial plan. There was pushback on a number of the operating assumptions. The company CFO did acknowledge that the debt management suggestions were valuable inputs for their forward contingency planning, albeit unnecessary for the time being. In the end, no concrete action was taken. Later, when the pro-forma quarterly results confirm the covenant breach, the CFO called the bank and suggested they meet "urgently" to discuss the situation. The financial reports were due to be published within mere weeks. Trouble is anticipated. The lender agrees but recommended that National Goods engage a reputable external restructuring advisor, "just in case."

By the time the meeting takes place later that week, the advisory firm is on board. Building on the lender's work, the advisors have prepared a restructuring plan. The fundamental premise of the plan is that the breach of the debt service coverage covenant reflects a structural imbalance that will only worsen over time. Drastic measures are required. As a result, the scope is broad and encompasses operational reforms and steps to address the debt problems.

National Goods will sell its international operations, stop the domestic retail expansion program and explore partnerships to reduce the financial burden of the retail network, securitize its current and future retail receivables book, and undertake a substantial rights issue to pay down debt. In return, the lenders will be asked to move amortizations back by two years, agree to a modified covenant package on the existing debt, and contribute to an emergency revolving line of credit meant to bridge the company's working capital requirements over a transition period.

The lender's reaction is overall positive, save for the revolving line of credit. The team expresses skepticism that all lenders will go along. A back-up plan? A shareholder's backstop is suggested instead. The company indicates this will be forthcoming, if necessary. The discussion turns to the question of how to approach the remaining lenders. There are twenty of them. The advisor suggests two cohorts: (i) eighteen reliable counterparties, large commercial banks, and asset managers all known for acting responsibly in these situations; and (ii) two potential problem creditors whose behavior cannot be predicted or are known or feared to be disruptive.

In terms of exposure, the first group accounts for roughly 85% of the debt. The agreed course of action is for the CFO and the advisor to reach out informally to all lenders bilaterally to inform them about the situation and the plan. In anticipation of an all-lenders meeting in two weeks, a detailed information memorandum and restructuring proposal will be sent. Additionally, face-to-face meetings will be held with the two "questionable" lenders to ascertain their likely position.

By the time of the meeting, National Goods has received feedback from all lenders. The revolving line of credit is off the table. All the lenders, save for one of the two questionable creditors, have expressed a generally favorable response to the plan. The holdout (3% of the debt)—an asset manager with an "end of fund" problem[12]—cannot delay the repayment schedule but would nonetheless agree to the new covenant package. A quick straw-poll of the major lenders indicates they will not oppose allowing the one party to maintain their original amortization schedule due to the "end of fund" problem (which is not merely due to lender obstinacy). The meeting comes and goes successfully. The lenders are critical of the original business strategy that led the company to the current situation. There is a consensus to proceed on the basis of the modified plan.

To support the process, a set of requisite organizational elements are agreed or work begins to put these in place. These include the following actions: (i)

---

[12] An "end of fund problem" arises when an extension of the original maturity date goes beyond the date by which the relevant investment fund must return the capital to investors.

a steering committee is established, its members are nominated and governance/communication rules are agreed; (ii) search processes for legal counsel and a technical market advisor are organized; and (iii) working groups on key process functions (e.g., modeling, legal, etc.) are founded; and (iv) an initial process timetable is fixed and agreed with the borrower.

## 2. The "Bad" (or the "Ugly")

For our second (or third) lender, there is no time machine in this case. National Goods' weakening operational performance has been observed by the markets, but it has not produced serious concerns or any reaction on the part of the lenders. Quarterly reviews of the financial statements and covenant checks are the extents of the lenders' activities.

Inside the company, most believe the problems are more cyclical in nature and will be cured without too much trouble.

When the quarterly numbers are distributed internally and the covenant breach is evident, opinion remains divided. Some managers persist in the view that the slower sales, narrower gross margins, and need for deferred payment terms are "growing pains" of the new, retail strategy, and hence a reasonable response is to request a waiver and move on.

In contrast, a minority led by the CFO argues that the problems are structural. Too much capital has been invested in a retail business that will never produce as projected with the current product mix. To survive, the CFO believes: (i) the international expansion should be stopped and the operations sold; (ii) the domestic retail network has to be reassessed and likely cut back; (iii) the explosion of working capital requirements has to be contained, probably best though a receivables securitization program. There is no discussion about new equity or other debt reduction efforts. The "let's carry on" team wins the match.

Thereafter, the company sends our lender a waiver request, sandwiched between an upbeat commentaries on the future outlook. The response is mixed, but it is generally supportive of the company. After several weeks, all the waivers are in place, but the climate has changed. There are more pointed questions than ever before. There are even some warnings that the next quarterly report will be pivotal. Should there be no improvement, then National Goods could "lose its audience."

As the date approaches, the evidence is increasingly clear. The numbers are moving in the wrong direction. In fact, cash levels have declined to a point where a payment default in the next month or so could not be dismissed as a real possibility.

The CFO reiterates his views from the previous quarter. This time, there is more support. The CEO acting with the support of the shareholders decides to adopt a "we are all in this together" approach with the lenders. National Goods will ask the lenders to affirm their support for the company's strategy, through a set of concessions (modification of covenants and extension of terms) to facilitate new debt and equity raises. The CFO dissents, arguing that getting the concessions from the existing lenders is a fool's errand and, even should they succeed, the markets will not be receptive to new money until there is clear evidence the company is turning things around.

A new waiver request is sent. The blowback is severe. The lenders demand a meeting with the company. The CEO remains defiant but agrees to meet. Certain of the lenders have been talking amongst themselves and have drafted a plan, not materially different from the "Good" case above. The company pushes back at the meeting, rejecting the draft plan, but critically it offers no alternative whatsoever. Worse, a division develops amongst the lenders. A subset of the lenders adopts a confrontational approach. They demand the company immediately pay down debt to permit a return to compliance. Otherwise, they will declare a default and move against the company.

The meeting breaks up with warring camps of lenders pursuing different approaches. The deal now risks moving from the financiers to the lawyers.

## Summary

There are multiple differences between the "Good" and the "Bad" initializations. These include: (i) the quality of the credit monitoring; (ii) the proactivity of the lender; (iii) the response of the borrower; and (iv) the initialization meeting. Let's look at each in turn.

1. *Credit Monitoring*: In the Good, one lender undertakes intensive and continuous credit monitoring, including forward-looking modeling, which will eventually benefit all, whilst in the "Bad," we get the sense that until if and when there is an actual covenant breach, there is no need to look further.
2. *Proactivity*: In the Good, when the forward-looking analysis triggered the amber warning light, the lead lender discussed its concerns with the borrower (and possibly with contacts at the other lenders) and came equipped with specific recommendations for remedial action, whilst in the "Bad," a real reaction did not happen until the second covenant breach.

3. *Borrower Reaction*: In the Good, whilst the company was initially skeptical about the lender's forecast and discounted some of its recommendations, they nonetheless reacted responsibly once the looming covenant breach provided clear evidence of a need to undertake a course correction, whereas in the "Bad," the attitude was defiant and dismissive throughout.

From the first three, we reconfirm a major takeaway from Chapter 5, namely: *(i) a well-informed lender raising credit concerns early with realistic borrowers, and (ii) having these two sides working together proactively on a viable resolution plan are the foundation stones of a successful restructuring.* The house itself of course still needs to be built. But the wooden frame for the house is made up of the various tasks completed during the initialization phase.

4. *Initialization Meeting*: In the Good, the frame is well constructed: a plan, the various organizational elements, and a compromise to neutralize a lender all agreed. In contrast, in the case of the "Bad," the foundation stones and the lumber lay scattered haphazardly around the building site, with worse than no progress being made as a result of the first meeting.

## Conclusions

Let's now consider the above. Once again, we will recap our opening narrative on Kristi and her plight with the Bank of Commerce at the Case Set-Up Phase.

Imagine we are walking in from the rain-swept entrance to the hotel with Kristi and Maya.

- Todd has reasons for being angry. JK appears to have misled him. Based on JK's assurances, Todd pushed through a twenty-five million dollar loan. Now, he is very frightened about losing his job. As a result, Edinburgh Partners is a genuine threat to the deal.
- Kristi has failed to engage with Ursula on the "way forward" despite repeated attempts over the past several months. And she knows why—JK! He has spent a lifetime trying to roll over people or, in his own words, to "subsume" them. With very few exceptions, he has always won the first battle and then also the war. When he has lost the initial skirmish, he has rallied his forces and then crushed the other side with excessive force, even cruelly, to prove to others the foolishness of their opposing him in the future. He expects this to be so this time around, and he is probably

right in his mind. Like Todd, Kristi also knows what's coming. She has the air-cover to fight back. Her question is how many other lenders will join her.

Once inside:

- Over Ursula's objections, JK's advisor presents the lenders a Hobson's Choice: "our way" or "here are the keys," confident the lenders will crumble.
- The lenders' reaction is volcanic. The meeting descends into chaos. Kristi calls for a recess. No one can mistake Todd's intentions as he once again leaves.

The two sides separate.

- That the lenders are unhappy does not concern JK. They will vent. In the end, they will realize that without him, the Bank of Commerce fails. They will then crawl back. Anyone who does not do so? Well, like politicians who have their Twitter, JK has a direct line to the boss of everyone in the room. He has destroyed the careers of a multitude of people who have dared to cross him.
- That Kristi opposes him is insufficient. She needs allies. Maya of course is one. There are others. Of them, probably the most important is Martin—the board representative of the International Development Fund, New West's co-shareholder in the bank. Martin's shareholders in turn represent the major global economies. Not even JK can out-shoot them, should they decide to unholster their gun. When Ursula joins the lenders after the meeting, she recognizes this and breaks with JK, despite the risk to her career.
- JK and his entourage return to San Francisco confident of a "mission accomplished," ignorant of Ursula's efforts (which, had he known of them, he would have considered a betrayal). Ursula, Martin, and Kristi are risking a lot. All are uncertain of the support of their respective senior managements. The lender group is deeply fractured. One (Todd) is already working to force liquidation. Given the Bank of Commerce's rapidly deteriorating financial condition, the chances of avoiding a wind-down, orderly or not, are actually quite low in reality.

What are our "takeaways," our "lessons learned"?

- **Agree a script in advance—"One Chance to Make a First Impression."** Whilst Ursula's agreement to work with Kristi and Martin to fashion a compromise solution was "better late than never," the process got off to a very poor start. Ideally, a high-level restructuring design and a common strategy to achieve it should have been hashed out way before the meeting. At a very minimum, the two sides should have walked into the kick-off meeting or call with an agreed upon script that acknowledged their differences and expressed a common willingness to work together in good faith. But JK had prevented Ursula from engaging with the lenders. As a result, no such "script" had been prepared in advance for the meeting—neither a rough plan nor even the bare minimum "we all must work together" platitude. Instead, JK and his advisor Stephen presented the lenders with a one-sided solution, one that clearly favored the borrower and its shareholders, delivered in a harsh, "take it or leave it" style. The reaction of the lenders was predictable: emotions frayed, positions hardened, and clear and constructive thinking challenged. Opposing arguments across a wide division of opinions and interests are a natural beginning of a restructuring. These must be managed by both sides, to facilitate a smooth beginning toward a solution. Otherwise, the negotiations can become more acrimonious and ultimately futile. JK's strong-arm tactics did just the opposite.
- **Personalities matter—"Don't Overdress (or Underdress) for the Occasion."** New West is the product of Wall Street. The lenders come from the emerging- and frontier market development sector. Each side has its distinct culture. The former is brash, loud, short-term focused, and biased towards zero-sum outcomes. The latter is measured, working with a longer-term and more consensus-focused perspective. JK's advisor dressed in a 3,000-dollar custom-made suit, whilst the relaxed attire of Kristi and her colleagues more resembled the dress of a university faculty. The glaring clash of the "win-at-all-costs" versus "economic-and-social-development" cultures had to be softened in order to give the parties the chance to work well together. In laying the necessary groundwork, the messenger is equally as important as the message. In our case, Ursula or even better, Martin should have been the messenger. Having the Wall Streeters in control of the dais was a serious miscalculation that could have derailed the process. The quick rebound, where Ursula, Martin, and Kristi—better-matched personalities—met afterwards, saved the process.
- **Be realistic—"Don't Try to Revive the Dead."** Can the Bank of Commerce actually be saved (as a going concern)? This is a critical

threshold question for each and every workout. The answer may not immediately be apparent, but lenders must keep it first on their lists. Here, our borrower institution seems to have a viable business, but it requires a significant amount of new equity, without which the institution surely will fail (the regulator will take it over). Given the shareholder's financial situation, they clearly cannot do it alone. The lenders could top off the needed capital by converting a portion of their debt into equity, but this would be hard for a number of legal and/or strategic reasons. JK's clumsiness has made this already slim possibility even more improbable. Further, there is a combination of uncertainty and asymmetric information. As the macroeconomic crisis continues to unfold, how big a hole needs to plugged? For whatever total needs to be raised, the lenders still believe Ursula can write the check. They therefore believe they need not contribute themselves. Being asked to do so will make them suspect they are being gamed. Deep down, Ursula knew the answer to this fundamental survival question was "no." Kristi and Martin suspected the same. The parties would merely waste time (and hence dissipate value) by pursuing a going-concern plan with little or no chance of working.

In the next Chapter 7, we will move onto the heart of the process—the work of Structuring and Negotiation, in determining the substantive content of the restructuring.

# 7

# Structuring and Negotiation

**Abstract** The fox threatens the group and is expelled from the refuge, ending up in a far less secure place. The animals were obliged to make a difficult decision for the good of the group. Like the animals, lenders must take hard decisions, often confronted with a series of negative outcomes and finding themselves forced to opt for the least bad alternative. The discussion in the chapter focuses on: (i) the main goals of a workout; (ii) elements of cost–benefit analysis in transaction structure analysis (including judicial versus nonjudicial restructurings); (iii) the building blocks of restructuring; and (iv) requisites of transaction leadership. Thorough and updated planning, maintaining control, dealing with detours, accepting compromise, but sticking to principles when necessary are amongst the key learnings that are reinforced through a return to the manufacturing case study and the opening Bank of Commerce Tale.

**Keywords** Balance sheet · Bankruptcy · Borrower · Consensual restructuring · Coordinating committee · Corporate debt · Debt · Debtor · Cash flow · Cost-Benefit Analysis · Distressed debt · Foreign exchange · Emerging market · Frontier market · INSOL II · INSOL principles · Insolvency · Lender leadership · Non-performing loans · Pre-insolvency · Restructure · Restructuring · Restructuring plan · Standstill · Steering committee · Workout

© The Author(s), under exclusive license to Springer Nature Switzerland AG 2021
R. Marney and T. Stubbs, *Corporate Debt Restructuring in Emerging Markets*,
https://doi.org/10.1007/978-3-030-81306-2_7

*"An intricately-woven tapestry can be unwound with the pulling a single thread."*
*Anonymous*

## Preface: The Stork and the Fox—Part IV

*The stork soared into the air and circled for a moment. She then swooped back, closer to the ground. "I see him." She pointed with her wing, "He is in this direction."*

*The foxes and the elks started down the mountain side, walking in the direction indicated by the stork.*

*After a time, the stork called out. "He is there! Just ahead, beyond the next thicket of trees."*

*The animals moved cautiously midst the trees. Soon they saw the fox.*

*The father fox approached his cousin.*

*"Hello there!"*

*The bedraggled fox looked up, appearing relieved. "I am near the sanctuary?"*

*The father fox stood in front, accompanied by his wife, the ancient elk, and his brothers and sisters. "Yes, you are."*

*A sly smile creeped over the wily fox's face. "Oh, good! I am tired and hungry."*

*"We need to talk first."*

*The wily fox eyed him suspiciously. His wariness increased as he saw the elks surrounding him.*

*"Eh? Why?"*

*The father fox spoke out, "We have escaped the flood waters, all of us, big and small. We have come to this mountain for safety. We have dry places under the trees to rest. We can stay here until it is possible to return to our homes. All must be kept safe. You are welcome to join us, but you must agree to respect our rules."*

*"But how will I eat?"*

*"There are nuts, fruits and berries for all."*

*"Eating those is not my custom!" cried the wily fox.*

*"All must adapt and conform," countered the father fox. "My family and I have promised. So too have the cougar and bear families. We have to change our usual habits so that the elks, deer, squirrels, and the birds are made safe." Then, motioning to the sky. "None wanted this to happen. All have to accept that now, only through compromise and cooperation will we all make it through this catastrophe."*

*The wily fox shook his head.*

*At that moment, the stork dropped to the ground, next to the strongest elk.*

*"I know you wanted to trick me the other day when you invited me to share a visit to the berry farm." She said. "Still, when you were in danger, I pointed the way."*

*The wily fox looked around the group. He eyed the stork hungrily.*

*"Enough!" It was the ancient elk. She stepped forward. "My family will not allow you to come until you are willing to live by our rules."*

*The wily fox tried to dart from the circle of animals, up the mountainside.*

*The strong, young elk stood in his way, his horns lowered menacingly.*

*The stork spoke out. "There is a knob, over there. It may enough to keep you safe." She pointed down to the right.*

*The father fox shouted, "You will go there!" His voice competing with the increasingly blustery wind and rain.*

*"But, if the rains return, I will not be safe!" Pleaded the wily fox.*

*"You have chosen. You cannot come with us."*

-&-

The animals have reached an imperfect compromise. All have agreed to live in close proximity on the mountain until the rains have subsided, save for the wily fox. Unlike the rest, he has refused to promise not to prey on his fellow-refugees. As a result, he has been excluded from the larger group. More to protect themselves than out of pity for the wily fox, the animals have pointed out an alternative refuge, less secure but far enough away from the main group to ensure their safety as much as possible.

The solution is flawed, but it may represent the least bad one available. For the larger group, the risk exists that the wily fox will sneak into their refuge and eat one of the vulnerable animals. They will have to guard against this threat. For the wily fox, with the storm on the rise, he may well not be safe even in his alternative refuge. He also has no certain source of food there. But should he try to leave and sneak into where the rest are staying, he will be attacked by the larger animals.

The best outcome is the two groups respect their spaces and hope the floodwaters do not threaten the wily fox and, indeed, the rest. The less good is bloodshed, should the wily fox feel he has no option but to infiltrate the others' refuge, whilst the worst is the floodwaters threaten all.

For our broader purpose, the message is clear. The more elevated refuge area with its rules and the active support of the animals represents a restructuring process. In both cases, the objective is clear—survive the floods in the case of the animals, maximize value in the case of the Bank of Commerce. There are diverse constituencies whose interests may not be identical in all respects—foxes, bears, elks, and storks don't always co-exist well any more than all creditors agree on tenors, pricing, and covenants—but who must compromise to permit a successful outcome. There is no assurance either process will be successful even when all parties are acting in good faith.

However, when there is an outlier, a rogue creditor (the wily fox in our parable), the heightened risk is introduced.

To neutralize his threat, the rest of the animals have found this particular fox a separate refuge, just as lenders may devise a parallel arrangement to accommodate a nonparticipating creditor. The solution is far less attractive for all the animals, but it may be the only possible compromise.

-&-

As we are now focused on the Structuring and Negotiation Phase, let's outline in more detail the main elements of the Structuring and Negotiation Phase. We will revisit the issues raised in our opening narrative of the Bank of Commerce and continue to apply these elements in practice with our other case studies.

# Main Elements of the Structuring and Negotiation Phase

## The Main Goals of a Workout

As the World Bank concisely stated in its Toolkit for Out-of-Court Work-outs,[1] a properly structured restructuring process (whether judicial or consensual) will achieve the following two main goals simultaneously:

1. obtaining *debt sustainability* by reducing the debt burden of the enterprise in an orderly manner, whilst
2. protecting the *value of the assets* and the *rights of the creditors* in order to *avoid litigation*.

These two goals must be achieved as quickly as possible to preserve enterprise value, prevent business disruption, and regain access to financing options.[2]

The first goal need not be a long-term goal. It may also be short- (or medium-) term, i.e., the restructuring need not be aimed at rescuing the enterprise entirely but may instead, if appropriate, be aimed solely at an orderly wind-down of the enterprise outside of a formal insolvency.

The second goal presupposes a fair distribution of value and loss between all classes of fund providers—from equity holders to senior or super-senior debt holders. The relative positions of classes of funds providers, combined

---

[1] *See* A Toolkit for Out-of-Court Workouts, The World Bank, 2016.
[2] *Ibid*.

with an accurate assessment of the likely outcome for each class if an insolvency were to occur under the applicable insolvency law, form the touchstone of "fairness."

Hopefully, all sides will agree that a consensual restructuring (workout) is more preferable than a formal insolvency process, which would likely result in greater losses for all funders (save perhaps secured creditors).[3] That said, residual subjectivity amongst some participants can sometimes present a formidable obstacle to achieving this common understanding.

Although each workout is unique (with its own underlying business, unique financial structure, issues driving distress and funds providers), keeping these core goals in sight and approaching them through a *shared conceptual framework* (e.g., the London Approach or its successor INSOL II) can make the negotiation process easier. INSOL II Principles and their accompanying official commentaries provide a wealth of guidance which may be used in emerging markets, with important caveats. Other resources, such as the World Bank Toolkit,[4] also provide invaluable know-how for leadership (the Toolkit includes a number of useful observations on workouts as well as a separate, additional set of commentaries on INSOL II).

## Cost–Benefit Analysis

As recognized in INSOL Principle One, one of the main entry hurdles will be to determine whether a workout is *most appropriate* in the given case.[5] Although as a general rule it is often more likely that a workout will be preferable to formal insolvency, probably including a full judicial restructuring (and give better returns), this will not always be the case.[6,7]

---

[3] As discussed in Chapter 11, enforcement of security and recovery of proceeds therefrom is not necessarily a "slam dunk" for a secured lender in an emerging market. Secured creditors must approach valuation of their likely recovery realistically in terms of value, time, effort, and obstacles.

[4] *See* A Toolkit for Out-of-Court Workouts, International Bank for Reconstruction and Development (World Bank 2016), https://openknowledge.worldbank.org/handle/10986/28953.

[5] It will be recalled, INSOL II Principle One includes this key carve out: "unless such a course is inappropriate in a particular case." *See* Chapter 11.

[6] A reflected in Annex 1, local business and legal culture will also impact on the choice and practical likelihood of whether a workout is feasible. For example, in certain emerging markets, there is an assumption (on both lender and borrower side) that resolution of distress should always be done via courts, and not consensually. By contrast, in other emerging markets the judicial restructuring procedures are novel and/or otherwise rarely used for a variety of reasons.

[7] The challenge for foreign plaintiffs in local legal systems should also not be underestimated. The reality exists that in many (but not all) emerging markets, *local parties may receive preferential treatment* in regulatory and other procedures.

Accordingly, transaction leadership must face the threshold issue of a *cost–benefit analysis* of pursuing a workout versus initiating or permitting a formal insolvency. This usually requires detailed input from local counsel on the relevant emerging market's insolvency and judicial systems. Also, where a sufficient jurisdictional nexus exists with a developed country whose law permits foreign debtors to file (e.g., the USA, the UK, and/or Singapore[8]) then such options should also be considered. It is said, a workout transaction "lives in the shadow" cast by insolvency law—i.e., *the workout's outcome must reflect approximately the same proportionate pay outs to funders as they would receive if the borrower went into a formal insolvency.*

Against this touchstone, the leadership must then assess *whether a workout in the case at hand will be more or less beneficial to the funders.* The *benefits* of a workout will usually include:

- avoidance of damage to goodwill (stigma) and business atrophy of the borrower—no matter how efficient a particular country's insolvency system may be, an insolvency proceeding is likely to damage the business and lead to deterioration in value;
- avoidance of loss of talent—management may be quicker to jump from the "sinking ship" of an insolvent enterprise than in a workout; whereas a proper workout may envisage incentive programs for loyal managers;
- a more orderly sale of assets as opposed to a forced "fire sale";
- velocity and flexibility of process—a workout often can be achieved in a quicker, more flexible process than a formal insolvency proceeding;
- lower cost—the total aggregate cost of outside professional advisors (particularly lawyers) to all parties to achieve the restructuring is likely to be far less than that in an insolvency;
- original currency maintenance—many insolvency systems convert foreign-currency-denominated claims into the local currency, thus creating local currency risk for claim holders;
- continued interest accrual—many insolvency systems will not permit interest to continue to accrue in accordance with the original loan terms;
- no loss of set-off—creditors will retain set-off rights (which may not be possible under the local insolvency regime);
- preservation of contracts—contracts with counterparties often identify insolvency as a basis for unilateral termination; in a workout, the borrower may preserve desirable key contracts in place;

---

[8] *See* discussion, Chapter 11.

- lighter regulatory impact—the borrower is less likely to risk the loss of necessary business licenses (e.g., as a regulated institution); and
- confidentiality of process—the workout process (e.g., size and conditions of claims, state of the borrower's business, etc.) enjoys greater confidentiality.[9]

The above said, a workout *may not always be the best solution* for lenders, e.g., where:

- the business is not viable in the first place, and a liquidation of assets is most appropriate (that said, it may still be preferable for an orderly wind-down outside insolvency to take place on a consensual basis[10]);
- the main value of the business has been pledged as collateral to one or more secured lenders, who may be less inclined to enter into a workout in lieu of merely foreclosing on their collateral;
- the requisite creditor aggregation (bulk of claims held by like-minded creditors prepared to act unanimously) is not possible (e.g., there are too many nonfinancial creditors such as diffuse bond holders, tax authorities, tort claimants, employees, trade creditors, etc.);
- the required level of commercial/financial information and proactive management cooperation is not present (or cannot be obtained quickly enough during a reasonable standstill period),[11] or there has been a serious breakdown in trust in the borrower's management and/or its shareholder(s);
- one or more holdout (rogue) creditors persist in pursuing enforcement, triggering the need for protection of an automatic stay (i.e., a moratorium on enforcement) in a formal insolvency;
- the borrower is a party to onerous executory contracts which cannot be renegotiated and must be avoided;[12]
- prior or ongoing leakages calls for invalidation of antecedent transactions and/or imposition of vicarious liability on controlling persons (shadow directors);

---

[9] *See* P. R. Wood, *op. cit.*; J. Garrido, *op. cit.*

[10] *See* discussion of orderly wind-downs in Chapter 11.

[11] A number of senior restructuring specialists have observed that with closely held businesses in emerging markets where the controlling shareholder simultaneously manages the business, achieving progress in a workout can pose challenges. The owner-manager may be less inclined to act objectively in reaching compromise, fighting against dilution/loss of control and/or other concessions benefiting lenders. Possibly this might be explained by Kahneman's and Tversky's loss aversion concept.

[12] *Cf.* desirable valuable contracts, where a workout may be better (see discussion immediately above).

- the required corporate, regulatory, and/or other approvals required for the borrower to conclude a workout are not available; and/or
- the relevant legal system has a well-developed hybrid insolvency proceeding (e.g., allowing pre-pack/cramdown), or a developed market with such a proceeding likely to accept jurisdiction is available (e.g., the USA, UK, Singapore).

## Impact of the Emerging Market Environment

What makes an emerging market different than a developed market in applying the above threshold test?

Most of the above-enumerated issues will (more or less equally) apply in an emerging market. However, their *impact* is likely to be *amplified*,[13] due to the *state of development* of the emerging market's insolvency system, judicial system, professional insolvency office holder network, and general legal protections.[14] The lender leadership team must therefore carefully consider this when taking the decision.

In particular, the following additional considerations may arise:

- lack of well-developed insolvency law and practice—many emerging markets' insolvency systems are still under development, including as regards judicial restructuring proceedings,[15] the ability to effectuate group restructurings and/or other critical aspects;

---

[13] For example, even in those emerging markets who have made advances with their insolvency systems such as Poland, administrative problems like backlog and overloaded court dockets can make insolvency proceedings drag out far longer.

[14] *See* EBRD Core Principles, *op. cit.*

[15] As mentioned in Chapter 5, there is a *wide degree of non-homogeneity* in the extent of development of emerging markets' insolvency systems. Accordingly, sweeping generalizations must be avoided. Each emerging market's insolvency system must be assessed on a *case-by-case basis*, and lender leadership will need competent advice from local counsel on these issues. But even where emerging markets' bankruptcy laws do include judicial restructuring procedures, *these are not always widely utilized* for a variety of reasons. For example, they may only be relatively recent, and due to lack of court practice the stakeholders may not wish to be a "test case"; they might fail to include key tools (e.g., pre-packs and/or cramdowns); there may be such distrust by stakeholders in the judiciary that filings are made only when it is far too late to save a business. Some countries have not established separate bankruptcy courts, with the result that judges in the courts of general jurisdiction are unfamiliar with application of bankruptcy principles. Other countries might have overly long statutory "observation periods" (mandatory waiting periods) or delays (e.g., from overloaded dockets) during which the debtor's business atrophies and ends in the slow, painful death of the patient on the operating table (e.g., Romania, Russia). The reasons vary. As a general observation, and subject to exceptions, judicial restructurings appear to be *widely under-utilized* in many emerging markets. For highlights on the judicial restructuring regimes of the 46 emerging markets surveyed for this book, *see* Annex 1.

- professional insolvency office holder infrastructure—the infrastructure of local professional insolvency officeholders may be insufficiently developed, nontransparent or otherwise unreliable; and/or
- unpredictability of the local judicial system field—in many emerging markets the local judiciary will not offer the required independence from other branches of government and/or from outside influence; the maturity of legal development; the objectivity and commerciality of the bench; the transparency; the predictability; or the level playing field found in more developed legal systems.[16]

These additional factors alone can often provide even greater incentive to pursue a workout in many emerging markets.

At the same time, certain emerging markets can also pose greater cultural challenges to successful workouts. For example, there may be a business of culture in some emerging markets of *less transparency* and greater secrecy in business dealings. External oversight of financial reporting may be less developed. Some borrowers and/or shareholders may not be prepared to have open and honest discussions with their lenders. Some borrowers and their management may be overly suspicious of sharing information outside their trusted circle or have a propensity to hide problems until it is too late to fix them. A successful restructuring will usually require quite early, open and frank discussions and collaboration, which may be fundamentally inconsistent with local business culture.

These local cultural hurdles impact not only on the borrower/shareholder side, but also on other relevant players. For example, *local lending institutions* in emerging markets are often less familiar with application of INSOL II Principles. There can sometimes be an intractable attitude of "every man for himself" or "law of the strongest" which informs local lender behavior. There may also be unwanted political or regulatory consequences if local lenders face unsatisfactory recoveries.[17] Restructurings in emerging markets where local banks (and/or bondholders) own a large share of total claims against

---

[16] The authors have observed this phenomenon on numerous occasions and in a number of emerging markets. Indeed, this may be one of the greatest obstacles toward the development of some emerging market insolvency systems, particularly when large, local "heavy hitters" are aligned with the borrower, its shareholder, and/or a competing creditor. Large, state-owned creditors often leverage their advantage by influencing the judiciary (or, in the parlance of the Russian-speaking states of the former Soviet Union, "*telefonnoe pravo*" or "telephone justice"). Similarly, the state itself can sometimes play a role as a predator of valuable assets and use the local insolvency system for political and/or corrupt motives. Judges' behavior is often motivated by self-censorship and a desire to play by "unwritten rules." *See, e.g.,* K. Hendley, "'Telephone Law' and the 'Rule of Law': The Russian Case, Hague Journal on the Rule of Law," 1: 241–262 (2009); *see also* A. Ledeneva, "Telephone Justice in Russia: An Update," EU-Russia Centre Review, XVIII, pp. 4–22 (2011).

[17] There may also be adverse regulatory or tax implications for local lenders.

the borrower face special challenges—either the transaction leadership must either convince the local lenders to go along with a group solution or craft a solution which excludes or neutralizes those lenders (e.g., by ensuring local lenders are paid in full).

Each of these considerations will drive the decision as to whether in a given case a workout will be achievable.

## Building Blocks of a Restructuring: Business and Balance Sheet

In addition to the above factors will be the feasibility in a given case of the actual *substance* of the restructuring. What measures must we take, to achieve our main goals as articulated above?

These measures will vary considerably, depending on the particular situation. That said, restructuring measures may generally be broken down into two basic categories—(1) *business* (or operating) restructuring measures, and (2) *balance sheet* (or financial) restructuring measures.

*Business* restructuring measures will range from relatively simple measures such as installing new management, refocusing operational strategy on more profitable business activities, to more complex ones such as asset sales, winddowns, hive offs and other corporate restructurings, and introduction of new product or service lines in line with shifting market demand.[18]

As simple as this sounds, in practice these measures may pose enormous challenges. For example, a sale of a distressed business unit or nonperforming assets will require finding a willing buyer, agreeing a fair price in the circumstances (which will usually be well below the lenders' and shareholders' expectations), ensuring that no residual liability remains for the borrower (e.g., on representations and warranties and/or indemnities to the buyer[19]), completing on the sale before the buyer changes its mind and/or some additional exogenous events occur hampering or scuttling completion entirely, and many more.

---

[18] A prime example of an event driving introduction of new product and/or service lines was the COVID-19 pandemic. Following COVID-19, many businesses' existing (pre-COVID) product and service lines had to be revamped, often fundamentally, to adapt to shifting market demand.

[19] The provision of suitable representations, warranties, and indemnities to a buyer of assets is often critical in enhancing the value of the assets in their disposal. This raises the conundrum of providing meaningful assurances to buyers whilst limiting the borrower's post-completion exposure. A possible solution for some emerging markets is M&A warranty and indemnity (W&I) insurance, which a number of global insurers now offer in some emerging markets. W&I insurance provides the policyholder with a standard suite of warranties and general tax indemnity, subject to some exclusions. It may be taken out by either seller (e.g., the borrower) or buyer. Although naturally it comes at a cost, nonetheless in many cases it expands the potential buyer market and sales price.

The introduction of new product or service lines adapting to radically shifting market demand introduces a new element of added risk, as well as recruitment and/or training of appropriate talent, funding of substantial investments in such new lines, and the like.

*Balance sheet* restructuring measures could include extension of lender maturities, rollovers, currency conversions, interest rate holidays or other alterations, forbearance of penalties, alteration of covenants, swaps (debt-equity, debt-debt [e.g., senior to subordinated], equity-equity), issuance of convertible debt, payments in kind, new loans (new money), restructured security, equity infusions, guarantees or other credit support (from existing or new shareholders), forgiveness of interest and/or partial or total debt write-downs (haircuts).

Often a restructuring will include a selection of various elements from both categories. There is no one-size-fits-all approach, and leadership will probably need to tailor a specific structure for each case. Leadership (usually with the assistance of outside financial advisors) must make a careful analysis of the factors leading to distress and solutions to eliminate these and stabilize and strengthen the borrower's financial position in a well-developed restructuring plan.

The measures themselves are not so different from those applied in more developed economies, though transaction leadership will be challenged to apply them in the context of the local business customs and legal system, so necessarily a fair amount of adaptation will arise. Local counsel will play a key role in ensuring that these comply with legal and regulatory requirements.

## Transaction Leadership

Given the combination of a greater impetus and at the same time the greater challenges of pursuing a workout in an emerging market, it is imperative that transaction leadership be well organized and prepared to devote substantial time and energy to the transaction. Strong leadership (or cat-herding skill) is essential.

A restructuring transaction will require overcoming major challenges, such as convincing parties to *agree to take losses* (often considerable) and *neutralizing holdout (or rogue) lenders*. On balance, sometimes the task of convincing parties to take a loss will be modest and simple math—better to take some loss than to lose everything entirely. With equity holders who stand last in line, leaving some value on the table often helps. But lenders will (rightly) see this as a zero-sum game with any such value coming from their pockets. At the same time, lenders must realize that taking too firm a position can lead to a total loss where this results in formal insolvency. Hence, they must be prepared to be flexible, and lender leadership will be challenged to help them appreciate this.[20]

By comparison, the challenge with neutralizing rogues can be daunting. A rogue often appreciates its bargaining power and will endeavor to use this to its maximum advantage (knowing it can easily trigger an insolvency).[21,22]

Lender leadership must be creative in its approach to dealing with these and other challenges as they arise in the workout.

-&-

Let's return now to some of our narratives, to see how we can apply these concepts in practice.

## Application in Practice: Case Studies

### Bank of Commerce Recap—Structuring and Negotiations

Let's look at the situation as it developed in Bank of Commerce, between the borrower and the shareholders. How did our negotiations proceed? Let's consider the main elements of structuring and negotiation outlined above and consider how our friends fared.

We had started off with JK's disastrously delivered Hobson Choice at the kick-off meeting with all lenders. This was rejected. Subsequently, he was forced out, when the board realized his tactics risked damaging New West's public image at a time when it faced a grave, potentially existential threat due to a failed refinancing of a recent acquisition.

With JK side-lined, a draft restructuring plan devised by our players was floated again with the lenders. This plan assumed the Bank of Commerce would continue as a going concern, with no change in control. Despite Edinburgh Partner's fireworks, the proposal gained traction when Ursula was forced to advise the lenders she could not raise the initial large sum of new equity, nor commit to the ongoing contingent capital envisaged under the plan.

In the meeting's dangerously volatile aftermath, the parties stumbled to the broad, charcoal strokes of a new plan. This time it was an orderly wind-down,

---

[20] Again, the concept of loss aversion—that losses loom larger than gains, and people are by nature averse to losses—is demonstrated by party behavior during workout negotiations. *See* D. Kahneman and A. Tversky, Prospect Theory: An Analysis of Decision under Risk, Econometrica (1979).

[21] This is discussed in more detail in Chapter 11.

[22] As shown in Bank of Commerce, rogues appeared a number of times before the deal was successfully closed.

with all parties facing losses. Their initial thinking was to work transparently with the local government. The local CEO knew better but said nothing. Off screen, Kristi and Ursula worked to refine the proposal, which Ursula's local CEO ran by a friendly, confidential senior contact within the local government. As he expected, the government would simply intervene, with local parties in and out of the government sharing the spoils. The result of their collective work was what Kristi shared with Martin in her weekend call. Everyone had given far more than they had been prepared to consider at the outset.

For Ursula, the fifteen million were good money after bad. Under only the most optimistic scenario would she see any part of this rescue amount again. Her argument to the board was two-fold—first, protect their relationship with Martin and his development finance institution employer, and second, safeguard their market reputation, already dangerously frayed by JK's recent missteps. She still needed a last push from Martin, but she was confident they would cross the finish line.

For Martin, five million was peanuts as an absolute amount but carried significance as a potential bad precedent. He argued to his investment committee that the shareholders have a duty to contribute to an orderly wind-down or risk reputational damage. More than that, he convinced a very wise managing director that this public contribution was a pittance when compared to the amount of private capital that might flee the sector were the Bank of Commerce to go up in flames.

For the lenders, the outcome was a grave let-down from the initial, albeit ultimately unrealistic hope that Ursula would rescue them. Maya and Kristi saw the possibility of a total loss, should the local government intervene to succor the depositors. The compromise plan meant a loss, but one estimated in the neighborhood of 75% in the base case. With this choice: a near certain 100% loss behind door number one versus a moderately high probability 25% loss behind door number two, our players appeared to have secured the agreement of the remaining lenders to go with door number two!

Now, let's examine the situation amongst the lenders themselves. Two elements warrant comment here.

*First*, lender leadership was faced with the task of *acclimatizing the lenders to losing money*. The moment a lender faces the unavoidable certainty of a loss is always painful. Depending on the relevant individual's (or individuals') involvement in creating the asset (exposure) in the first place, it is potentially damaging (and even fatal) to career prospects. In practice, many lenders and their representatives thus resist until it is futile. We have all witnessed the cascade of emotions and recriminations.

At the meeting where Ursula nixed the going-concern alternative, what would have followed in real life would probably have been longer and more colorful than we depict. Indeed, days or weeks depending on circumstances could pass before resistance to the evitable collapses. There would have been renewed demands for shareholder money, threats of acceleration, and calls between C-suites. The end of the tarmac would be reached eventually and a decision necessary. Most lenders will choose a small or even a big loss over a total write-off. They will moan and groan, group relationships will be strained, but finally, agree they will. Keeping the dialogue going and the parties engaged, much like managing an irascible adolescent, is the task for the "adults in the room," our players in this case.

*Second*, lender leadership was faced with *neutralizing the rogue lender*. Not all rogues are created equal. Some outliers are constrained by factors outside their control (e.g., end of fund requirements, external investment committee decisions, etc.). Acting in good faith, some reach different conclusions about the borrower and/or deal. These two groups can be "dealt with." The ones who defy cooperative effort are what one might call the "kidnappers." These are the creditors who, when confronted with a potential loss, engage in behavior to force other lenders to take value out of their own pockets to sweeten the kidnapper's recovery. In our parable, this is the wily fox. In the Bank of Commerce narrative, it was Todd and his boss Colin. Their underlying motivations are diverse and often not worth debating.

What is crucial in all cases is how to deal these parties effectively. The first question is how much leverage does the rogue lender actually have? In the case of Colin and Edinburgh Partners, we have agreed they can throw the Bank of Commerce into liquidation if they want. But were they really prepared to do this? Martin concluded that they were, but that there were guardrails, if you will. He subtly succeeded in ascertaining that Colin was prepared to "play along" with the lenders subject to two conditions: (i) that he could delay classifying the loan as non-performing until some point in the future, and (ii) that he signed no debt restructuring agreement. In other words, that the proverbial "can could be kicked down the road" on some inevitable loss.[23]

Now, let's look at the local regulatory landscape and how the negotiated solution fits into it. Even after having acclimated lenders to losing money and neutralizing the rogue creditor, lender leadership faced further obstacles.

---

[23] A reasonably delivered request by a small lender to deal with, say, their end-of-fund deadline may well elicit flexibility and take the form of, say, a discounted buyout. But this was not Edinburgh Partners' case. Instead, they were a large creditor. Our sense was they wanted to be paid out in full. To accommodate this demand seemed improbable, without risking destabilizing the rest of the group.

*First*, the players would have to run the bank down to nothing (or nearly nothing), but without the local authorities getting wind of their intentions, at least until the depositors are paid off in full. There could be no leaks to the market. Local management and their staff had to be incentivized to *maintain secrecy throughout the process*. The messaging to clients had to be consistent with a going concern, albeit an institution whose scale and business focus was undergoing modification to comport with a post-crisis world. This would be a ticking time bomb throughout the process.

*Second*, let's not forget the *wrongful trading* threat.[24] The local board members have a legal obligation to declare the bank insolvent when circumstances warrant. Arguably, should all loans be provisioned adequately, capital could be negative. The market volatility was generating a lot of smoke about true conditions in the financial markets. The local regulator knew this and sent the message that banks should forbear, avoiding the over-reaction which could transform a passing, minor disruption into a debilitating, systemic crisis with broad and lasting economic scarring. Therefore, for the moment, the bank would have more flexibility than in normal conditions to keep loans in the performing category—restructurings, new credits to fund debt service, etc. Further, the players clearly stated the intention to convert liabilities into equity as necessary to maintain regulatory solvency. As a result, the directors were restrained from declaring an insolvency. However, given potential personal vicarious liability (and even possible criminal liability), the risk would be ever present that an individual director could act to declare the bank insolvent. As with the management and staff, the directors had to be managed.

*Third*, the length of the recovery process and the acute and escalating uncertainty around recovery values raised the specter that one or more lenders could *abandon the process* over its life. People's minds can change, intervening events can occur, parties' commercial objectives can change. A long recovery period invariably evokes these and similar rights.

*Fourth*, once there were proceeds available for the offshore lenders, the wire transfers would require local foreign exchange approval. There are full means to do this. These wire transfers were the life blood of the whole structure. Either the growing foreign exchange crisis of the country or bureaucratic delay/blockages are non-mitigatable risks.

-&-

Before continuing, let's ask ourselves a question. When reflecting back over the whole of the Bank of Commerce case, what is the single most important

---

[24] *See* discussion on wrongful trading, Chapter 11.

lesson we have learned? Or asked another way, what is the one element or action you would change?

We'll cheat a bit. Our suggestion is we consider two parts. They are related, so perhaps we are still conforming to our original question.

One is: *be realistic about the solution*. The design should be *what works for all*, not one that exploits the other side's temporary weakness. The other is a precondition to the "intellectual honesty" required for the first. Be willing to accept a loss, a negative number if you will, if that is necessary to balance the equation.

Over the years, we have often observed an almost visceral reaction on the part of some lenders when a credit goes bad. Point fingers at the borrower. Accuse them of faults ranging from rank incompetence to even outright fraud in some cases, and ask them how they plan to fix matters. What often does not happen is an act of *introspection* on the part of the lender. Did the lender help lay the groundwork that led to the problem by poor analytics and/or structuring? Or during the life of the loan by failing to provide adequate oversight?

None of this changes the legal obligation for repayment but should *shift the perspective about how the parties work together*. If possible, the two sides should engage in a cooperative effort to fashion a going-concern solution. To do this, each side must be prepared to give a bit.

In the Bank of Commerce case, initially the two sides each wanted the other to shoulder the burden alone. Eventually, after much theatrics, the two sides recognized that a going-concern outcome was impossible and stumbled toward a structure agreed by all, save for Colin. After the fact, it is glib to imply the parties could have gone directly to the right answer. That would be otherworldly. However, we believe it fair to say that by accepting the principle of burden sharing from the outset, the parties may (and probably would) have reached a workable structure faster. In the end, the timing is secondary to the outcome. Within reason, getting there is the key. It is often better late than never (provided that the resultant delay has not prejudiced the restructuring, e.g., by the accumulation of greater losses, value leakage, exposure to intervening events or changes in circumstances, etc.).

To reinforce this concept, let us return to the National Goods case.

Recall that in the most favorable scenario (in Chapter 6), by the time the lenders meet, National Goods' advisor has consulted bilaterally with all the lenders. The major financial elements are generally agreed. The objectionable element—new money in the form of a revolving credit—had been dropped. One lender with an end of fund problem has been allowed not to participate. Underlying the financial restructuring is a series of significant corporate restructuring measures. The two major elements are: (i) the sale of the foreign and domestic retail networks; and (ii) the development of a more eco-friendly line of white goods to replace their legacy line of less-energy efficient models. The proceeds from the first will contribute to the funding for the second. A condition precedent to the overall restructuring is the signing of one or more binding memoranda of agreement on a sale of the retail networks. The sales process does not progress well. Whilst there are offers, the economics are not attractive. Buyers have adopted a very cautious valuation of the retail business. The best offer is at roughly 50% of book value. The company refuses to sell at these levels. As time passes, the lenders are forced to confront a decision: change the agreed workout terms or just foreclose on the company (hence landing them all in insolvency proceedings).

The retail sales network expansion is the proximate cause of National Goods' present financial challenges. The company cannot afford to keep the network without substantial reductions in their debt service burden combined with new working capital lines of credit. The current restructuring plan accomplishes neither of these necessary outcomes. Sell the network cheap and restructure is the lenders' mantra. The company's response is that this approach buys some time but does not solve the longer term problem of the increasingly uncompetitive wholesale product line. Both sides have arguments on their side. The current restructuring plan only works without the financial requirements of the retail network, but the forced sale does result in leaving significant value on the table.

From a birds-eye view, the lenders appear to have given very little and are the block to a successful outcome. The totality of their "give" is the extension of repayment terms and a relaxation of covenants. There is no new money, nor a reduction in interest rates. The company has agreed to "eat humble pie" and abandon their much-ballyhooed vertical integration and regional expansion programs. Their resistance to the bargain-sales price is arguably not a question of "wounded pride." Instead, the realistic short timetable imposed by the lenders has allowed bidders to low-ball the price. National Goods needs to get a better price in order to generate proceeds for the product reengineering, without which the longer term viability of the company is in question. National Goods' advisor suggests a compromise amongst the following alternatives:

- Eliminate the CPs, continue with the retail business, and have the lenders recommit to a new revolving line of working capital credit; or

- Agree the sale with one of the existing buyers, satisfy the CPs, and have lenders commit to a new financing package to help the research and development effort on the new product line.

As an exercise, which of the two would you chose and why? Spoiler alert (suggested answers below)!

The second strikes us as the better alternative. Why? The retail business requires excessive capital. The operations lose money and require an increasing volume of working capital to support sales. Based on current projections, there is no prospect of these trends reversing in the medium term. National Goods can't support the current debt burden, and new voluntary financing is not available. The working capital line will only dig a deeper hole. To survive, the business needs to be sold or, failing an attractive buyer, closed down. As such, the first alternative is not feasible. The second alternative has its drawbacks for both sides. But still, it is a sounder approach under the circumstances. First, National Goods divests the unprofitable, cash flow-negative business at roughly 50 cents on the dollar. Yes, admittedly, it is a loss. But it stops the bleeding, pays down a small (symbolic) amount of existing debt, and funds a part of the early research and development budget. This eliminates a key risk confronting the company and hence the restructuring. Overall, group operating cash flow returns to a slight positive balance. Second, with these actions, the lenders are induced to commit new money to complement the company's investment in the new product line. The new funds will increase each lender's overall exposure by roughly 1/5. A fair amount, but a necessary concession to induce the company to sell the retail operations quickly.

In both the Bank of Commerce and National Goods cases, we see each side compromising, moving on from their initial positions where a deal could not (or should not) be done to new ones where deals were possible. The ability to see beyond winning each point requires courage and confidence. Head offices are rarely forgiving of giving up value in order to allow a transaction to proceed. Had the deal person only negotiated better, then the "give" would not have been necessary, so they say. More junior staff are notoriously cautious, fearful that the perception of weakness will stunt their careers. In a sector becoming notoriously younger by the year, the grey hairs in finance tend to be better catalysts to progress in transactions. This reflects not just battle-earned knowledge of "what works," but the self-confidence to accept opposition and criticism, from both inside and outside the institution, and the courage to face the possibility that a bold step could imperil the whole transaction or elicit severe reprimand from one's paymasters.

In the case of the Bank of Commerce, we assume Ursula and Martin faced intense internal pushback on putting in "good money after bad," once the decision was made to proceed to a wind-down. At the same time, Kristi and Maya managed to bring along hesitant lenders to accept some loss via the debt forgiveness/recapitalization mechanism. Each side gave something up in order to ensure the overall deal happened. Had either side balked, intervention and a likely total loss would have followed. As individuals, all four could have sat back and blamed others, rather than risking personal political capital. Instead, they acted.

What happens when the parties cannot reach common ground? In an emerging market restructuring, often the most dreaded message a lender can hear is, "They filed for bankruptcy today." A failed negotiation resulting in one of the parties' hitting the panic button and forcing the borrower into court-administered bankruptcy happens. In many emerging markets, the underdeveloped nature of the courts means that this usually translates into a far less attractive outcome than a consensual restructuring (indeed, insolvency proceedings in these markets most frequently lead to liquidation and pennies on the dollar). Hence, such a direction should be avoided whenever possible.

There are also cases where the fundamentals of the borrower defy a going-concern outcome. The reader is invited to turn to Part 3 of the *Country Telecom case in Annex 4* before moving on.

## Conclusions

We have examined two cases in this chapter. In one—Bank of Commerce (orderly wind-down)—the borrower will not survive as a going concern. The parties succeeded in maintaining control of the process (in the form of an orderly wind-down), although the road ahead will not be easy. The success was built on cooperation between the two sides. The parties recognized there would be long memories about how they acted in the process. Ursula and Martin in particular demonstrated their understanding of this fact by investing hard cash in the orderly wind-down.[25]

---

[25] For those readers who have gone through the Country Telecom case in Annex 4, they will note that it, too, will not survive. Years of poor business judgment in an era of frothy markets dug a hole from which there was no private market escape. Were we to play the tape forward, the core mobile cellular assets and licenses of Country Telecom would have been purchased out of bankruptcy by one of the new entrants, and the local government would have nationalized the broadband network and assumed the debt.

In the second, the National Goods case, there is the prospect of a going-concern solution. Cooperation between the parties and a potentially viable long-term business model are the building blocks.

Before we move onto Chapter 8 (where we explore the work of transforming good intentions and term sheets into concrete deals in the Implementation Phase), let's consider the main "lessons learned."

We have already touched on several, including acclimating lenders to the possibility of financial loss and dealing with a rogue lender. There are others which emerge from the vagaries of the negotiation process and highlight the need for both flexibility and courage. These include:

- **Be proactive and adaptable—"Deal with Detours."** Circumstances change—market conditions, borrower financials, lenders' positions. The deal blueprint at the outset and the final form of the deal are rarely identical. The transaction leadership team—that is, the representatives on both sides—must anticipate these detours and change course as warranted. Often a deal continues to take shape as discussions proceed and diligence is done. Maintaining some particular structure, or aspects of a structure, as an *idee fixe* can even prevent finding a solution. The parties' representatives must be open minded and prepared to consider change. In Bank of Commerce, Ursula's financial inability to support the going-concern solution necessitated a pivot to an orderly wind-down. The parties skillfully succeeded in navigating this change of direction, without losing momentum. Given the need to maintain the public appearance of a going concern, this change was essential.

- **The virtue of compromise—"You Can't Always Get What You Want" (*Sir Michael Philip Jagger and Keith Richards*).** One rigid, uncooperative lender can jeopardize all. All parties start a process with a target outcome. These goals may well vary from lender to lender, and from the lenders and the borrower group. Imagine a list of a dozen "wants." Are all of these really essential, and is their absence really a deal breaker? Unlikely. Participants in a workout must consider the difference between the "want to have" and "need to have" items. They must be prepared to drop the former and be flexible about the latter (and crucially, about their exact form). In our Bank of Commerce narrative, the parties reached an agreement, save for the lenders requiring equality of treatment on proceeds. Holding on to issues merely for the sake of scoring points (or worse, settling scores) can kill a deal. Be flexible. Focus on the most fundamental issues. Insisting on wants (instead of needs) can also provoke mirroring behavior by other parties. Drive the deal forward—and drive the other parties' demands as well—by focusing solely on the absolute musts (and even then being prepared to compromise on these). What seems like an "unacceptable" outcome is often far preferable to the looming alternative (insolvency proceeding in a local court with pennies on the dollar).

- **Risk a breakdown sometimes—"On Matters of Style, Swim with the Current, on Matters of Principle, Stand like a Rock" (*Thomas Jefferson*).** The softening of the Edinburgh Partners position was not a solution, a viable compromise. The rest of the lenders, including Kristi, would be hard pressed to permit this rogue lender to exit unscathed. Perhaps Colin and Todd were just negotiating and would settle for something less? Time would tell. What was clear is that the lenders had to send the message that the Edinburgh Partners' ask was not acceptable. To be credible, the lenders had to be prepared to walk away, risk a breakdown in the process, even to the point of the Bank of Commerce's liquidation. That having been said, there are often circumstances where one or more lenders get a sweeter deal. More typically, this occurs when dealing with smaller lenders and/or where the ask is more reasonable, such as a very deeply discounted buyout (e.g., where there is an end-of-fund problem). This is not one of those cases. Should Edinburgh Partners persist in their demands, the ending would not be a happy one. The other lenders had to make this clear to Edinburgh Partners. The question was, how?

# 8

# Implementation

**Abstract** In our fable, the fox regrets his behavior and is allowed back into the group, hence allowing the whole community is safe. As a moral of the story and of relevance to restructuring is the willingness of the group to stand up to the fox, whilst still allowing him a way back. As we saw in the Bank of Commerce tale, the lenders had to confront first JT and then Edinburgh Partners to lead an unruly lenders group through many execution challenges to what would become the only viable outcome—an orderly wind-down. The main elements of the implementation phase are reviewed, again with a reliance on the manufacturing case study as well as the opening Bank of Commerce tale to identify the governance and execution challenges and evaluate possible solutions. There are many important lessons, but perhaps foremost is that experienced, committed transaction leadership must take full ownership of the deal to ensure that it is executed properly. For this purpose, constant communication, pro-activeness, flexibility, and speed are essential.

**Keywords** Balance sheet · Bankruptcy · Borrower · Consensual restructuring · Coordinating committee · Corporate debt · Credit monitoring · Debt · Debtor · Distressed debt · Emerging market · Frontier market · INSOL II · INSOL principles · Insolvency · Lender leadership · Non-performing loans · Pre-insolvency · Restructure · Restructuring · Restructuring plan · Standstill · Steering committee · Workout

*"United we stand, divided we fail."*
John Dickinson, 1768

## Preface: The Stork and the Fox—Part V

*The storm returned with relentless fury. The rain fell in horizontal sheets, propelled by sharp gusts of wind that shook branches and stripped their leaves. The wet soaked the ground. The raindrops painted circles in the puddles that appeared. The puddles soon swelled into ponds.*

*The wily fox searched for a place to shelter. He espied a small rocky outcrop nearby. It would give him some relief, at least for the moment.*

*Once there, he waited and waited. The storm did not abate. Still, he hunched, looking with increasing hopelessness into the grey, sunless day.*

*By nightfall, he was sorely hungry. In this weather, he despaired of finding anything to eat and so chose to stay under cover. He soon fell asleep. But his rest was fitful, dominated by dreams. He thought of days in the lowlands, playing in sunny fields, surrounded by the other animals, seeing birds coasting in the breezes that touched the trees with delicate caresses. He saw the stork leap into the sky and circle him, her pained, sad expression accusing him. Then, off she flew.*

*The water was now creeping up the slight incline to the outcrop.*

*Still he slept. He saw the stork circle in the air and point her wing up the side of the mountain. The wily fox was jerked from sleep. Had she returned? He realized it had only been his imagination.*

*Fear and even some small amount of remorse filled his heart.*

*It was dawn. Seeing the rain and the rising waters, he realized he could not stay here much longer. But he was weak from not having eaten in several days. Without food, he was trapped.*

*Later in the morning, the sky lightened and the rain slackened.*

*The wily fox looked out. No, he thought, this was another dream. A few paces down the hill, ankle deep in water, stood the stork.*

*She held a bundle in her mouth. Fearlessly, she waded up to the entrance of his shelter and dropped the bundle at his feet.*

*"You must be very hungry," she said.*

*"Yes, I am." the wily fox replied. "But why are you doing this for me? After all I did?".*

*Motioning to the outside, she explained patiently, "Do you not see? We all must find a way forward together or we all fail."*

*The wily fox's throat tightened. At length, he managed to say. "I do now."*

*"Do you, really?" Inquired the stork, eyeing him judiciously.*

*The wily fox pleaded, "I will."*

*At length, she continued. "You are welcome only on the understanding that you obey the rules."*

*"I promise."*

*The stork nodded. "We will see. The others trust my judgement, but some do not trust you."*

*The wily fox swallowed hard.*

*"Eat and then we will go the others." Said the stork. "You will be safe there and amongst friends."*

-&-

A corny ending or just another clever trick by the wily fox? Only time will tell. Indeed, the stork herself is not yet convinced. Why then help the wily fox? Would it not be better to be careful and let him drown? So why? In the past, this community of animals had lived in balance, held together by an agreement to adhere to rules and customs. The flood had not changed this. The catastrophe of the rising waters had actually intensified the need for common action. The more mature members had accepted that all had to compromise their behavior to protect the group. They mobilized the rest to make the best of a very bad situation. Should the end be a happy one, then the lesson for the self-centered wily fox will be that a collective solution, which safeguards and maximizes the common good, is superior to an outcome where one party, either by strength or guile, ruthlessly pursues their own self-interest. That is, no wily fox behavior.

As we now enter the final Implementation Phase, the same uncertainty is present. Yes, at a high level, the terms have been agreed. However, the path from a summary terms sheet to a set of definitive legal agreements is not straightforward or certain. There are hidden dangers. The topography is not flat. The journey's precise course is not known. Not all travelers share the same commitment to reaching the end. All the readers can share many stories of transactions which failed to reach closure even after lawyers were hired and drafting began. *"There's many a slip twixt the cup and the lip."*

In the case of the Bank of Commerce, we had a wily fox—Colin. What was really his game? What did he want, and how far would he go to get it? How would any accommodation provided to this one creditor affect the rest of the group, which we recall is hardly cohesive? Kristi and Maya were "herding cats" from the very beginning of the narrative. Any small fissure could quickly turn into a wide fracture threatening the structure of the whole deal.

On top of all the rest, there was the local depositor issue. As long as the parties ensured the Bank of Commerce remained fully in compliance with its regulatory requirements, then this risk could be mitigated. To do this, Ursula and Martin had to come through with their financial commitments.

At the same time, Kristi and Maya had to bring the lenders into a process of periodic debt forgiveness to maintain minimum solvency. All the whilst, they had to hope and pray the limited resources available were not overwhelmed by the deepening economic crisis and any adverse spill-overs into the financial system.

Let's now review the main elements of the Implementation Phase and then see how these are put into practice with some of our earlier narratives.

# Main Elements of the Implementation Phase

## Main Steps and Actors

The main steps in the Implementation Phase will comprise primarily:

- if not already done during case set-up, the drafting, negotiation, and execution of the formal *standstill agreement* (amongst the borrowers, lenders, main shareholders, and equity creditors [if any]),
- the commencement of the required *information flow* from the borrower to the external financial and legal advisors,
- based on such information, the analytical work and formulation (or re-confirmation) by the external financial (and legal) advisors and lender leadership of possible solutions, and the agreement with the borrower and main shareholders on *the most appropriate solution,*
- the *distillation* of such solution into a (more developed) term sheet for the final restructuring agreement, and addressing all relevant substantive commercial, financial, legal, and regulatory issues,[1]
- the drafting, negotiation, and execution of the *final restructuring agreement* and related ancillary documentation and parallel implementation of relevant *conditions precedent (CPs) to effectiveness,* as well as
- the planning and implementation of all *post-closing steps* for the restructuring, including post-closing monitoring (and if an orderly contractually

---

[1] As mentioned above, an initial term sheet may well have been signed in the Case Set-Up Phase. Such first term sheet however may be of more tactical importance for creating cohesion amongst lenders and the borrowers. In any event, it may have been signed prior to proper due diligence during a standstill, and it would need to be vetted as feasible and appropriate following such diligence. *See also* the discussion on term sheets in Chapter 11. Accordingly, it may be necessary or useful at the Implementation Phase to sign a second, more detailed term sheet outlining the agreed main substantive characteristics, actions, undertakings, and milestones of the restructuring, to be reflected in the main restructuring documentation (e.g., an overlay agreement). At the same time, if this can be avoided then proceeding to the final restricting agreement could save time and costs.

agreed wind-up is under way, the agreed distributions of funds and creation of any indemnity reserve).

The restructuring of a regulated borrower may well include a parallel dialogue of agreeing the overall restructuring with the *regulator*, as well as making all required formal *regulatory filings* (e.g., for any equity and/or management changes which form part of the restructuring).

This process requires a high level of coordination and management of *many different players*, including:

- the various lenders themselves (possibly also broken into classes of lenders),
- external legal advisors to the lenders (or classes),
- external financial advisors to the lenders (or classes),
- the borrower and its management,
- main shareholders of the borrower,
- equity creditors (group companies) of the borrower,
- external legal and financial advisors to the borrower and main shareholders,
- local regulators,
- nonparticipating creditors and other stakeholders whose interests must be accounted for (e.g., depositors (in the case of a credit-institution borrower); tax authorities, bond or other securities holders, employees, depositors, customers, suppliers, lessors of equipment, real estate and/or other assets; etc.).

Those parties on the borrower side (including the main shareholder(s) and equity creditor(s)) who will be signatories to the final legal documentation must be carefully diligenced, to ensure their capacity and authority to enter into the restructuring agreement and ancillary documentation is appropriately vetted (ordinarily diligence will not be carried out on lenders). In some cases, certain lenders may require formal legal opinions to be issued on these parties' capacity and authority and/or the validity and enforceability of the main restructuring documentation.[2] If any additional new security or other credit support is provided as part of the restructuring, this must be diligenced, executed, and perfected.[3]

As a workout always bears the risk that it may unwind (e.g., if the restructuring plan is not adhered to or some other event leads to termination of the standstill [if it continues after financial close under the main restructuring

---

[2] *See* more detailed discussion on legal opinions in Chapter 11.

[3] *See* more detailed discussion on hardening periods for antecedent transactions, as well as the corporate benefit doctrine where third-party credit support is given as part of restricting.

agreement, e.g., in the case of an orderly wind-down]), then the lenders must also be prepared to deal with the impact of any subsequent insolvency proceedings on arrangements under the restructuring (e.g., possible claw-backs of payments, avoidance of security for new money, potential risk of claims of shadow directorship/vicarious liability, etc.). Accordingly, a broad understanding of the local insolvency regime is critical, and risk-mitigation measures must be taken.

Since a workout is a voluntary contractual arrangement requiring the unanimity of all signatories, the management of the process of drafting and negotiating legal documentation amongst a large number of signing parties assumes a paramount role. Transaction leadership and their external counsel must therefore be vigilant in keeping this process under strict control—or it will easily get out of hand, driving costs up and possibly impacting on timing.

Whereas cross-border loan documents, despite their impressive length and complexity (and sometimes appearing in unfamiliar languages), have tended to become standardized in recent years with the use of well-developed precedents (such as LMA standardized lending documentation), restructuring arrangements are often *highly bespoke and complex*. Each transaction is unique and will usually attract a high level of attention from various departments of lender institutions (legal, banking, credit). Counsel cannot count on lenders to digest restructuring documentation quickly and quietly. The process of document circulation often results in a swell of comments, questions, and queries.

Lender leadership must drive home to the greater lender group the need for an *appropriately limited level of comments* aimed at big-picture issues only, on all workout documents (including the standstill and final restructuring document[s]). That said, the process of lender leadership's review of rounds with counsel in advance of circulation to the larger lender group will usually assist in minimizing the nature and number of comments from lenders (though not always).

## The Role of Lender Leadership—The Driving Force

Lender leadership must demonstrate to resolve and cultivate the larger group's trust and confidence in managing the process and mastery of commercial, financial, and legal issues. Although the lender leadership does not occupy a legal fiduciary position as such,[4] nonetheless they should strive to demonstrate to lenders that they are in control of the issues and de facto acting

---

[4] This should in any event be disclaimed in the coordinating committee appointment.

diligently, selflessly, and neutrally, in the best interests of all lenders. To quote Maestro Dudamel once more, they must *guide and inspire.*

Lender leadership must be prepared to maintain control of the process, to monitor implementation, and continually communicate with individual lenders. They must speak frequently, divide tasks between themselves, and operate a communications strategy aimed at guiding and inspiring all parties to play their required parts in harmony. A high level of so-called "*emotional intelligence,*" listening and communications skills will play to the leadership's advantage.

A successful closing will also require a *high level of availability* by lender leadership to work on the transaction. Certain leaders may have stronger relationships with some lenders, and thus identifying these "right chemistry" relationships at the outset can be useful. The lender leadership will also act as a sounding board for each other on key issues as the restructuring proposals and final agreement are negotiated with the borrower, its shareholders, and their counsel. Accordingly, regular meetings and discussions of negotiation issues between the lead lenders are critical. In this respect, a well-organized coordinating committee may well achieve success more quickly than a sole lead lender.

The personality traits and the behavior of a leader in a restructuring deserve a brief comment. As in many other activities, the best leaders are informed and confident, but not overbearing. They build consensus on the objectives and work alongside the other parties to get there. They moderate and facilitate. They encourage all to participate in the discussion. They listen far more than they talk. They don't impose their positions on the group. They respect other's opinions. When necessary, they deliver the bad news and demand hard decisions. Think about Kristi versus Ursula's Advisor. Or Martin versus Colin. That gets the point across.

## The Role of External Counsel

Likewise, it is essential that external counsel apply effective modern *legal project management (LPM)* practice to achieve an appropriate balance of quality, cost, and time and meet the critical path for implementation of the restructuring.[5] The establishment of a properly broad and detailed scope of works, capped budget and reasonable assumptions is essential. The use of planning templates and reports (e.g., Gantt charts, project plans, and

---

[5] Effective LPM is generally considered to enhance the delivery of legal services by using appropriate talent, technology, and processes. It can be critical in complex transactions.

roadmaps) can be helpful. A high level of coordination must take place between the two main legal teams (the lender and borrower side, respectively), and any negotiation impasses should be handled immediately by calls between principals with their counsel (the lender leadership on the one hand and borrower/main shareholder management on the other).

The level of specialization and seniority of the staffing of the external counsel's team of lawyers, and their capacity and commitment to work on the transaction, will be critical. Although it undoubtedly bears on legal costs, it is far preferable for lenders and borrowers alike to have senior, experienced counsel than less expensive—but less experienced—juniors. That said, the justifiable delegation of responsibility for more clerical and administrative tasks (e.g., running CPs, administering circulation and assembly of execution copies, etc.) will be critical for keeping legal costs down.

As an aside, the authors have observed, there can be a tendency in some outside law firms toward "over-lawyering" and "one-upmanship."[6] In the context of a restructuring transaction, such a proclivity can be counterproductive and generate much higher costs and delays. It is imperative that the transactional leadership instruct outside local advisors to avoid such behavior and to come to quick, practical solutions. The ability of counsel to do so is essential in a workout. They must avoid wasting time on trivial issues and instead focus on key business and legal issues.

Structuring and drafting solutions must be appropriate to the size and nature of the restructuring and also feasible in the context of the emerging market and its legal and regulatory framework.

The agreement at the outset of the transaction (at case set-up) of a detailed, broad *scope of work with capped budgets (subject to reasonable assumptions) for both lenders' and borrower's counsel* can help to control this tendency. At the same time, the structure of having a single external legal advisor for all lenders (or a class of lenders) usually results in substantial client value for the lenders.[7]

-&-

Now let's look at how these concepts may be applied in practice during the Implementation Phase.

---

[6] In one transaction on which the authors collaborated, opposing counsel reverted with so many additional comments in each drafting round, that the authors could not help but chuckle and be reminded of the well-known children's book, "If you Give a Mouse a Cookie" (L. Numeroff, 1985). Each time an issue was addressed, it seemed opposing counsel would revert with a hydra of multiple additional new, often unexpected comments. The process of trading drafts can sometimes present a slippery slope—where the principal negotiators must be prepared to step in and ensure that the process remains on track.

[7] In the authors' experience, lenders' external counsel's fees in workouts can often be relatively modest when compared to the fees of counsel for the borrower.

# Application in Practice: Case Studies

At this point, it might appear logical to think back over the whole of our journey with Kristi and the Bank of Commerce and the rest, and then consider the various lessons learned.

But this time, in lieu of delving directly into our case studies, let's first focus on the main "takeaways"/"lessons learned" which we hope to impart to the reader during this last phase of closing and implementing the restructuring agreement. Let us highlight three and then return to the National Goods case, then two further short episodes for reinforcement.

In the Bank of Commerce case, these were:

- **Rogue creditors (holdouts)—"Don't Hesitate to Pull Strings if Needed."** Edinburgh Partners present the quintessential rogue creditor phenomenon. Before Monique's intervention, Colin and Todd's disruptive behavior was not just a minor obstacle, but indeed an existential threat to a consensual restructuring.[8] Even afterward, with or without Colin's complicity, Todd's play to achieve a superior outcome relative to the rest of the lenders would have likely derailed the process. Kristi and Martin recognized this danger. To have begun intensive negotiations on transaction documentation and operational governance under the circumstances would have been futile at best. Edinburgh Partner's action had to be neutralized. Fortunately, Peter was true to his word. The moral suasion of the leader of a major global, public-sector financial institution, from whose goodwill Peter's business could benefit in future, played a significant role. Perhaps in the real world, we cannot imagine chief executives of development finance institutions involving themselves in such detail in a simple private-sector restructuring case. That aside, the message is that C-suite or other senior-level influencers' intervention can break logjams when nothing else can. Use it sparingly, but do not hesitate when absolutely necessary.
- **Unexpected threats—"It Ain't Over till It's Over"** (*Yogi Berra*). Until the ink on the definitive, binding agreement is dry, assume nothing. Things can change in a split second. For justified or opportunistic reasons, lenders (as well as borrower and shareholders) do drop bombs in this very last phase. Changes in external circumstances (negative market developments), and/or in the borrower's financial or operating condition (updated financial results) may well justifiably warrant the reopening of negotiations. Further,

---

[8] Recall, when one rogue lender calls a default, accelerates and enforces, this will ordinarily trigger a domino effect of cross defaults, landing the borrower in formal insolvency proceedings.

the laborious process of converting summary terms into the detailed, final documentation can uncover issues that force renewed debate. These are all reasonable and justifiable causes to question the original deal blueprint. However, there are parties who consciously play a game of demanding preferential concessions at the last moment. Their inspiration is the belief that the other parties may be more accommodative when the finish line is within sight. The "new guy on the block" syndrome (when a lender changes staff on the deal and the new individual[s] move to reopen negotiations on material elements, or when a lender sells its loan on the secondary market[9]) can crop up. This does happen, thankfully not in every deal, but enough to be wary. For example, the authors collaborated on one transaction where a lender demanded changes to the deal on a perfunctory call intended merely to confirm the delivery of execution copies and to thank all parties for their cooperation, literally 37 minutes before a central bank-imposed deadline to avoid liquidation. After running the clock down to roughly 15 minutes to the end, the lender yielded in the face of a willingness of the other lenders to blow the deal up on a matter of principal. Not all sneak attacks are so close to the wire and may necessitate flexibility, when possible.

- **Operational governance and performance—"Boots on the Ground will Drive Success."** Many transactions contain two distinct elements, "financial" and what we will call "operational." The first are the standard balance sheet actions such as, for example, extending maturities, adjusting interest rates, even new money. The second, the operational, consists of actions such as corporate restructurings, M&A transactions, products re-engineering, and the like. In our Bank of Commerce case, these latter elements were: (i) the wind-down of the loan book; (ii) paying off or transferring the depositors to another bank; and (iii) the closing down of the bank at the end of the process. To complete these actions, the parties had to maintain the Bank of Commerce as a fully regulatory-compliant, going concern until the very end, which required maintaining liquidity and solvency levels, the borrowers' belief that their obligations needed to be honored, and commitment of staff. As described above, the parties agreed on the objectives, the process, and, crucially, the governance (i.e., the decision-making) of the process. The process worked well. The deposit issue was resolved (they were transferred to another bank as a part of the divestiture of the branch operations in the capital city). The loan book

---

[9] In some more developed emerging markets, the appearance of a secondary market has resulted in the situation where lender parties can and do change regularly. The final holders of claims under the loans do not necessarily share the same long-term goals of the original lenders. Alliance of interests can become a major issue when reaching a deal.

was run down in a way that maintained the illusion of a going concern (selective new lending) from close to the end, when a sale of the "rump" bank to local investors was closed (and hence achieved a premium for the lenders and neutralized the risk of residual tax and other local liabilities). In closing, the authors (a banker and a lawyer) stress the need for *lenders to know their limits*. Some lenders lack the necessary operational experience to manage a wind-down like the Bank of Commerce. In this case, the Lenders engaged a specialist firm to act as liquidation monitor to administer the process. This firm was mandated to monitor the local staff of the Bank of Commerce and to liaise with the lenders. In conformity with regulation (and to avoid shadow director liability), they did not actually replace the local executives, nor did they make operating decisions or have the right to give binding directives. Instead, they strived, on the one hand, to inspire the local management to act in the interests of all parties to the wind-down, and on the other, to persuade lenders not to force counterproductive actions on local management. When considering the great success of the Bank of Commerce recovery efforts, the true heroes were not the lenders, but rather the local management and the external specialist.

## Continuation of National Goods Case: Implementation

In the National Goods case, we saw that the first two issues appear to have been effectively neutralized before the documentation phase. This positive outcome reflected the realistic and cooperative approach employed by the company and the lenders. Lender "issues" were identified early and resolved. All the parties displayed flexibility in addressing potential problems by reaching practical compromises.

In this case, these two proved easy, but the third figured as a K2 peak to be summited. Recall that following the decision to exit the retail business segment, the company had to face the daunting task of developing a new line of environmentally friendly white goods to compete with the new entrants. Can they actually do this? The failure to reverse the loss of market share will threaten National Good's future. The ultimate success of the financial restructuring is therefore dependent on the success of the company's product re-engineering.

The lenders may believe they understand how the company's operations should appear once the re-engineering is completed. However, their knowledge and practical experience in the specific industry are limited. As a result, they must resist the temptation to act in an area where they are not competent. It is essential that they find and empower qualified outside parties to be their eyes and ears and (when necessary) their mouthpiece in the company-led process of operational restructuring and product re-engineering.

In what follows here, we argue that this is the correct approach. The failure of the lenders to engage such external experts to monitor the operational restructuring a product re-engineering is a serious flaw in the approach to the restructuring.

In our discussion in this chapter, we will not venture into the "kitchen" to see how their work proceeds on a daily basis. Instead, note will only be taken when the financial implications of the work are inconsistent with a successful outcome to the restructuring solution.

With this introduction, let's now take a quick look at how National Goods plays out during its Implementation Phase.

Subject to diligence and negotiating binding agreements, the company was supposed to undergo a joint operational/balance sheet restructuring: (1) operational: selling all international operations, curbing domestic retail expansion, and exploring partnerships to reduce retail burden, and (2) balance sheet: securitizing receivables, undertaking a rights issue to pay down debt, together with lenders (all but one) moving amortizations back by two years and agreeing modified covenants, and receiving a new working capital cash injection from shareholders.

What now awaits us, and how do the "Good, the Bad and the Ugly" differ in their approaches?

# The "Good"

## Organization and Governance

### Organization

The lenders establish a four-member steering committee. The steering committee in turn creates working groups on key process functions. These functions include: (1) legal, (2) technical market advisors, (3) financial modeling and structuring, and (4) communications. A member of the steering committee acts as the chair of each such working group and calls in other lenders to participate in the work.

The respective working groups immediately begin their work.

**Legal:** The day the standstill is signed, the working group immediately sits down with one or more lenders' in-house counsel to short-list law firms based on their prior experiences. Open to the possibility of working with new firms, still, they know that tested firms with solid track records are preferred. Yes, cost is a factor. But far more critical are: (i) proactive, pragmatic, results-driven service, (ii) a team of senior lawyers (partner/of counsel) who play an active, hands-on role (not delegating to unexperienced juniors), (iii) expertise in cross-border emerging markets workouts, (iv) in-depth knowledge of insolvency, corporate, and other relevant local-law issues (either via a local subcontractor or more preferably (if adequately qualified) a local branch), (v) ability to deal effectively with a group of disparate lenders, and (vi) ability to collaborate well with the borrower's external counsel (whom she has already sussed out and even interviewed). They narrow the options down, picking either a single favorite tested firm (or a small group of firms) meeting these key criteria. Having elaborated a scope of works with her in-house counsel, they finalize a well-drafted RFP with the maximum amount of available information in it, attach the term sheet and hit "send." The engagement (with suitably capped budgets and reasonable assumptions) is closed expeditiously, with the understanding that the process also ensures that the borrower undertakes binding cost-coverage obligations and pays deposits against fees. Post engagement, this working group oversees outside counsel's drafting of documentation, negotiation with the borrower, and the lenders' approvals.

**Technical Advisor(s)**: With equal urgency, the working group undertakes their search for one or more technical market advisors. Similar process steps are present, with an enhanced emphasis on the ability of the advisor to interact constructively with their counterparts at the borrower level, under operating principles agreed between the lenders and the borrower, covering access, monitoring, consultation, and reporting. In-country experience is highly important, as language and cultural affinity are crucial to a successful mandate. Post engagement, this working group oversees the work of the external technical advisor's work and keeps the other working groups informed. The fundamental principle underlying the work is a reliance on expert opinion and professional fulfillment of these commercial and market aspects of the transaction.

**Financial Modeling and Structuring**: Whilst much would have already been done, it is essential that there be a coordinated effort amongst the lenders and with the borrower, under which the parties create and maintain one version of the "truth" (a financial model) to permit all to talk the same language when undertaking the structuring work which will form the basis of the restructuring terms and conditions. The lenders' working group and a designated team drawn from the company combine to carry out these tasks and to consult with/seek approval from their respective stakeholders. This working group liaises closely with the legal and technical working groups throughout the development of the final restructuring plan.

**Communications**: This working group has two major functions: (i) it centralizes the input of the various working groups into timely and coherent summaries for the steering committee and the full-lenders group; and (ii) it coordinates formal steering committee and/or full lender group communications with the borrower and external parties. Timely and transparent communications amongst the lenders are an essential building block of a successful restructuring effort.

Following their formation, the steering committee has a videoconference with the borrower's CEO and the relevant staff to underscore the need to instruct all stakeholders to work constructively with the lenders' representatives and advisors to ensure successful work and the avoidance of roadblocks/needless "point scoring." The message is sent: "We are one team now." A communications policy and procedure is agreed between the two sides.

Subsequent steering committee meetings are used as a forum for working group reports and discussion of their input, from which updates and requests for approvals to the full-lenders group are formed. Timing of all meetings and calls follow no preset formula, but reflect the requirements of the transaction. Normally, a weekly regime at the least is seen. The frequency of meetings is critical to ensure that the process is kept on track and to mitigate against the risk of intervening circumstances which might derail the process.

## Governance

The formation of the steering committee and the working groups was the result of informal conversations amongst the lenders, with the largest creditors volunteering. An informal charter is agreed and circulated in email form.[10]

Ultimately, decisions must be unanimous. One lender objecting to a matter, however trivial, can block a restructuring agreement. However, efforts are made to arrive at a working arrangement amongst the lenders whereunder individual lenders agree to defer to the majority on less important matters,

---

[10] The establishment and governance of such creditor committees can be more formal, documented by a binding legal agreement (e.g., based on LMA precedents—see Chapter 11), or not, depending on the circumstances and the requirements of the lenders.

whilst retaining their rights to object on what they perceive as material ones (i.e., to require unanimous consent).[11] For several "high-maintenance" lenders, the steering committee assigns "buddies" from the group. The selection reflects the committee personalities who are best "suited" to those lenders (e.g., age, nationality, past relationship, etc.). The designated buddy is to make regular, individual calls to their assigned lender, to listen carefully to the lender's concerns, and to implement these (where practicable), reminding the lender, the alternative of a National Goods bankruptcy would be disastrous for all, and recoveries would be far less (possibly zero). The lender's organizational structure and decision-making process should be understood, so that in the future if escalation is necessary, a roadmap is at hand.[12]

## Execution

The transaction's blueprint had been elaborated and agreed at a high level in the earlier discussions with the National Good's management. However, the execution process will take time. A formal three-month standstill agreement is drafted and signed.

The next task is to set this previous understanding to paper in the form of a term sheet, to be drafted by counsel. The input of the working groups' diligence and analysis (technical/market and financial structuring teams) to the legal working group and counsel is used to refine certain details of the transaction blueprint, most notably key elements such as funding (e.g., the required rights issue and shareholder-funded new working capital facility, both of whose completion will be made a condition precedent to the overall restructuring agreement) and refinancing (e.g., existing senior debt) types and amounts, repayment schedules, economic terms, covenants, undertakings, and the like.[13] The term sheet is discussed initially "informally" between the steering committee and the company, before being circulated to the full-lenders group.[14]

---

[11] What distinguishes "less important" from "substantive" matters? This will vary according to the deal, the circumstances and the personalities of the lenders (institution and people). However, as examples, a choice of the precise value in a financial covenant may be something the lenders can likely agree goes according to the majority view, whilst the exchange ratio in a debt to equity swap needs unanimous consent.

[12] Think back to the Bank of Commerce case and the "escalation" first by Maya with Todd's boss, Colin, and eventually by Martin and Monique with Colin's chief executive, Peter.

[13] For example, to cover the sale of the retail operations and ensured these are treated either at least on "as is" terms or where possible covered by suitable M&A warranties and indemnities (W&I) insurance, leaving zero post-closing residual liability of the borrower from those sales.

[14] This order of review depends on the parties and the transaction. If the steering committee feels it more prudent then the full-lenders review can predate sharing the document with the borrower.

Once the term sheet is agreed, the parties move to the drafting of the overall restructuring agreement and the ancillary supporting legal documentation (e.g., subordination agreement for the working capital facility, escrow accounts, inter-creditor agreement for the refinanced senior debt, etc.). Counsel will have already collected its diligence for appropriate legal opinions. The closing checklist and process documentation are finalized.

During the lender review of the term sheet and subsequently the restructuring agreement package, the legal working group aims continually to give the message to all lenders to focus on big-picture issues only. The process is of course far from perfect. As expected, there are delays along the way. The parties end up having to extend the standstill once during the process (this is not difficult, given that lenders see that progress on implementation is happening before their eyes). One raging fire occurs—two lenders' management nearly renege due to the one holdout's retaining its original repayment terms. After lengthy individual calls, these lenders are neutralized.

The final restructuring agreement is circulated, covered in a well-rehearsed all lenders' conference call with external counsel (for which a script has been prepared). The execution copy is finalized, circulated, and signed up. All CPs are met (including the new shareholder cash and the effectiveness of the subordinated shareholder working capital facility, backed by a local bank standby letter of credit), and the finish line is crossed.

External counsel submits its final bill (with modest, albeit justifiable overruns from the additional unexpected negotiations with problematic lenders). These are quickly settled by the borrower.

## Five Keys to Success

Although many elements assisted in the success of the restructuring, nonetheless we may summarize the main ones as follows:

- Achievement of a shared vision amongst the lenders and the borrower,
- Sound technical expertise (relevant, external advisors, and service providers),
- Strong transaction leadership (the steering committee),
- Establishment of an open communications channel between the lenders and the borrower, and
- Effective transaction management (the working groups).

## The "Bad" or "Ugly"

Not quite the same as above. The steering committee members forgot (or didn't know about) the Five Keys to Success (above).

Two full weeks passed after the standstill was signed before anything happened. No seasoned restructuring specialists were involved. Rather, relationship bankers remained the principal decision-makers and transaction leadership. They managed to engage an external firm between them, but they did not do their homework on the firm or put reasonable control measures in place over it. The firm had worked with one of the lenders previously on its original loan to National Goods Company (and hence had some cross-border finance experience). But it had never done a multi-lender workout deal before and had limited knowledge of the local legal system.

Poor instructions were given, no capped budget was established, cost-recovery obligations of the borrower were never put in place, the steering committee members did not maintain regular contacts, and lenders were unable to keep the process on track.

A draft restructuring agreement was produced, but after two rounds, no progress had been made. National Goods Company's and the lenders' group had run into impasses in drafting, engaging in legal "one-upmanship." A loose plan for sales of international retail assets was produced, and a buyer was found. But the sale price was subject to substantial hold-backs to cover post-closing liabilities on reps and warranties. More time passed.

As one could guess, in a blink of an eye the standstill period ran out. Would the lenders agree to extend the standstill at this point, given the clear lack of transaction leadership and virtually no progress? They went back and forth on this by email for several weeks. More time passed. Two lenders then backed out, stating that their management had no confidence in the process (the lenders had some collateral and counted on foreclosure).

National Goods Company's CEO then emailed the lenders, informing them of his obligation to file for voluntary bankruptcy, citing rules against wrongful trading, and his personal liability. The company went into a 6-month "observation" period under local bankruptcy rules. At the end of the day it was liquidated, with (woefully) insufficient assets to pay creditors. In the meanwhile, quickly following the CEO's email the lenders' external counsel sent its bill to the steering committee member who had arranged its engagement. The invoice exceeded the firm's original estimate by multiples.

## Further Cases to Illustrate

To reinforce how these differences can play out, let's consider two episodes and examine each using our "Good, Bad and Ugly" approach.

## First Case

A capital-constrained corporate borrower announces a moratorium of principal payments. The solution requires debt reduction and/or a combination of new external equity and a significant extension of the repayment tenor.

## The "Good"

A core group of lenders step up to address the situation in a coordinated manner. A standstill is agreed to avoid acceleration. The core group (i.e., the steering committee) identifies an impasse very early. They determine that the existing shareholders are not capable of subscribing to a sufficiently large rights issue today. Moreover, at current valuations, they are opposed to external equity. At the same time, certain lenders are not willing to consider the debt reduction alternative, and others indicate, for questionable reasons, that they are not prepared to participate in a restructuring.

A diligence exercise by an external team, well experienced in the geography and industry of the borrower, demonstrates that the fundamentals of the business are sound and the longer term prospects promising. Following a series of frank and open discussions between the steering committee and the company, the parties sketch out a plan consisting of: (i) neutralizing the uncooperative lenders by an agreement to have the borrower buy back their debt at a deep discount at the time of completion of the overall restructuring, using existing shareholder funds; (ii) hiring an investment bank to raise hybrid capital in the form of convertible, subordinated debt, market soundings around which are promising; (iii) obtaining a shareholder commitment for a limited rights issue; and (iv) having the existing senior lenders agree to refinance their debt for a longer tenor.

The steering committee approaches the rest of the lenders to sell them on the deal. When one of the uncooperative lenders refuses to wait and threatens to accelerate their debt immediately, a member of the steering committee arranges a successful intervention at the lender's executive management level.

Working groups are organized to oversee the execution of the new funding elements and the debt buyback, and to document the overall transaction.

Periodic calls with the mandated investment bank, amongst the lenders, and between the steering committee and the borrower/shareholders drive an orderly process. Despite the usual hiccups, the parties achieve closure with only one extension of the standstill to give the investment back sufficient time to complete their mandate.

## The "Bad" or the "Ugly"

A leadership cohort (a steering committee) fails to coalesce out of the broader lender group. Whilst several calls amongst the lenders are held, there is no coherence in the discussions. No agreement is reached with respect to organization, governance, objectives, etc. Separate conversations develop between lenders and the borrower.

The threatening tone from the uncooperative lenders results in a hardening of the position of the borrower and its shareholders. After a period of time egged on by the threat of default notices, a subset of lenders attempts to engage with the borrower. Operating without an independent view of the business to support a realistic financial solution, the two sides talk across a wide divide. They fail to agree a common vision of the future, without which the outline of a solution is elusive.

The borrower then engages an external advisor whose restructuring plan is submitted to the lenders. This acts as a catalyst for the lenders to convene as a group and engage with the borrower. The plan calls for an immediate standstill and a definitive agreement under which a portion of the debt to be forgiven and the tenor for the remaining debt to be extended. No allowance is considered for potential rogue lenders. This impasse results in several lenders declaring defaults and accelerating their debt.

Before the more sober lenders can intervene, the borrower enters into a form of protective formal insolvency proceeding in local courts.

Consider: (i) no one took charge; (ii) the two sides did not establish an effective working dialogue; (iii) through inaction to inform an updated, objective, and informed view of the borrower's future business prospects, the lenders failed to achieve confidence in a going-concern scenario; (iv) the more responsible lenders and the borrower did not address adequately the threat of rogue lenders; and (v) once the threat of acceleration materialized, the lenders lacked the means to intervene in time.

## Second Case

A second-tier commercial bank has experienced a slow and steady loss of deposits over the past year, reflecting an industry wide flight to quality. Borrowings from the country's central bank's discount window have compensated for the deposit loss. In local banking circles, it is well known that the discount window is intended for temporary and occasional liquidity support, but not to be a source of structural liquidity.

## The "Good"

The shareholder reaches out bilaterally to a core subset of their lenders to discuss solutions. One lender suggests a more coordinated approach, drawing on the bank's major lenders. Whilst at first the bank demurs, eventually they agree. The parties decide to engage a well-known regional financial sector advisory firm to undertake an analysis of the local banking market and the strategic alternatives available for the bank.

Two months later, their detailed report is submitted. The crux of their findings is the bank will face a challenging future without a strong, strategic, or financial partner. A change in control is likely in both cases, given valuations. The alternative however is the untenable continuation or even increase in the dependence on central bank liquidity support. It is only a matter of time before the central bank intervenes.

These core funders agree to support this effort by maintaining their outstandings, whilst the bank discreetly pursues a merger. The leading local, financial institutions M&A house is engaged for this purpose. The management of the bank confidentially advises the central bank of this action, a step which is well received. In time, a buyer is identified. Following exploratory diligence, an offer is made. The buyer requests that a critical mass of the existing lenders commit to remain with the bank, post-transaction. This requirement is fulfilled. Following confirmatory diligence, documentation, and regulatory approvals, the deal is done.

Post-transaction, the "new" bank pays off its central bank funding and separately is rewarded with a ratings upgrade.

## The "Bad" or the "Ugly"

The shareholder attempts to keep this potentially threatening development from their core lenders, for fear that this news might spark a run. Requests are made to lenders for increases in the existing facilities, with only modest success and to new providers, with equally unimpressive results.

Rates on deposits are increased as a means of slowing withdrawals, an action which is somewhat successful, but with the result that the bank's net interest margin begins to be pressured. And still the outstandings with the central bank remain too high. The lenders have failed to monitor the bank's financial condition with sufficient rigor to have detected these developments.

When the local deposit insurance corporation announces the decision to intervene and force a merger, the lenders are both shocked and unprepared. At this late date, they attempt to fashion a solution. The government rejects it.

The treatment of the senior lenders in the eventual acquisition of the bank by a larger competitor results in a write-down of the senior lenders debt.

Conclusions? The problems return us to one of the key early elements of the successful restructuring process, namely effective credit monitoring during the Pre-Restructuring Phase. Admittedly, the bank's shareholder's failure to come clean with its core lenders contributed to the fiasco. But the lenders should have been on top of the bank's deteriorating liquidity position. With a bit of sleuthing, all the information could have either been found in the public domain or discovered through rigorous reporting requirements. By the time the lenders woke up to the existential threat, it was too late.

# Conclusions

And what general conclusions might we draw from all of our case studies as regards the Implementation Phase?

There are several, but perhaps foremost is that experienced, committed transaction leadership must *take full ownership* of the deal to ensure that it is executed properly. For this purpose, *constant communication, pro-activeness, flexibility, and speed are essential*. The likelihood is that the transaction will not be simple. It will have many moving parts and a large number of players with divergent and often conflicting interests. Players can change their minds in a second. Exogenous events or other circumstances can intervene quickly. Lender leadership must drive the deal process forward. And the role of *experienced, effective external advisers* (legal and financial) in executing cannot be overstated.

Whilst these sound like platitudes, they are more important than ever in an emerging market consensual restructuring, where the supportive insolvency system infrastructure of developed markets is often absent.

# Part III

**Acts of God and Other Exogenous Events**

# 9

# A Practical Approach to Exogenous Events

**Abstract** At the time of publication of this book, many countries have experienced fresh COVID-19 lockdowns. New variants have started to develop and spread across the globe, driving a resurgence of further infections, hospitalizations, and deaths. Covid-19 represents an extreme example of an exogenous shock. Natural disasters (Acts of God), wars, revolutions, etc., are further examples and are often referred to in common parlance as "force majeure." This chapter lays out a methodology for approaching workouts in such situations. To frame the discussion, the chapter begins with a focus on the distinction between proximate and fundamental, and exogenous and endogenous drivers, relying again on the manufacturing case study and the opening Bank of Commerce tale. Thereafter, the two exogenous shocks (a tropical cyclone and the pandemic) are presented. In each case, the work analyzes the impact on and restructuring requirements of: (i) a financial institution; and (ii) a manufacturing and services company, respectively. The special characteristics of these cases include the: (i) the speed and pervasiveness of the shocks; (ii) the uncertainty of their degree and duration; and (iii) the challenges to devise effective mitigation techniques into the structure due to weak predictability of the subsequent income stream, liquidity, and solvency of borrowers. The chapter ends with a discussion of three basic alternative approaches for restructurings in cases of uncertainty.

**Keywords** Act of God · Antecedent transaction · Bankruptcy · Borrower · Consensual restructuring · Coordinating committee · Corporate debt · Debt · Debtor · Cash flow · COVID-19 · Credit analysis · Currency peg ·

Distressed debt · Financial statements · Exogenous shock · Emerging
market · Frontier market · Holdout lender · INSOL II · INSOL principles ·
Insolvency · Lender leadership · Non-performing loans · Pre-insolvency ·
Restructure · Restructuring · Restructuring plan · Standstill · Steering
committee · Workout

# Introduction

At the time of publication of this book, many countries have experienced
fresh COVID-19 lockdowns. New variants have started to develop and
spread across the globe, driving a resurgence of further infections, hospitalizations, and deaths. Premature relaxation of mobility restrictions and farcical
political opposition to sensible precautions such as facial masks and social
distancing has also contributed to giving the pandemic new legs. The vaccination campaign gives hope, although hoarding and export controls are leaving
many countries with inadequate access to supplies.[1]

This is especially acute in emerging markets, hitting many hard. Limited
financial resources prevent well-meaning governments from protecting their
populaces. The attainment of global, herd immunity, the likely impossible
but necessary condition for the elimination of the scourge, recedes into the
future.

Several weeks ago, one of the authors joined a restructuring meeting as
a nonpartisan restructuring advisor, a meeting moderator. Around the table
were the borrower and roughly a dozen lenders. A one-year deferral agreement
would expire in just over six weeks.

The borrowera diversified manufacturing and services company with international operations—painted a somber picture of the near-term outlook.
Sales were picking-up, but nowhere near enough to return the business to
pre-pandemic levels. Production was at less than a third of where volumes
were in December 2019. As worrisome was the increasingly unwillingness
of their customers to rebuild their inventories and commit to longer term
contracts. The future was simply too uncertain for them. Would their governments reimpose lockdowns? When would consumers be confident about their
economic prospects to begin spending again on nonessentials? When would
the pandemic be a memory and not a continued day-to-day threat?

The two sides expressed the same sense of near bewilderment. In normal
markets, the business could easily service its debts. Today, interest payments

---

[1] Vaccine distribution has also become subject to politicization, which has interfered in a rational and
unified policy approach by governments.

were being made, just barely, by drawing down cash balances. This would soon end without a pick-up in business activity. Principle amortization was out of the question. What to do?

One group argued for another deferral (albeit shorter and assuming the shareholders committed to keeping interest current). Most agreed with this position, arguing any other course was foolish given the uncertainty around the path of the pandemic and the economic recovery. Better to wait. Act only with facts in hand.

A second, much smaller group (actually, just one creditor) challenged this view. Yes, the representative admitted, the trajectory and timing of the pandemic were unclear. However, a return to pre-pandemic levels of sales and cash flow was unlikely, given the probable, long-term changes in consumption patterns as societies adapted to the post-COVID world. Better to "bite the bullet" now and begin the painful process of downsizing or even closing down selected businesses.

Two days later, after much drama, the first group's argument won out. Kicking the can down the road was clearly the expedient and politically prudent course of action. Moving today toward a corporate and debt restructuring with so much uncertainty was deemed imprudent. How would this all look if the economy and currently afflicted market segments snapped back and exceeded expectations? Investments lost, careers damaged. Only lawyers and the investment bankers would benefit.

Who was right? Time will tell, of course.

For our purposes, how do we characterize the outcome? Realistic and positive. The lenders' agreement to defer principle again in return for a maintenance of interest payments reflected the reality of where the two sides sat. Ultimately, the holdout lender agreed to conform to the consensus view, rather than going rogue and threatening the bigger picture. Additionally, the parties agreed that strategic planning to scope out potential downsizing and divestitures would continue, with lenders' representatives involved, should this become necessary. Lastly, a smaller working group was formed to explore financial solutions to the likely scenarios, again with representatives of both sides. The result was positive overall. The parties had met and, theatrics aside, worked together to find a consensual, interim solution which maintained an orderly path to an eventual "least bad" outcome for all parties.

To be sure, achieving a successful restructuring in the aftershock of an exogenous event, and in particular one whose effects continue to impact on an economy, the borrower, its suppliers, and customers, is a far greater challenge than restructuring when the impact has already subsided and a clear path forward is visible.

In this chapter we have endeavored to lay out a methodology for approaching workouts in unclear circumstances. As a first step, we will compare restructurings following Acts of God with other situations. We will then consider this by several case studies. Finally, we will lay out some thoughts on approaching workouts in the face of continuing uncertainty.

# Developing a Practical Approach to Restructurings Following Exogenous Events

In the prior cases discussed in the book, the story of the "why" a restructuring was necessary varied. Let's quickly review two of those cases to see how: the Bank of Commerce and the National Goods Company. Whilst there may be various alternative ways of analyzing each case, let us first consider the difference between "fundamental" and "*proximate*"[2] causes for each case.

In the Bank of Commerce case, we saw:

- a slowdown in global growth,
- a decline in the demand for copper,
- decreases in export revenues leading to a weakening in the country's balance of payments and FX reserves, with pressures building up on the currency peg (heightening the need for central bank intervention) to the point where the peg was abandoned,
- falls in copper-related tax proceeds and overall aggregate demand, employment, and the like, with a knock-on effect on operating cash flows within the commercial sector,
- the combination of the above exploiting structural balance sheet vulnerabilities in the financial sector, including the Bank of Commerce, hence resulting in increases in nonperforming loans, lower profitability, and the like,
- critically, the absence of corrective measures from shareholders and management to cure actual or prospective covenant breaches, which led to lenders' questioning the institution's future, and tightening of liquidity as a result, and
- payment defaults looming.

---

[2] We use these terms from the economic standpoint: fundamental meaning the deeper cause, and proximate meaning the more immediate cause. By way of example, Johnny loses his temper when his mother will not allow him to go outside and play with his friends. He throws a ball, and it knocks over a vase. The fundamental cause of the broken vase is Johnny's emotional reaction to his mother's action, whilst his act of throwing the ball is the proximate cause.

By contrast, in the National Goods Company case, we saw:

- a singular decline in competitiveness of the company's product line, as management ignored the need to adapt to increased public focus on ecologically friendly products,
- a failure to understand the growing need for retail outlets to support sales with discounts and extended customer financing terms,
- despite the foregoing, the managements launching a strategy to move into the retail space both at home and abroad,
- funding of expansion primarily by debt (rather than equity), which markedly increased leverage,
- underperformance of sales and tightening of gross margin, reflecting competition from more-energy and water-efficient products,
- a build-up of inventory and receivables,
- a plunge of operating cash flow due to the forgoing, and
- consequently an increase in working capital funding requirements combined with debt from the retail expansion, straining NGC's financial condition to the point of covenant breaches and approaching payment defaults.

In Bank of Commerce, the "fundamental" cause was the copper market's impact on the economy, whilst the "proximate" causes were the knock-on effects on the bank's financial condition and performance. For National Goods, a set of management failures arguably constituted both the "fundamental" and the "proximate" causes.

Another perspective from which to evaluate causality is the distinction between "*exogenous*" (i.e., external) and "*endogenous*" (i.e., internal) factors.

From above, we can surmise that the material driver for the Bank of Commerce was exogenous—global demand for copper—whilst for National Goods, endogenous—failure to adapt the product line to change and a misconceived expansion campaign.

The word "shock" is used frequently, along with the terms exogenous or external, to describe events that happen unexpectedly and outside the control of a business, household, or individual. In the Bank of Commerce case, the advisor said no one could have seen the Bank of Commerce's problems coming (or, to put it in the terms we are now using, "The bank's business was hit by an exogenous shock due to an unpredictable collapse in copper prices").

How fair is this? Are exogenous shocks really unexpected? Commodities like copper are cyclical. They rise and fall regularly. As an industrial metal, demand varies with the course of the global macroeconomy. Of course, the precise timing and the magnitude of volume and price declines can never be predicted with absolute certainty. Given this, can the management be excused for not seeing the problem coming? This is debatable.

Certainly, they can be excused for not knowing the exact timing of the coming shock, but not for having *failed to prepare* for the inevitability of the shock occurring at some point and taking steps to insulate their solvency and liquidity through a combination of a lower dividend pay-out ratio, building up pro-cyclical loan loss reserves and establishing longer duration, local currency funding in an economy so dependent on a single, highly cyclical export product.

Most of these "shocks" actually happen with some anticipation and some level of predictability. Hence, credit analysis and transaction structuring can and should focus on the potential vulnerabilities of these not entirely unexpected risk events (and ensure that they are adequately mitigated against).

But what about events that truly defy prediction (or at least are so rare in their occurrence that companies rarely take the extraordinary measures necessary to mitigate risk, especially if this would be enormously costly and/or highly impractical)? We typically think here of so-called "Acts of God." By this term we mean *events neither created nor controlled by humans*, that is, purely natural phenomena, which are both *extraordinary and unforeseeable*, and in respect of which it is *impossible or highly costly/impractical to prepare*. What are some examples of these?

In years past, we might have thought of a hurricane hitting the Caribbean, a typhoon ravaging the Philippines, the 2004 Indian Ocean earthquake and tsunami, more recurrent wildfires in the Western USA, and/or the 2011 Icelandic (Grimsvotn) volcano eruption which paralyzed air traffic. In the year 2020, we added the deadly global COVID-19 pandemic to the list.[3]

And are there others, where human beings play a role? Indisputably. Wars, terrorist acts, labor strikes, embargoes, riots, civil unrest, and other human-made occurrences abound. Their impact may not only be proximate for local businesses, but they may also play a fundamental role globally, when asymmetric information prevents market participants from not being aware until the event is already upon them. What is an example of this? Think of a

---

[3] One may of course look deeper into the question of whether the 2020 COVID-19 pandemic was truly "unpredictable" as such, given prior pandemics (most recently the 2002–2004 SARS outbreak, the 2009 H1N1 pandemic, the West African Ebola outbreak of 2014–2016) and global health authorities' steps to prepare for a global pandemic. Similarly, can climate change and its various impacts (increased heat, drought and insect outbreaks, electrical grid blackouts, flooding of coastal areas, increased wildfires, etc.) even be considered to be "unforeseeable," now that global scientists have irrefutably ascertained its existence and its trajectory of impact on human activity?

major terrorist attack which shuts down much of the productive capacity in Saudi Arabia and then causes a spike in world oil prices. These are likely less frequent than devastating weather or seismic events, but they still do happen. And in emerging markets, both natural and human-made exogenous shocks can have a brutal and immediate effect on domestic businesses.

There are distinct differences between human-made shocks and Acts of God. Let's continue with the discussion of oil. In the 2014–16 period, a combination of factors—some economic (supply and demand), some market-focused, arguably some political in nature—drove a severe contraction in global oil prices. Smart players saw it coming, months in advance. That's different from a tropical storm, where the warning period may be mere days. Additionally, Acts of God may be less discriminating than typical human-made exogenous shocks. A super-hurricane hitting the Bahamas devastates the entire economy, whilst an oil price spike might hit only parts of the economy, depending on the energy intensity of the sector, etc.

Our restructuring toolkit must make allowance for Acts of God and other exogenous events. The recommended approach must take into account key factors, to name a few:

- the *speed* with which such events hit,
- their *pervasiveness*,
- the *uncertainty of degree/duration* of impact on the *economy* and/or on the *borrower*,
- whether the borrower (or some third party) has acted *effectively to mitigate* the impact (and/or whether this may be done as part of the restructuring), and
- whether there will be a *clear, predictable stream of income and reliable expense/investment budget* allowing transaction leadership to determine whether the current debt is manageable or must somehow be modified—and if so, how.[4]

---

[4] The authors observe that Acts of God and other exogenous shocks frequently will prompt borrowers and lenders to refer back to their loan documents to determine how these documents (and/or applicable law) treat such events. On the borrower side, counsel will be instructed to examine whether some legal argument may be made to avoid a default and acceleration. On the lender side, counsel will be asked whether the event's impact gives rise to a right to suspend lending and/or call a default and accelerate (and, if present, to enforce on security or other credit support). The authors observe that although this depends on the specific facts of each case, as a general proposition, borrowers will probably be hard-pressed to find strong legal arguments in their favor. Likewise, lenders will ordinarily exercise great caution in exercising lending suspension and default/acceleration based purely on the provisions typically aimed at exogenous events (i.e., MAE clauses). Lender caution is even more salient in emerging markets, given the systemic issues we have discussed elsewhere in this book (imperfect insolvency and judicial systems). The authors have nonetheless included a detailed

# Case Studies

In this chapter, we will focus on two examples of such Acts of God. The first is a tropical cyclone that devastates the agriculture and tourism sectors of an island economy. The second is the 2020–21 COVID-19 pandemic and its impact on a middle-income economy. For each, we will analyze the Act of God's impact on a local corporate borrower on the one hand and a local FI borrower on the other in the affected country.

From this analysis, we will identify the restructuring prerequisites in each case. It will be evident that the restructuring process outlined in previous Chapters *must be modified* to accommodate the particular characteristics of this shock type. Additionally, the corporate finance and legal structural elements in the solutions will display some marked differences from the earlier standard cases (such as the Bank of Commerce and National Goods).

As a preliminary to our discussion, we will outline the key facts of the cases.

## A. The Tropical Cyclone

### 1. Background

The economy of this island country consists primarily of two major activities—coconut production and tropical beach holidays for foreign tourists. In the country, absentee landowners and large agribusinesses control the coconut industry. The coconut farms vary in size from a few to a hundred hectares. They customarily employ local peasants to collect coconuts on piece-rate basis. Coconut production is aggregated by a small number of local agents, who sell to processing companies whose output consists of coconut oil, copra (dried coconut), and desiccated coconut. There are about a dozen local processing companies. International agri-business companies purchase almost all of the production, with only a small share kept for local consumption. In the latest year for which data is available, the coconut industry accounted for 15% of GDP.

The country's tourism sector is dominated by international hotel chains. However, there are many local businesses which provide goods and services to this sector. Overall, well over half of the labor force is directly or indirectly involved in the tourism sector. Recognizing the potential for such events, the government has built up a contingency fund to provide financial support for

---

summary of some key legal issues surrounding exogenous events (e.g., force majeure, MAE clauses, government relief programs) in Chapter 11.

disaster recovery, including loans and loan guarantees to the financial and commercial sectors.

## 2. The Cyclone

A cyclone categorized as "extremely severe," with sustained winds of 190 km/h hit the island. There was only a week's warning. The eye of the storm took two days to pass over the island, with residual rain and winds persisting for three days. Some flooding occurred. It was the first such direct hit in over a decade. The damage was material. Experts estimate that approximately one third of the country's palm trees were lost. With proper care, coconut palms produce their first fruit in six to ten years, taking 15–20 years to reach peak production.

The hotel sector escaped serious damage for the most part. However, repair work will take an average of between 3 to 4 months at a minimum. Overall, whilst the impact on the economy is material, the magnitude appears within the range of the country's capacity to remedy.

## 3. The Business Impact

We will assume two borrowers: one a coconut processing company, a second a local bank whose portfolio is divided between companies in coconut processing and those providing goods and services to hotels.

### The coconut processing company:

- Revenue dropped by 75% in the first year. A return to pre-cyclone levels is unlikely in the medium term. Despite cost cutting, net income turned negative in year one and is projected to remain in the red through year 3.
- Capital will decline, pushing the debt to equity ratio from 3:1 to 9:1 at its peak, with the debt service coverage ratio ("DSCR") falling from 2:1 to negative 1.75:1 in year 1, with projections pointing to a return to positive coverage only in the range of years 4–5.
- With these developments, the company announced it would cease normal debt service and requested that lenders enter into discussions.

### The bank:

- NPLs spiked, rising from 5 to 40% within the first six months following the cyclone. Half of the remaining book was restructured, with the principal deferred for two years subject to a continuation of interest payments.

- Minimum capital requirements were suspended for a 12-month period for the four privately owned banks (including this one), during which the shareholders were either to raise new capital or be nationalized. Against a regulatory capital minimum of 10%, the bank's pro-forma capital is estimated at -10%.
- The bank's liabilities are divided between deposits (25%; insured) and debt (75%), with the latter contracted principally with foreign banks and funds. The bank announced it would cease normal debt service and requested that lenders enter into discussions.

4. The Restructuring

**The coconut company:**

- The long-term outlook is sound, assuming the recovery in the coconut palm population progresses as hoped. Belief in this outlook is key to the agreement below.
- The challenge is to calibrate operating and financial costs with cash flow during the recovery period.
- To achieve this, the parties agree to: (i) a rights issue to be subscribed by all the shareholders; (ii) a multi-year deferral/restructuring of principal payments; and (iii) a shorter-term capitalization of interest payments, with the objective of maintaining the DSCR at a level of no less than 1.25:1 throughout the restructuring period.

**The bank:**

- The challenge is to recapitalize the bank sufficiently to cover eventual loan losses and to ensure compliance with minimum solvency requirements.
- Given the size of the new capital requirements, the shareholders asked the lenders to cooperate in the recapitalization. The agreement consists of: (i) the shareholders' subscribing to a rights issue; (ii) the lenders' converting a portion of their senior debt into Tier 2 qualifying subordinated debt; and (iii) the lenders' also agreeing to extend the repayment term of the remaining senior debt, with a partial government guarantee.

B. **The COVID-19 Pandemic**

1. **Background**

The country is a fast-growing, middle-income economy, which sits at the crossroads of trade for the surrounding area. Using foreign capital, the government has invested in the development of land, sea, and air transport and logistical assets, and factories for intermediate manufacturing components for global supply chains. National income has skyrocketed, as have the fiscal deficit, public debt, current account deficit, and the external financing gap. The country remains dependent on external financing for the foreseeable future. The banking system is highly dollarized.

## 2. The Pandemic

The first detected cases were registered in late February. Within a month, the upsurge of infections forced the government to impose restrictions on restaurants, stores, offices, and schools. By June, cases declined to levels that allowed the government first to relax and then to eliminate mobility restrictions entirely. The respite was short-lived. By late summer following the pattern seen elsewhere, infections surged. Total infections reached the range of 6000 cases per 100,000. Rising hospitalizations have strained the country's public health facilities. The government reacted with renewed restrictive measures, as it continues to struggle with flattening the curve.

## 3. The Economy

GDP fell by a record 40% in the second quarter, reflecting the pandemic-related restrictions at home and the slowdown in global trade. With the lifting of domestic restrictions and a moderate recovery in trade, national income rebounded in the third quarter, notching a 50% rise. Capital flows declined precipitously in the second quarter, as financial flows into the banking sector reversed, and new foreign direct investment was delayed. Over the course of the summer, a slight rebound ensued but quickly stalled. Overall, net capital flows for the year are forecast to decline by several percentage points of GDP. The central bank has been forced to intervene aggressively in the exchange markets to limit the depreciation of the currency.

As the aforementioned financial pressures built up and FX reserve levels slipped into dangerous territory, the government negotiated a Rapid Financing Instrument (RFI) arrangement with the IMF. With the resurgence of infections and renewed mobility restrictions, the economic recovery stalled, and fourth-quarter GDP is forecast to decline by up to 10%, with the first quarter of 2021 likely to be breakeven at best.

## 4. Business Impact

We will assume two borrowers: one a trucking business, operating out of the country's major facility, a second a local financial leasing company whose portfolio is diversified between small and medium real estate and equipment leasing.

### The trucking company:

- The onset of the pandemic-induced economic slowdown began in mid-March. On a year-on-year basis, first quarter revenue was essentially unchanged, down only 3%. By mid-April the port traffic had declined by half, and by end-May by 90%, with the result that first quarter sales decreased by roughly two-thirds. The company's drivers are contracted on a "job" basis (drive to be paid), but with the trucks themselves being company-owned. Hence, the significant level of variable personnel costs could be reduced. Notwithstanding, net income fell by a half, and cash flow from operations turned strongly negative.
- The company's leverage is moderate, predominantly in the form of capital lease financing for the truck fleet. The duration of the debt is just over one year, reflecting the age of the fleet. At the time of the pandemic's outbreak, the company had plans in motion to replace a third of the fleet, as breakdowns were frequent and represented a critical threat to the business.
- In the spring, the company approached its creditors requesting a six-month deferral of principal payments. This was quickly accepted. When the pandemic appeared to be abating, the company resumed principal payments as an incentive to the banks to allow a partial fleet replacement, financed with three-year capital leases. Shortly after the effectiveness of this new financial package and the purchase of the new trucks, the daily infection rate surged, and the parties met to anticipate the impact on the company's debt service capacity.

### The leasing company:

- The leasing portfolio is divided into thirds between commercial and industrial real estate, equipment, and consumer durables. Equipment and consumer durables leasing is short duration with the capital leasing tenors of up to three years, with commercial and operational real estate longer duration in the five-to-eight-year range. Loan to value ratios is conservatively managed, with a maximum of 75%. The external funding consists of senior debt contracted with a combination of local and foreigner lenders, with approximately half denominated in foreign currency.

- When the first COVID-19 wave hit, the leasing company acted in proactive manner, coordinating with both their funders and their lessees to anticipate potential liquidity stresses. On both sides, the objective was to maintain interest payments current, whilst deferring principal when necessary. Roughly a third of principal installments of the local leasing book was deferred for periods ranging from 3 to 9 months, whilst a commensurate amount of principal was deferred with foreign lenders.
- As noted above, by autumn the rising infection rate forced the government to reimpose restrictions on local businesses and individual mobility, and again domestic business struggled. In the global economy, activity began to soften, and this generated further adverse economic headwinds, especially for trade and logistics-dependent companies and households.
- Coming on the heels of six months of anemic business activity (which had weakened the financial resilience of many lessees), this second shock drove a rapid deterioration in the debt service capacity of many lessees. Nonperforming asset figures quickly spiked and required intensive and immediate remedial action. This development also alarmed the leasing company's domestic and foreign creditors. Meetings were called to address the situation.

## 5. The Restructurings:

### The trucking company:

- The central questions underlying the approach to the restructuring are: (i) do the company's future prospects support the current size of the business; and (ii) if not, or if the return to a sustainable business will be protracted, what to do in the meantime?
- Analysis concluded that under the baseline projections: (i) there is likely to be excess capacity in the business through 2022–3; (ii) operating cash flow cannot service the current debt burden until this time frame; and (iii) even at the lower level of activity, the truck fleet requires new investments.
- The parties face a sustainable business, but one that needs both sides to help. The company needs to downsize (assets and people). The lenders need to extend the principal maturities of the debt. There is also the additional matter of the modernization of the fleet.
- The agreement reached consists of: (i) the company to undertake a large reduction in operational expenses, mothball processing facilities, and place

redundant trucks with a reseller; (ii) all debt maturities to be refinanced for three years; (iii) interest to be serviced as per the existing contracts; (iv) all fixed assets to be placed in a common security pool; (v) an excess cash flow arrangement to be established to allow capex for fleet modernization and debt prepayment; and (vi) the ownership family to pledge certain additional fixed collateral to be added to the common security pool.

## The leasing company:

- The questions facing our trucking company above are typical of the situation with the leasing company's customers. In a renewed downturn with a lack of certainty about the course of the pandemic and therefore the timing and strength of the eventual economic recovery, creditors must make a determination of the sustainability of their customers. Restructure or foreclose. Additionally, the local government may have established guidelines concerning the treatment of borrowers during the pandemic period.
- In the first phase as described above, the leasing company agreed payment delays with both of its customers and funders. In this second phase, the work is more complex and the creditor action is less controlled by the government. The leasing company divided its clients into three groups: (i) normal servicing; (ii) restructuring cases; and (iii) problem credits. The first are strong credits whose ability to service their debt has not been impeded. The second group consists of customers like the trucking company. The third are cases where there will be a potential loss.
- Following an asset quality review, it is determined that 65% falls in group one, 25% in group two, and 10% in group three. Even should the full 10% be written off, the net impact (after expected collateral collection) on solvency will still leave a buffer above the minimum regulatory capital requirement. For the restructuring cohort, the average required refinancing term is 24 months.
- Based on this analysis, the leasing company agrees with its funding creditors: (i) the shareholders commit sufficient capital to ensure compliance with the minimum regulatory solvency; and (ii) principal installments to be extended by 30 months, but with a prepayment mechanism.

Having now outlined the key facts of these Acts of God cases, we will consider the similarities and differences between them and cases like the Bank of Commerce and National Goods. First, let's recall the five major characteristics of Acts of God we cited earlier:

1. **Speed**,
2. **Pervasiveness**,
3. **Uncertainty of degree/duration**,
4. **Effective mitigation**, and
5. **Predictable income stream and expense/investment budget**.

How do these affect the restructuring process?

## 1. Speed

We define "speed" here as the time from the first signals of an event to when its impact on financial condition requires a restructuring response. As expected, speed increases remarkably in the case of an Act of God.

In both the Bank of Commerce and National Goods episodes (our "standard" cases), the problems were a long time coming. They should have been seen (and could arguably have been avoided) in advance. The first was an exogenous shock, but one with sufficient warning signals well in advance of the event. The second was a self-made problem, simply a set of very bad business decisions. More astute analysts should have uncovered their threats to the company's investment program. These stand in stark contrast to our Acts of God cases, where there was no real warning (or at least a very short one).

For the Bank of Commerce, that a copper demand shock would happen was never in doubt. The question was when. The end of the long, super commodity cycle as Chinese growth peaked and then decelerated had been extensively discussed in economic circles. To the vigilant observer, the writing was on the wall several years back. Kristi undoubtedly had irritated her colleagues with her Cassandra-like warnings. The precise timing of the jump from slackening fixed investment in China to a collapse in demand for industrial metals, including copper, defied facile predictions. But as the build-up of technical, factors pointing to copper market weakness progressed, market specialists and speculators narrowed their timeframes for a correction. The rise in market-shorting trade volumes would soon become the talk of traders over their end-of-day lagers at the local pub, even before the occasional article in the financial press.

Kristi had picked up on the trend by this time. She had incorporated the potential terms of trade shock into the macroeconomic modeling used to stress her firm's portfolio. This analysis had underlain her initial conversation with Ursula. The first "it's going to rain" warning coming on a sunny day had been dismissed, we will recall. Only thereafter, when the adverse impact of collapsing copper prices on the Bank of Commerce's home economy was unmistakable, did our players wake up to the threat. Still, Kristi's admonitions fell on deaf ears. Had New West reacted appropriately even at this late date, the Bank could have been saved.

In the National Goods case, the company's management had failed to see the market moving to more energy efficient products and that their recent sales through third-party retail outlets had to be supported with discounts and generous deferred payment terms. That a young analyst sitting thousands of miles away was able to uncover these facts highlights that human error lay at the base of National Goods' problems. Being self-made, this financial car wreck should have been seen and avoided.

In the case of the Tropical Cyclone, countries in the storm zone accept their vulnerability. However, the incidence, timing, force, and precise impact are all unknowns. As such, basic precautions—including building codes, sea walls, insurance when available, and the like—are taken. But at the enterprise level, managers don't typically work a severe category storm into their financial planning. Modern meteorological advances have given humankind the capacity for more timely and accurate storm predictions. However, in the end, these exercise an immaterial effect on the economic fallout.

Despite SARS and Ebola, virus-driven pandemics have never been a meaningful input into forward business planning, at least until COVID-19 hit the world in 2020. The pandemic was not seen coming—at least by most in the global business community.[5] The first reports of a new coronavirus outbreak in China emerged only in December 2019. Within a few months, much of the globe was under some form of lockdown. The second quarter 2020 economic downturn broke records. The summertime lull (largely in the northern hemisphere) caused some to conclude that the virus would "burn itself out" as some past episodes had done. The ferocious resurgence may have been predicted by many in the public health sector, but the premature relaxation of mobility restrictions belies current claims that the second wave was ever taken seriously.

The impact of these differences in "speed" on the restructuring process is obvious. Let's recall our five basic phases of restructuring. The *first two phases*, Pre-Restructuring and Decision to Restructure, can disappear entirely or be quite short-lived. There may be cases where a borrower's particular circumstances allow it to absorb the effects of the Act of God, without restructuring

---

[5] Only a relatively small number of high-profile businesspeople seem to have foreseen the COVID-19 pandemic, though global public health and intelligence experts had been predicting it. See, e.g., Hillary Hoffower, "*Bill Gates has been warning of a global health threat for years...*", Business Insider, December 15, 2020.

its debts or where downsizing, application of insurance proceeds (if any), and/or other actions allow a successful recovery or adjustment to the new reality. The determination of this status may require time. The length depends on the nature of the shock and the borrower's idiosyncratic characteristics.

In our Tropical Cyclone case, the coconut processing company had the strengths of flexibility with respect to its labor force and strong financial buffers. Still, given the severity of the damage to the coconut palm population, the need to recalibrate the debt payments to the reduced revenue outlook became quickly apparent. For the local bank, the process of ascertaining the nature of the impact may require more time. Individual credit files must be updated to take into consideration the impact of the storm.

In a simplified case where a bank has just two borrowers—the coconut processing company and a hotel's external laundry service—the nature of the restructuring request to the bank's funders would reflect the coconut processing company's refinancing terms and the impact of the laundry service's estimation of the timing of the reopening of its hotel customers and the resumption of foreign tourist arrivals. Additionally, the impact of loan loss provisioning and write-offs, etc., must be forecast to determine capital requirements. The work period can range from days to weeks, but will be shorter, all things being equal, than a standard case.

In the case of COVID-19, the considerations are similar at this stage. But as will be discussed below, the uncertainty around the *duration* of the episode adds a unique degree of complexity to the forecasting exercise.[6]

The *third phase*—the Case Set-up—remains as a distinct stage in all cases. The major difference between the standard and the Act of God cases is the optics. In the latter, the magnitude of the shock and its pervasiveness will often dispel the illusion that the parties have any option but to restructure. JK and Ursula's procrastination and Edinburg Partners' morality play would be less likely in a case where half the country has been flattened by high winds, or where a public health crisis has closed down businesses and emptied the streets. That is, the parties are typically forced to admit there is no alternative but to engage constructively to fix a problem, rather than wasting time debating who is to blame and posturing for initial negotiating advantage.

The *fourth and fifth phases*—Structuring and Negotiation and Implementation—present the same substantive challenges in both the standard and Acts of God cases. Indeed, the breadth of the economic disruption in both Acts

---

[6] The authors observed that in the case of the 2020 COVID-19 pandemic, during the first wave (Q1–2) lenders tended to act more quickly flexibly in alleviating debt service burdens (e.g., granting interest holidays and/or extending maturities for a short period, e.g., 3–6 months, waiving covenants, etc.), whilst in the second wave (Q3–Q4) many appeared to embrace the more customary (or "standard") negotiating positions.

of God scenarios and the unique uncertainty of the pandemic's duration and severity arguably increase the technical difficulty of the design of the restructuring solution. Further, as we discuss below, there may be an intermediary step where a temporary moratorium is established to preserve liquidity whilst the definitive agreement is formulated and approved. Again as before, the urgency of the situation should exercise a positive influence.

## 2. Pervasiveness

By "pervasiveness," we mean the breadth of the impact of an event (or series of its after-effects). Individual bankruptcies of course happen for a variety of reasons. With an exogenous shock, sometimes its effects are felt more intensely in one region or sector or class of companies than others. It can affect an entire population of businesses. In the case of Acts of God, the degree of pervasiveness can vary, from being geographically and/or politically contained to being far-reaching, if not all-encompassing.

The exogenous shock (copper price collapse) that brought down the Bank of Commerce did weigh heavily on the local economy. The Bank of Commerce had aggravated its own vulnerability by continuing to upstream profits at a time when it should have been preserving them to prepare for a largely anticipated copper correction. However, most other banks weathered the storm. There was no systemic crisis. The other banks' superior pre-shock financial condition allowed them to continue to service their liabilities without seeking a restructuring.

National Goods' troubles were by contrast entirely self-inflicted (expansion into retail, maintenance of an outdated product line) and not indicative of a wider market problem. Competitors with newer, more environmentally friendly product lines did perfectly well. National Goods represents a garden-variety example of company-level mismanagement leading to financial stress.

Overall, we can characterize these cases as idiosyncratic in nature and isolated. Whilst their occurrence could generate negative externalities for the broader economy, they are not part of an economy-wide episode where many if not most parties are affected in a similar manner at the same time.

By contrast, this limited pervasiveness does characterize the impact of Acts of God. Wind, rain, and viruses usually do not discriminate. The impact of the shock is virtually universal. All are exposed. In our Tropical Cyclone case, the caprice of nature might spare some structures. Some businesses may have also partially (or even completely) covered their capital and/or income losses by way of insurance. But still, the after-effects of the storm will be felt throughout the economy to varying degrees and will affect most (if not all) businesses. That said, the Tropical Cyclone like many other Acts of God will as a general matter be geographically contained to the storm's footprint. This is often similar to many other exogenous events whether natural (earthquakes, hurricanes, floods, fires, etc.) or human-made (wars, terrorist acts, strikes, etc.).

The COVID-19 pandemic has demonstrated morbidly that in the case of some Acts of God, no quarter is insulated.[7] Even national borders and oceans have failed to block a virus's spread. The spread's velocity might have been slowed down by some governmental measures (e.g., imposition of travel restrictions, lockdowns, social distancing, mandatory masks, and the like), but it nonetheless marched forward. The whole global economy fell under its shadow. Moreover, the pandemic occurred in slow-motion and in multiple waves. The loss of critical time by governments in effectively dealing with the virus early on and in a decisive manner gave the virus the time to mutate in new, apparently more infectious strains, further exacerbating its pervasiveness.

How does this pervasiveness in the case of COVID-19, influence the restructuring process? *First*, the negative multiplier effect of this global-economy-wide episode risks intensifying the adverse financial fallout, hence adding to the imperative to act quickly.[8] *Second,* the volume of restructuring cases will be markedly higher, thus requiring a greater application of resources on the part of lenders, both on the cross-border and local levels. *Third*, a degree of standardization in approach, structure, and even documentation may become inevitable, due in part to the time pressures, and in part to a concept of fairness. *Fourth*, the science (or art) of restructuring has never had to deal with such a scope of a crisis. Experimentation and boldness are necessary, to arrive at new and pertinent solutions.

By phase, how do the COVID-19 effects vary? In the *first (pre-restructuring)*, monitoring is transformed into an urgent and rapid evaluation of the current and (based on highly speculative and uncertain forecasts of the course of the pandemic) projected impact of the public health restrictions on economic activity.[9] Uncertainty permeates the macroeconomic outlook, the true exposure of individual borrowers, their ability to adapt, etc. To get the analysis right the first time has proven impossible in most cases, reflecting not

---

[7] Though as mentioned above, certain business segments actually thrived as a result of the pandemic.

[8] At the same time, due to the unpredictability of degree/duration, clarity on an appropriate solution (apart from extensions and covenant waivers) is compromised. *See* below.

[9] No doubt other factors also contribute, e.g., the virus's impact on the health of the work force, the local consumer population's perception of personal health risk, etc.

just the evolving COVID-19 picture, but also inadequacies in the capability of analysts to decipher the future under these unique circumstances.

In the *second and the third (decision and case set-up)*, the decision to do "something" and the management of the preliminaries to the process are broadly similar to what we see in standard restructuring cases. As we discuss in greater detail below, the difference is the unique challenge of what comes next? What's the deal? What problems are to be addressed? How quickly might all this change? How do we provide in the restructuring agreement for the likelihood that the parties may have to come back to the table?

To explore these and other questions, we will punt down to the next section where we focus on the *fourth and fifth phases (Structuring and Negotiation and Implementation)*. In this discussion, we will combine the remaining three major characteristics of Acts of God we cited earlier[10] into one question: "How to design and implement a restructuring plan in the midst of an evolving pandemic?"

## 3. Uncertainty of degree/duration

The two clear differences between the standard restructuring cases and those arising in the context of many exogenous events are *first* the "speed" with which the fundamental causation event triggers the need to restructure and *second* the "pervasiveness" of the resulting financial stresses.

As we have noted previously in the case of the Bank of Commerce, there was a full year between the inception of copper market down-cycle and the deterioration of the institution's financial condition. And not all banks in the local market were as seriously affected as Bank of Commerce. By contrast, the period from the first coronavirus outbreak in Wuhan (December 2019) to the wave of lockdowns took merely weeks. Further, the scope of the financial fallout, whilst not universal, was far, far greater. It produced historical records for the severity of the decline in economic activity in the second quarter of 2020.

Arguably, however, an even starker distinction is the degree of clarity (the lack thereof) with which we can model the future and hence craft the elements of a restructuring solution.

In the case of the Bank of Commerce, Kristi did not attempt to predict by when, if ever, the price and volume of copper exports would return to pre-crisis levels. Undoubtedly, she recognized the causes of the downturn and argued that the cycle would turn in time through some combination of

---

[10] Uncertainty of degree/duration, effectiveness of mitigation, and predictability of income and reliability of investment/expense budgets.

increased demand, decreased production/lower inventories. Within a time-range, she was confident that the country's export revenue would recover. In her analysis, she was positing market direction rather than a precise price by some date certain. Given the size of the export shock and an estimation of its length based on past experiences, she also felt comfortable with fore-casting the broad trajectory of the external accounts and national income and forming a view on when the trend in the deterioration of asset quality might begin to reverse.

Based on these assumptions, Kristi designed an initial recapitalization program for the bank. Whilst the failure of New West—the bank's majority shareholder—to commit the requisite equity doomed the plan, there were enough credible data points to create a plan.

In the case of National Goods, the restructuring plan's assumptions were supported by historical market data, consumer surveys, and the like. The precise outcome of the reengineering of the product line was uncertain at the time the parties signed on to the deal. However, a reasonable range of revenue scenarios could be elaborated, around which the terms of the transaction structured.

Midst the restructuring negotiations, the future for both the Bank of Commerce (even after the orderly wind-down decision) and National Goods remain uncertain. The precise outcome in each case will be unknowable until the very end, but the *range* of the financial results can be forecast with a reasonable degree of confidence. The same may be said for our Tropical Cyclone case and the restructurings of our local coconut processing company and bank.

In contrast stands the "radical uncertainty" of COVID-19.[11] To borrow John Kay's words,[12] *"COVID-19 is absolutely an example of radical uncertainty. The pandemic is not what Nassim Taleb calls a Black Swan, an event you can't anticipate because you can't imagine the event. You definitely could imagine a pandemic; indeed, we somewhat presciently wrote in the book (Radical Uncertainty) that a pandemic would happen. But we didn't know when or where, and we certainly couldn't have sensibly responded to the question: 'What's the probability a global pandemic will start in Wuhan in December 2019.'"*

Not only is the initial outbreak of the pandemic an example of such radical uncertainty, but (at least at the time of publication of this book) the *future course* of the virus falls into the same category. This is true even when layering on the effects of individual governments' public health responses. Defects

---

[11] John Kay and Mervyn King, Radical Uncertainty (Norton, 2020).

[12] John Kay, www.suerf.org (22 August 2020).

in their design, rule-breaking by citizens of various countries, foreign traveler contamination, and premature relaxation due to political pressure have contributed to the virus winning the match to date. Moreover, mutations of the virus in late 2020 and early 2021 further obscured the picture.[13]

## Restructuring in a State of Uncertainty

Over the months immediately preceding publication of this book, even when faced with this highly uncertain future, noteworthy economists have continued to issue authoritative growth forecasts. This year, the revisions in their numbers have come more frequently than ever before. The drastic change in their view of growth in the fourth quarter of 2020, in particular, reflected the third quarter's unexpectedly strong upsurge in infection rates in many countries. The economists' experience is instructive for the restructuring professional in the era of COVID-19.

Until the combination of widespread vaccinations and herd immunity allows a return to some degree of normalcy, there will be a degree of uncertainty—in John Kay's words, "radical uncertainty" ("*not all outcomes known*"),[14] with respect to commercial and financial performance across the global economy.

In such an environment of uncertainty, how do lenders rationally approach restructuring, when it is no longer possible to "extend and pretend," when local COVID-19 moratoria no longer apply, and when borrowers are already a heartbeat away from the insolvency court?

The authors contend that in such a state of uncertainty restructurings can be undertaken, but they must be approached with the realization that the objective will be to achieve the *best possible solution at the time, based on then-available information.*[15]

---

[13] In late 2020 and early 2021, as countries rolled out newly developed vaccines, new strains of the COVID-91 virus started to mutate in a number of countries, some with apparently greater transmission advantages and severity than prior variants of the virus.

[14] Kay, op cit.

[15] This requires a de novo real-time (or "tabula rasa") analysis of the borrower's current financial condition and projected future income stream, based on the nature, extent and duration of the relevant exogenous event, with limited (if any) reliance on prior years' financial performance. For example, as a result of the COVID-19 pandemic, many businesses which previously had successful commercial operations may no longer survive. Or they may survive only by undergoing a substantial business restructuring (re-profiling), development of new product or service lines, etc.. Lender leadership must ask uncomfortable questions and base its answers on today's relevant information: will the borrower's business survive in the new post-COVID-19 world?

Effectively, the authors suggest *three basic alternative approaches* when the nature of an exogenous event (e.g., COVID-19) does not provide sufficient clarity on expected duration, effectiveness of mitigation and/or predictable income, and reliable budgeting:

1. **Status quo approach**: this would involve maintaining a *standstill* in place, with revolving short-term extensions of maturities and waivers of covenants, provided certain basic parameters are met (e.g., no leakage, no super default events, nonparticipating creditors continue to be paid, etc.). The parties would delay any actual restructuring until sufficient clarity is achieved;
2. **Buffer approach**: this would involve the parties' negotiation and implementation of an actual restructuring, but with a sizeable buffer built into the restructuring terms, so that the restructuring agreement can adapt to changing assumptions without further amendments (or with limited actions, e.g., based on majority lender decisions); or
3. **Flexible approach**: in this approach the parties would negotiate and implement a full debt restructuring but would simultaneously agree that they are prepared to *return to the negotiating table* if and when the course of the pandemic invalidates past assumptions.

Admittedly, the *status quo* approach *per se* is not a "restructuring" at all—rather, it is a conscious decision to maintain one of the key initial elements of a restructuring (the standstill) in place on an extended, revolving basis. In effect, the patient is maintained in suspended animation on the operating table on life support, monitored constantly by the medical staff. The benefit of such an approach includes the rather modest cost of putting it in place (from the standpoint of external advisors' fees) and the flexibility it preserves for taking future action, as and when such action ultimately becomes appropriate. That said, it may not meet short-term liquidity requirements. It will also require an analysis to determine other risks, as it is not a restructuring *per se*.[16]

---

[16] Ordinarily, standstills in workouts are established on a short-term (e.g., 3–4 month) basis for the purposes of conducting due diligence, determining whether a workout can be achieved and negotiating its terms. See Chapter 11. In this case, the standstill would be a medium-term (e.g., 6-month) measure specifically aimed at waiting for greater clarity on how the business will ultimately be impacted and whether a workout will indeed be viable after the dust settles. This assumes the business will continue to survive during the interim period. This assumption may something of a stretch unless equity holders are prepared to inject further cash or a particular lender has already provided (or is prepared to provide) some form of emergency financial relief which reduces liquidity problems. By way of example, in 2020 during the COVID-19 pandemic a number of DFIs (led by EBRD) rolled out emergency financing packages. The EBRD's Solidarity Package provided short-term financing for

For the *buffer* approach, as an illustration let's use our trucking company case outlined above. The lenders agreed a three-year refinancing tenor. Underlying this duration selection were certain assumptions, most notably concerning: (i) the course of the pandemic at home and abroad; and (ii) trade volume through the port. Let's assume the original assumptions for each were: (i) vaccinations contain the global pandemic within a 12–18-month period; (ii) this success results in a progressive return to pre-crisis levels of global economic activity and trade by the end of year 3. Aided by its cost cutting program and flexible arrangements with its driver force, the company's baseline financial projections showed repayments could begin by month 30 (year 2 ½). The parties agreed to build in a 6-month buffer for the inception of repayments, but with the provision of an excess cash flow mechanism to allow repayments to start earlier if conditions warrant. If all goes as forecasted, debt repayments will begin by year three at the latest.[17]

For the *flexible* approach, let's consider our same trucking company case. But instead of the 6-month buffer and excess cash mechanism, the parties recognize that there is uncertainty now. So they include a clause expressly recognizing that the pandemic is continuing and agreeing that if the borrower continues to underperform due to specific continuing effects of the pandemic, the parties will reconvene their negotiations in good faith to determine whether and how the main restructuring agreements must be further modified. The global vaccination program indeed fails to achieve its objective, and the global economy continues to underperform as lockdown restrictions persist. It becomes clear that our trucking company's debt must be restructured further. The parties then sit down to talk. Where all parties are flexible, comfortable working together (e.g., from prior workouts), and prepared to accept this approach, it may well work.[18]

---

borrowers who were existing clients with strong business fundamentals experiencing temporary credit difficulties. *See* https://www.ebrd.com/what-we-do/coronavirus-solidarity. However, not all borrowers will necessarily have been fortunate enough to have had such emergency funding in a given case.

[17] In the authors' view, if achievable, this approach may be preferred over the status quo approach, as the parties will have put the restructuring in place (rather than merely an extended standstill). From a tactical standpoint, lender leadership may be better-placed to convince lenders to make any required future "tweaks" should these become necessary (if the buffer proves too small). The main contractual framework of the restructuring would have been put in place. Lenders and their management may find it more palatable (and speedier) to approve modifications to a formal existing workout structure.

[18] One legal difficulty here is in ensuring that all parties do indeed come back to the table and agree the necessary amendments. Under many systems of law commonly used in workouts (e.g., English law, New York law), *an "agreement to agree" is generally unenforceable due to the lack of certainty on essential terms. See* McKnight and Zakrzewski, On the Law of Loan Agreements and Syndicated Lending, Oxford University Press, 2019, Section 1.17 (under English law, an agreement to negotiate in good faith is unenforceable and will fail for certainty). By contrast, under New York law, in certain cases a preliminary agreement may be enforceable—at least to the extent that it can oblige the parties to negotiate open terms in good faith and to refrain from actions contravening the negotiations. *See*

To be sure, where the *buffer* or *flexible* approach is applied, lenders should recognize a greater risk of *unwinding* of the restructuring (insolvency of the borrower) due to the continuing uncertainty. Accordingly, issues such as the potential application of antecedent transaction rules to distributions made, and/or to new security from the borrower, during the restructuring (and consequent claw-backs) may require more attention than in restructurings achieved during a situation of higher certainty. To mitigate against such risks lenders may wish to delay or back-load lender distributions under the terms of the restructuring to lessen financial pressure on the borrower.

---

Teachers Insurance & Annuity v. Tribune Co., 670 F. Supp. 491 (S.D.N.Y. 1987); Vacoid LLC v. Cerami, 545 F.3d 114, 124 n. 2 (2d Cir. 2008). This can at least limit bad-faith actions by and a level of comfort knowing they will continue to be incentivized to agree terms given the likely alternative (insolvency of the borrower in the local courts of the emerging market).

# Part IV

**Reference Toolkit**

# 10

# Macroeconomics and Credit Analysis

**Abstract** This chapter elaborates the simplified macroeconomic analysis methodology conducted by Kristi in the opening Bank of Commerce tale. The content is not meant to be a summary of a macroeconomics textbook. Instead, a simple (non-mathematical/econometrics-based) practical method to incorporate macroeconomics into credit analysis is introduced. The Bank of Commerce case fact set is used as the foundation. Thereafter, four brief new cases are reviewed using this approach to reinforce the learnings.

**Keywords** Balance sheet · Bankruptcy · Borrower · Consensual restructuring · Coordinating committee · Corporate debt · Debt · Debtor · Cash flow · COVID-19 · Credit analysis · Currency peg · Devaluation · DFI (development finance institution) · Distressed debt · Financial statements · Foreign exchange · Emerging market · Exchange rate · Frontier market · INSOL II · INSOL principles · Insolvency · Lender leadership · Loan loss provision · Macroeconomics · Non-performing loans · Pre-insolvency · Restructure · Restructuring · Restructuring plan · Shareholder(s) · Standstill · Steering committee · Workout

© The Author(s), under exclusive license to Springer Nature
Switzerland AG 2021
R. Marney and T. Stubbs, *Corporate Debt Restructuring in Emerging Markets*,
https://doi.org/10.1007/978-3-030-81306-2_10

This chapter is not meant to be a summary of a macroeconomics textbook. We assume the reader has at least an elementary grasp of macroeconomics, in particular international and monetary economics. Hence, we do not devote much ink to the standard underlying theory and empirics.[1] Instead, we suggest a simple, practical method to incorporate macroeconomics into credit analysis.[2]

# Introduction

Let's think back to Kristi's conversation with Ursula at the New West headquarters early on in the Bank of Commerce narrative. In the months before the call, global demand for copper had fallen dramatically. This development reflected slowing economic activity in many countries, with the knock-on effect that industrial metal requirements in manufacturing and construction activities fell. The Bank of Commerce's home country's economy was highly dependent on copper exports. When the world cut back on its copper purchases, the country suffered. On the external side, exports fell, trade and current account balances deteriorated, foreign exchange reserves declined, and currency selling pressures heightened.

Domestically, the dramatic fall in export activity spilt over into the broader market in waves, first hitting companies and households directly linked to the sector, before reverberating outwards in second and third waves lowering employment and aggregate demand throughout the economy. Government revenue decreased, as did revenue from excise taxes on copper exports (and subsequently from income taxes), as the pace of economic activity faltered. Debt service capacity weakened for both the government and the private sector. Financial institutions began to see a rise in loan delinquencies. This development raised the specter of a cycle of loan portfolio quality deterioration leading to higher loan loss provisioning, reduced profitability, and weakened capitalization.

Foreign capital providers viewed these developments with intensifying concerns about issuer insolvency and the possibility of the breaking of the currency peg. Capital flows slowed then reversed. The central bank increasingly intervened to counter increasingly panicked selling in the exchange

---

[1] We provide at the end of the section a suggested bibliography for those who need or want a quick refresher.

[2] As we have discussed in Chapters 3 and 4, credit monitoring during the Pre-Restructuring Phase is an essential tool for "seeing problems before they become problems."

market. Foreign exchange reserves continued to decline. The high degree of dollarization in the financial system exacerbated the vulnerabilities for banks like the Bank of Commerce.

The shareholders prioritized profitability over prudent risk management and operated with a sizeable open currency position. Additionally, a material volume of lending denominated in foreign currency went to borrowers with no natural hedging. As the management of the Bank of Commerce had previously warned Ursula, and Kristi had been persistently reminding anyone who would listen, the breaking of the currency peg could create an existential threat, due to the double impact of currency translation losses at the bank level and an unmanageable spike in debt service costs at the end-borrower level. The day that Kristi reached out to Ursula followed the government's fateful decision to devalue the currency. Already, the Bank's solvency was below the regulatory minimum, and lender panic was building. A liquidity crisis threatened. A duration mismatch left the Bank's survival vulnerable to an outflow of deposits and foreign lenders, like Kristi, accelerating their loans. Recall her admonition to Ursula:

> *The country's financial system has been one big carry trade. Cheap dollar funding, a fixed exchange rate, high local interest rates all built on blind faith that nothing will change. Once this faith is questioned, and the 25% devaluation did this, nothing short of drastic medicine will have a chance to stabilize the capital flows. The 25% devaluation did not stop the panic; it has accelerated it. Their FX reserves are reaching critically low levels. I think they will be forced to approach the IMF and in so doing let their exchange rate float. The fundamentals are showing signs of improvement, so that will help. I believe there'll be enormous volatility for a few months but the situation will eventually stabilize with maybe another 10% -20% depreciation.*

This all played out as Kristi had predicted. Events flowed from an exogenous market shock to economic weakening to pressures within the financial system. And, as she feared, the Bank of Commerce became a casualty.

In this section, we will attempt to answer two questions: *First*, when Kristi puts on her economist hat, what is the objective of the work? *Second*, how does she go about her analysis?

## Overview

Kristi's role within her firm is that of a risk officer, not an economist. However, economic analysis is central to performing her role. Macroeconomic and market factors are significant explanatory factors of operating performance and hence financial outcomes. To evaluate credit risk, underlying macroeconomic and market developments must be understood. Therefore, she will be judged not by the precision of her economic forecasts, but by how well she translates a view of the macroeconomy into credit analysis of her house's investees. The focus of her doctoral program classmates working at the IMF or the BIS is generally limited to macroeconomic (e.g., national economic aggregates), macro-financial (systemic risk), and other sectoral analyses. Kristi's focus is more granular. She does not stop with, for example, the question of how a more restrictive monetary policy stance will affect growth in financial system credit levels or, using the Bank of Commerce case again, how the decline in export tax revenue affects public debt affordability. Instead, she evaluates the impact of the monetary policy stance on the net interest margin of specific financial institutions or the ability of white-goods producer or a mobile telecom operator to close a financing round, and how a rise in sovereign risk premia affects the renewal cost of foreign-sourced funding for her in-country counterparties.

And at this stage, her work is only beginning. Her end-game is to collate the various sets of macro-phenomena/enterprise-level impacts into a holistic credit narrative on which her colleagues on the investment committee can predicate their portfolio construction decisions. In summary, exact predictions are secondary to capturing the correct trend, tracing the impact along their transmission channels, and evaluating the effect on the capacity of her investees to service their obligations fully and on a timely basis.

In addressing the question about how Kristi went about her work, we should recall her doctoral supervisor's admonition of "countries are best analyzed as companies." What does this mean? How is it relevant to our current discussion?

*First*, it helps to suggest a structure of the economy. For illustrative purposes, consider this "Six Panel" format (Fig. 10.1):

This simplified structure divides the economy into domestic and external sectors. The domestic sector covers real-economic, monetary, and financial activity taking place within the national borders of the country, but excludes international trade, investment, and other financial activities in which domestic economic agents are involved.

|  | Domestic Sector | External Sector |
|---|---|---|
| **Real Sector** | • Output<br>• Investment & Savings<br>• Consumption<br>• Government – Spending & Taxes | • Exports<br>• Imports<br>• Investment |
| **Monetary Sector** | • Money Supply<br>• Central Bank Assets & Liabilities<br>• Policy Interest Rates | • Capital Flows<br>• Foreign Exchange Reserves<br>• Exchange Rate |
| **Financial Sector** | • Private Assets & Liabilities<br>• Public Assets & Liabilities<br>• Market Interest Rates | • Private Assets & Liabilities<br>• Public Assets & Liabilities<br>• Market Interest Rates |

**Fig. 10.1** Six Panel macroeconomic summary

In turn, within each of these two sectors, the economy is divided into the three (sub-) sectors: real, monetary, and financial. As noted above, the real sector consists of the standard components of national income, output ("Y") on the supply side and investment ("I"), consumption ("C"), government spending ("G") and net trade, exports ("X") less imports ("M"). Savings ("S") and taxes ("T") are noted. These elements are important to our subsequent analysis. The relationship between G and T determines the fiscal balance and is the major driver of public debt levels.[3] The relationship between S and I is a fundamental determinant of the level of the current and capital accounts. When national fixed investment exceeds national savings, the country turns to foreign markets to cover the deficit in the S-I balance and drives these external balances. The monetary sector centers on the central bank balance sheet and monetary policy activities, policy interest rates, and the money supply within the domestic sector, whilst we place foreign capital flows, foreign exchange reserves, and the rate of exchange. In the financial sector, we include borrowing and lending (assets and liabilities) for both private and public agents and lending conditions (market interest rates and credit standards).

*Second*, let's consider tools. The building blocks of enterprise credit analysis are the income, balance sheet, and cash flow statements. Whilst labelled differently, these statements and their underlying nature and logic are quite similar at the sovereign level. Examine the following (Fig. 10.2):

---

[3] The fiscal balance, the differential between interest rates and the growth rate of the economy, and the effect of changes in exchange rates and market values of tradable debt are the primary drivers of public debt levels.

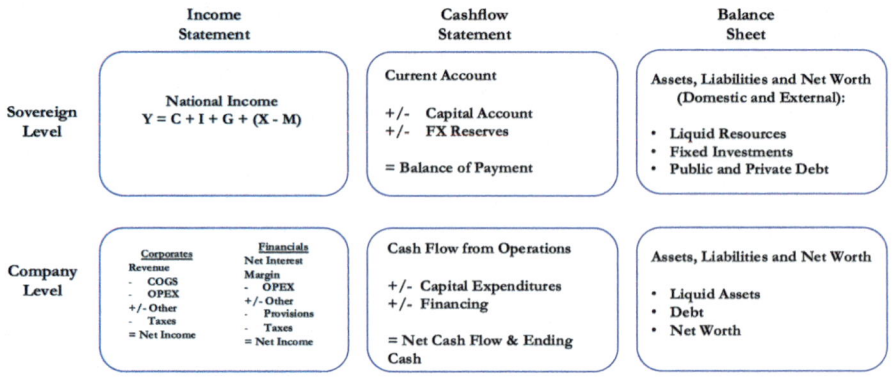

**Fig. 10.2** Financial statements: sovereign versus company levels

We observe that both countries and companies generate income and expend resources to support this effort. For the sovereign, the national income accounts depicting gross domestic product (GDP). First year economics students can cite the basic national income identity of GDP being the sum of consumption, investment, government, and net trade (exports less imports). For enterprises, the profit and loss (or income) statement reports revenue and expenses to arrive at net income. All things being equal, there is a positive correlation between GDP and net income for the average company or bank. Rising national income is good for business on the whole.

Both government and individual enterprises fund their operations from internally generated (or primary) resources and borrow to cover any shortfall. In the case of the government, the funding comes in the form of taxation and other sources (revenue). In cases where expenditures exceed revenue, the government borrows. This debt can be raised from a variety of sources.[4] Similarly, to the extent that cash flow from operations is insufficient to cover capital, financial, and/or other expenditures, enterprises access external funding. In cases when there is an overall shortfall or deficit for the sovereign, the government draws down on domestic reserves (or prints money) or foreign exchange reserves, depending on whether the shortfall is domestic or international. When the sovereign's reserves run out, there is a default. In the case of an enterprise, bankruptcy follows.

The interaction between these cash flow factors at the sovereign and enterprise levels is indirect and more complex than the simple "more GDP is good for business." The implications of a near or actual sovereign default on the

---

[4] The sovereign's resulting "cash flow statement" must be broken down into domestic and foreign components to reflect the sources and nature of the liabilities.

exchange rate (depreciation) and the availability and cost of foreign capital (less supply at a higher price) are both unambiguously negative for enterprise cash flows on the whole. The precise impact will vary of course widely from case to case, depending on the idiosyncratic characteristics of each company's business mix, capital structure, operating performance, and the like.

*Third*, both sovereigns and enterprises have balance sheets, which present summaries of assets, liabilities, and net worth. All things being equal, interpretations of leverage, solvency, funding structure, and liquidity metrics are similar, although the power of the government furnishes the sovereign with far greater flexibility than in the case of an enterprise.

*Overall*, the application of the standard tools of enterprise credit analysis provides a useful analogue to evaluate the critical risks of growth/profitability, fiscal strength/cash flow, debt sustainability, and liquidity in the case of a sovereign. The relevance for this discussion is that by reversing the direction we can enhance the effectiveness of the work of tracing the impact of macro and market developments through their transmission channels to the individual credit at the enterprise level. This is what Kristi did in the Bank of Commerce case.

Consider (Fig. 10.3):

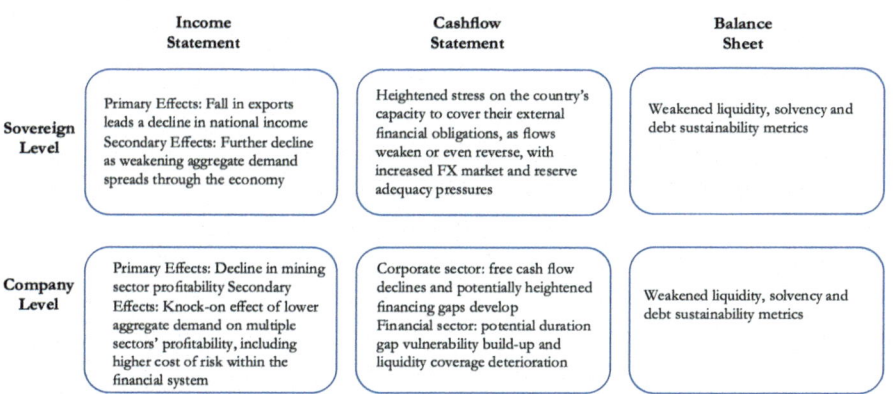

**Fig. 10.3** Copper market—terms of trade shock's effects on financial statements

Let's go a little deeper. For companies *first*, at the base of the analytic pyramid lies growth. To state the obvious, companies with rapidly increasing sales and net income today are likely to be sounder overall credit risks than those losing money. But what about tomorrow? How secure is the current trajectory for sales? Are market conditions—technology, consumer preferences, competition—changing? What is the outlook for operating margins? *Second,* how is the company funding its business? By a conservative blend of debt, equity, and internally generated funds or by a highly leveraged approach? Is today's funding structure sustainable in the future given company operations and market conditions? Are currency, interest rate, and duration mismatches encouraged to achieve short-run gains, but at the risk of financial stress, should market conditions turn? *Third*, do the company's asset-liability and liquidity management approaches provide protection against unforeseen financial market events? What contingent sources of emergency funding exist, should this become necessary?

This set of considerations can be easily tweaked, of course, for a lender to reflect the differences between a company selling white goods (think of National Goods) and a bank extending credit (think of Bank of Commerce, as below). For countries, these credit analysis considerations are similar. GDP growth is the analogue to gross revenue or sales. Cash flow for the government is the sum of taxes and new debt less budget expenditures and debt service, and for the private sector the aggregated cash flows of firms and households. Debt (domestic and external, respectively) to GDP represents a proxy for leverage/solvency, expressible either for the government or the sovereign. To explore further these concepts, let's consider the following "mind map" (Fig. 10.4):

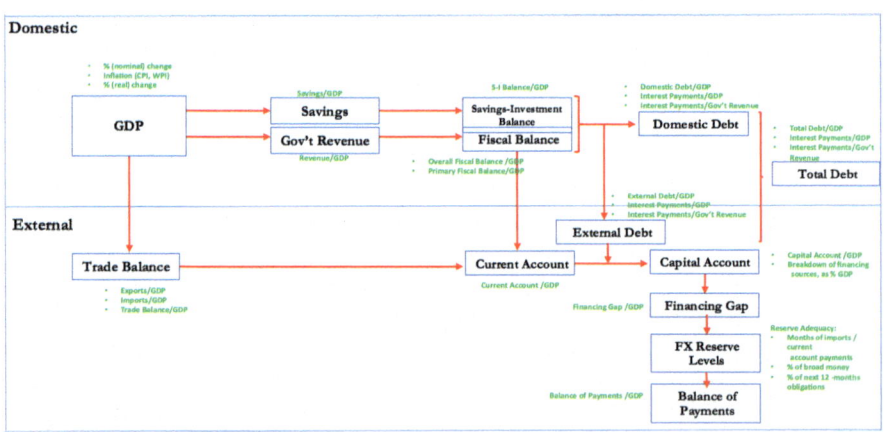

**Fig. 10.4** Analytic mind map

*First,* growth is evaluated by the level, rate of change, sources, and volatility of gross domestic product ("GDP"). Are the drivers of GDP vulnerable to near-term changes in domestic or external conditions? How much policy space does the government have to mitigate these cyclical or structural risks to growth? Are institutions equipped to address these challenges?

*Second*, are national savings sufficient to fund investment? Can the government balance its books? If not, how big a hole is there, and why? In both cases, the deficit must be covered by borrowing. What are the conditions of market access? Are current and projected debt levels sustainable? Is there an excessive dependence on external sources? Does the government confront the same currency, interest rate, and duration mismatches as in the enterprise case?

*Third*, is the external balance compatible with economic fundamentals? Is the near-term external funding gap manageable? Is total foreign debt sustainable over the longer term? Does the country have sufficient liquid foreign exchange reserves to deal with unexpected external shocks? If not, does it have access to emergency liquidity support?

We know in the case of the Bank of Commerce, the exogenous terms of trade shock flowed through several channels, as shown above, using the financial statements taxonomy, which can be traced again using the mind map above.

In the mind map above, we note a number of concepts (e.g., GDP, Savings, Fiscal Balance, etc.), and analytics (ratios, etc.). These data and calculations form the basis of the analysis. There are numerous public and private databases, which furnish the numbers we need. These include: (i) multilateral organizations such as the International Monetary Fund, the World Bank, and the various DFIs; (ii) rating agencies; and (iii) host country sources such as the central bank, ministry of finance, and national statistics offices (Fig. 10.5).

*Fourth*, how do we tie these together as credit analysts?

In the macroeconomic sphere, the credit analyst's objectives are to: (i) identify critical macroeconomic risk elements, which could translate into materially adverse effects on the capacity of an individual borrower to service its indebtedness according to its contractual terms; (ii) estimate the severity of their impact; (iii) as possible, speculate on the likelihood of their occurrence; and (iv) based on available policy and external financial support mechanisms, establish a baseline scenario of the residual risks to be incorporated into the baseline financial projections. To see this, let's consider Kristi's Bank of Commerce case.

In the run-up to her warnings to Ursula, Kristi undertook an in-depth risk analysis of the Bank's host country. Two elements are presented below: (i) Model-Summary Output (Year "Y" covers the year in which Kristi approaches Ursula); and (ii) a "Risk Matrix" (Table 10.1).

| Real-Domestic | Monetary-Domestic |
|---|---|
| Real GDP (% change) | Money and Credit. (% change) |
| GDP Deflator (% change) | Broad Money (% change) |
| Consumer Price Index (% change) | Reserve Money (% change) |
| Total Investment (% GDP) | Credit (% change) |
| Government Investment (% GDP) | Policy Rate (%) |
| Private Investment (% GDP) | **Monetary-External** |
| Total Savings (% GDP) | Capital Account (% GDP) |
| Government Savings (% GDP) | Financial Account (% GDP) |
| Non-Government Savings (% GDP) | Foreign Direct Investment (% GDP) |
| Central Government Budget (% GDP) | Assets (% GDP) |
| Total Revenue (% GDP) | Liabilities (% GDP) |
| Tax Revenue (% GDP) | Portfolio Investment (% GDP) |
| Non-Tax Revenue (% GDP) | Assets (% GDP) |
| Total Expenditure (% GDP) | Liabilities (% GDP) |
| Current (% GDP) | Equity and Investment Funds (% GDP) |
| Capita (% GDP) | Debt Securities (% GDP) |
| Primary Balance (% GDP) | Other Investments (net) (% GDP) |
| Overall Balance (% GDP) | Net Errors and Omissions (% GDP) |
| **Real-External** | Overall Balance (% GDP) |
| Total Exports (% GDP) | Gross Reserves (months imports) |
| Merchandise (% GDP) | **Financial-Domestic** |
| Services (% GDP) | Public Gross Nominal Debt (% GDP) |
| Total Imports (% GDP) | Public Net Nominal Debt (% GDP) |
| Merchandise (% GDP) | Gross Domestic Debt (% GDP) |
| Services (% GDP) | **Financial-External** |
| Trade Balance (% GDP) | Public Gross Nominal Debt (% GDP) |
| Net Investment Income (% GDP) | Public Net Nominal Debt (% GDP) |
| Current Account Balance (% GDP) | Gross Domestic Debt (% GDP) |

**Fig. 10.5** Macroeconomic data headings

# Risk Matrix[5]

Recall that the country in which the Bank of Commerce is located is a high-growth (5% p.a. range historically, but slipping to just under 4% in the last year), middle-income country dependent on copper exports for nearly all of its exports, well over half of government revenue, and roughly a quarter of GDP. An effort has been made to diversify the structure of the economy through the encouragement of foreign direct investment (FDI) in related copper processing and diversified manufacturing activities (Table 10.2).

---

[5] A generic definition of a risk matrix can be found at: https://en.wikipedia.org/wiki/Risk_m atrix. Additionally, highly instructive examples of the application of risk matrices in the context of country macroeconomic and financial sector analysis can be found in Article IV Consultation reports of the International Monetary Fund at https://www.imf.org/en/home, in the country section/publications.

**Table 10.1**  Bank of Commerce—home country model

| | Y-3 | Y-2 | Y-1 | Y | Y+1 | Y+2 | Y+3 |
|---|---|---|---|---|---|---|---|
| **Real-Domestic** | | | | | | | |
| Real GDP (% change) | 5.0 | 5.2 | 3.9 | 2.1 | (0.6) | (1.5) | (0.2) |
| Inflation (CPI, % change) | 6.5 | 7.1 | 5.8 | 5.6 | 4.3 | 3.9 | 3.1 |
| Total Investment (% GDP) | 24 | 26 | 24 | 22 | 20 | 20 | 20 |
| Total Savings (% GDP) | 15 | 14 | 12 | 12 | 12 | 12 | 12 |
| Savings - Investment Balance (% GDP) | (9) | (12) | (12) | (10) | (8) | (8) | (8) |
| Total Revenue (% GDP) | 18 | 19 | 21 | 20 | 20 | 20 | 20 |
| Total Expenditure (% GDP) | 23 | 25 | 26 | 25 | 25 | 25 | 25 |
| Primary Balance (% GDP) | (3) | (4) | (4) | (4) | (4) | (4) | (4) |
| Overall (Fiscal) Balance (% GDP) | (5) | (6) | (5) | (5) | (5) | (5) | (5) |
| **Real-External** | | | | | | | |
| Total Exports (% GDP) | 23 | 25 | 24 | 20 | 18 | 15 | 16 |
| Total Imports (% GDP) | 20 | 21 | 21 | 20 | 19 | 18 | 18 |
| Trade Balance (% GDP) | 3 | 4 | 3 | 0 | (1) | (3) | (2) |
| Investment Income (net; % GDP) | (5) | (5) | (5) | (5) | (5) | (5) | (5) |
| Current Account Balance (% GDP) | (2) | (1) | (2) | (5) | (6) | (8) | (7) |
| **Monetary-Domestic** | | | | | | | |
| Broad Money (% change) | 9 | 11 | 12 | 7 | 7 | 7 | 7 |
| Reserve Money (% change) | 7 | 8 | 9 | (6) | 5 | 5 | 5 |
| Credit (% change) | 12 | 16 | 18 | (9) | 3 | 3 | 3 |
| Policy Rate (% p.a.) | 4 | 4 | 4 | 5 | 5 | 5 | 5 |
| **Monetary-External** | | | | | | | |
| Foreign Direct Investment (% GDP) | 3 | 2 | 2 | 2 | 2 | 2 | 2 |
| Portfolio Investment (% GDP) | 1 | 2 | 0 | (2) | (3) | (1) | (1) |
| Equity and Investment Funds (% GDP) | 1 | 1 | 0 | (0) | (1) | (1) | (1) |
| Debt Securities (% GDP) | 2 | 2 | 1 | (1) | (3) | (1) | 0 |
| Overall Balance (% GDP) | 4 | 5 | 1 | (7) | (11) | (9) | (7) |
| Reserves (gross) (months of imports) | 17 | 18 | 18 | 14 | 5 | 3 | 1 |
| **Financial-Domestic** | | | | | | | |
| Public Gross Debt (% GDP) | 25 | 25 | 30 | 32 | 35 | 38 | 40 |
| **Financial-External** | | | | | | | |
| Gross External Debt (% GDP) | 35 | 40 | 45 | 48 | 53 | 57 | 60 |

With an overall fiscal balance, which has slipped into deficit in recent years, the government began to supplement its tax revenue with long-dated maturity debt issuance, much of which has been sourced in the global markets. Its public debt to GDP ratio is still low at 30%. The banking sector has grown rapidly over the last decade, supported by external funding to a point where approximately half of the banking system liabilities are foreign-sourced and denominated in US dollars. This stock of private, external debt is of relatively short duration of approximately 18 months. Total external debt (public and private) is moderately high at 45% of GDP. The current account deficit is low (2% of GDP).

To encourage FDI and external borrowing, especially to the fast-growing domestic banking sector, the central bank has established a 1:1 FX peg to the

**Table 10.2**  Risk matrix (selected excepts from Kristi's document)

| Risk Type | Probability of Occurrence | Timeframe | Potential Impact | Policy Response |
|---|---|---|---|---|
| **(1) Growth** | | | | |
| (i) Structurally weak growth in key advanced economies. | Medium | Medium-Term | **High.** This would negatively affect (i) the trade balance and current account of the balance of payments by reducing copper and other exports; (ii) the financial account of the balance of payments by reducing foreign direct investment and portfolio inflows; (iii) a reduction in export tax revenue, with an adverse impact on the government's fiscal and debt positions; and (iv) weaker domestic economic growth. | (i) Move progressively to a regime of exchange rate flexibility and engage in liquidity support with multilateral institutions |
| (ii) Significant slowdown in China and other key import markets and their spill overs. | High | Short-Term | | (ii) Accelerate reforms to increase competitiveness of non-copper exports . |
| **(2) Weak demand for copper** | High | Short-Term | **High.** This could occur as part of (1) above, but has potential to occur as a result of technical and other factors. | See (1) above and undertake measures to bolster precautionary FX reserves |
| Risk Type | Probability of Occurrence | Timeframe | Potential Impact | Policy Response |
| **(3) Financial conditions** | | | | |
| (i) Direct impact of currency depreciation on financial institution funding costs and capitalization | High | Short-Term | **Medium.** The impact would vary across the financial system, depending on the idiosyncratic characteristics of individual institutions and their capacity to raise new capital to counter pressures on liquidity and solvency. | (i) Strengthen financial sector supervision and liquidity support mechanisms. (iii) Strengthen policies to bolster macroeconomic fundamentals and growth in small- and medium-sized businesses |
| (ii) Indirect impacts of slowing growth and reduced export proceeds on asset quality. | Medium to High | Short- to Medium-Term | | |
| **(4) Breaking the USD peg** | High | Short-Term | **High.** This could occur as part of (1) and (2) above, should the capacity of the central bank to defend the currency peg be exhausted. solvency. | See (1)(i) above. |

US Dollar. The country has substantial foreign exchange reserves (8 months of imports) to support the exchange rate.

In the Risk Matrix (see above), Kristi had identified the price and volume of copper exports as the key to the country's economic health. A material decline would exploit external, fiscal, and financial vulnerabilities. Her downside scenario eventually played out. With a slowing in global economic activity, especially in major copper importers like China, demand for copper followed, with predictable knock-on effects on the country's economy and financial sector. Growth fell. Lower export proceeds led to reduced FX reserves and more frequent market intervention to support the currency peg. The decline in export tax revenue necessitated higher levels of government borrowing at the very time that there was a discernible slackening in capital inflows.

These developments also created stresses on the financial sector. Higher interest rates pressured lending margins. Asset quality began to show signs of deterioration as economic activity slowed. As NPLs and provisioning spiked, foreign lenders began to cut back their exposure to the local banks, which forced a curtailment in credit, as well as exacerbating the increasingly tight liquidity. The impact of these lower credit volumes, higher loan loss provisions and, once the currency peg broke, FX translation losses weighed on systemic solvency, with weaker institutions like the Bank of Commerce forced into liquidation.

From a collapse in global demand for copper to a bank being liquidated—Kristi had warned her business colleagues this could happen. Their credit decision was based on a view that such a scenario would not play out. And in terms of the frequency (hence the likelihood) of these events actually occurring, the business side was more right than wrong, until it actually happened.

# Cases and Learnings

In this section, we present a set of brief cases. The objective is to reinforce certain learnings for the analyst when interpreting the impact of macroeconomic trends or shocks on credit risk. For each, we provide a background snapshot of the country and borrower, a catalyst, and the impact of the catalyst on the borrower. At the end, we summarize the key takeaways.

## Case 1

### Taper Tantrum

*Background*

Country

- An BBB-rated emerging market sovereign with significant foreign portfolio capital flows and in whose highly dollarized domestic financial markets non-resident investors represent a significant portion of total systemic funding.

- Foreign bank branches constitute roughly one-third of banking system assets.
- The ratio of external short-term financial obligation to liquid foreign exchange reserves is roughly 1.25 to 1.
- The exchange rate regime is floating, with historically limited central bank involvement.

Borrower

- A mid-size chemical Borrower, which imports much of its raw materials and sells exclusively into the local market.
- The Borrower has moderately high leverage, but has pursued a funding strategy of borrowing in the form of short- and medium-term, foreign currency-denominated, floating (quarterly re-set) rate credits from a combination of local/foreign bank branches, and foreign-based funds. The average duration of the funding book is roughly two years. Over the next six months, roughly one-third of the funding book will roll over.

*Catalyst*

After a multi-year period of highly accommodative monetary policy, the US Federal Reserve signals an eventual, slow transition to a more normalized policy stance. Markets overreact. Capital flows out of the EM space, with intense selling pressure on local currencies. Domestic monetary and financial conditions tighten. Central banks raise interest rates to defend their currencies. With funds flowing out of financial systems, credit availability decreases and cost of funding spikes.

*Impact*

- The immediate impact of the depreciating exchange rate on the cost of goods sold is limited, but the effect on debt service costs is instantaneous and severe.
- The refinancing exercise confronts strong headwinds, with immediate renewals or replacement funding only possible on about three quarters of the requirements, albeit at higher costs and with shorter duration.

- The Borrower's available cash reserves will just cover the next three months, but thereafter a liquidity crisis looms. After this point, should the adverse conditions persist, cash flow from operations will be depressed, further exacerbating their situation.

## Case 2

### Drought

*Background*

Country

- A low-income, primarily agricultural economy, with a burgeoning free-port manufacturing center.
- Farming has been dependent on the annual rainy season, as the development of water storage and irrigation infrastructure was constrained due to a paucity of public resources. Crop–weather insurance is not available due to lack of requisite infrastructure and institutions. Government revenue as a percentage of GDP is amongst the lowest in the frontier market space and is spent predominantly on current outlays.
- The government took advantage of a recent wave of investor interest in frontier market debt issues and raised funds aimed at further developing the country' manufacturing capacity and to address shortfalls in the operating budget. This debt issuance combined with heightened foreign lending into the country's banking and microfinance sector raised the Debt to GDP ratio into the low 40% range, a high level when compared to similar countries. FX reserve levels are modest, covering only a few months of imports.
- A loan program from a DFI was contracted to address the vulnerabilities of the agricultural sector, most notably that of water security.

Borrower

- A non-bank financial institution focused primarily on small and medium holder farming and microenterprises.
- The institution operates with only a moderate equity buffer above the regulatory minimum. Funding is exclusively in the form of medium-term senior, unsecured loans from private impact investment funds and DFIs.

Liquidity coverage and stable funding ratios are within prudential ranges. The institution has been consistently profitable, albeit at a modest level.
- Shareholders are led by two international charities, whose capability to raise new equity is questionable.

*Catalyst*

A severe drought hit the region. Both food security and cash crops were affected. Estimates placed the decline of overall agricultural production at roughly 30%.

*Impact*

- NPLs spiked as farmers' harvests were insufficient to cover their obligations.
- The combination of the reduced interest income, higher debt service expenses (due to a depreciation in the local currency), and an increase in the cost of risk (provisioning) pushed the institution's net result into a loss and solvency close to the regulatory minimum.

# Case 3

## Inflationary Spiral

*Background*

### Country

- A low-investment grade credit, with a long history of a modest, but steady growth, a nearly balanced budget, a stable external position with adequate reserves, low levels of foreign debt, and a moderately positive current account.
- Since last year's election a new, populist government has pursued an economic program aimed at achieving greater income and wealth distribution. To fund the effort, the government has begun to run a quite sizeable fiscal deficit, to increase the rate of expansion in the money supply to several times above the historical norm, and to encourage business and personal lending, whose totals also rose to record levels.

Borrower

- A nationwide budget-electronics retail sales company.
- The offer of deferred payment terms to buyers has been an important catalyst for sales, but does create a heavy working capital finance burden.
- The size of the store network has doubled over the past year, as the management took advantage of the easy money and strong growth environment to expand their market coverage. The capex was exclusively debt-financed.
- Total leverage is high, but given the Borrower's robust operating cash flow, debt affordability is manageable.

*Catalyst*

Excess aggregate demand builds up, with the result that inflation rises sharply to 25% per annum and the current account slips into negative territory, as imports surge. The government responds with a series of measures to cool down the economy, including a rise in interest rates, a siphoning off of liquidity in the financial system, and a cutback in government spending. The contractionary policies succeeded in dampening the inflationary pressures, but these come at the cost of a severe decline in economic activity, with falls in investment, industrial production, and consumption, and an upwelling in unemployment.

*Impact*

- The strong decline in the Borrower's sales and increased financing costs resulted in a net loss.
- Operating cash flow was halved, reflecting the weaker operating result and an increase in accounts receivable average collection period and inventory days on hand, and combined with tighter financial conditions which limited access to refinancings and new credits, leaving the Borrower with insufficient liquidity to meet its debt obligations.

## Case 4

### Pandemic

*Background*

<u>Country</u>

- A middle-income country.
- Over the past decade, the country has consistently grown by roughly 5% each year. The economy is highly diversified amongst mining, manufacturing, and services. The current account deficit has increased progressively to just under 10%. Debt capital into the local banking sector and foreign direct investment into the mining and manufacturing sectors have covered this deficit and permitted FX reserves to accumulate into the range of 6–7 months imports. External debt to GDP has remained in the mid 50% range for the past several years. The financial system is moderately dollarized (40–45% assets and liabilities). The exchange rate is loosely pegged to the US dollar and has traded within a narrow band for the last two years.

<u>Borrower</u>

- A commercial bank focused on SME lending.
- The institution is conservatively leveraged (20% capital to total assets), maintains a disciplined credit and lending practice, which has resulted in a low level of NPLs, and has been consistently profitable over the recent past.
- The shareholders' capacity and willingness to provide equity support is graded as low to medium.
- One area of weakness is the concentration of its sources of funding. On the deposit side, 10 institutional depositors account for roughly 50% of the deposit book (one-third of liabilities) and 8 lenders for all of the borrowed funds (two-thirds of liabilities). As a mitigant, most of these parties have been creditors to the bank for a longer period and hence are deemed to be highly secure sources of funding.

*Catalyst*

Due to a dangerous rise in the level of COVID-19 infections, the government was forced to impose a lockdown on the economy. With the exception of essential services (medical, food, etc.), all commercial and financial establishments were closed. The measures will be relaxed and eventually lifted entirely once the incidence of infections declines to a manageable level as determined by the government.

*Impact*

- The Central Bank announced a policy of forbearance to address temporary loan payment problems, under which all borrowers current in their payments could request a six-month deferral of principal, and in exceptional cases, the capitalization of interest. At the time of the government action, the bank's NPLs amounted to 3%. Roughly one-half of the remainder of the portfolio availed themselves of Central Bank's restructuring (deferral) program, with half of these requesting the capitalization of interest. The net effect was to lower cash inflows.
- For the economy as whole, speculative investors anticipated domestic and external financial stresses and began to withdraw funds. As a result, selling pressure developed on the local currency. The central bank intervened to limit depreciation. Still, the currency lost 10% of its value within the first two months of the crisis.
- For the bank, certain of the non-resident depositors withdrew their funds, further exacerbating the bank's liquidity position. The lenders' obligations were medium term in nature and hence positions could only be reduced through the declaration of a default.

## Summary—Key Learnings

1. **Case 1 (Taper Tantrum)**
   The identified vulnerability is the country's acute exposure to adverse developments in global financial markets. We see this from the high external debt levels and the short duration and foreign currency of liabilities for both the sovereign and the private sector. When the supply of foreign capital declines rapidly and its cost escalates, domestic liquidity tightens, and debt affordability decreases. In this case, the impact is studied in the corporate sector, but it has similar effects within the financial system. For the corporate sector, debt service coverage and refinancings could become problematic. In the financial system, threats are at two levels. The first is the bank's own liquidity management. The second

is the impact on its borrowers' debt service capacity and eventually on the bank's asset quality, profitability, and solvency.

2. **Case 2 (Drought)**

The identified vulnerability is twofold: first, a heavy dependence on one sector or activity, agriculture in our case and, second, the lack of public and private resources to address the gravest potential threat of drought. The sovereign's limited fiscal space and low domestic savings are to blame. When the rains fail, the economy suffers grievously. For our financial institution, widespread ruined crops translate into widespread defaults within its loan portfolio, with predictable knock-on effects to profitability and solvency, as well as setting on motion a liquidity crisis, should funders retreat from supporting the institution.

3. **Case 3 (Inflationary Spiral)**

Business cycles are "part of the landscape." However, the greater the boom, the greater the bust. In this case, the government pursued overly aggressive expansionary policies, which created a potential threat of hyperinflation. The medicine to counter this threat was stiff and threw the economy into a deep recession. Seasoned risk managers on both the borrower and lender sides would have realized that the government's economic policies were unsustainable and acted to insulate themselves from the inevitable hangover. Rates of increase in the money supply and credit that jump quickly into the realm of multiples of GDP growth alone should set off red warning lights, and especially as in our case when combined with substantial deficit spending.

4. **Case 4 (Pandemic)**

This is of course the reality of 2020 and 2021. We repeat the case here to re-emphasize the unique nature of the pandemic's macroeconomic fallout and to highlight the special credit management challenges. The duration of most garden-variety recessions can be forecast within a reasonable range. And occasionally, there are double-dip recessions. In these cases, well understood, traditional tools can be employed and the outcome is fairly predictable. The COVID-19 downturn is different. As goes the virus, so does the economy. Multiple waves of infections may mean multiple lockdowns and multiple growth downturns. The depth and the breadth of the economic fallout resemble something akin to war or a tropical cyclone. Combined, these characteristics would have presented a daunting challenge even to our Kristi. The first wave was unforeseen, subsequent waves unknowable. Hence, as discussed above in Chapter 9, the restructuring solution requires bold and creative thinking.

# 11

# Legal Issues in Restructurings

**Abstract** The chapter gives a high-level review of recurrent key legal issues in emerging markets restructurings. Whilst many of the issues have been touched on in prior chapters in the book, the reader is given the opportunity to consider these legal issues in greater detail. The discussion covers the interface of multiple legal systems, the INSOL II Principles, the rule of law, the nature of local legal systems, standstill agreements, confidentiality and bank secrecy, term sheets, governing law and dispute resolution, antecedent transactions, availability and jurisdictional hurdles of international hubs for judicial restructurings (USA, UK, and Singapore), debt to equity swaps, equity creditors, third-party credit support, new money, syndicated lenders, bondholders and liability management, secured lenders, vicarious liability, wrongful trading, overlay restructuring agreements and overlay wind-down agreements.

**Keywords** Antecedent transaction · Balance sheet · Bank secrecy · Bankruptcy · Borrower · Confidentiality · Consensual restructuring · Coordinating committee · Corporate debt · Debt · Debtor · Debt to equity conversion · Cash flow · COVID-19 · Credit analysis · Credit checks · DFI (development finance institution) · Distressed debt · Equity creditors · Emerging market · Frontier market · Holdout lender · Hybrid restructuring · INSOL II · INSOL principles · Insolvency · Judicial restructuring · Lender leadership · New money · Non-performing loans · Pre-insolvency · Rescue proceeding · Restructure · Restructuring · Restructuring plan · Rogue lender · Scheme of arrangement · Shadow

© The Author(s), under exclusive license to Springer Nature
Switzerland AG 2021
R. Marney and T. Stubbs, *Corporate Debt Restructuring in Emerging Markets*,
https://doi.org/10.1007/978-3-030-81306-2_11

director · Shareholder(s) · Standstill · Steering committee · US Chapter 11 · Vicarious liability · Wind-down · Workout

## Introduction

This chapter gives a high-level review of some of the main recurrent legal issues in emerging markets workouts, from the standpoint of the practicing transactional lawyer.

Issues will of course vary from deal to deal, and country to country (depending inter alia on the nature and stage of development of its laws, its courts, its insolvency system, etc.).

The reader may already be fluent in some or all of these issues (e.g., if (s)he is a more experienced in-house counsel, a credit/restructuring officer with prior emerging markets workout experience, etc.) and may wish only to consult the topics below on a selective basis.

The authors' intent is to provide a broad set of legal reference points for appreciating the case studies and discussions in the earlier chapters of this book and moving on to future restructurings. Many of the issues have already been discussed to some degree in Chapters 3–8. This chapter is not intended to be an exhaustive list of the issues but rather to highlight the main issues which typically arise.

As previously mentioned, legal issues play a fundamental role in an emerging market restructuring, at all phases—from Pre-Restructuring through to Implementation. Competent international and local legal support are essential.

Although each restructuring transaction will be different from the one before it, nonetheless, the authors observe that many of the practical and substantive legal issues which arise are similar in theme and nature. Depending on the particular transaction, its stakeholders, the financing structure, the jurisdiction, and the causes of distress, some of these issues may play a more prominent role in a particular transaction, whilst others less so.

These issues will emerge under (and usually involve some interface between) various different legal systems, such as:

- that of the *borrower's jurisdiction*, which will usually drive the tax, corporate, securities, financial/regulatory, insolvency, real estate, employment/pension, IP, competition, operational, customer/supplier, litigation, and other legal issues;

- where offshore equity structures (e.g., a holding company, a shareholder finance vehicle, etc.) are used, such *offshore jurisdictions' legal systems* will also come into play[1];
- the applicable law of the *loans and other finance documents* (e.g., security, guarantees, and other credit support) with the lenders;
- those of relevant *third parties* (e.g., shareholders offering credit support, off-takers, suppliers, contractors, licensors, guarantors of concessions, landlords, etc.) and their contractual arrangements with the borrower;
- those of *the lenders* and other financial counterparties (e.g., hedging, ECAs, etc.);
- those of any parties providing *new capital or other new money*, such as lenders, buyers, investors, etc., and the law of relevant documentation underlying such new money; and
- the applicable law of the *restructuring agreements*, e.g., standstill agreements, overlay restructuring agreements, and the like.

Of the above issues, *insolvency law issues* are often the most critical and will require thorough knowledge by the transaction leadership's advisors (even though, again, the goal will be to avoid a judicial insolvency proceeding via a successful workout). These issues will impact on the proposed allocation of lender concessions and cash distributions, priorities of new moneys, contingency planning for risks, and the like.

It will be recalled, certain lenders (and/or equity holders) such as DFIs will not be subject to any sovereign nation's legal system but rather to their own constitutional documents, that is, the international treaties and other instruments which create them under general *international law*. They may also enjoy key privileges and immunities under those instruments, which must be acknowledged and respected in the workout. Similarly, ECAs will have their own special status. These organizations will not be driven solely by profit motives, but rather by their respective development mandates.[2] They

---

[1] In many emerging markets it is common to see offshore special purpose vehicles (or SPVs) frequently used for M&A and financing structures. It is commonly perceived (particularly post-Panama-Papers) that this is predominantly for unlawful tax evasion purposes. However, on closer legal analysis there is often a legitimate motive for using these SPVs in lieu of local corporate structures. For example, they may provide a far better framework for ensuring enforceable *corporate governance* arrangements, for ensuring meaningful *dispute resolution* provisions in the form of an international arbitration clause between equity JV partners, and/or for *easier and quicker enforcement of security* over a lower asset structure (e.g., via a holding company share pledge).

[2] By way of example, the European Bank for Reconstruction and Development (EBRD), established in 1991 to help build a new, post-Cold War era in Central and Eastern Europe, has a special mandate combining support of its countries of operation for progress toward becoming market economies committed to and applying the principles of multi-party democracy and pluralism. In recent years EBRD's mandate has expanded to ensure that countries of operation are inclusive,

can indeed play a critical role in many emerging markets workouts, given that they are often prepared to step into a transaction leadership position and/or otherwise act to ensure the success of a workout. They are also often seen by investment funds and commercial lenders as non-biased and hence attractive candidates for lender leadership in workouts.[3]

The challenge of structuring, agreeing, and implementing a consensual restructuring against this complex and multidimensional legal background becomes all the more formidable in the emerging market setting, given the particularities of emerging markets discussed previously.[4]

There are already tomes of professional materials available on legal issues in restructurings generally (and a multitude of precedent documents to implement them, e.g., reservation of rights letters, waiver letters, pre-negotiation letters, coordinating committee appointment letters, standstill agreements, and the like). Most international law firms who advise on cross-border workouts will also have their own internal precedents and well-developed practice notes to guide them and their clients.

---

well-governed, green, resilient, and integrated. EBRD furthermore places strong emphasis on the environment and sustainable energy. By 2019, climate finance accounted for 46% of EBRD's total annual investment. Finally, in 2020 with the onset of the global COVID-19 pandemic EBRD responded by committing all its activity in 2020–2021 (expected to amount to Euro 21 billion) to countering its economic impact. See www.ebrd.com. The mission of the Black Sea Trade and Development Bank (BSTDB) is to contribute effectively to the transition process of its member states toward economic prosperity of the people of the region. See www.bstdb.org. By contrast, the Asian Development Bank (ADB) is committed to achieving a prosperous, inclusive, resilient, and sustainable Asia and the Pacific, whilst sustaining efforts to eradicate extreme poverty. In 2020 ADB deployed an assistance package of $20 billion to help its members counter the severe impacts of COVID-19. See www.adb.org. The African Development Bank (AfDB) has as its mandate to contribute to the sustainable economic development and social progress of its regional members individually and jointly. It is focused heavily on poverty reduction, with particular emphasis on water, including agriculture, energy, environment, water supply, and sanitation. See www.afdb.org. Similarly, a triumvirate of DFIs in Latin America and the Caribbean provide market leadership in the development and integration of the region: the Inter-American Development Bank (IDB), CAF—Development Bank of Latin America (CAF), and FONPLATA. See www.iadb.org, www.caf.com, and www.fonplata.org. Most recently, the Asian Infrastructure Investment Bank (AIIB) was founded in 2015 to foster sustainable economic development, to create wealth and to improve infrastructure connectivity in Asia. See www.aaib.org. The European Investment Bank (EIB), the lending arm of the European Union (EU), is also active in various emerging markets. It advances a broad mandate to support continued development and integration and build a stable and open world economy. See www.eib.org. And, of course, the International Finance Corporation (IFC), one of the oldest global development banks founded in 1956, has as its mandate to promote economic development by supporting productive private enterprise in its developing member countries in partnership with private sector clients. See www.ifc.org. This is by no means meant to be an exhaustive list but rather to flag some of the larger, more well-known multilateral DFIs operating in emerging markets.

[3] This is not to say that DFIs will support a workout in every distress situation. DFIs do permit their borrowers to enter formal insolvencies when they see this as appropriate. Critically, a DFI must be convinced that survival of the borrower by restructuring is consistent with its respective development mandate.

[4] See, e.g., Chapter 7 above.

Accordingly, the authors will forego providing or repeating what is already available for legal practitioners.[5] We will instead try to outline some of the more common "big picture" legal problems encountered in emerging markets workouts, with observations on possible strategies for solutions.

As a first step in this process, the authors see merit in reminding the reader of the basic guidelines for multi-creditor workouts, as embodied in the INSOL II Principles. We mentioned the INSOL II Principles a number of times earlier in the book.[6] But we believe it is worth the reader's time to read and digest the actual text of the Principles, so as to reinforce their main conceptual framework. Thereafter, we will delve into some common legal issues in emerging markets in the consensual restructuring context.

As a reminder, the INSOL II Principles are not a set of rules intended to have binding force per se under any country's legal system[7]; nor are they intended to constitute themselves any form of contractually binding obligations (though the Principles will often be clearly reflected in the operative terms of the relevant legal agreements and the process by which these are negotiated and agreed).[8]

Rather, they are a set of *conceptual principles* developed by restructuring specialists in the course of decades of workouts. If voluntarily applied by all stakeholders,[9] they provide a rational common framework for approaching

---

[5] In any event, this book is not intended to be a legal treatise for lawyers but rather a practical guide for restructuring specialists.

[6] *See* Chapter 5.

[7] The authors and other practitioners have observed that the non-binding nature of INSOL II Principles may well be one of the reasons they are not readily understood in certain emerging markets, where market participants (entreprenuers, lenders) prefer the formality of a rules-based approach. This has led to certain initiatives (adoption or recommendation) of the INSOL II Principles by regulators. See, e.g., https://www.ebrd.com/news/2016/hungarian-reg ulator-to-adopt-best-practice-guidelines-for-corporate-outofcourt-restructuring.html (reporting on the EBRD's project with the Hungarian National Bank).

[8] The World Bank Toolkit includes a letter of intent (or term sheet) reciting the INSOL II Principles (virtually verbatim) and which the parties undertake to observe. *See* A Toolkit for Out-of-Court Workouts, *op. cit.* In the authors' experience, it is probably counterproductive to try and impose such an approach in practice. Firstly, a term sheet's utility is in its brevity (it should be kept to a minimum, at least prior to due diligence during standstill). Second, the INSOL II Principles themselves are too broad to serve as the text for a term sheet. Including them verbatim would likely raise various concerns by lenders and their legal departments (who ordinarily are extremely hesitant to undertake contractual obligations which might form the basis for a claim for breach of contract later, e.g., the alleged failure to observe INSOL II Principles recited verbatim in a term sheet). Finally, even if a term sheet refers to and/or recites INSOL II Principles verbatim—and expressly stipulates that these are non-binding on the parties—the utility is limited. The authors believe merely referring to the INSOL II Principles on an *informal verbal basis* as a voluntary conceptual framework for collaboration between lenders, a borrower and its shareholders is probably the most practical approach.

[9] It is critical that not only lenders, but *borrowers, their management, shareholders, and UBOs* must also embrace the INSOL II Principles. Often one of the greatest obstacles to a successful workout will be the borrower's own willingness to engage in good faith in workout discussions and to abide

the myriad of legal and financial issues whilst trying to rescue a distressed business on a consensual basis.

In the authors' personal experiences, knowing and applying the Principles in practice will heighten the likelihood of a successful outcome for all stakeholders.

## INSOL II Principles[10]

**FIRST PRINCIPLE**: Where a debtor is found to be in financial difficulties, all relevant creditors should be prepared to cooperate with each other to give sufficient (though limited) time (a "Standstill Period") to the debtor for information about the debtor to be obtained and evaluated and for proposals for resolving the debtor's financial difficulties to be formulated and assessed, unless such a course is inappropriate in a particular case.

**SECOND PRINCIPLE**: During the Standstill Period, all relevant creditors should agree to refrain from taking any steps to enforce their claims against or (otherwise than by disposal of their debt to a third party) to reduce their exposure to the debtor but are entitled to expect that during the Standstill Period their position relative to other creditors and each other will not be prejudiced. Conflicts of interest in the creditor group should be identified early and dealt with appropriately.

**THIRD PRINCIPLE**: During the Standstill Period, the debtor should not take any action which might adversely affect the prospective return to relevant creditors (either collectively or individually) as compared with the position at the Standstill Commencement Date.

**FOURTH PRINCIPLE**: The interests of relevant creditors are best served by coordinating their response to a debtor in financial difficulty. Such coordination will be facilitated by the selection of one or more representative coordination committees and by the appointment of professional advisors to advise and assist such committees and, where appropriate, the relevant creditors participating in the process as a whole.

**FIFTH PRINCIPLE**: During the Standstill Period, the debtor should provide, and allow relevant creditors and/or their professional advisors reasonable and timely access to, all relevant information relating to its assets, liabilities, business, and prospects, in order to enable proper evaluation to

by those aspects of the INSOL II Principles geared toward transparency and value preservation for lenders.

[10] *See*    www.insol.org/_files/Publications/StatementOfPrinciples/Statement%20of%20Principles%20II%2018%20April%202017%20BML.pdf.

be made of its financial position and any proposals to be made to relevant creditors.

**SIXTH PRINCIPLE**: Proposals for resolving the financial difficulties of the debtor and, so far as practicable, arrangements between relevant creditors relating to any standstill should reflect applicable law and the relative positions of relevant creditors at the Standstill Commencement Date.

**SEVENTH PRINCIPLE**: Information obtained for the purposes of the process concerning the assets, liabilities, and business of the debtor and any proposals for resolving its difficulties should be made available to all relevant creditors and should, unless already publicly available, be treated as confidential.

**EIGHTH PRINCIPLE**: If additional funding is provided during the Standstill Period or under any rescue or restructuring proposals, the repayment of such additional funding should, so far as practicable, be accorded priority status as compared to other indebtedness or claims of relevant creditors.

-&-

These Principles will drive the nature of the legal issues, the structure of the workout, and the substantive content of the legal documentation.

At the same time, the authors observe from their experience and research that INSOL II Principles are *not* strictly followed in all emerging markets.[11] On the contrary, there can sometimes be great differences between the approaches of international lenders (financial institutions, debt funds, DFIs,

---

[11] As discussed in Chapter 5 above, familiarity with INSOL II Principles varies greatly in emerging markets. This depends inter alia on the level of relative development of the market's financial services and legal community, its depth of integration into the global economy, its historical and cultural ties to global financial capitals, the extent to which its academic institutions, government authorities and/or regulators may have promoted consensual workouts, and the like. In some markets, the Principles may be well known (or at least recognized as reflecting common-sense). In others, the concepts embedded in the Principles might have even been reflected to some extent in the law itself. For example, Uzbekistan's Bankruptcy Law of 2003 has a separate chapter devoted to workouts (*dosudebnaya sanatsia*). And in 2002 Argentina reformed its insolvency system to promote workouts ("*Acuerdo Preventivo Extrajudicial*" or "APE"). Workouts then became increasingly common, especially with larger corporate borrowers (e.g., Telecom, CTI, Autopistas del Sol and Multicanal), who suffered from the 2001 financial crisis and resultant peso devaluation. The Principles are now more frequently used as a roadmap in APE negotiations. In another example from Ukraine, in 2016 the National Bank of Ukraine and the Ukrainian Ministry of Finance requested EBRD's support in creating an out-of-court debt restructuring mechanism to address the high rate of non-performing loans. EBRD's collaboration with Ukrainian authorities resulted in enactment of the Ukrainian Law on Financial Restructuring in June 2016 (as amended), establishment of an administrative Secretariat and an Arbitration Committee for disputes, two new institutions created by the Law, arbitration rules and Restructuring Guidelines for stakeholders. As of March 2021, 41 cases (more than USD 2.258 billion) were successfully restructured under the new framework. Almost all restructurings were bilateral and by one public bank (Oschadbank).

etc.) on the one hand and local lenders on the other hand.[12] The latter are likely to be less familiar with the INSOL II Principles, and there may also be a tendency to see individualist behavior, free riders, and holdouts amongst such lenders. Furthermore, some borrowers' management and shareholders can, in more difficult legal environments (where there is a lower level of rule of law, immature legal systems, etc.), treat lenders with impunity knowing that the lenders have limited negotiating leverage. This attitude can act as a barrier to effective workouts and lead to long delays in resolution of distress. In cases where a distressed debt market is limited, this often leaves lenders stuck in limbo and willing to accept temporary solutions such as merely refinancing with a longer maturity—"kicking the proverbial can down the road"—in lieu of properly restructuring the borrower's business or balance sheet.[13]

This is not to say INSOL II Principles are irrelevant in emerging markets. Quite the contrary. Rather, their acceptance and utility as a guide will depend on the parties themselves and most importantly lender leadership, through whose guidance and inspiration compromise may be reached. The Principles can and indeed are used, often successfully, *when advocated by lender leadership*. The authors believe they should thus be referred to by lender leadership as starting point whenever possible and be adapted as circumstances dictate.

## Some Common Legal Problems in Emerging Markets Restructurings

### The Rule of Law and Its Impact on Restructurings

Having made the conscious decision to lend to the borrower in the first place, it is assumed lender leadership will have been previously introduced (at least in theory, if not in actual practice) to the realities of working in an environment where there may be weak institutional "buy-in" to the rule of law and varying degrees of accountability on the part of public servants. The regulation, legislation, and judicial practice may be nascent or still under development. The law may also be applied differently in practice (as between

---

[12] In some emerging markets, local lenders may be wary of workouts, fearing repercussions and/or even liability for acts taken outside of a more formal framework. For example, Turkish banks prefer to use the Framework Agreements established by the Banking Association in cooperation with the BRSA regulator, which benefit from an exemption from various taxes and also offer protection against a potential charge of embezzlement under Article 160 of the Banking Law by virtue of Provisional Article 32 (of the Banking Law).

[13] In the words of one emerging markets restructuring consultant, "Sometimes it is just a question of getting lucky" in dealing with a given situation.

international and local parties) than is apparent from the plain statutory language.

Unfortunately, unlike more developed legal systems, in emerging markets justice does not always wear a blindfold—frequently, one senses she rules with her eyes wide open and the occasional wry wink.

This is not to say that the legal systems of all emerging markets are void of the rule of law or that all individual judges on the bench, regulators, or other governmental officials (or the bar or insolvency office holders) are rotten apples.

Quite the opposite: the dedicated work of many jurists and public servants has resulted in major improvements over recent decades. The work of the World Bank, various DFIs, non-governmental organizations, international law firms and accounting firms, universities, academic and professional exchange programs, and exchange of information in the last decade (via the internet) have had a distinctly positive impact on attitudes toward the rule of law in emerging markets.[14] Advances in promoting rule of law have also been reflected in the ratings by organizations that track corruption, such as Transparency International in its annual corruption perception index (CPI) and the World Bank in its Doing Business survey.[15]

A number of emerging markets have made genuine improvement in their legal systems and their ability to assist commercial parties in the efficient enforcement of contracts. For example, it may surprise some that countries often associated with high levels of corruption are advanced in the ability of their judicial systems to enforce contract rights efficiently.In the authors' experience, in the absence of elements which introduce risk of political or other interference, it may indeed be preferable for smaller, run of the mill commercial disputes to be processed by local courts in lieu of alternative dispute resolution such as arbitration.

That said, many countries still lag behind in terms of separation of power (e.g., interference by the executive branch in the work of the judiciary). Many of the problems observed are political in nature (rigidity against democratic

---

[14] *See* https://www.worldbank.org/en/topic/governance/brief/justice-rights-and-public-safety.

[15] *See* https://www.transparency.org/en/cpi/2020. The CPI index measures perceptions of public sector corruption in countries on a comparative basis (with corruption being defined as "abuse of entrusted power for private gain." *See* https://www.transparency.org/en/blog/cpi-2012-what-is-public-sector-cor ruption). A number of emerging markets have made substantial progress in the CPI at the time of publication of this book—e.g., Uruguay, Singapore, Hong Kong. Also, others have also demonstrated an upward trend, e.g., Armenia, Kosovo, Seychelles, Botswana, Cabo Verde, Rwanda, Mauritius, UAE, Qatar, and others. The World Bank enforcing contracts indicator (one of its Doing Business indexes) "measures the time and cost for resolving a commercial dispute through a local first-instance court, and the quality of judicial processes index, evaluating whether each economy has adopted a series of good practices that promote quality and efficiency in the court system." *See* https://www. doingbusiness.org/en/data/exploretopics/enforcing-contracts.

development; retrenchment and consolidation of political power; oppression of political opposition; appointment of pro-government judges; flawed elections with limited oversight by the judiciary; abuse of criminal justice system for political purposes and other human rights violations).[16]

For a lender, this also creates the risk that in certain cases these flaws can occasionally impact on the conduct of financial transactions and in particular the resolution of commercial disputes, debt/security enforcement, and insolvency proceedings. In many countries, having "friends in high places" can give an unfair advantage and sometimes even be a deciding factor in a purely commercial dispute. The unwary foreign investor or lender may also be surprised by sudden turns of event.[17,18]

Informal (including political or commercial, often both) power structures may overrule formal constitutional power structures. The machinery of the state may be used not to further the official legal or regulatory mandate of the office, but rather to promote unofficial interests (whether personal "nest-feathering" within accepted limits [if any] as imposed by the informal hierarchy [often with tribute], or interests dictated by the informal hierarchy or its master of the moment). The hierarchy may also have (or be linked to) competing economic interests (e.g., businesses and financial institutions owned by the state or by well-connected owners) which impede any fulfilment of an official legal mandate inconsistent with such interests.

Judges on an emerging market's bench may be severely underpaid (thus not always attracting the best candidates). Given that insolvency is often a highly complex area requiring a mix of different skill sets (often far broader than purely legal), the bench may simply not be up to the task of administering a complex insolvency matter effectively. Often insolvencies are administered by courts of general jurisdiction and hence do not have regular involvement in insolvency concepts.

---

[16] *See* www.brookings.edu/wp-content/uploads/2019/02/illiberal-states-web.pdf. *See also* discussion above at footnote 95 regarding so-called "telephone justice" in the former Soviet Union.

[17] By way of example, a prominent American businessman Michael Calvey (founder and CEO of Baring Vostok, a leading Russian private investment fund) was arrested in February 2019 along with three other Baring Vostok executives on (what were generally considered on the market to be) trumped-up charges of embezzlement from an investee of the fund, Vostochny Bank. The arrests arose out of a commercial dispute with the fund's co-investor, Artem Avetisyan (who reportedly had high connections in the state security apparatus). Though Calvey's imprisonment was relatively short-lived (February–April 2019) nonetheless, the other fund executives remained imprisoned for much longer. Calvey himself was then subjected to extended house arrest, which was lifted in December 2020 (following settlement of the commercial dispute between the co-investors).

[18] Where DFIs are involved as stakeholders in an emerging market finance structure (on the loan and/or equity side), the authors have observed anecdotally that judicial abuse seems to be much less recurrent.

This situation places a premium on transaction leadership's "being informed" and "knowing the lay of the land." Such a survey should be part of the due diligence process, and questions/risks from the work must also be considered as integral elements of the credit analysis. Relationships of counterparties (be they the borrower, its shareholders or management, or competing creditors) must be scrutinized carefully and in real time (particularly during the Pre-Restructuring Phase). Where an individual lender does not have local mastery of these issues, it should quickly endeavor to obtain this (by outsourcing) or rely on suitably experienced lender leadership. Identifying stakeholders often goes well beyond persons with a direct or obvious commercial interest—often one needs to understand which way the political wind is blowing (or who may in fact be "pulling the strings").[19]

Ideally, KYC, integrity, political and other risk checks would have already been made at origination stage regarding the borrower, its management, and UBOs (but the situation can change, so these checks should be regularly updated in real time during monitoring as well as at the first moment the amber light on a loan flashes). The views of nationals familiar with navigating these risks (business and/or legal side) should also be heeded. Local financial and legal advisors working with lender leadership may be in a position to advise on risks and mitigation measures.

The implications of these issues on reliability of the legal system cannot be overstated, from the standpoint of influence on:

- the system of contract enforcement, insolvency law practice, and impartial justice within the legal system,
- the comportment of judges, bailiffs, insolvency office holders, and other government servants involved in any insolvency or enforcement proceedings,
- the potential outcome of the creditors' claims and the proposed restructuring, and
- other individuals involved, e.g., lender or borrower staff posted in-country.

The potential for abuse is greatly enhanced in contentious situations. Accordingly, leadership should avoid viewing litigation as a suitable and easy option

---

[19] In the authors' experience, having a DFI in the finance structure tends to play a positive role in deterring abuse. Many countries' embassies will also have commercial attaches who are willing to intervene in discussions with local government provided that they have the comfort that the financing transactions and businesses involved are legitimate and do not raise transparency concerns. Finally, where actions by the local government are tantamount to an expropriation, then a bilateral investment treaty (a BIT) may provide an avenue for recovery where the BIT's language is sufficiently broad to protect loans and other debt instruments.

and instead consider it judiciously. This is not to say that a lender should be afraid to enforce rights in a court or tribunal if necessary, but rather *do so judiciously.*[20]

This in turn creates a significant conundrum for lender leadership: if the lenders have little or no bargaining power in a given jurisdiction due to their inability to obtain recourse through the judiciary (or via self-executing security interests and other credit support), how can they negotiate a meaningful workout with the borrower?

Not every emerging market will necessarily encounter all of these problems, and thus an individual assessment of the relevant emerging market and magnitude of these (or similar) issues must be made on *a case-by-case basis for the country in question. Moreover, the level of risk may vary depending on regions* within a given country (with capital cities or larger cities often tending to reflect more efficient and objective functioning of the judiciary).

Finally, the position of the equity shareholders as last in line in the waterfall of pay-out priorities in a formal insolvency, as well as the threat of potential vicarious liability against management and/or shareholders, may help in negotiating a favorable outcome for lenders even where the rule of law in a given country may be weak.[21]

## Nature of the Local Legal System and Law on the Books

Legal systems in emerging markets are often still under development, that is, "works in progress." Thanks to the active support of DFIs and other international organizations, a number of emerging markets have made excellent progress in drafting their laws to reflect a rational approach to financial and insolvency issues, more in harmony with those of developed markets.[22] That said, the judiciary and regulatory regime may still be playing catch-up in understanding and applying insolvency concepts on a rational, impartial basis with commercial practicality.

---

[20] Arbitration clauses in loan documents may mitigate to some extent against rule of law issues in a host country. Critically, in a solvent enforcement proceeding they will provide a neutral arbiter of fact and law. An arbitral award must then be enforced where the borrower (or other entity providing credit support) has assets. The process substantially narrows the possibility of abuse. But importantly, arbitration clauses lose their force in the insolvency setting, as local courts will have exclusive jurisdiction over their legal entities' insolvencies (subject to some possible exceptions such as UK/US/Singaporean restructuring proceedings where jurisdiction can be obtained and where such proceedings will be recognized by the borrower's home courts).

[21] The authors would not wish to overstate this, however. Vicarious liability tends to be a far more prominent issue in more developed markets. In a less developed emerging market, it is likely to be of less concern to borrower management.

[22] *See* more generally Annex 1. Chapter 11.

In certain emerging markets' legal systems, there may still be a high degree of rigidity and formality in applying legal concepts. This may particularly be the case in civil-law systems, which tend to be more rigid than common law systems.[23]

Whilst these topics may be the subject of fascination for legal theorists, what does this really mean for the lender from a practical standpoint?

First, each individual lender must do its utmost to be ready *to document and present its claim in the event of an insolvency.* A successful outcome for a consensual restructuring will always be the hoped-for, "best case" scenario. However, each lending institution must be prepared for the possibility (and in some cases, likelihood) that the restructuring will *not* be achieved. It may fall through prior to execution of the restructuring agreement. It may even fall apart subsequently.

In such case, judicial insolvency proceedings (possibly of a rescue nature, but more likely, insolvent liquidation) will take place.

International lenders from developed markets may be taken aback by the high level of legal formalities involved in assembling and proving their claims (including the underlying basic credit claim, as well as rights under available security). The time and effort required to put these documents together may be substantial.

Insolvency office holders, as well as competing creditors (in particular local creditors), may act aggressively and use sharp tactics to resist the inclusion of a lender's claim and rights into the registry of creditors. Often, a seemingly small formal defect (where the proverbial T has not been crossed or the I dotted) may prejudice the filing. Some emerging markets' legal systems place a heavy emphasis on form over substance.[24]

Foreign-law claims may also require support in respect of the validity of the underlying loan obligation under the substance of the foreign law. Where the claimant is not the original lender (e.g., it is an assignee of the debt) then one needs to be prepared to prove up valid assignment to the current

---

[23] The fundamental nature of an emerging market's legal system is likely to depend on its historical political/legal legacy—e.g., (1) the English common law system for former members of the British Empire; (2) the Napoleonic system for countries with a strong Gallic connection; and/or (3) the Roman-Germanic system, including for post-Communist system of Central and Eastern Europe, Central Asia and Caucuses. *See* P. R. Wood, *op. cit.*, Ch. 3.

[24] Insolvency office holders may also be more inclined to take 'the easy way' of merely liquidating the debtor in lieu of supporting a judicial restructuring, given a lesser workload and more favourable remuneration structures *See, e.g.,* the EBRD's Insolvency Office Holder Assessment at https://www.ebrd.com/what-we-do/sectors/legal-reform/debt-restructuring-and-bankruptcy/sector-assessments.html.

claimant (in form and substance).[25] Where the document is foreign-language (e.g., English), then observance of local language requirements (including at the original execution stage, if applicable) may need to be proven.[26]

Given this, it is imperative at the Pre-Restructuring Phase (or latest, Decision to Restructure Phase) that each lender's in-house counsel commission a *full legal audit of the initial loan transaction* (including all finance documents, corporate approvals, registrations, notarizations, and/or other formalities, legal opinions, etc.) and ensure that original wet-ink execution copies (and if necessary, translations, which may need to be notarized) are ready to be submitted in insolvency proceedings. Counsel should also undertake its own debt mapping exercise to ensure a full understanding of the competing claims of which it knows (though a more reliable and comprehensive view may only be available after completion of diligence by lender leadership and its financial advisors, following implementation of the standstill).

Issues of due execution, proper corporate authority, proper registrations, stamps, and other formalities regarding the original loan merit extreme scrutiny in this audit exercise. Local counsel should be consulted on all substantive and procedural formalities related to filing and enforcing a claim in insolvency (including enforcement of any security or other credit support). In respect of any relevant registries (regarding perfection of security, such as corporate shareholders' registries, central national security registries, land registries, etc.), where possible, official excerpts confirming due registration of the lender's security should be obtained.

This will all be a critical exercise, to test the existence and strength of the lender's claim as well as the availability of any possible defenses by the insolvency office holder or competing creditors. It is also likely to be time-consuming. It is far better to uncover these deficiencies well in advance and then to be prepared to deal with them than to be put on the back foot by the insolvency office holder and/or other creditors following the filing. A sober understanding of costs and difficulties of security enforcement is also important.[27]

The importance of this exercise cannot be overstated. The sooner each lender starts it, the better. Lender leadership in a restructuring will serve its

---

[25] One of the authors recalls an insolvency case where local competing creditors claimed that an English-law deed of assignment in favor of the author's client was invalid due to "lack of consideration" (an absurd position from the standpoint of English law). The client-creditor had to incur unnecessary legal costs and delay in fighting against this meritless claim.

[26] Some emerging markets (e.g., the Republic of Kazakhstan) may have local "laws on language" requiring documents signed between local companies and foreign counterparties (e.g., international lenders) to be in the country's official language.

[27] *See* discussion below on secured lenders.

lender base well by *reminding each individual lender to undertake this exercise as early as possible.*[28]

## Standstill Agreements

As stated in the INSOL II Principles, a standstill arrangement plays an essential role in a consensual restructuring, for a variety of reasons. Indeed, the standstill is the very core mechanism of INSOL II (notably, it is mentioned as an essential element of all eight Principles).

Firstly, it "takes the heat off" of the borrower in its concern that one or more lenders may call a default and accelerate, triggering the dominos of cross-default (and the usual subsequent filing for insolvency by the borrower and/or unpaid creditors). Depending on the manner in which the local wrongful trading rules are drafted, it may provide legal justification for the directors to forego filing for voluntary insolvency.[29] It also gives the parties "breathing room" to obtain enough information and to perform proper financial analysis, to ascertain whether a consensual restructuring really is possible. It allows, from the psychological standpoint, emotions to "cool down" and sober logic to prevail.

Indeed, even where things might seem hopeless at the outset, once the standstill is achieved, often the parties will be in a far better position to resolve their differences and come to an agreement, particularly where talented lender leadership steps in to provide the guidance, counsel, and inspiration to the borrower and/or less experienced lenders to make required compromises. When combined with a term sheet,[30] the act of signing the standstill and term sheet will promote an enormous amount of goodwill and propel the parties forward.

As with other contractual arrangements, a standstill creates an essential *quid pro quo*: in simple terms, the lenders mutually agree to *forbear from demanding repayment and/or enforcing* against the borrower (absent "super default" type events), in consideration for which the borrower agrees to *forbear from depleting value and/or favoring one lender over others.*[31] The parties

---

[28] Whilst it is highly unlikely an individual lender will expressly share with lender leadership, other lenders and/or the borrower the details of any uncovered defects, nonetheless, the lender's learning of these may serve to soften its resistance to compromise during the workout process. It is therefore in the group's overall collective interests for lender leadership to promote all lenders' taking an informed view of their respective claims.

[29] *See* discussion on wrongful trading below.

[30] *See* discussion on term sheets below.

[31] Ideally, the borrower's majority shareholders and other affiliates with whom the borrower has contractual arrangements (e.g., under management service and/or other group company arrangements)

may also appoint the lender leadership in the context of the standstill, include important disclaimers and/or other provisions (such as cost coverage).[32] The agreement will critically establish the ground rules for open flow of information to the lenders and their professional advisors and their rights to share such information with each other, subject to agreed confidentiality assurances to the borrower.

Two critical legal elements of the standstill agreement will be the *applicable law* and *dispute resolution* clauses. Like the term sheet,[33] agreeing these issues in the standstill is likely to be treated by the parties as a precedent on these issues for the main restructuring agreement (e.g., an overlay).

The law of a well-developed legal system, flexible enough to accommodate restructuring transactions and predictable enough to provide a reliable legal regime for resolution of issues, is critical. In many emerging markets (perhaps depending on the particular hemisphere involved) this will be English law or New York law.[34,35]

Whilst most international legal practitioners will appreciate the difference, it is not uncommon for lawyers unaccustomed to cross-border transactions and/or non-legal staff (e.g., bankers, credit and restructuring specialists, etc.) to conflate "choice of law" (or "applicable law") on the one hand with "choice of jurisdiction" (or "dispute resolution") on the other.

---

should also be a party(ies) to the standstill and undertake not to deplete value from the borrower (or to take other steps contrary to the intent of the standstill). The lenders may also wish to require the majority shareholders to undertake to procure the borrower's observance of its standstill covenants.

[32] The lack of cost coverage can contribute to severe in a restructuring—where the borrower refuses to cover lenders' costs, this is far more likely to result in severe inaction, delay and a failed workout. One restructuring specialist known to the authors referred to Asian cultural attitudes toward workouts as a "make-it-or-break-it" issue. ("Cost coverage is the binding glue of successful workouts. If everyone rides free, nothing gets done.")

[33] *See* discussion on term sheets below.

[34] English law has become the law of choice for global cross-border financial transactions given inter alia its transparent, large body of precedents, its pro-creditor approach, the consistency and fairness of the English courts, the general notions of freedom of contract (including ability to declare a trust) and bias against speculative or punitive damages. English law has also developed a high level of acceptability in the financial markets (in terms of asset quality for debt investors), in turn driving its usage. *See* P.R. Wood, "Ten Points for Choosing the Governing Law of an International Business Contract," www.ibanet.org (2020). English law is also highly conducive to multi-creditor restructurings. By contrast, New York law tends to be more frequently encountered in Latin America and the Caribbean but (as a common law system) nonetheless shares many of the favorable aspects of the English system of law. It is highly promoted by the US legal community. *See* A.R. Jaglom and M.W. Galligan, "New York Law as the Gold Standard Choice for Global Business Contracts," New York State Bar Association www.nysba.org (2019).

[35] Another reason for English law or New York law is that standstill arrangements may be more enforceable under these systems than under the borrower's own domestic legal system. Whilst the position may be untested by the courts, some local practitioners from emerging markets have argued that standstill arrangements, if governed by the law of the domestic legal system might be unenforceable.

The former ("choice of law"/"applicable law") determines the *substantive law* which the parties agree will govern formation of the contract in question and how its terms and conditions are to be interpreted and applied as between them (including in the event of any dispute); the latter ("choice of jurisdiction"/"dispute resolution") determines *by which court or tribunal* and *where* any dispute which arises will be heard (with the carve out being if and when a formal insolvency proceeding is commenced regarding a party (e.g., the borrower).[36]

As regards the latter issue ("choice of jurisdiction"/"dispute resolution"), it should *never* be assumed that just because English law or New York law is chosen as the applicable law, that the disputes should be heard by English courts or New York courts (respectively). On the contrary, subject to the lender leadership's taking specific advice on this issue for the particular circumstances of the restructuring in question, it may be preferable to *avoid* choosing any particular country's state courts in favor of some form of *international arbitration* (whether institutional or ad hoc).

Many emerging markets have joined the 1958 New York Convention,[37] making international arbitration a rational choice for solvent dispute resolution of cross-border restructuring documents involving emerging markets borrowers.

The use of an arbitration clause will also usually be required where a DFI is participating in the restructuring transaction.[38]

One of the most essential elements of the standstill agreement will be the *agreed period* (which should be relatively short, but long enough to do meaningful diligence and agree the terms of the main restructuring agreement, e.g., 3–4 months, though this will be determined on a case-by-case basis) and when such period may be *prematurely terminated* (usually by a short list of "super default" type events, such as insolvency, attachments, breach of the borrower's undertakings in the standstill and/or a majority vote by the participating lenders).

Another common issue which arises in approaching the issue of a standstill arrangement will be whether the arrangement should be a *formal* legal

---

[36] Again, an arbitration clause will fall away on insolvency, and local courts of the borrower will be vested with exclusive competence over the insolvency (unless some global or regional insolvency hub such as the US/UK/Singaporean system will support a filing and such proceeding will be recognized in the borrower's home jurisdiction.

[37] The United Nations Convention on the Recognition and Enforcement of Foreign Arbitral Awards (New York, 10 June 1958), www.newyorkconvention.org.

[38] As international organizations, most DFIs will safeguard their privileges and immunities from legal process (lawsuits) in the courts of sovereign nations and, as an alternative, agree to resolution of disputes by international arbitration.

agreement (with the elements described above clearly laid out) or an *informal* arrangement (aka the "handshake standstill" or "email standstill").

In the authors' view, there is no "one-size fits all" solution here. Clearly, the jurist's preference is always that arrangements be as clear, precise, reliable, and enforceable as possible. At the same time, lawyers must recognize that legal issues sometimes need to take second place to commercial issues and practical expediency.

There are indeed situations where the handshake standstill is acceptable. Let's say a core group of lenders know each other and have a common history of collaboration on multiple prior workouts. They know it is highly likely none will step out of line. Their borrower's parent is a trustworthy, dependable partner (e.g., from prior workouts in other jurisdictions).

In such a case, the handshake may be fine.[39] It may even be preferred. Dispensing with the formal legal document in the circumstances allows the parties to focus on more critical issues and reach the finish line of the restructuring more quickly. It also saves costs and preserves the legal budget for other elements of the restructuring.

The authors also observe that in certain emerging markets jurisdictions where the reliability of enforcement and recovery measures is limited (e.g., due to a low level of rule of law, unreliability of the judiciary, dysfunctionality of enforcement procedures, and the like), the threat of action by any one lender in a distress situation may be relatively low. In such cases, the parties may well engage in lengthy negotiation of possible workout plans without invoking the need for a formal standstill agreement.

That said, depending on the circumstances, the risks of an informal standstill must not be discounted:

- **Enforceability**—in the informal arrangement, there is a question over whether the standstill is even enforceable (and under what law),
- **Breach**—what actions will constitute a breach? Will such breach give rise to a claim for damages against the breaching party?
- **Wrongful trading**—Will the handshake alone give the borrower's directors a sufficient legal justification under the local bankruptcy law to forego filing for insolvency?
- **Terms**—due to the shorthand nature of most handshakes, the terms governing the standstill are likely to be vague and unclear—what did the parties really intend?

---

[39] As the head of the restructuring legal team of one major lending institution put it, "Sometimes a note on the back of a packet of fags" will be fine, where lenders have collaborated in the past, feel comfortable with each other and know the drill.

- **Dispute resolution**—in which venue would disputes be heard? It is possible (indeed likely) that the parties have not agreed on a proper international arbitration clause, and
- **Termination**—although the parties may have agreed to some period, will they have clearly agreed the bases for premature termination of that period? Or will their hands arguably be tied from taking action for the entire period?

Due to the many possible legal issues arising in respect of the informal approach, and absent unique circumstances (e.g., a history of successful collaboration), there may be a preference for going the more formal route. Lender leadership must consider this on a case-by-case basis with the input of external counsel (who should understand the merits of each approach and not merely advocate the formal approach due to its own bias).

## Confidentiality and Bank Secrecy

As mentioned earlier, confidentiality of the information a borrower supplies in good faith to its lenders is an essential element of a successful workout. Indeed, this subject is even given special standalone status as one of the eight INSOL II Principles.[40]

Borrowers typically supply substantial non-public information to lenders in the course of a credit relationship. However, in a financial distress situation, the lenders may need more detailed strategic commercial, operational, and financial information on the borrower and/or on its shareholders and other affiliates. The borrower is being asked to provide this information at a time when potential litigation (in the form of a contentious, zero-sum insolvency proceeding) looms over the parties' heads.

Borrowers' trust that lenders will not abuse this sensitive information (or allow it to fall into the wrong hands, such as a competitor or predator) is essential to their decision to disclose the required information.[41]

Without the specific authority from the borrower, lenders may not have access to the requisite information for a workout. Timely and complete information sharing is crucial. Delays or opacity become dangerous obstacles.

---

[40] *See* INSOL II Seventh Principle.

[41] In one case of which the authors are aware, an international lender transmitted sensitive information on its distressed borrower to a local prospective purchaser whilst negotiating a distressed sale of the borrower (to be used to pay off the lender's loans). The lender was then surprised to see the prospective buyer abandon the negotiations and instead pursue a hostile takeover of the borrower using (i.e., abusing) the insolvency courts. Borrowers can hardly be blamed for their suspiciousness in such a predatory environment.

Workable rules governing information management represent a fundamental building block of the restructuring process.

Lenders' underlying loan documents may well already include confidentiality obligations. Moreover, certain of the lenders who are licensed financial institutions may already be subject to statutory (or common law, as the case may be) obligations of bank secrecy.[42]

The borrower may wish to have these assurances of confidentiality repeated or strengthened, if it deems that the lender group includes lenders whose statutory or contractual obligations are not strong enough to protect it.

Where all lenders already have confidentiality obligations in place, one can and does encounter restructuring documents where such obligations are not expressly set out. However, it is also common to see overt detailed confidentiality ("disclosure") provisions in restructuring documentation.

By way of example, the LMA precedent forms for coordinating committee appointments include detailed non-disclosure provisions. Notably, though, the LMA form footnotes stress that these disclosure provisions are meant primarily to *authorize disclosure* by the coordinating committee to other lenders, not to create *new* restrictions, given that lenders are already under existing restrictions under their facilities agreement.[43]

At the same time, in the authors' experience, it is common to see confidentiality restrictions expressly laid out in restructuring documentation, on the basis that not all lenders' documents may have these and/or that the borrower is highly sensitive to this issue at this particular time.

The authors have further observed that emerging market borrowers generally tend to be more sensitive to issues of trust and confidentiality. This becomes more acute in times of distress. This enhanced sensitivity probably

---

[42] *See* McKnight and Zakrzewski, On the Law of Loan Agreements and Syndicated Lending, Oxford University Press, 2019, Sections 4.42–44, pp. 249–250 (banker has a duty to maintain the confidence of information concerning its customer's affairs which becomes known to the banker during the course of the banking relationship between them). *See also* Godfrey, Newcombe, Burke, Chen, Schmidt, Stadler, Coucouni, Johnston and Boss, Bank Confidentiality—A Dying Duty But Not Dead Yet? Business Law International, Vol. 17, No. 3, September 2016 (an article considering similarities and differences concerning bank confidentiality in six jurisdictions [England, USA, Austria, Cyprus, Ireland and Switzerland]). Many emerging markets will have analogous bank secrecy rules to those in developed countries. Finally, with standardization of lending documents, many intentional lending forms include non-disclosure obligations on the finance parties. *See*, e.g., LMA syndicated facility forms as well as various DFI loan forms. These loan forms will often impose a general contractual obligation of confidentiality which is subject to certain agreed exceptions, e.g., to affiliates, to advisors, to assignees of its loan rights, to sub-participants, to authorities, to other loan parties, etc.

[43] The form states, "Prima facie there is no reason why the Co-ordinating Committee and ultimately the lenders should accept additional restrictions even though the debtor's sensitivities about confidentiality may well be heightened at this time. In some circumstances, additional confidentiality restrictions may be considered appropriate and in the interests of both the debtor and the Lenders. Any such restrictions should be balanced. The Co-ordinating Committee should not accept liability or responsibility for the conduct or actions of other Lenders as regards any confidentiality restrictions."

results from weaker institutional protections. Accordingly, lenders should be willing to accommodate and repeat or reconfirm these obligations.

The sooner confidentiality obligations are put in place (or reconfirmed) between the parties (e.g., in semi-binding term sheets, pre-negotiation letters, standstill agreements, and/or coordinating committee appointments), the more quickly the parties can start the diligence process required to corroborate the appropriateness of a restructuring plan.

Where lenders have multiple layers of commercial relationships with the borrower, e.g., they have both a lending relationship and also an equity desk trading in the borrower's securities, then the information required to be circulated in the diligence process may well be price-sensitive, and unless effective information barriers can be established between departments, the lenders may be hesitant to undertake robust confidentiality provisions unless these reconfirm existing ones.[44]

At the same time, the question arises, what can and what should lenders do in the meanwhile (pending implementation of a confidentiality clause enabling effective information sharing with and between lenders)?

Can, and should, lenders discuss the borrower's situation amongst themselves? What risks do they run in doing so?

As mentioned in our earlier discussion, it is indeed highly desirable for a lender to seek information from a multitude of sources which is relevant to its borrower's financial health—both before and after the proverbial amber light flashes. Otherwise, the lender may not be making full use of various sources of potentially critical information on the borrower. As a practical matter, these conversations do happen ("bankers talk"). In periods of distress, discretion should be exercised given the potential downside of litigation.

Each lender (subject to the advice of its in-house counsel) must determine to what extent it is comfortable in approaching other lenders to discuss a borrower. Notably, the very act of asking for another lender's view on the borrower's financial situation may not in and of itself constitute a breach of the lender's confidentiality or secrecy obligations. The lender is not necessarily sharing information which it has in its possession, but the contrary—it is *asking* another lender for its view. There would certainly seem to be little or no harm in listening.[45]

Moreover, questions need not be directed at the borrower itself but can concern the market, the macroeconomic situation in the country and a host

---

[44] E. Saunderson, The Bare Necessities: Disclosure of Confidential Information in Corporate Rescue, Journal I'd International Banking and Financial Law, 6 JIBFL 375, June 2014.

[45] That said, the lender must be cautious about being seen to provoke a breach of contract by the other lender.

of other issues which are directly relevant to the borrower. Great utility may also come from "reading between the lines" of the messages other lenders may give. Often what is not said can be just as important as what is said.

As noted above, these "credit checks" are a market staple. Where the contacts are on an informal, discreet basis, in a face-to-face setting (not evidenced by correspondence), the risk may well be deemed acceptable for the lender. In the authors' experience, some lenders take a practical view— that the likelihood of detection of such discussions is low (or even remote), and a borrower would in any event be obliged to bring an action at great cost, prove a breach and prove up damages arising from the breach. Some lenders see this as a rather low risk, and in view of the potential benefit of gleaning useful information from off-the-record discussions, it is worth taking.

In any event, this should be seen as a grey area, to be tread cautiously. In short, each lender must make its own decision, on a case-by-case basis, to what extent the limited and discreet receipt or sharing of information in any given case is to be pursued.[46]

## Term Sheets

As mentioned in Chapter 6, the utility of a succinct, well-drafted term sheet outlining the elements of a standstill and the intent to explore the parameters of a potential restructuring (at the earlier stage) and/or the substantive elements of the restructuring agreement (at the later stage) assumes great significance in an emerging market workout. It will be essential for lender leadership to collaborate closely with its financial and legal advisors on this goal.

The term sheet will *ordinarily be expressly non-binding* except in respect of a limited number of legal issues (e.g., confidentiality of information supplied by the borrower to the lenders and their advisors, applicable law and dispute resolution).

The term sheet will serve as a roadmap for the parties and drafting of main documentation, e.g., the standstill and (once the parameters for the restructuring are determined) the restructuring itself.

When drafting the term sheet, the goal is *not* to address each and every possible commercial, financial, legal, or operational issue, or to make the document overly legalistic or complex. A balance must be struck between

---

[46] As mentioned earlier in Chapter 5, where the borrower is already in distress and amenable, it may be desirable for the banker to obtain the borrower's verbal agreement to discuss its situation on a discreet basis with one or more other key lenders, and for the banker/restructuring officer then to make a record of this discussion with the borrower.

conciseness and comprehensiveness, with the preference to apply the "KISS" formula ("Keep It Simple, Stupid"). Often external counsel (on the lenders' and/or borrower's side) can lose the plot in keeping things simple—perpetuating that old adage that lawyers act as if they are "paid by the word." Transaction leadership must remind their external counsel to keep things as simple and straightforward as possible at term sheet stage. Brevity will result in a speedier term sheet signing (which itself has great significance) and lower costs. Legal budget must be economized at this stage.

Given that the term sheet is generally non-binding, getting it signed up by all of the parties usually is much less time-consuming and bureaucratic than getting authority for signature of a fully legally binding agreement, such as a standstill agreement and/or the actual restructuring agreement. Financial institutions will usually have bureaucratic administrative requirements for signing binding legal agreements but less rigid requirements for non-binding documents such as term sheets. The document's non-binding nature may also support counsel's "taking a view" on capacity and authority, supporting a less rigid approach to signing formalities (such as corporate resolutions, etc.).

The very act of signing the term sheet also gives the parties a *sense of accomplishment and solidarity of purpose.* The sudden change in attitudes and dynamics, between pre-term sheet and post-term sheet stage, can often be remarkable. The signing of the term sheet will usually speed the process of agreeing the main legal documentation for the restructuring (even if there are a number of details to be worked out). Having the term sheet signed up will often change the parties' mind-sets and lessen the "us versus them" attitudes which may pervade the Decision to Restructure and Case Set-up phases. This gives lender leadership the opportunity to strengthen relationships with all parties (lenders and borrowers alike) further and move toward bringing the parties together for the main restructuring.

As regards *applicable law and dispute resolution* in the term sheet, these issues do play a critical role at the term sheet stage. Often the term sheet will be treated as a *precedent* for deciding on the applicable law and dispute resolution principles to govern the main restructuring documentation.[47]

From a practical standpoint, although the commercial terms of the term sheet may be brief, the applicable law and jurisdiction clauses will (like in the standstill agreement, as discussed above) merit close attention from counsel and must be coordinated with legal departments of all parties.

---

[47] Again, as mentioned above, in many emerging markets the applicable law would likely be English or New York law.

## Deal Follow-Through

An essential element of any workout is ensuring that agreed actions are followed through on. *Purposeful deal follow-through* is one of the most critical elements of the Implementation Phase. But it also must be anticipated and *built in early on during negotiations and documentation.*

The authors have observed a number of cases where lenders and the borrower have engaged in lengthy and painful negotiations, finally agreed terms for a restructuring and started to put these in place, and perhaps even partially succeeded. Then, due to lack of purposeful follow-through, the situation has unraveled, and the parties have found themselves exactly in the same place they were at the beginning of negotiations, or worse.

What happened? Did the parties merely assume that once they had agreed everything, it would get done? Where lender leadership assumes that "things will go as planned" this can be a recipe for disaster.

In emerging markets and particularly in distress situations, it is quite the opposite. Lender leadership must assume that Murphy's Law can and will operate to the maximum possible capacity. Each day of delay in a restructuring can lead to cold feet, changes of mind and potential new exogenous events.

Given this, transaction leadership and counsel must carefully plan ahead and use the broadest possible tools for transaction implementation, including regular (e.g., weekly) multiparty conference calls between lender leadership, the borrower and their advisors, action plans, transaction checklists (pre-closing, closing, and post-closing) and other organizational tools. Each meeting, conference call, or other communication must stipulate the relevant follow-through from such communication, what actions need to be taken and who is responsible for taking them. This then must be confirmed immediately in writing (email) and closely monitored. Transaction leadership and their advisors must be prepared to be vigilant in ensuring that agreed pre-signing schedules and deal milestones are observed, and where delays or divergences do occur the course must be reset immediately.

Failure by transaction leadership to insist on purposeful follow-through by all parties to the restructuring (including lenders, the borrower, shareholders, and all advisors) can have disastrous ramifications for all parties and is likely to contribute to a failed transaction. External counsel for the lenders must also back the lender leadership up in this role.

Although this all may sound rather elementary, it is especially critical when dealing with distressed borrowers in emerging markets. They may well have a less disciplined, "more relaxed" business culture, and their management may be less attentive to purposeful follow-through than in more developed economies.

The (unfortunately common) phenomenon of lack of follow-through also underscores the need to ensure several things when establishing the *chronology for performance of obligations* in the main restructuring agreements:

- firstly, where critical elements of a restructuring can feasibly be made into conditions precedent (*CPs*) to the restructuring (and in particular to lender concessions, whether these are in the form of new repayment schedules, forgiveness of interest, haircuts, relaxed covenants, or other significant concessions), lender leadership and its legal advisors must be vigilant in ensuring that these elements be CPs, rather than conditions subsequent (*CSs*), in the main restructuring agreements.
- secondly, where such critical elements cannot be made CPs and may only operate as CSs, then lender leadership and its legal advisors must find a meaningful way of ensuring that such CSs can and do actually occur. This can be done in a variety of incentives and disincentives, or "carrots and sticks." For example, lender concessions may be divided into phases, so that each next concession (the "carrot") occurs only once the borrower achieves the relevant CS milestone, and some serious negative consequence (the "stick") occurs if such CS milestone is not achieved by its relevant longstop date. Ideally, the stick should be something *other than a default* (leading to borrower insolvency), which would only put the parties back in the same position (or worse) they were in at the outset. If possible, the stick should be directed against the equity (shareholders) or their affiliates, rather than the borrower itself (which may be meaningless or only slightly better).

The role of borrower management in achieving CPs and CS milestones cannot be overstated. Lender leadership must make a sober and realistic assessment of whether borrower management and shareholders are able and willing to ensure deal follow-through at the Implementation Phase. Where lender leadership is on notice as to a poor track record in follow-through and/or worse (e.g., an attitude of impunity amongst local management, prior mismanagement, self-dealing and/or value leakage, etc.), they must either approach the overall workout structure differently, insist on change in management or decide that a consensual approach is not likely to succeed. A local insolvency proceeding may well be the lesser of evils.[48]

Sometimes key follow-through actions can be achieved via the use of an independent third party, such as a project monitor. This may be combined with special escrow accounts over which such third party may have some element of control (e.g., sole or joint signature power).

## Selected Insolvency Law Issues Impacting on Lenders

Again, depending on the particular market and state of its development, there may be varying degrees of risk arising from a restructuring transaction and the consequences of a subsequent insolvency.

Firstly, if the borrower is de facto insolvent from the balance sheet or cash flow standpoint, then the borrower's directors may already (or soon) be under an obligation to file for voluntary insolvency under local insolvency law. These rules merit close attention, as they may impose broad liability on the directors for wrongful trading.[49] Some emerging market's insolvency systems will have imported this concept from developed legal systems. That said, the speedy signing of a standstill agreement may also be a mechanism to absolve them from liability at least as regards cash flow insolvency.[50] This issue should be quickly dealt with at term sheet stage by the lender leadership and its counsel together with counsel for the borrower, and it may serve as an argument to convince the lenders to sign the standstill more quickly.

Secondly, it is possible the standstill and/or even the restructuring transaction itself might be executed and implemented to some degree, only to reach a subsequent point of failure resulting in a formal insolvency proceeding. (Just because the agreements are signed does not mean the parties are "out of the woods.")

In such case, there could be the risk of unwinding of steps taken to implement the transaction, and/or other risks, e.g., to name a few:

---

[48] *See* discussion in Chapter 7 regarding the utility of judicial insolvency proceedings for purposes of pursuing claims of vicarious liability, piercing the corporate veil and unwinding antecedent transactions.

[49] *See* discussion of wrongful trading below.

[50] In a member of transactions on which the authors have worked, local management and their external advisors have concluded that the standstill was sufficient from the legal standpoint to suspend the obligation to file for insolvency.

- **claw-back** of distributions to the lenders, as antecedent transactions within the relevant hardening period,[51]
- **invalidation of security** given previously and/or as part of the restructuring by the borrower (e.g., to secure new monies), as antecedent transactions within the relevant hardening period,
- questions as to the **enforceability of any arrangements intended to address stakeholder priorities** (e.g., subordination provisions, distribution sharing and balancing payments, security-sharing arrangements),
- **claims against the lenders** for acts which ostensibly damaged creditors (e.g., on the basis of alleged vicarious (controlling person/shadow director) liability and/or agency) for their own acts or the acts of advisors (e.g., a project monitor),
- **Recharacterization risk** where the loan, if not properly documented and if extended by an affiliate, for example, could be deemed an equity contribution as opposed to a bona fide loan,
- **Valuation** of the security may result in a portion of the lender's claim being classified as unsecured.

The lender leadership should therefore instruct external legal advisors (and in particular competent local counsel from the relevant jurisdiction) to advise on these risks early on (e.g., at structuring/term sheet stage) and ensure that the restructuring agreement and other relevant agreements (e.g., the agreement retaining any project monitor who plays a role on-site) are drafted so as to mitigate against such risks, to the greatest extent possible.

A careful analysis must also be made of the general appropriateness of use of a multi-creditor restructuring agreement with so-called *"override" provisions* amending terms and creating consistency across all the loan agreements. The authors have found that where the override approach is possible and consistent with the law of the borrower's jurisdiction and various loan agreements (and their relevant applicable laws), it may be preferable to making individual amendments to underlying loan agreements.[52]

---

[51] A "hardening period" is a period of time prior to commencement of an insolvency proceeding (and stipulated by a country's insolvency law) for purposes of the court's determining whether a particular act or transaction taken or entered into by the debtor prior to such proceedings should be unwound by the court as an antecedent transaction (e.g., as a preference or undervalue transaction). Initiation of such a process can take place, e.g., at the behest of a court, an insolvency office holder and/or one or more of the debtor's creditors, depending on the law's wording. Such periods of time are referred to as "hardening periods." They vary depending on the relevant law, with undervalue transactions (particularly those with counterparties who are affiliates or insiders) often being accorded longer periods. The risk for a counterparty in such case is that it may be obliged by the court to return the value it received (e.g., payments received, assets received [or their value], etc.).

[52] *See* discussion on overlay restructuring agreements below.

The process of having to draft and negotiate individual amendment agreements can be time-consuming and increase costs. Speed and simplicity play a crucial role in getting the parties over the finish line. The simpler the approach which may be taken, the more quickly it is likely to be implemented to achieve the goal of the restructuring.

## International Judicial Debt Restructuring Hubs: A Viable Alternative?

As mentioned earlier, the legal systems of certain developed nations which act as international or regional financial centers—such as the USA, the UK, and Singapore—allow use of their courts for judicial restructurings of *foreign* debtors and the recognition of foreign restructurings by the respective courts.

Hence, these countries' courts can accept and preside over judicial insolvency proceedings for borrowers from emerging markets. In this manner, they may also act as regional or international hubs for debt restructurings. The relevant regimes include, e.g.:

- **US** Chapter 11 and Chapter 15[53] proceedings under the US Bankruptcy Code,
- **UK** schemes of arrangement (and more recently restructuring plans under the UK Corporate Insolvency and Governance Act 2020) and the Cross-Border Insolvency Regulations of 2006 ("CBIR") (the UK adoption of the UNCITRAL Model Law on Cross-Border Insolvency), and
- **Singaporean** judicial management/schemes of arrangement (first under the Companies [Amendment] Bill 2017 and more recently the omnibus Insolvency, Restructuring and Dissolution Act [2018]) including the wholesale adoption of the UNCITRAL Model Law on Cross-Border Insolvency.

Where cross-border workouts are difficult to achieve (e.g., due to an inability to obtain a critical mass of participating lenders, uncooperative holdout creditors, etc.) and the local courts are unpalatable (e.g., due to systemic problems discussed earlier in the book) such international insolvency regimes may well

---

[53] The United Nations Commission on International Trade Law ("UNCITRAL") promulgated the Model Law on Cross-Border Insolvency (the "Model Law") to provide a framework for international cooperation on insolvency related matters. The Model Law has been adopted in the USA and is included under Chapter 15 of the US Bankruptcy Code. A Chapter 15 case is commenced by a "foreign representative" of a foreign debtor for recognition of a foreign proceeding, and of times, orders of foreign courts. *See generally In re PT Bakrie Telecom TBK*, 601 B.R. 707 (Bankr. S.D.N.Y.2019).

offer viable alternatives. They should be considered carefully by transaction leadership with the help of external counsel.[54]

The *pluses* of such regimes can include:

- strong value-preservation measures (e.g., moratoria (automatic stays), vicarious liability (including wrongful trading), avoidance of antecedent transactions, assumption or rejection of executory contracts),
- well-developed insolvency rules,
- fairness in treatment of creditors and other stakeholders,
- super-priority for new moneys (DIP finance),
- pre-packs, cramdowns (e.g., to neutralize minority holdouts), and streamlined proceedings,
- not least importantly, an independent, commercially oriented and efficient judiciary, and
- an ability to recognize and enforce foreign orders and thereby constrain adherence to the overall restructurings from abroad.

Lenders and debtors alike should thus bear these alternatives in mind when encountering difficulties in achieving a consensual restructuring.

Although it is not the objective of this book to go into the fine details of each such regime's judicial restructuring rules,[55] nonetheless, the authors believe one key threshold issue merits brief discussion in this chapter: *jurisdiction.*

In other words, will these venues' courts formally recognize and accept their competence to adjudicate insolvency proceedings for the particular foreign (emerging market) borrower in question?[56]

These jurisdictional rules will vary from venue to venue. However, they share similar concepts, such as whether the borrower has some substantial nexus (connection) with these venues.

We outline below a brief synopsis of the jurisdictional rules:

---

[54] It will be recalled from our Bank of Commerce case, it was only after the Bank threatened US Chapter 11 that transaction leadership was able to convince the remaining rogue lender to go along with the workout at the eleventh hour.

[55] Transaction leadership should take advice from external counsel in each individual case.

[56] A related and *certainly no less important threshold* issue will be whether the laws of the borrower's own emerging market (and/or other relevant jurisdictions where the borrower's assets are located) will recognize and enforce such proceedings (and accommodate and support required actions by the insolvency office holder), e.g., under the UNCITRAL model law on cross-border insolvency. This is a critical issue to be discussed with external counsel when considering usage of such international venues. A number of emerging markets' insolvency systems have *not* implemented the UNCITRAL model law or analogous provisions. This issue must be securitized in each individual case.

## US Chapter 11 Proceedings

The USA has acted for many years as a popular and effective international restructuring hub. A company may file a US Chapter 11 bankruptcy petition if it "resides or has a domicile, a place of business, or property in the United States...."[57] US courts broadly construe these eligibility standards. For example, cases have found companies may file US Chapter 11 if they have a *minimal amount of property in the USA*, such as a retainer paid to US external counsel.[58]

Beyond having property in the USA, a company's *connections with the USA* is relevant to its eligibility for US Chapter 11. For example, courts have stressed the importance of the debtor's principal creditors being located in the USA so that the court has jurisdiction over those creditors.[59]

However, even where a company is eligible to file for US Chapter 11, *a party may still move to dismiss the company's filing under other two other relevant sections of the Bankruptcy Code*. Thus, the filing of a US Chapter 11 case is not necessarily a "slam-dunk," and the parties must bear in mind the possibility of challenge. The relevant challenge sections are namely:

*Section 305(a)* grants US bankruptcy courts broad authority to dismiss or suspend proceedings where "*the interests of creditors and the debtor would be better served by such dismissal or suspension.*" To be clear, the test is whether *both* the creditors and the debtor would be "better served" by dismissal.[60]

*Section 1112(b)* allows a US Chapter 11 case to be dismissed or converted to a liquidation under Chapter 7 "*for cause, including* (1) continuing loss to

---

[57] 11 USC. § 109(a).

[58] *See In re B.C.I. Finances Pty Ltd.*, 583 B.R. 288 (Bankr. S.D.N.Y. 2018) (retainers deposited in trust account in the USA was property of foreign debtors located in the USA, and sufficient to satisfy statutory eligibility requirement); *In re Ocean Rig UDW Inc.*, 570 B.R. 687 (Bankr. S.D.N.Y. 2017) (attorney retainer held by foreign debtors' New York counsel qualified as property of foreign debtor which was present in the United States); *In re Octaviar Admin. Pty Ltd*, 511 B.R. 361, 372 (Bankr. S.D.N.Y. 2014) ("Octaviar also has property in the United States in the form of an undrawn retainer in the possession of the Foreign Representatives' counsel"). Also, "Section 109(a) does not specify how much property must be present or when or for how long property has had a situs in the U.S.]." *In re Foreign Econ. Indus. Bank Ltd., "Vneshprombank" Ltd.*, 607 B.R. 160, 166 (Bankr. S.D.N.Y. 2019). Accordingly, courts have found that "there is virtually no formal barrier to a foreign entity commencing a case under title 11 in the United States." *In re Aerovias Nacionales de Colombia S.A.*, 303 B.R. 1, 13 (Bankr. S.D.N.Y. 2003) (*quoting* 2 L. King, *Collier on Bankruptcy*, ¶ 109.02[3] (15th ed. rev. 2003).

[59] *In re Aerovias Nacionales de Colombia S.A.*; *see also In re Enron Corp.*, 274 B.R. 327, 347–348 (Bankr. S.D.N.Y.2002).

[60] *In re Aerovias Nacionales de Colombia S.A., 303 B.R. 1, 9 (Bankr. S.D.N.Y. 2003); See also In re Compania de Alimentos Fargo, S.A.*, 376 B.R. 427 (Bankr. S.D.N.Y. 2007).

or diminution of the estate and absence of a reasonable likelihood of rehabilitation; (2) inability to effectuate a plan; (3) unreasonable delay by the debtor that is prejudicial to creditors."[61]

Accordingly, transaction leadership must consult external counsel on the likelihood of a successful challenge to US Chapter 11 jurisdiction in each instance.

## The English Schemes of Arrangement

Similarly, the UK has also acted as an international judicial restructuring hub and most recently (in 2020) seen an expansion of its judicial rescue proceedings.

Available to both solvent and insolvent companies, a scheme of arrangement (a **Scheme**) is a company law process under Part 26 Companies Act 2006. A Scheme is a compromise or an arrangement between a company and its creditors (or its members), or any class of them. It is a statutory procedure that requires both creditor approval and court sanction. The creditor voting requirements are for a simple majority in number and 75% by value of those present and voting (either in person or by proxy) in favor at each class meeting.

Although not an insolvency proceeding per se, only a company capable of being wound up by the English court can enter into a Scheme. In practice, many (but not all) non-English companies can be wound up in England as unregistered "overseas" companies.

Where a company is not incorporated in England and Wales, the test is whether the company has a "*sufficient connection*" with the jurisdiction for it to be the subject of a winding up in England and Wales and therefore susceptible to a Scheme. It is clear from recent English court cases that the sufficient connection test can be satisfied simply by the governing law of the

---

[61] For example, the court in *In re Yukos Oil Co.*, 321 B.R. 396 (Bankr. S.D. Tex. 2005) found that "cause" existed to dismiss a US Chapter 11 case filed by a Russian company with only minimal contacts with the USA, based largely on its deposit of funds in USA bank less than a week before petition was filed in apparent attempt to create jurisdiction in US bankruptcy court, for purposes of substituting USA law in place of Russian law, European Convention law and/or international law, and to utilize judicial structures within the USA in an effort to alter creditor priorities that would apply under the law of these other jurisdictions. The court also reasoned that the debtor could not reorganize without the cooperation of the Russian government because the debtor's large oil business was a central part of the Russian economy and the Russian government was the debtor's largest creditor. Also, the funds were primarily transferred to create jurisdiction in the US. On the other hand, the court in *Northshore Mainland* explained why it was improper to dismiss the case under § 1112(b) (although the court ultimately dismissed the case under section 305(b)). *In re Northshore Mainland Servs., Inc.*, 537 B.R. 192, 203 (Bankr. D. Del. 2015). *See also In re Cenargo Int'l, PLC*, 294 B.R. 571, 603 (Bankr. S.D.N.Y. 2003).

debt being English law.[62] The English court may consider a range of other factors relevant to establishing a "sufficient connection," including:

a. The restructuring has been negotiated in England;
b. The documents contain a jurisdiction clause in favor of England[63];
c. The company has migrated its COMI to England[64]; and
d. A sufficient number of creditors are domiciled in England.[65]

In order to be satisfied that it has jurisdiction to sanction a Scheme, the English court must also be satisfied that the Scheme will have substantial effect, i.e., that it will be recognized in all relevant jurisdictions, for example, where the company has material assets, the location of the company's COMI and the jurisdiction of the company's incorporation. The English court will usually require expert evidence from counsel in any relevant jurisdiction regarding the likely recognition of the Scheme overseas.

Companies do not automatically benefit from a moratorium on creditor claims when proposing a Scheme. However, the English court does have general discretion to stay court proceedings, and this discretion has been used to stay dissentient creditor claims to enable a company to negotiate and finalize its Scheme.

## The English Restructuring Plan

The Corporate Insolvency and Governance Act 2020 inserted a new statutory restructuring tool into Part 26A Companies Act 2006 (a "Restructuring Plan"), intended to supplement the existing Scheme legislation.

Like a Scheme, the Restructuring Plan is a court process. There are considerable similarities between the two tools. As such, the English court is expected to draw on the existing body of Part 26 case law in relation to

---

[62] *See* the judgment of Richards J in *Re Vietnam Shipbuilding Industry Group* [2013] EWHC 2476 (Ch) (which case involved a single set of bonds all governed by English law) and other, subsequent cases concerning liabilities governed by English law, including a case where the original governing law of the finance documents was not English but, in accordance with the amendment provisions of the finance documents, the governing law was changed to English before the scheme was proposed (*see Apcoa Parking (UK) Ltd* [2014] EWHC 997 (Ch)).

[63] However, this does not need to be an exclusive jurisdiction clause. In the *Vietnam Shipbuilding* case, the court considered, obiter, that even a non-exclusive jurisdiction clause alone would be seen as a sufficient connection with the jurisdiction.

[64] The term "COMI" means a "center of main interests," that is, the jurisdiction with which a company is most closely associated for purposes of cross-border insolvency proceedings. *See, e.g., Re Magyar Telecom BV* [2013] EWHC 3800 (Ch).

[65] *Ibid*.

Restructuring Plans under Part 26A.[66] Accordingly, an English court will have jurisdiction to sanction a Restructuring Plan in relation to an overseas company provided the "sufficient connection" test is satisfied.

There are a number of important differences between a Restructuring Plan and a Scheme, including:

i. The financial difficulties threshold which require a company proposing a Restructuring Plan to have encountered or be likely to encounter financial difficulties affecting its going-concern business, and the purpose of the Restructuring Plan must be to address those financial difficulties;

ii. The Cross Class Cram Down provisions, which mean the Restructuring Plan can bind dissenting creditors provided certain conditions are met. In short, if a class does not vote in favor but the court considers the class would not be worse off under the Restructuring Plan than in any relevant alternative, and a class of creditors with a genuine economic interest in the relevant alternative has voted in favor of the Plan. Note, the relevant alternative is usually insolvency;

iii. Approval by 75% in value of creditors present and voting (in person or by proxy) at the class meeting (no requirement for approval by a majority in number) and

iv. The ability for the court to exclude from the class meeting any class of creditors without a genuine economic interest in the company.

## Singapore's Improved Insolvency Regime

Singapore is increasingly seen as a regional restructuring hub in Asia. Slightly less than two years after it was passed in Parliament, Singapore's Insolvency Restructuring and Dissolution Act 2018 ("IRDA") came into force on 30 July 2020. Prior to the passing of the IRDA, the insolvency regime was governed by a platter of legislation.[67]

The IRDA now consolidates personal and corporate insolvency laws and the laws relating to debt restructuring by individuals and companies. At the same time, it also brings with it notable developments in the following areas:

a. Judicial management;

---

[66] *Re Virgin Atlantic Airways* [2020] EWHC 2376 (Ch).

[67] This included the Companies Act (Cap. 50, Rev Ed. 2006), the Companies (Winding Up) Rules and the Bankruptcy Act (Cap. 20, Rev Ed. 2009).

b. Schemes of arrangement;
c. Winding up;
d. Receivership;
e. Personal bankruptcy;
f. New licensing and regulatory regime for insolvency practitioners; and
g. Ipso facto clauses.

## Singapore Judicial Management

Notwithstanding the sweeping changes that accompanied the IRDA's introduction, the option to put a company under judicial management is no stranger to Singapore's insolvency regime. Briefly, judicial management is a method of debt restructuring where an independent judicial manager is appointed to manage the affairs, business, and property of a distressed company. The company also benefits from a temporary respite from legal proceedings by third parties whilst it attempts to rehabilitate itself.

With the IRDA now in force, a company may place itself into judicial management as long as a majority in number and value of the creditors present and voting agree to it. Under IRDA Section 94, companies can now be placed under judicial management through a creditors' resolution without a court order. The company can propose to its creditors that it enters judicial management and with the approval of a majority in number and value of the creditors present and voting, be placed under judicial management. Once the company enters judicial management, the judicial management process will proceed under the Court's supervision in the same manner as a court-commenced process.

The 2017 Amendments to the Companies Act meant that *foreign companies* doing business in Singapore could also apply for judicial management, as long as they could show that they had a "*substantial connection with Singapore.*" In this regard, a foreign company is likely to meet the requirements if it can demonstrate that:

i. It has assets in Singapore;
ii. It has substantial business in Singapore;
iii. Singapore law had been used in as the governing law for its business transactions;
iv. The foreign company has submitted to the jurisdiction of the Singapore Courts for the resolution of disputes arising from its business transactions; and/or
v. Singapore was the company's COMI.

## Singapore Schemes of Arrangement

Another popular mechanism for debt restructuring in Singapore is the scheme of arrangement. Like judicial management, this option enables companies to rehabilitate whilst a moratorium on proceedings (automatic stay) is in place.

However, there are a few notable differences which may inform one's decision on which option to choose:

a. In a scheme of arrangement, the company can "cram down" dissenting creditors as long as a statutory majority in each class of creditors vote in favor of the scheme. This is a process not available to a company undergoing judicial arrangement;

b. A company retains control whilst during a scheme of arrangement, whereas during judicial management an independent third party steps in as a judicial manager to take over the running of the company; and

c. Judicial management is often preferred as a mode of restructuring in those situations where there are allegations of fraud or financial misconduct.

Again, one key advantage of proceeding with a scheme of arrangement is the "cram-down" regime.[68]

Similarly, the 2017 Amendments to the Companies Act furthermore mean that a foreign company doing business in Singapore can apply also participate in a scheme of arrangement as long as it can demonstrate a *"substantial connection with Singapore."* In this regard, a foreign company is likely to succeed if it can demonstrate the same elements mentioned above regarding judicial management.

# Legal Opinions, Capacity, and Authority Issues

It is essential that the capacity and authority of the borrower and its participating group companies (e.g., parent and/or majority shareholder, other equity creditors) be properly determined restructuring workout.

This will ordinarily imply at least a full *capacity and authority* legal opinion on the borrower itself (sometimes also a full validity and enforceability opinion on the restructuring agreement, but not always[69]).

---

[68] Section 70(4)(b)(ii)(B) of the IRDA provides the much needed clarification that shareholders are not required to divest their shares before a cram down can be made.

[69] Requiring a full validity opinion on a restructuring agreement (e.g., an overlay) can be a two-edged sword. This can impact heavily on both timing and costs. Unlike a loan or facility agreement, which is likely to be fairly standardized (e.g., based on some market precedent such as an LMA facility

A less thorough approach to the parent and equity creditors may be appropriate, for example if they are not providing credit support as part of the restructuring or if their covenants are not core to the deal (see discussion below on third-party credit support). In such case, a less formal check of capacity and authority (e.g., review of corporate resolutions) may be appropriate.

Whilst some legal systems (e.g., common law systems) may have doctrines of apparent authority which support enforcement of a contract against a party that was standing the absence of authority by its signatory, nonetheless, a number of emerging markets' legal systems may not have this. The results of absence of authority can be severe. It is therefore preferable to ensure that due capacity and authority to enter into the restructuring documentation has been suitably diligenced and confirmed by external counsel to the lender leadership.

This process should not be left until the last minute, and lender leadership should instruct external counsel to start work on draft opinions (and the required diligence for them) as soon as possible following term sheet signing.[70]

Legal opinions should also include required customary ancillary opinions such as no license required, no taxation of lenders,[71] choice of law, arbitration, and the like.

Notably, formal legal opinions will *ordinarily carve out (as qualifications) insolvency issues*. Because of this, the importance of separate parallel written advice from external counsel on insolvency issues, such as those outlined in this chapter, cannot be overstated.

---

agreement, a DFI standard loan agreement, etc.), a restructuring agreement will be a *bespoke instrument* calling for heightened attention by counsel. The authors would therefore advise that as a general matter lenders consider the possibility of proceeding without it, absent special considerations. For a general discussion of the role of legal opinions in international financial transactions *see* McKnight, Paterson & Zakrzewski, The Law of International Finance, 2nd Ed., Oxford University Press (2017).

[70] The authors have observed, it has become increasingly common in cross-border financial transactions to see parties requesting the use of eSignature platforms, such as DocuSign and/or its equivalents. This issue must be considered carefully. Not all emerging markets' legal systems will recognise such a signing procedure as valid. Although as a general matter *contract formation* should be a matter of the substantive law of the contract (e.g., if English law applies, then formation should merely meet English-law requirements), nonetheless, the absence of a wet-ink signature by the borrower (and/or its affiliates giving credit support or other key covenants) could prove problematic later on, e.g., if (despite the workout) the borrower (and/or such an affiliate) goes insolvent. The authors advocate prudence (at a minimum, standard electronic pdf circulation followed by assembly and circulation of wet-ink signed originals). Whatever method is used, advice of transaction counsel and local counsel must be carefully coordinated.

[71] Ordinarily transaction legal opinions will not opine in detail on tax matters, though opinions often do confirm the lenders will not incur taxation in the local jurisdiction by virtue of conclusion and performance of the agreements. There is no reason why this cannot be done in a workout.

## Debt To Equity Swaps

Where lenders swap their debt claims for equity in a restructuring, a myriad of issues, of both a strategic commercial and a regulatory nature, will arise.[72]
In terms of strategic commercial issues, these may include:

- the threshold issue of whether lenders may indeed accept equity interests in lieu of their debt interests, under their respective local regulatory regime, constituent documents, policies, or other applicable limitations,
- the pricing of the equity and the level of dilution of existing shareholders,[73]
- the likelihood of exit from the trade, and whether this may be imposed unilaterally by the swapping lenders on the existing stakeholders (borrower, its management, and other shareholders), e.g., by way of puts, drags, tags, and the like,
- how corporate governance and shareholder rights are generally treated by local corporate law during the period when the lenders hold their shares,
- whether exit rights and/or existing statutory corporate governance protections should be strengthened by a *shareholders' agreement (SHA)*,
- whether the local legal system will recognize and enforce such SHA as well as its governing law and arbitration provisions,
- to what extent the borrower's constituent documents (e.g., *memorandum and articles of association, or MAA*) need to be aligned with the SHA, and
- whether in lieu of equity at the local level it may be preferable to put equity in at the offshore level.

For lenders, a debt-to-equity swap is a necessary evil in certain cases. However, not all lenders, especially funds where holding equity is not permissible, can even consider this option. Certain lenders merely do not have the expertise or the existing internal infrastructure to close the structure and effectively manage the investment thereafter. For those who do, the commitment of time, resources, and expense are significant and must be weighed carefully against the likely recovery versus acceleration or a deeply discounted secondary market sale. In some cases, it may be possible to find so-called "loan-to-own" investors interested in acquiring control of a borrower and/or

---

[72] Although debt for equity is not frequently encountered in judicial restructurings, it is seen in workouts.

[73] It will be recalled in the Bank of Commerce case, this was of the key sticking points. New West Investments was unrealistic in the level of equity and the pricing it was prepared to offer the lenders in the proposed swap.

its assets. This may prove more of a challenge in an emerging market than in a more developed country.

In any equity swap, the lenders will effectively end up in *joint venture (co-investment) relationships* in the relevant emerging market with the existing shareholder(s) and other lenders. Where the borrower is a publicly traded company, the room for negotiation of revamping corporate governance arrangements may be limited.

Where the borrower is a closely held business with a limited number of shareholders, the post-swap equity structure will merit careful consideration of both statutory and contractual instruments which will provide corporate governance rules.

Although the lender leadership should vet these issues with external counsel, ultimately they may decide that the new co-investment relationships are best dealt with by a *detailed SHA (or revising an existing SHA, which may be sub-standard)*, and in particular where the borrower is not publicly listed. The texts of the SHA and MAA must be carefully aligned to avoid discrepancies, and certain key provisions in the SHA (e.g., veto rights, supermajority or unanimity provisions (so-called 'reserved matters'), restrictions on shares, etc.) must be appropriately set out in the SHA and mirrored in the MAA. (The mirroring exercise will likely be important, as where a violation of the SHA takes place, it generally gives rise only to an action for damages for breach of contract, whereas a violation of the MAA should give rise to an action to invalidate the infraction (e.g., the relevant shareholders or board decision). This provides important protection for the new shareholders.)

Depending on where the borrower entity is located, the issue may arise as to whether local company law will be of an acceptable standard to protect the new shareholders' interests as investors and to allow the flexibility needed in tailoring this relationship in the SHA (e.g., departing from rules under local company law which might otherwise govern their relations and/or supplementing those rules to the extent that they unclear, inadequate or unworkable). This may be a key issue in many emerging markets, where the law and practice on SHAs may still be relatively new and untested. In a number of emerging markets, companies laws have been reformed to recognize the validity of SHAs. Still, the rules may remain skeletal and untested in the courts. Typical protections one would ordinarily expect to see in a well-drafted SHA—e.g., share transfer restrictions, drag-along and tag-along rights, puts and calls, voting agreements, and the like—may risk being unenforceable. Moreover, the enforceability of restrictive covenants (non-competition, non-solicitation, etc.) may remain untested.

Consequently, it may be more prudent for the lenders to consider a re-organization whereby the *main equity relationships are relocated to another, more developed legal system* (such as an offshore jurisdiction), the company law of which allows flexibility in SHA arrangements and recognizes and enforces SHAs and accompanying governing law and dispute resolution arrangements.

In the cross-border equity investment context, the lender may wish to require that the SHA be governed by the law of a well-developed legal system (e.g., English or New York law). However, the enforceability of the choice of a foreign law to govern the SHA must be vetted with external counsel. The same may be said for the dispute resolution provisions (where an international arbitration clause may be favored).[74]

The regulatory issues will also present challenges. Some jurisdictions' laws may still prohibit straight debt-to-equity swaps and thus require the use of special mechanics for the swap. Also, regulatory issues may arise in the intro-duction of new shareholders (e.g., competition law, foreign investment law (including limitations on issuance of equity to foreign parties), financial regu-latory law requiring special filings or approvals, and the like. Key corporate issues (such as shareholder approvals, pre-emotive rights [and whether these can be waived]) and others often raise unexpected obstacles in emerging markets. The process of issuance of equity shares can often be extremely burdensome under local laws of emerging markets. Accordingly, this aspect of any restructuring merits detailed attention by local counsel, as well as accurate description in the drafting and mechanics of financial close in the restructuring agreement.

Not least importantly, a full legal opinion under local law regarding the due issuance of the new shares should be required for the benefit of the new equity holders (swapping lenders).

As mentioned in other parts of Chapter 11, shareholders may bear special risks (e.g., as equity creditors and/or as controlling persons). Accordingly, these issues should be considered by lenders and external counsel to the lenders prior to conversion. The resultant equity share of each converting lender should be considered in this context. The larger the resultant equity shares (particularly where these result in formal control or cross thresholds stipulated in the law), the more likely they will cause concern. A related issue, as with any equity investment, will be the impact of any required regulatory approvals at the local level (e.g., foreign investment approvals, competition

---

[74] In some emerging markets, civil procedure rules may prohibit referring shareholder disputes (including under an SHA) to international arbitration (i.e., such disputes may be "non-arbitrable" and hence not recognizable and enforceable by local courts notwithstanding that the emerging market in question may well be a party to the 1958 New York Convention).

approvals, regulated financial institution approvals, etc.). External counsel must advise here as well.

## Equity Creditors—Justifiable Support Versus Value Leakage

It is not uncommon, when structuring direct investments into emerging markets, for an investor to put in place multiple commercial relationships between the target (i.e., the borrower) and the investor's other group companies.

These can take various forms, such as:

- Royalty agreements for the use of valuable IP rights (including trademarks, service marks, know-how, and the like),
- Management service agreements,
- Technical support and/or shared services agreements,
- Equipment and/or other leases,
- Shareholder or other group company loans,
- Supply or off-take arrangements, and
- Others.[75]

This can occur when the target is a wholly owned subsidiary as well as in the case when it is a functioning joint venture of several investors. It can also be seen in companies with multiple shareholders and even in public companies (though in a well-regulated market, the exigencies of securities regulations may mitigate against abuse).

Certain lenders may be strict in their approach to policing the borrower's involvement in such relationships, e.g., requiring borrower to conduct its business on "arm's length terms and for full market value."[76] At the same time, arrangements which might seem as arm's length in a non-distressed scenario might be viewed quite differently in a financial distress scenario, when the borrower's business needs to be saved. Are these contributing to, or are they depleting, the borrowers' value?

Depending on the emerging market, its tax rules may regulate transfer pricing, thin capitalization, and other issues thus de facto mitigating against abuse. International audit companies (e.g., the big four and/or mid-tier) may

---

[75] Shareholders may be in the loan structure (e.g., in prepay structures), which may raise issues re information flow and voting.

[76] This covenant will often be seen in DFIs' standard loan documents and is also in the standard LMA facility documentation for developing markets.

also have scrutinized intragroup relationships and advised their clients to follow a rational approach, particularly when tax rules are involved.

At the same time, not all emerging market borrowers will apply the same level of scrutiny in structuring their intragroup relations objectively. Frequently, investors will put these relationships in place as a means of extracting value from an investment structure for various reasons (e.g., to implement tax minimization and/or create hidden dividends).

These relationships may be put in place at the outset of the investment and/or during its life. Occasionally, during times of distress one may also observe various levels of group financial support actually flowing to the borrower entity (e.g., in substance, an emergency capital injection).

Lender leadership should commission an *in-depth due diligence investigation* by its financial and legal advisors to determine the extent, nature, and other relevant circumstances relating to all intragroup commercial relationships, in order to have a full understanding of these and their relevance to the debtor's financial distress and the proposed restructuring. Even if there are no covenant breaches under existing loans (since intragroup arrangements may be characterizable as "arm's length"), nonetheless these must be scrutinized in light of the distress situation and the spread of losses amongst stakeholders to rescue the borrower's business. It is likely this investigation will only happen during standstill stage, once more complete information is available.

Lender leadership must then consider with its advisors:

- To what extent are these intragroup commercial arrangements necessary for the continued successful carrying out of business by the borrower, and hence to what extent should they remain in place,
- To what extent should these be modified (e.g., should pricing be revisited and/or should the scope of services be reduced and/or otherwise modified to enable the borrower to remain viable),
- Do these relate to some aspect of the business which will undergo an operational restructuring, and hence should these be revisited,
- Are more competitive alternatives available,
- Are these merely a form of hidden dividend which should be terminated entirely (or at least suspended), as otherwise their continued existence may jeopardize successful restructuring of the borrower,
- Should the borrower's payment obligations under these arrangements continue in place and/or be suspended (e.g., with capitalization, deferral, and/or subordination of payment to the lenders[77]), and

---

[77] Notably some emerging markets' legal systems may not recognize (or have sufficient experience in enforcing) subordination arrangements, so this issue should be confirmed by local counsel.

- How will the local insolvency law regime of the borrower view these arrangements?

In this latter respect, the local insolvency rules may either be silent on treatment of affiliates with claims against a debtor, or they may have developed a position which either treats such claims on par with third-party creditors or worse.

-&-

In this latter aspect, many developed economies' insolvency laws have special rules for affiliated creditors (also known as "*equity creditors*"). The concept may be found, e.g., in the legal systems of Denmark, Germany, Greece, Slovenia, Portugal, Austria, Spain, and others. The laws of these countries implicitly recognize that the *special position of a shareholder in and of itself justifies scrutiny* in a subsidiary's insolvency, especially regarding *loans* made by a shareholder to its subsidiary.[78]

In the USA, courts can characterize shareholder loans as equity under state laws, including treatment of interest payments as dividends subject to avoidance and recovery (e.g., in the case of inadequate capitalization of a legal entity or inadequate documentation). Moreover, Section 510(c) of the US Bankruptcy Code also has special provisions on "equitable subordination" of individual creditor claims to the claims of all creditors where such creditors (including shareholders) have, by their wrongful or oppressive conduct, interfered in the management or business of the debtor to the prejudice of other creditors.[79] Likewise, the insolvency regime may treat an equity creditor's rights differently in the insolvency process (e.g., depriving it of voting rights at creditors' meetings).[80]

By contrast, not all developed countries have uniformly approached this issue. For example, there is no provision for subordination of shareholder loans in France. Nor do the laws of England recognize equitable subordination as such.

An emerging market's legal system may well follow the lead of a related developed economy (e.g., from its colonial legacy with such other economy).

---

[78] *See* P. R. Wood, Principles of International Insolvency, Ch. 11–069.

[79] This issue may pose a risk for a senior lender lending to a parent or holding company and relying on security over (e.g., an assignment of) the sub-loan from the parent or holding company down to the operating company.

[80] E.g., this is the case in Argentina, which deprives controlling shareholders from the right to vote on a judicial restructuring proposal. Nonetheless, as a general matter its law does not differentiate affiliates' claims from those of arms' length creditors. (*See also* Poland.)

Some emerging markets have also started to develop their own special rules for equity creditors.[81]

If the borrower's respective insolvency regime has special rules on equity creditor claims which subordinates them and/or allows their re-characterization as equity, then effectively this means that under the substantive terms of the restructuring, there will be a strong argument for subordination of their claims to those of the lenders.[82] Otherwise, it may be difficult for lender leadership to persuade the lenders to treat such claims as *pari passu* to the lenders' own claims. Lender leadership must therefore consult with local external counsel to determine whether such an approach is warranted.

Equity creditor issues in an emerging market restructuring will therefore merit close attention, for the reasons outlined above. Transaction leadership will wish to find the balance between continued rational support of the borrower's operational needs and fair treatment of the lenders.

## Third-Party (Intragroup) Credit Support

It is common in financing structures for one party to give credit support for the obligations of a third party in the form of a guarantee, suretyship, pledge, mortgage, or other security interest. Often, the third party who is the principal obligor/borrower (hence beneficiary of the credit support) may be a parent, subsidiary, or other group company of the party giving the credit support.

Most legal systems will not expressly prohibit such arrangements (and often codes of law in civil-law systems will explicitly recognize that one party may guarantee or give security for another's obligations).

The existence of such arrangements and their impact on a debtor often draw close scrutiny under the insolvency rules of many countries. The set of

---

[81] E.g., in January 2020, the Russian Supreme Court Presidium established special new rules for equity creditors. The rules presented a major step forward in crystallizing Russia's judicial practice with equity creditors, permitting debt characterization and/or statutory subordination of claims of both controlling and other non-controlling affiliates. Some other emerging markets' laws also treat equity creditors differently, e.g., Azerbaijan (treats parent-lenders to their corporate subsidiaries differently); Brazil (subordinates equity creditors); Chine (subordinates equity creditors); Egypt (equity creditors are most likely to be subordinated); Hungary (subordinates equity creditors); Kazakhstan (deprives equity creditors of vote); Mexico (subordinates equity creditors); Panama (scrutinizes connections of interest and makes such claims vulnerable to challenge); Poland (subordinates shareholder loans in certain cases and can deprive equity creditors of a vote on judicial restructurings); Slovak Republic (subordinates equity creditors); Uruguay (subordinates equity creditors). At the same time, a number of emerging markets treat equity creditors on par with arms' length creditors (e.g., Cayman Islands, Honduras, Jordan, Malaysia, Qatar, Saudi Arabia, Singapore, Turkey, UAE, Uganda, Uzbekistan, Venezuela, Zambia).

[82] Again, the restructuring should *replicate more or less the likely distributions in an insolvency.*

insolvency rules which come into play are often referred to as the "*corporate benefit doctrine*"—in other words, has the debtor received sufficient reciprocal value for its undertaking an obligation on behalf of a third party beneficiary (including an affiliate)? The categories of group credit support commonly encountered will include "upstream," "downstream," and "cross-stream" credit support (e.g., a guarantee from a parent will be "downstream," a pledge or other security from a subsidiary to its parent's lender will be "upstream," etc.).

*Downstream* credit-support arrangements generally tend to be viewed by insolvency systems as benefiting the party giving the credit support (e.g., a subsidiary's financial health will usually be to its parent's advantage, so the parent benefits economically from guaranteeing its subsidiary's obligations).

The same is not necessarily true for *upstream or cross-stream* arrangements. Nevertheless, a subsidiary guaranteeing its parent's or another affiliate's obligations may benefit from on-lending by the parent or other affiliate under the facility being guaranteed or benefit in some other meaningful way.

In short, a factual and economic analysis must be done, on a case-by-case basis, to determine in each instance whether real, tangible economic benefit flows to the supporting party.[83]

Many emerging markets' insolvency systems have imported these concepts and include some form of corporate benefit doctrine in their insolvency regimes. The corporate benefit doctrine will generally be found in the rules on *antecedent transactions* in its insolvency regime (and in particular, rules on undervalue transactions).[84] If inadequate benefit flows to the party giving the credit support, then the credit-support arrangements (guaranty, suretyship, pledge, etc.) risk being challenged (e.g., by an administrator and/or competing creditor) as invalid in insolvency proceedings involving such party as a debtor.

Again, as a core concept, a workout should ideally reflect (as closely as possible) the prospective distributions which would be made if the borrower were to go into judicial insolvency proceedings. These issues are thus directly relevant to determining those distributions.

In emerging markets' legal systems, due sometimes to vaguely written rules, the absence of well-established judicial practice and/or other factors, it can be

---

[83] Note here the relevance of directors' fiduciary duties (under local corporate law of the borrower) as well, to ensure that decisions are made in the interests of the company.

[84] The doctrine is distinct from the rules requiring due corporate approval of entry into the relevant transaction under the respective companies law of the debtor (e.g. as a significant and/or interested part, transaction)—the issue is also ordinarily excluded in practice from legal opinions by way of the usual "insolvency qualification" of standard legal opinions.

difficult to gauge the likelihood that existing credit-support arrangements of the debtor may be challenged as antecedent transactions.

Lender leadership must therefore instruct external local counsel to analyze whether and to what extent claims against the debtor under its credit-support arrangements might be challenged, if the debtor were to go into insolvency. If such arrangements risk challenge under such analysis, then lender leadership may have an argument that the lenders (or other claimants) benefiting from such arrangements should be treated differently under them than other lenders of the debtor. At the same time, as this analysis may be speculative, particularly if the rules on corporate benefit are not clear in the relevant emerging market, a more nuanced approach may be required. A lender benefiting from credit-support arrangements of the debtor (where strong corporate benefit rules threatening the lender's claim are absent) may need to be treated as a holdout, with some commercial arrangement achieved to get it to agree to waive or terminate its claim against the debtor under the relevant credit-support arrangements.

As a separate issue, where a lender has a claim against a borrower (e.g., under a loan) but that claim also benefits from third-party credit-support arrangements (e.g., from an affiliate of the borrower), this will raise issues of potential conflicts of interest amongst the lenders. One of the core concepts under INSOL II is that conflicts of interest in the creditor group should be identified early and dealt with appropriately (Principle Two). A creditor who benefits from security arrangements which decrease the risk on its claim against the borrower (or which may be prejudiced if the claim against the borrower is discounted in the restructuring) may be less inclined to agree to restructuring terms which give it less of a return than it might have if it retains its full claim against the borrower and pursues remedies under third-party credit support, whether these pose risks to lenders relying on them and whether these risks can be mitigated against.[85]

Finally, corporate benefit rules must be borne in mind when lender leadership is arranging new third-party credit support of the borrower's obligations as part of a restructuring. In some cases, for example, the current shareholder(s) and/or new investor(s) may undertake recourse and/or provide other credit support for the borrower's restructured obligations. In such case, it is essential for lender leadership to instruct external counsel to make a detailed analysis of corporate benefit issues applicable to the new credit support.

---

[85] For example, one of the authors was involved in a restructuring where the parent ultimately (after lengthy negotiation) agreed to give an indemnity for the relevant hardening period, to mitigate against the risk arising from cross-stream credit-support arrangements entered into by the subsidiary.

It goes without saying that there will be a compelling interest in ensuring that full capacity, authority, and enforceability opinion(s) are commissioned regarding such new credit support and that such opinions operate as CP(s) to effectiveness of the restructuring.[86]

## New Money

In many (if not most) distress situations, *the borrower's liquidity will be dire* and may even be the most pressing issue of the day. Despite the good-will afforded by those cooperative lenders who may agree to modify loans to improve the balance sheet and/or reduce debt service (e.g., by adjusting repayment schedules, forgiving interest, converting or partially converting to equity), the borrower's prospects for survival may be tenuous without needed cash.

The bridging requirements may be short term (i.e., during the standstill only) or more long term (e.g., as part of and for some period following closing on the restructuring).

The need to fund operating expenses may be further aggravated by having to repay substantial claims from creditors not participating in the workout, e.g., back pay to employees, trade creditors, tax authorities, and the like.[87] In such case, additional funding (or "new money") will be indispensable.

Of course, the borrower may be able to take certain measures to generate cash, e.g., reducing overhead, selling non-core assets, and the like. At the same time, such measures may simply require more time than the borrower has. Time may be of the essence.

On top of this will be the understandable concern of the borrower's directors to avoid personal liability for wrongful trading if they do not file for voluntary insolvency as required by law.[88]

Whilst the ideal solution for lender leadership will of course always be to secure either equity capital or junior (i.e., subordinated) debt infusions from the borrower's own major shareholders and/or from new investors,[89] this may not always be possible. As was seen from Kristi's case with Bank of

---

[86] Again, the corporate benefit analysis is a separate exercise and will not be part of these legal opinions; the latter will ordinarily include blanket insolvency qualification(s).

[87] Again, ordinarily non-financial creditors will not participate in a consensual restructuring.

[88] Some insolvency systems extend this liability to controlling shareholders, so just directors.

[89] The reader will recall, as a universal concept equity is last in priority in insolvency.

Commerce, the shareholders themselves may be dependent on upward cash flow from the borrower or otherwise unable to contribute.[90]

It is a fundamental concept of INSOL II that providers of additional debt funds during a standstill should (insofar as practicable) be entitled to *priority status*, as compared to other indebtedness or claims from relevant creditors.[91] This is furthermore consistent with the general proposition that the treatment of relevant creditors' claims in a restructuring should (more or less) reflect the resultant priority distributions if the borrower entered formal insolvency.

Many insolvency systems will grant statutory super-priority to new money advanced during formal insolvency proceedings and which meets the relevant eligibility requirements (e.g., judicial approval to ensure fair terms). This is also known as bankruptcy financing, or *debtor-in-possession (DIP) financing*. DIP financing is widely used for example in US Chapter 11 proceedings, and this approach is often also now reflected in emerging markets' insolvency systems.[92]

However, super-priority status is not generally granted by insolvency rules for non-judicial workouts. This is because workouts are voluntary contractual arrangements and thus not regulated by insolvency laws. There is consequently a certain level of risk for those lender(s) who consider providing new money, due to the absence of statutory protections.

Super-priority status must therefore be agreed on *contractually* by the parties in the standstill and/or restructuring agreement, by way of the participating lenders' entry into *inter-creditor arrangements*. These arrangements are ordinarily provisions included within the main restructuring agreements, providing inter alia:

- the new money lender will be repaid in *priority* to the payment of other claims,
- the other lenders' claims will be *subordinated* to those of the new money lender (including in any subsequent insolvent liquidation or other formal proceedings concerning the borrower),

---

[90] At the same time, ultimately in Bank of Commerce, Martin's DFI shareholder institution, the (fictitious) International Development Fund, was prepared to bridge the gap for the sake of market stability, consistent with its greater development mandate. This is not to say that in every case a DFI will be the knight in shining armor. But DFIs can often be helpful in finding solutions (where this promotes their mandate).

[91] INSOL II, Eighth Principle.

[92] *See* P. R. Wood; *op. cit.* DIP finance in developed economies such as the USA (under US Chapter 11) is increasingly recognized as an attractive financial activity, given the priority status and more enhanced level of control over US Chapter 11 proceedings afforded to DIP lenders. *See*, e.g., Kenneth Ayotte and Jared Ellias, 'Bankruptcy Process for Sale,' UC Hastings Research Paper No. 382, August 2020.

- any distributions to the other lenders contrary to this arrangement will be held in *trust* for the benefit of the new money lender,
- the other lenders will *share proceeds* of such distributions with the new money lender to effectuate such super-priority status, and
- the other lenders undertake certain negative covenants (e.g., against demanding payment, taking collateral, enforcing, etc. whilst the new money loan is outstanding).

The super-priority claim of the new money lender may also be supported either by new security from the borrower or security or other credit support from a third party (e.g., a parent or other affiliate).

So, what are the risks in putting these new money arrangements in place?

**Inter-creditor arrangements**—It will be essential for lender leadership to instruct external counsel to draft appropriate inter-creditor provisions and to confirm their enforceability, including under the applicable law of contract as well as the borrower's local insolvency law. Most likely a well-developed legal system (again, English or New York law[93]) will allow the creation of enforceable inter-creditor arrangements. This will not usually be problematic in the cross-border restructuring scenario in an emerging market: the main restructuring documentation will ordinarily meet these criteria. However, enforceability should also be vetted under the local law of the borrower's jurisdiction. The local legal advisors to the lenders may take the view that in the absence of unclear laws or well-developed judicial practice (a common situation in emerging markets), enforceability of inter-creditor arrangements is dubious or untested at best. For example, they may advise that such arrangements risk invalidation due to their violating public policy or other mandatory norms of the local laws and may be challenged later on at the insolvency stage. Some lenders may take a view on this and proceed to lend the new money in the given case (e.g., the amounts involved may be relatively small compared to existing exposures; there may also be other mitigating factors, e.g., the identities of counterparty lenders, the presence of an arbitration clause, etc.), whilst others may not.[94]

**Security and other credit support**—Where security for new money comes from the borrower, then obviously it must meet the legal standards expected for security (e.g., bona fide title, proper capacity and authority,

---

[93] *See* discussion above.

[94] In the authors' experience, in practice many international lenders are generally willing to accept subordination provisions, knowing in practice it is highly unlikely that other reputable international lending institutions participating in the workout as lenders would agree to undertake these now but then later argue that they should be disregarded.

due registration and other formalities for enforceability and perfection, etc.). Moreover, it must be remembered that the security will in any event be subject to the risk of subsequent invalidation as an antecedent transaction during the relevant hardening period, if the borrower enters formal insolvency proceedings during such period. If the security (or other credit support) comes from a third party, then in addition to the above, issues will likely arise under any corporate benefit doctrine of the jurisdiction of the party providing such support.[95] Local counsel from such jurisdiction should be instructed to advise on these risks.

Where the level of comfort as regards inter-creditor agreements is insufficient to move forward with the new money, then other alternatives may be available. For example, one approach may be to request all participating lenders to participate in the new money arrangements *proportionately* to their current exposures, hence spreading the risk. If the required amount of new money is relatively modest, then this approach may work in a given case.

Alternatively, the new money might be lent to one or more affiliate(s) of the borrower who are not obligors on the borrower's current loans and which may thus provide *structural seniority* to the existing debt claims (with separate collateral arrangements thus not risking invalidation as antecedent transactions in a subsequent insolvency of the borrower).

Whatever the case, lender leadership will face a challenge in ensuring any new money needs are met.

## Syndicated Lenders

It is of particular importance for transaction leadership to understand the manner in which *syndicated* lenders (as opposed to bilateral lenders) hold their claims against the borrower and the consequences of this from the standpoint of organization and documentation of the workout.

From a historical perspective, cross-border loans in emerging markets have predominantly been made on a bilateral basis—by a variety of DFIs, international commercial banks, specialized impact investment funds, and other lenders. The usage of cross-border bilateral loans as one of the primary sources of finance for emerging markets borrowers remains highly relevant today. Accordingly, much of the discussion in this book has focused on consensual restructurings of bilateral loans and their lending representatives' interaction with each other and the borrower.

---

[95] *See* discussion on third-party credit support, above.

That said, to be sure the growth of syndicated lending generally as a convenient financing method (combined with the march of globalization and the rise of emerging markets as profitable lending destinations) has considerably increased the prevalence of syndicated loans in these markets—and particularly over the last two decades.[96]

Indeed, the London-based LMA[97] has even developed its own suite of facility agreements especially tailored for use in developing markets.

A plethora of supplemental materials has also been written on the drafting, negotiation, and usage of the LMA standard loan forms generally. These materials are directly applicable to the use of LMA forms in emerging markets. Many may be found on the LMA's own website, as well as in articles by lawyers, law firms, and professional organizations.[98]

Of particular relevance to workout exercises, the LMA has published a useful guide for agent banks on dealing with amendments and waivers.[99]

This section of the book is not intended to replace a thorough study and mastery of such materials, particularly where the reader is regularly and directly involved in negotiating such loans for his or her financial institution, for a borrower or as a professional advisor.

Rather, the authors wish merely to provide a high-level summary of some of the big-picture issues for transaction leadership to bear in mind, where a syndicated loan is part of the greater debt package to be restructured.[100]

As a fundamental concept, a syndicated loan is a *collection of loans* made by individual lenders under a *single loan agreement* (the facility agreement). Each lender's loan legally constitutes an *independent debt claim* against the borrower, should it ever need to be enforced. That said, in practice in an LMA syndicated facility the decision to accelerate the loan will require majority lender (i.e., 66 2/3%) consent, and acceleration would then be coordinated

---

[96] Syndications provide considerable benefits for a borrower, in the relative ease of having to negotiate a single set of terms for a large volume of debt finance with a larger group of lenders. *See* M. Gruson, Restructuring syndicated loans: the effect of restructuring negotiations on the rights of the parties to the loan agreement (summarizing the position under New York law), International Law Revista Colombiana de Derecho Internacional, num. 3, junio 2004, pp. 322–342 Pontificia Universidad Javeriana, Bogota, Colombia.

[97] *See* discussion in Chapter 6.

[98] *See*, e.g., The ACT Borrower's Guide to the LMA Facilities Agreement for Leveraged Transactions (September 2008), prepared by the London-based Association of Corporate Treasurers (ACT), at www.treasurers.org. *See also* D. Newcomb, Recent Trends in Senior Loan Negotiation, A Practitioner's Guide to European Leveraged Finance, at www.lw.com/thoughtLeadership/recent-trends-in-senior-loan-negotiation.

[99] *See* Dealing with Requests for Amendments, 2019, at: www.lma.eu.com/application/files/2615/5654/7521/LMA-Dealing-with-requests-for-Amendments.pdf.

[100] Transaction leadership in emerging markets restructurings will often include representatives of impact investment lenders and/or DFIs who do not regularly work in the syndicated lending field. It is hoped that for readers from these institutions this summary is useful.

via the facility agent. Thus, if acceleration has not already occurred, the lenders in a particular syndicate will only be able to enforce their rights if the majority lender threshold is met.[101]

Moreover, the "sharing" provisions of the LMA form can discourage individual lenders from lodging enforcement actions, inasmuch as such provisions oblige an individual lender taking such action to *share the enforcement proceeds* proportionately with all other lenders.[102]

---

[101] As a general matter, the international financial community and the most relevant legal systems' courts have looked at lenders' rights under syndications as separate and independent. Individual lenders are not legally obliged to forbear or to agree to restructurings and may individually enforce their rights against borrowers. *See*, e.g., M. Gruson, op. cit. (regarding New York law).

As an exceptional matter, in 2015 a Hong Kong court issued a judgment contradicting this general consensus. *See Charmway Hong Kong Investment v Fortunesea (Cayman) Ltd & Ors* [2015] HKCU. Following the Charmway case, the LMA subsequently issued guidance and a conclusion that were the matter to come before an English court, it would not likely follow such an approach. The LMA also made subsequent clarifications to its loan forms to reinforce the doctrine of separate, independent rights. The LMA developing market facility agreement form reads in relevant part:

**2.3 Finance Parties' rights and obligations.**

(a) The obligations of each Finance Party under the Finance Documents are several. Failure by a Finance Party to perform its obligations under the Finance Documents does not affect the obligations of any other Party under the Finance Documents. No Finance Party is responsible for the obligations of any other Finance Party under the Finance Documents.

(b) The rights of each Finance Party under or in connection with the Finance Documents are separate and independent rights and any debt arising under the Finance Documents to a Finance Party from an Obligor is a separate and independent debt in respect of which a Finance Party shall be entitled to enforce its rights in accordance with paragraph (c) below. The rights of each Finance Party include any debt owing to that Finance Party under the Finance Documents and, for the avoidance of doubt, any part of a Loan or any other amount owed by an Obligor which relates to a Finance Party's participation in the Facility or its role under a Finance Document (including any such amount payable to the Agent on its behalf) is a debt owing to that Finance Party by that Obligor.

(c) A Finance Party may, except as specifically provided in the Finance Documents, separately enforce its rights under or in connection with the Finance Documents.

[102] Clause 27 provides in relevant part:

**27.1 Payments to Finance Parties.**

If a Finance Party (a "Recovering Finance Party") receives or recovers any amount from an Obligor other than in accordance with Clause 28 (Payment mechanics) (a "Recovered Amount") and applies that amount to a payment due under the Finance Documents then:

(a) the Recovering Finance Party shall, within three Business Days, notify details of the receipt or recovery to the Agent;

(b) the Agent shall determine whether the receipt or recovery is in excess of the amount the Recovering Finance Party would have been paid had the receipt or recovery been received or made by the Agent and distributed in accordance with Clause 28 (Payment mechanics), without taking account of any Tax which would be imposed on the Agent in relation to the receipt, recovery or distribution; and

(c) the Recovering Finance Party shall, within three Business Days of demand by the Agent, pay to the Agent an amount (the "Sharing Payment") equal to such receipt or recovery less any amount which the Agent determines may be retained by the Recovering Finance Party as its share of any payment to be made, in accordance with Clause 28.5 (Partial payments).

\* \* \*

**27.5 Exceptions.**

The notable exceptions to independent lender enforcement rights would be in the case of a relevant inter-creditor agreement (which may create further relevant conditions or limitations), a moratorium imposed by relevant insolvency proceedings or by applicable law (e.g., COVID-19 relief measures) and/or by a standstill arrangement which the facility agent has formally joined as a party (for which the facility agent will have needed to obtain majority lender approval, inasmuch as a standstill arrangement is a waiver of rights[103]).

Nonetheless, the lenders are all legally bound by the facility agreement, which not only governs the commercial and legal terms of the lenders' loans, but also the lenders' relationships with each other and with the facility agent, who has undertaken to represent them. Whilst the facility agent acts for the lenders primarily as an administrator, it retains certain discretion to act (or not to act), including to call an event of default, to accelerate and to enforce the loan and any relevant credit support, subject to *two key caveats.*[104]

*Firstly,* there will be a number of decisions which are expressly solely within the competence of a *"majority" of the lenders* (usually 66 2/3% of commitments) to decide, and who may also require the facility agent to act in certain cases. These include many types of amendments and waivers.[105]

*Secondly,* there will be a number of decisions which are solely within the competence of a *unanimity of the lenders* (100% of commitments) to decide.

In a given restructuring, therefore, transaction leadership must understand *which proposed aspects of the restructuring* requiring modification of the loan relationships (e.g., as one or more amendments or waivers) *will require a majority and which will require unanimity.* In this respect, the difference between these two categories can be quite substantial, as all-lender decisions can empower abusive holdout lenders (or at best present greater administrative obstacles and/or delays).

---

(a) This Clause 27 shall not apply to the extent that the Recovering Finance Party would not, after making any payment pursuant to this Clause, have a valid and enforceable claim against the relevant Obligor.

(b) A Recovering Finance Party is not obliged to share with any other Finance Party any amount which the Recovering Finance Party has received or recovered as a result of taking legal or arbitration proceedings, if:

(i) it notified that other Finance Party of the legal or arbitration proceedings; and.

(ii) that other Finance Party had an opportunity to participate in those legal or arbitration proceedings but did not do so as soon as reasonably practicable having received notice and did not take separate legal or arbitration proceedings.

[103] *See* discussion on lender consents below.

[104] As a practical matter, however, it is rare for the facility agent to exercise these discretionary acts without first seeking approvals under the caveats discussed below.

[105] In respect of a very limited number of technical matters, which are likely to be of limited relevance in a workout, the facility agent may also have individual authority to amend the facility.

Each syndicated loan facility will have been individually negotiated, and depending upon the success of the borrower and its counsel, the line between these two main categories of decisions may vary.

As a general rule, the un-negotiated standard LMA facility form provides that subject to the list of special matters requiring lender unanimity, any amendment or waiver of the terms of the facility agreement or other finance documents (e.g., credit support in the form of guarantees or security) will require majority (i.e., 2/3) lender approval.

The list of unanimous lender matters then includes the following:

a. changes to the definition of "majority lenders";
b. an extension to the date of payment of any amount under the finance documents;
c. a reduction in the margin or a reduction in the amount of any payment of principal, interest, fees, or commission payable;
d. a change in currency of payment of any amount under the finance documents;
e. an increase in any commitment or the total commitments, an extension of the availability period or any requirement that a cancellation of commitments reduces the commitments of the lenders ratably under the facility;
f. a change to the borrowers or guarantors other than as contemplated by the facility agreement;
g. any provision which expressly requires the consent of all the lenders;
h. clauses dealing with the several nature of the finance parties' rights and obligations, transferred mechanics, amendments, and waivers;
i. the nature or scope of (or releases of) guarantees or security; and
j. others, e.g., commitment to order of priority and/or subordination under an inter-creditor agreement.

Recent years have seen substantial negotiations on these points by borrowers and their counsel, e.g., to thwart anticipated minority holdouts, e.g., with the introduction of supermajority provisions, as well as so-called "snooze-you-loose" and "yank-the-bank" provisions.[106]

The relevant clauses of a syndicated facility thus merit close examination by transaction leadership with their external legal advisors to determine

---

[106] *See* D. Newcomb, *op. cit.* A 'snooze you lose' clause in a syndicated loan will disenfranchise a lender on a vote regarding a specific amendment or waiver request, if the lender does not respond to the syndication agent within a certain pre-determined time period. A 'yank the bank' clause will allow the borrower to replace a particular syndicate member with a new lender in certain limited circumstances.

whether the availability of such anti-minority-abuse provisions may facilitate obtaining syndicated lender consents for the workout.

As a general matter, transaction leadership must bear in mind that close coordination with the borrower and the facility agent will be essential. Obtaining syndicated lender consents relevant to the workout may require far more effort, administration, and time than bilateral loans. This must be built into the milestones for the workout.[107]

Lender leadership can take some comfort in the fact that they will, generally speaking, have a smaller number of banks to deal with directly when interfacing with the relevant parties—this will be the borrower and lead bank (if any), on the one hand, and the facility agent on the other hand. At the same time, the mere presence of an organized syndicate of banks will complicate the legal manner in which the workout is negotiated and implemented. There is likely to be a much more formal (legalistic) approach to the legal documentation (the standstill, the creation of the coordinating committee for the syndicate, the cost-coverage mechanisms, the standstill, and the main restructuring document itself [most likely an amendment or amendment and restatement, with ancillary documentation]), given the existence of what will probably be a rather lengthy and complex facility agreement, to begin with. The syndicate will most likely therefore have its own standalone set of legal documentation.[108]

In this respect, it may be said that the syndicate members will live in their own "restructuring microcosm"—but this must fit into the overall structure of the workout. Indeed, where bilateral and syndicated lenders are involved they and their external counsel must ensure careful coordination of the two sets of restructuring documentation.[109]

---

[107] Note the difference between a "facility agent," who acts purely as the administrator on the lenders' behalf, and a so-called "lead bank," i.e., a lender who will have been earlier approached by the borrower with the request to act as the borrower's representative to lead and liaise on the amendment process. This will usually be one of the original mandated lead arranger or book runner, but never the agent.

[108] *See* discussion above re LMA forms for restructuring syndicated loans.

[109] As one of the terms of the restructuring, or as an event that may occur after a restructuring, the borrower may well arrange to consolidate several of its existing loan agreements (whether syndicated or bilateral) into one new syndicated facility agreement so as to rationalize the terms of the debt and to bind as many lenders as possible to a single set of contractual provisions. This approach may be more acceptable to existing syndicated lenders in that they might be more comfortable in signing up to a new LMA syndicated facility agreement rather than signing up to an overlay restructuring agreement.

## Bondholders and Liability Management

Where a borrower has issued securities in the debt capital markets ("DCM"), then the approach to dealing with this class of creditors will be distinctly different from that employed for other lenders (e.g., bilateral, syndicated, or DFI lenders).

The reason is that unlike bilateral or syndicated loans where the borrower deals with a limited group of known lenders, debt securities (being negotiable instruments) are generally held by a much *wider class of creditors* with the composition of such class being much more likely to change, particularly in the context of more liquid debt securities. Thus, the actual identities of the creditors (i.e., the bondholders) are not always known to the issuer.

It is increasingly common in emerging markets to see companies who will have turned to DCM finance, either in the form of international debt instruments (e.g., eurobonds, often in a major international currency but more frequently in issuers' own national currencies[110]) and/or local debt instruments (e.g., domestic bond issuances, usually in the issuer's national currency).

At a time when developed economies' debt markets are providing less attractive returns, global fixed income investors have welcomed the higher returns emerging market bonds can afford. Reward and risk go hand in hand.

The trend picked up even greater speed in the year prior to publication of this book, when the liquidity being provided by global central banks to the market (to counter the global 2020–2021 COVID-19 pandemic) provided an attractive funding environment for highly rated issuers.[111]

Accordingly, it is not (and in future years will not be) uncommon to see an emerging market distressed situation where a *combination* of cross-border loans (e.g., bilateral, syndicated, and/or DFI) and DCM issuances must be restructured in tandem.

---

[110] Eurobonds initially developed as debt instruments by which issuers could tap international DCMs in a major international currency, e.g., EUR, USD, GBP. In addition to the fundamental issue of market supply/demand, an early functional limitation was the capability of the major eurobond clearing systems (e.g., Euroclear and Clearstream) to settle in international currencies. As international demand for more "exotic" currencies grew and the clearing systems increased the currencies they could accommodate, it has become more commonplace to see eurobonds issued for settlement in, and/or denominated in, the currencies of a variety of emerging markets. *See* https://www.clearstream.com/clearstream-en/products-and-services/cash-and-banking-ser vices/cash-and-banking-overview/eligible-currencies; *see also* https://www.euroclear.com/services/en/pri mary-issuance.html.

[111] *See* Emerging market eurobond volumes set for record year in 2020, Financial Mirror, 13 October 2020, at www.financialmirror.com/2020/10/13/emerging-market-eurobond-volumes-set-for-record-year-in-2020/.

In such case, it will be critical for transaction leadership to have a sound understanding of the options for restructuring the DCM issues (known as "*liability management*" alternatives) and how these will likely bear on the process and the milestones for the greater restructuring.

The purpose of this discussion section is not to provide the in-depth knowledge transaction leadership will need in such a case. Rather, it is to outline in "broad stroke" the likely steps toward restructuring the DCM tranche of the debt and to remind leadership to factor these steps into the action plan and milestones in advance.

The restructuring methods in a DCM liability management exercise will differ considerably from the negotiation and implementation of a workout involving purely loan relationships (the latter is effectively usually just an amendment exercise, albeit undertaken on a coordinated, multi-lender basis).

As a general matter, there are essentially *four (4) main types of DCM liability management techniques*, whether bonds are issued by a borrower from a developed nation or from an emerging market. In this respect, the two market categories are quite similar: both will involve a suite of lengthy, complex cross-border transaction documents (usually governed by English or New York law), a trustee arrangement and, to the extent the bonds are listed, various stock exchange notices and announcements.

In other respects, they may differ considerably. Critically, the emerging markets issuance will involve many of the same insolvency law and systemic questions we have discussed above—since ultimately, the local emerging market borrower (and/or its assets) will provide the main credit support for the bond holders, e.g., as a borrower, a guarantor, a pledgor/assignor, etc.

The four (4) main liability management techniques will be:

1. **consent solicitations**—the issuer's submission of a proposal to the holders to consider an amendment to the bonds' terms,
2. **open market purchases/bond buy backs**—the issuer's re-purchase of a portion of its bonds by inviting or accepting bids or offers on the secondary market,
3. **tender offers**—the issuer's offer to purchase its bonds by launching a public offer, and/or.
4. **exchange offers**—the issuer's offer to the holders to exchange them (in whole or in part) for new ones.

These four (4) techniques may either be used individually or on a combined basis with each other.

In a distressed situation where debt must be restructured, in the authors' experience, an issuer would frequently opt for a *consent solicitation or an exchange offer*. One might also see a so-called "*exit consent*" where the consent and tender offer are combined in one exercise and those bondholders who tender their bonds are automatically consenting to the proposal. However, these are not the sole options.

How does transaction leadership decide which option is best suited for a particular workout? This decision must be taken together with the issuer (i.e., the borrower) and those investment bank(s) assisting it to enhance interaction with bondholders to increase the success of the exercise, as well as with the issuer's specialized external DCM counsel. There is no "one size fits all" answer, and each solution will be bespoke.

The option chosen will ultimately depend on various factors (primarily the issuer's objectives, which must reflect the overall restructuring plan), including a careful legal analysis of the terms and conditions of the outstanding bonds and their applicable law. In addition, market factors (e.g., demand, pricing) will play a critical part in determining which path is most appropriate. Whether the issuer has already defaulted under the bonds or is merely trying to avert disaster looming on the horizon will also be relevant.

For example, one might see a combination of a *tender offer together with a new issuance*, so that a large portion of outstanding bonds are retired in a short time frame, by way of a public offer by the borrower to buy the bonds back for cash. The payment (likely to be made at a premium, as a "carrot" for bondholders to go along) is funded by way of a simultaneous issuance of new bonds. The new bonds will be more attractive to the borrower (and hence its other creditors, such as bilateral and syndicated lenders participating in the workout) from the standpoint of reducing its overall debt service requirements, e.g., by a lower interest coupon, a more extended repayment schedule, reduced financial covenants, and the like.

-&-

Because bonds are securities, the *regulatory framework* will be far more complex than that for mere loans. There will be a strict requirement to observe applicable securities law requirements in a number of relevant jurisdictions (locally and internationally). Indeed, this is one of the key differentiating factors from pure loans. Where a bilateral or syndicated loan is restructured, the lender is more or less free to negotiate and agree the terms for restructuring its loan. If the lender is a syndicated facility agent, its hands will be tied by the facility agreement—in that it will have to obtain the approval of the requisite portion of the syndicated lenders (some majority or possibly 100%) in accordance with the facility's relevant terms.[112] But even here, this is done on a consensual, contractual basis, more or less free of regulatory interference as such.

By contrast, the implementation of a DCM liability management exercise must observe the strict requirements of the various relevant securities laws. Interfacing with the trustee (who will have its own external counsel) will play a key role. And any relevant exchange procedures and applicable laws must also be strictly observed.

Certain international jurisdictions will also likely be highly relevant. As many emerging markets DCM issuances have existing US holders, US securities law requirements may need to be observed and may require exploring an appropriate exemption in the USA for the issuer to avail of. If a tender offer is used, the US tender offer rules may apply and impact heavily on the timetable, the process, and the disclosure elements (particularly where US holders have 10% or more of the bonds), unless the issuer elects to exclude the US holders from the tender. External counsel must advise on these issues (particularly, in light of not liability management exercises being capable of being executed on an exclusionary basis), and transaction management must factor these aspects into the overall timing and milestones for the larger workout.

Furthermore, where there is an English-law element to the bond issuance (many DCM issuances are done under English law), one would need to ensure that the bondholders are treated fairly and equally (as a class) and consider carefully whether there is any risk of claims of "oppression" or "intimidation" of a minority and how these could be mitigated.[113]

The authors have observed that where bonds have been issued on a purely local basis, the inclusion of such bonds into a workout can be quite cumbersome and even assume a highly sensitive political tone. Provided this does not impede the viability of the larger loans workout, it may be simpler for transaction leadership to try and restructure the international lenders' loans without modifying domestic bond terms (i.e., ensuring the local bonds are repaid in full, whilst international lenders restructure their own loans).

---

[112] *See* discussion on syndicated loans above.

[113] *See Asenagon Asset Management SA v Irish Bank Revolution Corporation Ltd* [2012] EWHC 2090 (Ch).

## Secured Lenders

Ordinarily in a developed economy's legal system, the presence of security plays a major role in driving a lender's position and whether or not to join with other lenders in a consensual restructuring.

In particular, other considerations aside (e.g., the broader customer relationship with the borrower and/or its major shareholders, the collateral coverage ratio, fluctuations in market value of collateral, etc.), the lender will usually differentiate itself from non-secured lenders and take the view that security enforcement affords a far better return on the trade than joining in a workout. Insolvency rules of most developed nations will give the secured creditor the exclusive right to receive proceeds from sale of the collateral and to apply these proceeds against its claim.

However, this assumption may not always be a "slam dunk" for the lender in an emerging market. It must therefore be tested in the given case: *how secure is the security*, and how quickly can the lender move forward with foreclosure? Will this be easy and straightforward? Will the lender be able to apply the full value of the proceeds against its claim? Will the proceeds be enough to settle the loan?

In many emerging markets, the bureaucratic obstacles, pitfalls, complications, and delays associated with creating, maintaining, and enforcing against various forms of collateral can create formidable barriers toward value realization during collateral enforcement.[114]

Lender leadership in a restructuring must therefore bear in mind that whilst individual secured lenders will publicly maintain that their security is valid and they are fully entitled to enforce, behind closed doors they may take a more nuanced view. Accordingly, there may be room for compromise and convincing a secured lender to join in a restructuring when they would otherwise not do so, if the borrower and the collateral were located in a more developed jurisdiction.

Some examples of possible issues bearing on security enforcement in emerging markets include:

- Certain secured creditors (e.g., DFIs) may take a less recovery-driven approach and may instead be willing, for purposes of their public mandate,

---

[114] In some emerging markets certain lenders may require offshore security structures to mitigate against local security enforcement risks (administrative burdens, delays, etc.), by creation of an offshore holding company whose shares (together with shares in the local operating company) are pledged to the lender to complement a local security structure over the operating assets (movables, immovables and main contractual rights). Note that not all lenders will necessarily have taken such measures.

market development, and support of the country in question, and/or of the particular borrower in question, to support a consensual restructuring.[115]

- The secured claim may only be a part of the lender's overall exposure to the trade. For example, there may be unsecured loans and/or even a piece of the equity, which the lender must include into its overall recovery calculations.
- The general negative impact of insolvency may bear on the prospects for the secured lender's realization of value in insolvency proceedings. The insolvency rules will likely create an automatic stay prohibiting enforcement other than through the proceedings, subjecting the secured lender to the value loss and systemic problems discussed earlier in this chapter (e.g., weak rule of law, nature of the legal system, etc.).
- The security may fall under rules on antecedent transactions (where it is in the relevant hardening period) or fall short of corporate benefit doctrine if it is third-party security.
- In some emerging markets, insolvency rules create a statutory waterfall for application of proceeds from security enforcement, which bite into the lender's value expectations.[116] The secured lender may take the view that this delay and/or statutory waterfall is unpalatable (particularly where the collateral's market value has reduced or is subject to the threat of future reduction), and the chances of recovery are better in a workout.
- In some emerging markets, due to the general systemic problems discussed earlier in this chapter (e.g., weak rule of law, nature of the legal system, etc.), the borrower may be able to create bureaucratic obstacles to successful enforcement outside of insolvency. For example, the rules on security may not permit self-help (or self-help rules may simply not be workable). They may require that for the particular security given, recourse to the local judicial system is required in order to enforce. The local rules may provide broad room for the proactive borrower to avoid or delay enforcement, and the risks of corruption of the judiciary and/or interference from "friends in high places" may create real threats to successful enforcement;
- there is the risk that due to the high level of formalities in the legal system for creation and/or perfection of security, the secured lender in question may have faulty security and/or ancillary documentation necessary to enforce such security (e.g., necessary perfection registrations may

---

[115] *See* discussion regarding DFI mandates above.

[116] E.g., in Russia, the bankruptcy law can require that secured lenders delay enforcement of security until a later stage of the proceedings and moreover that even then, once enforcement is permitted, up to 10% (and in some cases 20%) of proceeds from enforcement be paid to the administrator to defray costs of the insolvency proceedings and of enforcement (including fees of the administrator).

have been missed; ostensibly 'irrevocable' powers of attorney given to assist in enforcement may prove less irrevocable than previously believed; etc.).

Based on the above, lender leadership should test in each case whether the ordinary assumptions regarding secured creditors will operate in a given emerging market distressed situation. Lender leadership should have *frank discussions* with secured creditors on these issues. Having secured creditors on board the workout in a given case may help create the necessary critical mass of relevant creditors and may encourage others to join.[117]

The presence of existing security may also help the secured lender to play a more active role, e.g., in providing new money in the restructuring to meet cash needs (which will benefit from the existing security).

## Vicarious Liability (Shadow Directors); Wrongful Trading

As briefly mentioned above, various insolvency law issues will impact on lenders and/or otherwise raise risks in a restructuring. Despite the parties' good-faith efforts to reach a restructuring, there is always a significant chance that the transaction will not unfold as planned (or that other troubles might arise), as a result of which the borrower may still end up in formal insolvency proceedings. The parties must therefore always look ahead at this possibility.

One of the main insolvency risks here will be the doctrine of vicarious liability. This is sometimes referred to as "shadow director" liability (a term frequently encountered in common law systems), as "controlling person" liability or something similar.[118]

It will be essential for lender leadership to ensure that their *actual comportment* during the restructuring, as well as the *terms and conditions of relevant legal documentation* in the restructuring, mitigate against the risk of vicarious liability for the lenders.

The insolvency laws of many (though not all) emerging markets include provisions on vicarious liability (some in quite skeletal terms, others in far

---

[117] Notably, there may also be legal restrictions on foreclosure in the form of an emergency relief moratorium prohibiting foreclosure. For example, during 2020, in connection with the COVID-19 global pandemic, various countries' governments adopted emergency moratoria restricting foreclosure on collateral against businesses hit by the pandemic.

[118] Note that this is a different doctrine of law from say: (1) piercing the corporate veil/disregard of corporate form, and/or (2) breach of duties by officers and directors, which are also relevant. The doctrine of shadow director (i.e., vicarious) liability generally arises under the insolvency law of a jurisdiction, whilst these other two doctrines are ordinarily found in the jurisdiction's corporate (and/or civil) law and can be applied outside the context of an insolvency. Importantly, these two other corporate doctrines may provide an important sword against prior management and/or majority shareholder abuse (leakage), when the lenders decide to pursue a workout.

greater detail). Some such laws limit the liability to officers and directors alone. Others can give broad discretion to the court to determine if in a given case a third party (including potential lenders in the restructuring) may bear vicarious liability for the debts of the borrower, if the debtor goes insolvent and its estate is insufficient to pay claims.

The premise for such liability is that if a person was de facto in control of the borrower during a period when the borrower's financial condition was deteriorating, and as result of that person's wrongdoing the interests of creditors were harmed, then creditors ought to be able to recover the losses from the controlling person (including in particular the deficit on their claim recovery).[119]

The insolvency laws may expressly list those persons who qualify as controlling, e.g., the borrower's CEO, members of its board of directors, majority or even substantial minority shareholders, and the like. The law may also be broad enough to permit the court to find other persons as de facto controlling, even in the absence of formal legal relations with that person. In short, the law may cut a rather broad swathe, allowing for a wide range of candidates to bear liability.

Lender leadership should bear in mind that if sufficient evidence of abusive control exists and this may be used to broaden recourse on claims to cover de facto controlling persons, it may be worth considering whether a judicial restructuring (either in the relevant local courts or in an international or regional judicial regime [e.g., UK, USA, Singapore]) might provide a higher recovery. Even if this is not a viable alternative, its discussion as a potential option may still help expedite negotiation of a consensual restructuring.

-&-

At the same time, the vicarious liability rules are a two-edged sword. In some emerging markets, the provisions of the law and the discretion afforded to the court have led to troubling results, including imposition of vicarious liability on account banks and other arms' length contracting counterparties, who would never have expected such liability.[120] Moreover, in cases where the law

---

[119] Or "interlopers, usurpers, puppet-masters or string-pullers," in the words of P. R. Wood, *op. cit.*, 19–109, p. 589. Note that in at least one case in the English courts, Re A Company (No. 005009 of 1987 (1988) 4 BCC 424), it was held that a company's bank could be a shadow director of the company; but it has also been established that a bank will not be a shadow director if it sets out its requirements for continuing loan facilities as conditions, not instructions; *Re PFTZM Ltd* [1995] BCC 280. "[The] cases indicate that although shadow directorship is a concern for lenders who overstep the mark, the courts recognize that lenders are entitled to take steps to protect their rights as creditor without running the risk of being found to have acted as shadow directors." P. R. Wood *op cit.*

[120] For example, in 2017 in Russia the rules on vicarious liability were reformed to introduce a broad element of judicial discretion to determine de facto control and impose vicarious liability on

is broad, the approach of insolvency office holders and creditors has been overly aggressive—a "shot-gun" approach aimed at imposing liability on the broadest possible population of parties to make up for the shortfall in the debtor's assets.

Given this, the issue of potential vicarious liability in a workout, as applicable to the lenders, their professional advisors and other parties involved in the borrower's financial operations and restructuring efforts (e.g., project monitors), deserves the closest attention.

Lender leadership should instruct the lenders' external legal advisors at the outset (in particular, local-law advisors from the borrower's jurisdiction) to weigh in on such risks and confirm that the manner in which the restructuring is conducted and the terms and provisions of the legal documentation (including any overlay restructuring agreement) do not raise concerns. Documentation should be vetted for the absence of rights or authorities of the lenders to control the borrower and should furthermore include appropriate disclaimers.[121]

So, from a practical standpoint, is this a major issue? Should lender leadership lose sleep over it? Probably not, provided lender leadership and its counsel bear the issue in mind both as regards *comportment and documentation.* To be sure, many emerging markets' rules do allow judicial discretion. But to date, the authors have not encountered a case where a bona fide arms' length lender was held vicariously liable.[122]

That said, the authors have seen cases where lenders have made proposals which, if implemented, could tempt fate. One of the authors has encountered (a surprising number of times) cases where lenders demand the right to appoint the executive management and/or one or more members to the board of directors of the borrower (in a clear attempt to control the borrower's financial activities). The intention, of course, is understandable. By controlling the management the lender can stem leakage and ensure repayment of its loan.

---

third parties. *See* https://www.dentons.com/en/insights/alerts/2017/august/31/russian-insolvency-law-recently-amended-to-expand-vicarious-liability. Thereafter, as expected, the volume of motion practice expanded substantially, with insolvency officers increasingly relying on such motions as a mechanism to increase bankruptcy estates and satisfy creditor claims.

[121] Generally the assumption is that negative covenants (and other forms of negative control) in finance documents should not be sufficient to trigger vicarious liability, but this should be checked with local counsel in each case.

[122] *Cf.* one case in Russia, in which an account bank was deemed to be a controlling person of the debtor. *See* Supreme Court of the Russian Federation Decision of 6 August 2018 No. 308-ES17-6757 (2, 3). However, in the survey conducted especially for preparation of this book, none of the insolvency practitioners interviewed in any of the 46 emerging markets jurisdictions surveyed could remember such a case. Most agreed that based on the readings of their respective countries' laws, the risk was probably relatively low.

But is this level of control really worth it? And can it be implemented without exposing the lender to vicarious liability? The issue must be closely examined by counsel under the borrower's insolvency laws. Additionally, formal appointment as an officer or director may raise issues for the individual concerned.[123]

The safer route from the standpoint of avoiding potential vicarious liability would be instead to have *"eyes and ears" rights only*, i.e., monitoring, information, and attendance rights in respect of all correspondence, board meetings, and the like. An independent project monitor may also be well-equipped to play this role. But the rights and authorities of the project monitor must be scrutinized carefully to ensure that these avoid actual control and decision-making rights and include appropriate disclaimers.

Unfortunately, contractual indemnifications (and/or hold-harmless undertakings) from the borrower in the restructuring documentation may be ineffective as a mitigant. If vicarious liability is indeed imposed by the relevant insolvency law, then the court may well take the view that an indemnification or hold-harmless clause is contrary to the law or does not bind the administrator.[124]

Vicarious liability provisions in insolvency laws will also likely include so-called *"wrongful trading"* rules. Under such provisions, an officer or director (or even a controlling shareholder) will be under a statutory obligation to file for voluntary judicial insolvency within a prescribed period, if the borrower entity evidences indicia of insolvency (on a cash flow and/or balance sheet basis).

If the officer or director (or controlling shareholder) fails to meet this duty within this period, then (s)he (or it) will become personally liable for the debts of the borrower accumulating after the period expires. The rules and their judicial interpretation will of course vary from country to country. Some borrower's officers and directors (and/or controlling shareholders) may be understandably concerned as to their potential personal liability. They may demand the right to consult with independent legal advisors and/or their in-house counsel on the legal course of action they should take.[125]

---

[123] There may well be a conflict of interest for an individual appointed as a director of a borrower whilst maintaining employment with and/or a corporate or fiduciary obligation to another entity (such as a lender); an individual may also be concerned about potential criminal liability and/or the absence of effective D&O policies in certain emerging markets.

[124] Nonetheless, the authors have worked on several restructurings where they were able to create an indemnity fund structurally ring-fenced to ensure availability for indemnities to the borrower's officers, directors, the project monitor, etc.

[125] Notably, officers' and directors' attitudes toward the issue of wrongful trading vary widely in emerging markets. In some markets the law and practice is relatively underdeveloped, and local management may be far more relaxed about potential liability. In others they may be far more

The authors have successfully convinced officers and directors in a number of emerging market workouts that a formal standstill agreement is sufficient under the relevant rules to suspend this obligation. In a given market, the rules may well be properly interpreted in this manner. (In some cases, however, it may simply not be clear.) The position should be vetted with local counsel in advance to ensure whether it may be used to assuage concerns of the borrower's officers and directors.

In short, lender leadership should ensure that vicarious liability (and wrongful trading) issues are at the top of the list of issues on which external counsel are advising, from the very start of and throughout the workout transaction.[126]

## Building Blocks of Overlay Restructuring Agreements

As earlier mentioned in the book, each restructuring transaction will have its own particular set of facts and circumstances, lenders, investors, personalities, regulators, business, market, and legal issues which will drive the structure and implementation of the transaction. In this sense, one may say that each restructuring transaction is truly unique.

At the same time, indisputably many restructuring transactions will also share common features with others. And the legal agreements which implement them will bear similarities, often reflecting comparable legal style (not to mention many common boilerplate provisions). Just as an architect may assemble architectural elements from past projects together to make an entirely unique new construction, so, too, the lawyers tasked with drafting the documentation will often rely (with some overhauling) on concepts and provisions which may have worked well for them or their law firms in earlier restructuring transactions. "Hey, we did this the last time – let's use that (but...)" is a common theme when drafting.

Accordingly, the authors see some merit in describing for the reader some of the main principles or legal "building blocks" used in assembling restructuring agreements.

---

sensitive. The presence of expatriate independent directors on a board of directors may further influence the directors' attitudes generally.

[126] During the COVID-19 pandemic, various countries (including emerging markets) adopted insolvency relief measures suspending wrongful trading rules (hence relieving directors of the duty to file for voluntary insolvency). Whilst many such measures were intended to be short-lived, lender leadership should consult local counsel on whether these (or extensions or similar measures) remain in effect. Lender leadership may also wish to consult with the borrower's management as to whether a directors and officers (D&O) insurance policy is in effect and sufficiently broad to cover potential wrongful trading liability of the borrower's management.

It is assumed the lenders and borrower will have already put a standstill agreement in place at an earlier stage (unless one is not required). The parties may now be at term sheet stage (so the building blocks might be suggested only tentatively, subject to vetting during the diligence stage). Or they may already be at the stage of drafting the formal restructuring agreement.

The threshold issue will be whether the borrower and lenders prefer to proceed with the restructuring purely based on a *series* of parallel bilateral agreements (negotiated and executed by the borrower with each individual lender) or whether a *multiparty overlay* restructuring agreement may be acceptable and appropriate (negotiated by lender leadership with the borrower, for final approval and execution by all lenders).

Where a borrower attempts to negotiate bilateral arrangements with individual lenders (holding them at a distance from one another), this may not help to garner the trust and collaboration required to meet the challenges of a complex restructuring. Such efforts can be counterproductive, and though they may give the borrower some feeling or illusion of control, they can sometimes create more work and delays in negotiations.

In the authors' experience, multiparty overlay agreements can be extremely useful tools to coordinate the efforts and obligations of lenders, borrowers, shareholders, and other participating stakeholders in the restructuring. They can also be useful in dealing with local financial regulators, demonstrating a unified purpose amongst the borrower and its providers of capital, giving the regulator confidence that it need not step in to take over administration of the borrower's business, where the trigger for this is close.[127],[128]

In simple terms, an overlay agreement is a single contractual document in which:

- the parties re-confirm the amounts and other details of the loans outstanding;
- the all participating lenders, on the one hand, agree to the financial concessions they must make in order to meet the main goals of the restructuring, e.g., reducing financial pressure on the borrower by agreeing to modify the terms of their respective loans, waiving or reducing financial obligations, extending maturities, waiving or resetting financial covenants and the like,

---

[127] Where all participating lenders are part of a single syndicated facility, it will be sufficient to amend the facility itself (or to amend and restate it). That said, in the authors' experience emerging markets borrowers frequently have multiple bilateral loan facilities in place.

[128] It is further assumed that the parties will not have pursued hybrid options in certain developed jurisdictions such as the US, UK, Singapore, etc. and will be satisfied relying on a multiparty overlay agreement.

modifying the nature of their claims (e.g., re-characterizing senior debt as subordinated debt, swapping debt for equity, etc.), etc., and

- the borrower and its affiliates (e.g., major shareholders, equity creditors, etc.), on the other hand, undertake their own respective contributions to meet the main goals of the restructuring (this can be new equity from the major shareholders, various undertakings to restructure the business, etc.),
- other parties may also be signatories (e.g., a project monitor) and undertake certain functions, and
- other critical legal terms are agreed.

The lenders' concessions will not be granted unconditionally. On the contrary, they will ordinarily be *conditioned* upon the successful prior occurrence of the borrower's and its affiliates' respective undertakings, in such a manner that the lenders' concessions *will only become effective* (legally enforceable) once these borrower/affiliate undertakings and other conditions occur as conditions precedent ("CPs") to effectiveness (this is similar to CPs for a loan disbursement being met).

Effectiveness must occur by a certain longstop date stipulated in the overlay agreement (failing which, the restructuring is a nullity, financial close does not occur and the parties are free to take such steps as they wish, including to petition a local court for formal insolvency proceedings).

As a simple (and rather common) example, a group of lenders' partial forgiveness of their respective loans (or interest thereon) may become effective only once the major shareholder (or an identified new investor) has contributed an agreed sum of further cash to the borrower as equity capital (or agreed to guarantee the restructured loans upon effectiveness).

In addition to the conditionality of lender concessions based on key performance by the borrower and its affiliates, often the restructuring agreement will include *other key CPs* to effectiveness, such as the following, usually all "in form and substance satisfactory to the lenders":

- formal CPs which would be common for a facility document, such as extensive representations and warranties of the borrower/affiliates (including regarding information provided during the earlier standstill/diligence stage) continuing to be true and accurate as at the date of effectiveness, as well as documentary deliveries regarding the borrower and affiliates and duly executed originals of the overlay agreement itself,
- issuance of formal legal opinions from the lenders' external counsel, e.g., on the capacity and authority of the borrower and its affiliates and other

ancillary legal matters, and if required, the enforceability of the overlay agreement,[129]

- the absence of certain disqualifying events (or "super defaults") from having occurred,
- engagement (or continued engagement) of the project monitor to the extent the project monitor has been engaged by the borrower and must continue to play a key role following financial close (e.g., monitoring the borrower for a certain period),
- where a debt-to-equity swap is a part of the restructuring, the due issuance of new shares to converting lenders, due occurrence of any required regulatory approvals for such issuance, due execution of any new shareholders agreement (SHA) to meet lenders' corporate governance demands as new shareholders,[130]
- evidence of completion by the borrower/affiliates of any business or financial restructuring measures required as CPs to effectiveness (this might include further cash or credit support), and
- any other agreed CPs.

Upon achieving effectiveness, the lenders' respective loans are then deemed restructured (modified) as agreed. This is often helpful to document by way of attaching as schedules tables reflecting all lenders' current loans as at the moment of signing the overlay agreement and these loans are then restructured as a result of the restructuring transaction, including new principal amounts, new repayment schedules, new maturities, and new financial covenants. It can be helpful to have repayment schedules brought in harmony with each other. The agreement will likely also require that any further prepayments be made only pro-rata to all lenders.

The overlay will also include various typical provisions which one may see in financial agreements, such as detailed definitions of terms used in the agreement, extensive representations and warranties of the borrower and its affiliates, key undertakings by the borrower regarding further debt and security, as well as standard boilerplate.[131]

Where equity creditors are involved, as mentioned earlier in this chapter one may see rather detailed provisions on subordination of the equity creditors' claims to the participating lenders. Where new moneys are being

---

[129] *See* discussion, footnote 209 above.

[130] The lenders can be expected to require appropriate legal opinions including, e.g., on valid issuance of shares, due regulatory approvals and validity and enforceability of any SHA.

[131] The overlay is not intended to replace but merely to supplement and modify the existing loan agreements, accordingly it may not require many of the covenants usually seen in loans, e.g., affirmative/negative covenants, information covenants, etc.

provided, one would also expect to see inter-creditor arrangements (including subordination by existing lenders to the new money lender(s)). One may also see certain senior debt being converted into subordinated debt.[132]

The overlay would also typically include its own standstill (forbearance) provisions recognizing that absent certain disqualifying events (or "super defaults"), the lenders will not enforce whilst the parties are using their mutual efforts to achieve effectiveness (financial close) on the restructuring. These provisions may also require a majority or supermajority of lenders to take an action to terminate the standstill.

The document may also include certain conditions subsequent for the borrower and/or its affiliates, where these are not so essential to the financial close and/or impossible to be achieved before the longstop for effectiveness.

Where one or more holdout creditors are involved in the transaction and have agreed to be a party to the document, the document may include such parties as signatories and require the borrower to make payoffs to them at some agreed haircut.

The document will also usually include detailed provisions on costs and expenses of the lenders to be borne by the borrower, indemnities, provisions on disclosure (confidentiality), dispute resolution (ordinarily by international arbitration, as discussed above in this chapter), applicable law (as discussed above, e.g., often English or New York law) and the like.

Where DFIs are involved in the restructuring and signatories to the overlay, then it can be expected that these DFIs will require that certain standard provisions be in the document, such as express preservation of privileges, immunities, and/or other exemptions pursuant to their respective constituent documents and international law. They may also have other special requirements for their financial documentation which they require to be reflected, e.g., their own institutional approach to international arbitration agreements.[133]

It will be essential for each individual lender and its own set of legal advisors (often in-house) to determine that the overlay approach may be used, and this will be effective in amending its respective underlying loan document(s). This exercise would not ordinarily be undertaken by the external counsel to the lender leadership (the group of participating lenders as a whole).

---

[132] A common requirement may arise for subordinated debt to meet the local statutory requirements for subordinated debt to be treated as statutory capital where the borrower is a regulated entity (e.g., a bank). This must be checked with local counsel.

[133] In the post-Brexit world, the authors have observed an apparent move by some European DFIs away from London (e.g., LCIA) arbitration.

Ideally, unless required to preserve legality, separate individual amending agreements to implement the restructuring envisaged in the overlay document are best avoided. In the authors' experience, individual lenders can sometimes attempt to use these further amending agreements as an opportunity to "improve" their position vis-à-vis the borrower, and these can open a veritable Pandora's Box of issues. That said, some legal systems may require that some form of formal local-law document be signed. If possible, in such cases, individual amending agreements should follow a uniform approach.

## Building Blocks of Orderly Wind-Down Agreements

In certain cases, it may be clear that the borrower's business does not have a bright financial future. For example, there may be negative equity, and current shareholders may be unable or unwilling to support the business further. It may be difficult to find a buyer for or new investor into the business. Even so, it may still be far preferable for the lenders to collaborate with shareholders and keep the borrower out of formal insolvency proceedings, by agreeing an extended standstill and the terms for an orderly winding down and liquidation of the business.[134]

This might be done, for example, where the borrower has its principal value sunk into an asset which will take an extended period of time to recover fully, such as a loan portfolio. The "fire sale" of such an asset (by way of sale and assignment of the portfolio to a competitor) may be impossible, or simply undesirable given the heavy discount on a third-party sale.[135]

In such case, it may be far preferable just to slow (and ultimately stop) originating new loan business and merely collect the portfolio over time. Then, once the business is ready to be liquidated, the lenders can forgive the debt, and the shareholder may liquidate the entity on a fully solvent basis. The authors have done this with a number of microfinance and other financial institutions in various emerging markets.

In the case where the business must be wound down in this fashion, a number of key legal issues will arise:

- ensuring that the directors are relieved from any statutory obligation to file for insolvency (to avoid liability for wrongful trading),

---

[134] As was done in our opening narrative for the Bank of Commerce.

[135] This was the case in our Bank of Commerce narrative, where the loan book needed to be collected over time. A fire sale of the loan book would have resulted in a significant loss for the lenders.

- incentivizing management and key employees to stay on with the business during the wind-down period,[136]
- ensuring that the borrower, if a regulated entity (e.g., a financial institution), continues to meet all relevant local regulatory requirements to avoid being taken over by local authorities (this may also involve some level of discreetness to avoid attracting regulatory attention and/or triggering a run),
- ensuring that non-participating creditors (e.g., depositors, tax authorities, commercial landlords, etc.) and the borrower's current expenses are promptly and fully paid,
- providing for discounted payments of any lenders who wish to leave early,
- agreeing the terms of the extended standstill arrangement (this will be a longer period than the usual short-term standstill prior to a restructuring and hence may have special issues),
- agreeing lender consent requirements (and addressing these, e.g., with majority or supermajority provisions),
- agreeing the level of support from current shareholders and their affiliates (e.g., management and service arrangements, shared service arrangements, subordination of their equity creditor claims, etc.),
- agreeing the extent to which the lenders will be able to monitor the wind-down effectively (e.g., by an on-site, independent liquidation monitor approved by the lenders), and the collection and distribution of information on the wind-down amongst the lenders,
- agreeing on periodic distributions of available cash to the lenders (e.g., by the liquidation monitor),
- agreeing terms of indemnities to management who stay during the wind-down, as well as incentivization programs, to ensure management remain committed to the business and maximizing returns on the existing asset,
- addressing any sensitive commercial arrangements concerning the shareholders' re-entry into the market (the lenders may demand non-embarrassment provisions, requiring the shareholders to refrain from competing with the borrower during the wind-down and/or re-entering the market for a certain period of time following liquidation), and
- ensuring that adequate defensive mechanisms are built into the wind-down structure to fend off against predatory local creditors (e.g., overly

---

[136] In the authors' experience this can be critical to a wind-down's success, as otherwise management are not likely to want to stay with a "sinking ship."

aggressive tax authorities[137]). These can include foreign escrow account arrangements, to maintain a reserve of funds for indemnities and bona fide wind-down expenses, away from the borrower's balance sheet and not under its control, so that local predators do not see such funds as "low-hanging fruits").

These and other issues can be addressed in a well-drafted multi-lender wind-down agreement.[138] Many of the same issues which drive consensual restructurings can also drive consensual wind-downs, and INSOL II Principles and lender collaboration will be beneficial. At the same time, it is important to note that several of the other key legal issues described in earlier sections of this chapter will be relevant to such wind-downs. In particular, at any moment some exogenous event and/or other circumstances could arise whereby the wind-down is usurped by insolvency proceedings. Accordingly, it will be critical for external advisers to bear this in mind whilst structuring the wind-down.[139]

* * *

---

[137] In some emerging markets local tax and/or other authorities may exercise a strong hand in overseeing liquidations, imposing audits and making unjustified tax claims. When the courts do not provide on even playing field this case be problematic.

[138] An orderly wind-down may best be implemented in form of an overlay agreement—thus, it may be structurally similar to overlay restructuring agreements, as discussed above, except that the ultimate goal will not be to rescue the borrower's business but rather to wind it down in an orderly fashion.

[139] Clearly, if the borrower retains control over funds and/or an insolvency office holder (in a subsequent insolvency) claws funds back, this reduces the ability to use such funds for indemnities and/or payment of bona fide expenses. At the same time, some structures may be used to mitigate against such risk. One is the use of a special distribution in the nature of a *one-off* bona fide partial repayment to lenders of their debts (pro-rata), which *they* (not the borrower) then use to fund an escrow under joint control of a lender representative and a *shareholder* representative. The authors have used this approach in a number of orderly wind-downs.

# Part V

## Conclusion

# 12

# Closing Thoughts

**Abstract** As a recapitulation of the book as a whole, the chapter focuses on the Bank of Commerce narrative and engages in counter-factual musings for each of the five restructuring phases. The reader is encouraged to think back on our case studies and to consider the themes discussed and lessons learned—in particular, the need for strong skills in managing both people and process.

**Keywords** Bankruptcy · Basel III · Borrower · Consensual restructuring · Coordinating committee · Corporate debt · Debt · Debtor · COVID-19 · Credit monitoring · Distressed debt · Emerging market · Exchange rate · Frontier market · INSOL II · INSOL principles · Insolvency · Lender leadership · Non-performing loans · Pre-insolvency · Restructure · Restructuring · Restructuring plans · Standstill · Steering committee · Tier 1 Capital · Tier 2 Capital · Workout

To frame our closing thoughts, let's focus on our Bank of Commerce narrative and engage in some counter-factual musings for each of our five restructuring phases. Each should be treated as independent of the other four.

What would have happened if…

# Pre-Restructuring Phase

...the lenders had anticipated that New West's policy to dividend almost 100% of the Bank's net income (rather than building up pro-cyclical equity buffers) and to rely on short-duration, foreign currency funding (rather than employing a funding strategy that limited duration and currency mismatches) would leave it exposed to exchange rate crises and economic downturns?

Consider:

- The local regulatory minimum core Tier 1 capital was 7% (actually higher than the Basel III 6.0% requirement). Pre-crisis, Bank of Commerce's figure was around 7.5%. Since the New West acquisition, the Bank's average dividend payout ratio was in excess of 90%. Given the local economy's dependence on a volatile commodity, there is a strong argument favoring a much larger buffer. Additionally, the Bank's use of cheaper short-term foreign currency-denominated funding created perilous duration and currency mismatches.
- The lenders recognized this need and established:

  - Two solvency covenants: (i) minimum Tier-1 capital of 12%; and (ii) maximum dividend payout ratio of 15% and an undertaking that that on a quarterly basis the Bank will provide a forward-looking evaluation of capital adequacy, acknowledged by the shareholder who agrees to use reasonable efforts to maintain the capital adequacy;
  - A maximum open currency position[1] covenant of 25% of tangible net worth; and
  - A minimum net stable funding ratio[2] covenant of 125%.

---

[1] OCP or "Open foreign currency position" means an excess of assets (including off-balance sheet forward purchase contracts) over liabilities (including off-balance sheet forward sales contracts) (a "long position") held by a financial institution denominated a foreign currency, or an excess of liabilities (including off-balance sheet forward sales contracts) over assets (including off-balance sheet forward purchase contracts) (a "short position") held by a financial institution denominated a foreign currency. See http://www.cbsi.com.sb/financial-stability/prudential-supervision-policies/foreign-currency-open-positions/.

[2] The NSFR is defined as the amount of available stable funding relative to the amount of required stable funding. This ratio should be equal to at least 100% on an on-going basis. "Available stable funding" is defined as the portion of capital and liabilities expected to be reliable over the time horizon considered by the NSFR, which extends to one year. The amount of such stable funding required of a specific institution is a function of the liquidity characteristics and residual maturities of the various assets held by that institution as well as those of its off-balance sheet (OBS) exposures. See https://www.bis.org/publ/bcbs271.pdf.

- In retrospect, the size of the tsunami that hit the Bank might well have overwhelmed even these prudential measures. However, we suggest their presence would have limited the direct effect and had the further benefit of sensitizing both sides to the risks, hence encouraging early and cooperative joint responses.

## Decision-Making Phase

...Ursula had reacted positively to Kristi's approach well in advance of the situation turning critical and taken preventative measures, up to negotiating a balanced restructuring?

Consider:

- Kristi's analysis identified the potential copper price shock, the sovereign's external and domestic vulnerabilities to this event, and the transmission channels into the banking sector. Whilst the precise timing and impact could not be forecast with certainty, the "dark clouds and blustery winds presaged rain" with a high degree of likelihood.
- The response could have taken many different forms. Let's assume a combination of: (i) immediate hedging to cover the open currency position; (ii) a commitment of contingent capital (Tier 1 and Tier 2) to provide capital support up to some maximum; and (iii) discussions between New West/Bank of Commerce and the major lenders, perhaps facilitated by Kristi, to explain these steps and to enlist the support of the lenders during any future market turbulence.
- These measures should neutralize the institution-level FX effect. The impact on local borrowers with FX-denominated debt with no natural hedges will be adversely affected, and NPLs will mount. Profitability will decline, even to the extent to going into the red, with some capital reduction, but not enough to threaten regulatory solvency (especially given the contingent capital support). The forward communications with lenders served Ursula well as the community appreciated her proactive and constructive approach.

# Case Set-Up Phase

…when the crisis hit, JK had Ursula had reached out to Kristi and the other lead lenders to engage in a constructive dialogue, rather than merely adopt JK's confrontational posture, both before and during the initial creditor meeting?

Consider:

- The Bank was ill-prepared to absorb the blow of the copper market collapse. They can of course be criticized for having ignored Kristi's earlier warnings.
- However, the proactive and collegial approach of New West to work with the lenders to fashion a solution may well be effective in enlisting the cooperation of the lender group.
- The precise outcome of the process is secondary in importance to the fact that the positive attitude of the borrower and its shareholders created an environment where the parties were motivated to work together to achieve the best possible result.

# Structuring and Negotiation Phase

…Kristi, Ursula, and Martin had not played the constructive roles they did to keep the process on track?

Consider:

- Left to his own devices, JK would have most likely driven the Bank of Commerce into bankruptcy. In response to his "my way or the highway" approach at the meeting, at least one (possibly more), lenders to start with Edinburgh Partners, would surely have accelerated their debt. This would in turn have triggered a domino effect of cross-defaults, forcing the Bank to declare insolvency.
- Instead, in our original narrative, Martin had acted as a bridge between Ursula and Kristi. He helped Ursula climb down from the ledge which JK built. Kristi recognized this courageous step and moved to accommodate Ursula's constraints as much as possible.
- The successful outcome achieved thereafter in the original narrative would have been impossible without this cooperative trio.

# Implementation Phase

…Ursula had not kept the local management of the Bank of Commerce "on side" throughout the wind-down process?

Consider:

- The local management and supervisory board had a legal obligation to declare insolvency (and a compelling interest in avoiding personal liability for wrongful trading) under certain circumstances that were arguably present at times during the process (i.e., indicia of cash flow or balance sheet insolvency). Additionally, the maximization of recoveries and the final sale of the rump organization and license required the Bank of Commerce to retain the appearance of a going concern. Any one of these local individuals could have scuttled the process with a single phone call.
- Instead, they worked with dedication and great energy. Loyalty to Ursula, helped by a generous retention scheme, secured their commitments.

Each of our counter-factual musings demonstrates that the path a restructuring takes will depend largely on the *behavior* of the parties and their individual representatives and the extent to which they can *manage their own and others' human foibles*.

Careless credit monitoring and ignoring macroeconomic trends can lead to disaster or at best make a restructuring all the more challenging. A borrower's denial (or a lender's failure to speak and act decisively) during intervention can allow the borrower to career closer toward the cliff of insolvency. Aggressive posturing at the kick-off meeting can leave parties with no hope of a workout in sight. Lack of lender coordination toward the common goals can leave the ship without a rudder, drifting whilst the threat of insolvency looms (and usually then overtakes everything).

To capture the fundamental message of the book, we paraphrase James Carville's famous quip,[3] "It's the economy, stupid," to offer an alternative: "It's the people!".

There is nothing especially original about such a statement. From negotiating with our parents for more playtime as children, through angling for

---

[3] "The economy, stupid" was a phrase coined by James Carville in 1992. It is often quoted from a televised quip by Carville as "It's the economy, stupid." Carville was a strategist in Bill Clinton's successful 1992 presidential campaign against incumbent George H. W. Bush. His phrase was directed at the campaign's workers and intended as one of three messages on which they should focus. The others were "Change vs. more of the same" and "Don't forget health care.".

the career-transforming promotion as adults, we all can validate the importance of people management. In a professional setting (and in life generally), overcoming challenges or completing projects is far easier when all (or most) of the parties get along. Constructive relationships facilitate problem-solving. Respect serves to enhance resiliency to navigate crises.

As described above in the case of the Bank of Commerce, people's foibles (JK's steamroller arrogance, Colin's connivance, and the like) accentuated the transaction's challenges. At that same time, a combination of simple, positive personal characteristics (empathy, patience, courage, honesty, perseverance, industry, and the like) and effective people management, especially on the parts of Martin and Kristi, kept the process moving toward a successful end.

We can adapt Mr. Carville's quip once again to stress a second key message, "It's (also) the process." The answers to the "what, how, when, why, and by whom," questions underlying transaction execution form the process plan. These answers must be constantly reassessed and the plan adjusted to reflect changing circumstances and new information. Renewing stakeholder buy-in when there is change is essential. Process management is not just updating and distributing a Microsoft Project spreadsheet. Here is where people and process management merge.

Throughout the life of the deal, the lead financier or more broadly the steering committee (in either case, lender leadership as we have named it) must engage in a function that probably resembles that of a proactive "Agony Aunt."[4] Taking the Bank of Commerce case, we can imagine at each material step or change in the trajectory of the deal Kristi calling around to the other lenders to answer their questions about what was happening and why, as well as to allow them to vent about the Bank, JK, Ursula, etc. Kristi's aim was to *understand at every step where each lender was in their thinking.* This knowledge would allow her to anticipate problems and to frame appropriate solutions. Often emotions were at play as much as the numbers.

If asked, Kristi would joke: a command of behavioral psychology was as important for a successful workout as were well-developed corporate finance and deal management skills. How Kristi would go about structuring and managing the process often reflected this belief.

And what about the nuts and bolts of finance, credit monitoring, macroeconomics, loan documents, insolvency law and practice, business vs. balance sheet and the like? Where do these fit in?

To be sure, a thorough knowledge of these issues will critical. The manner in which they are addressed can make or break the successful restructuring.

---

[4] Someone commonly consulted for advice about problems.

Where inadequate care is given, at best this will delay the workout, at worst, derail it or leave a ticking time bomb (which can result in greater losses by all parties). The successful restructurer (banker or lawyer) must therefore understand and have thoroughly mastered these technical skills. They are indispensable.

In our narratives, we have endeavored to demonstrate how these skills should be applied in practice. Breaking the life of a restructuring down into five main phases, we hope we have provided the reader with a methodology for approaching restructurings. In Chapter 10 we have provided a more in-depth overview of some of the key macroeconomic and legal issues which arise in emerging markets. And to be sure, in the post-COVID-19 world it is critical to appreciate the impact of exogenous events, how these affect restructurings and how parties may (like it or not) need to act in situations of radical uncertainty.

But the authors postulate that in *getting the parties to sign up* to a workout, it will be the *people and process management skills* where lender leadership must focus its greatest attention. Understanding the individual predicament and motivations of each party (and its representative, including in particular their emotional and mental states) will be far more important than during earlier transactional phases. And communicating effectively in a manner most likely to elicit constructive responses from workout participants cannot be overstated. We have tried to emphasize these people management and communications skills in our "lessons learned" in the book.

To be sure, it is the marriage of these key technical, people management, and communications skills which make the successful restructurer.

Let's use a professional concert pianist as an analogy.

Our young pianist is booked to play Beethoven's Pathetique Sonata in London's Wigmore Hall next week. It is her first concert in such an esteemed venue.

She has worked years to master her technical skills through constant training: sight reading, scales, exercises, study of composition and theory, fingering and body technique, accumulation of repertoire, and the like.

The moment arrives. The hall becomes quiet. She walks out onto the stage to play.

At this moment, is she thinking about all those accumulated technical skills? What is on her mind, first and foremost?

It is the pure essence of the music and her artistic expression of it, how she *communicates* the language of music to the audience and becomes at one with them.

So, too, our successful restructurer in an emerging market borrower's distress must accumulate technical skills in finance, macroeconomics, and law, as relevant to emerging markets restructurings. She must have these skills and mastery, to the extent that they become second nature to her. And when it comes time to do the actual restructuring, she must then focus her efforts on *communicating with people and driving the process forward, guiding and inspiring.*

We close with a third version of James Carville's famous saying, which combines our first two, "It's the people and the process!".

# Annexes

## Annex 1: Law and Practice Summaries for Selected Emerging Markets

In researching restructuring and insolvency practice for this book, we prepared a detailed survey to a selected group of practicing banking and insolvency lawyers from a sizeable group of 46 emerging market countries.

Whilst far from comprehensive and scientific, we believe the survey represents both a *diverse group* of jurisdictions and *indicative snapshot* of law and practice as at the date of publication.

We have already accounted for the many detailed responses to the survey, in the main text of the book and footnotes thereto. In lieu of presenting detailed information on each country and its insolvency system in this Annex, we have distilled a handful of what we consider key issues, namely:

(i) general market familiarity with INSOL II Principles,
(ii) availability and prevalence of judicial and consensual restructurings,
(iii) observance of rule of law and other factors bearing on reliability of courts, and
(iv) availability of foreign law for cross-border transactions (e.g., for overlay agreements).

© The Editor(s) (if applicable) and The Author(s), under exclusive license to Springer Nature Switzerland AG 2021
R. Marney and T. Stubbs, *Corporate Debt Restructuring in Emerging Markets,*
https://doi.org/10.1007/978-3-030-81306-2

For speed and convenience, our choice of jurisdictions was based on the available network of offices in the multinational law firm in which one of the authors practices, *Dentons*. The authors are grateful to the Dentons lawyers who kindly participated in the survey and who are named as contributors below.

Naturally, we recognize that the survey reflects the views of a limited audience, based on their own individual experiences whilst practicing law in these countries. Hence, the answers are admittedly anecdotal in nature. Other lawyers may well have divergent experiences. A more comprehensive study of a larger sampling of lawyers could well present different results. Whilst we have tried to be fair in our assessments, we have also tried to be candid.

Moreover, this Annex 1 is not meant to represent a comprehensive description or analysis of the insolvency law and practice in these countries (which abound on the websites of international law firms and other consultants). Rather, it is meant to summarize some key issues salient to a decision on pursuing a consensual versus a judicial restructuring. Accordingly, it should be read together with the earlier discussion in the book on this topic (in particular, in Chapters 5 and 11).

No survey of global insolvency regimes would be complete without acknowledging the critical work done by governmental organizations and DFIs over many years, to improve these regimes. This includes in particular the World Bank, which publishes a comprehensive analysis of insolvency systems named 'Resolving Insolvency' (part of its 'Doing Business – Measuring Business Regulations' index—see https://www.doingbusiness. org/en/data/exploretopics). The Resolving Insolvency study measures recoveries by *secured* creditors in insolvency (i.e., fully secured by a mortgage [on an operating hotel property] and universal business charge [an enterprise charge]). The study thus by design excludes unsecured debt. Still, from a practical standpoint, it reflects the respective systems' *relative efficiencies and levels of development*.

Accordingly, the authors have supplemented the contributors' answers below with the respective World Bank Resolving Insolvency rank/score/recovery rate for each country at the time of this publication. (As a guide, the OECD high-income country region has a rank/score/recovery rate of 28/74.9/70.2, respectively.) The *lower* the first number (rank), the better (as it indicates a higher position in global rankings); the *higher* the next two numbers (score and recovery rate), the better.

The authors have further supplemented the contributors' answers below with the respective Transparency International 2020 corruption perception index (CPI) ranks. A lower CPI ranking number indicates less perceived corruption in a country (hence greater perceived success), whilst a higher ranking indicates more perceived corruption in a country (hence less perceived success). The authors acknowledge that the CPI is far from perfect. It has been the subject of often justifiable criticism (e.g., as unscientific, perceptually biased and re-enforcing stereotypes[1]). Still, the authors believe that as *one of multiple sources*, the CPI should not be completely disregarding when considering the issue of potential impact of corruption on rule of law in a given country.[2]

For purposes of discussion below, the INSOL II Principles are referred to merely as the "Principles."

| Region/Country | |
| --- | --- |
| *Central and Eastern Europe, Central Asia and Caucuses Region* | |
| Azerbaijan | The Principles are not widely known. The regulator has generally not actively endeavored to promote them publicly. That said, there may be a strong preference for workouts on the part of both local and international lenders, given the relatively undeveloped nature of the Azerbaijani insolvency system, unpredictable court practice, rule of law, and transparency |
| | Azerbaijan's main insolvency law (Law of the Republic of Azerbaijan *"On Insolvency and Bankruptcy"* No. 326-IQ) which applies to all corporates, except banks and public legal entities, and individual entrepreneurs was adopted in the late 1990s. Whilst it has undergone several revisions, it still requires considerable overhaul. The law includes judicial restructuring provisions. In practice, these are not widely used. Rather, most insolvencies end in liquidation. The insolvency office holder profession remains underdeveloped |

(continued)

---

[1] See, e.g., https://www.cmi.no/publications/file/2120-is-it-wrong-to-rank.pdf.

[2] Whilst the authors observed some general correlation between the views of the lawyers surveyed with the CPI ranks, there were a number of cases where their views diverged considerably from the CPI ranks. This may be explained by the fact that the CPI index is intended to measure *public sector corruption more broadly* (including grand corruption, petty corruption, public sector, bribery, embezzlement, patronage, nepotism, conflict of interest, and procurement), which may not necessarily carry over into the judiciary as impacting on the manner in which judges make decisions (including in particular in the insolvency sphere).

(continued)

| Region/Country | |
| --- | --- |

|  | (Azerbaijan has a separate insolvency regime for banks, which is set out in the Law of the Republic of Azerbaijan "*On Banks*" No. 590-IIQ, dated 16 January 2004. It was amended several times especially after plummeting oil prices in 2014 and the financial crisis of 2015 to introduce a voluntary debt restructuring regime under judicial supervision.) The restructuring regime does not yet appear to work in practice |
|  | Workouts are thus preferred, to overcome the above issues. There have been several successful sizeable workouts in Azerbaijan (via overlays). English law is often used for cross-border financial transactions |
|  | World Bank Resolving Insolvency rank/score/recovery rate: 47/63.5/39.7 |
|  | CPI 2020 Rank: 129 |
|  | Contributor(s): Ulvia Zeynalova-Bockin, Partner, Dentons Baku |
| Czech Republic | The Principles are known in the professional community but not customarily used in practice. Several attempts were made to implement a set of "Prague Rules" (based on London principles), but those efforts stalled. Whilst there are some attempts to promote the principles, local lenders tend to be individualistic and opportunistic. The regulator has not actively promoted the Principles |
|  | Czech Republic's insolvency law (Czech Insolvency Act) has US Chapter 11 type judicial restructurings (including pre-packs). But the vast majority of distressed borrowers go into insolvent liquidation, often due to parties' waiting too long to seek rescue. A long observation period also hinders the process. The country is now in the process of implementing the 2019 EU Directive. There is a relatively reliable rule of law. The insolvency office holder profession has been criticized by some for being overly formalistic and not business oriented. But there has been some positive development in this area, especially after introduction of specialized professionals to handle more complex insolvencies |
|  | Some major workouts have been achieved (largely driven by the large Czech banks, major international banks or their Czech subsidiaries). But the lack of alliance between lenders frequently prevents successful conclusions. Accordingly, a distress situation would likely be addressed via a judicial insolvency. English law is regularly used in cross-border financial transactions |
|  | World Bank Resolving Insolvency rank/score/recovery rate: 16/80.1/67.5 |
|  | CPI 2020 Rank: 49 |
|  | Contributor(s): Jiří Tomola, Partner and Head of Restructuring and Insolvency, Dentons Prague |

(continued)

(continued)

| Region/Country | |
|---|---|
| Georgia | The Principles are not widely known in Georgia. Nor has the regulator actively endeavored to promote them |
| | Georgia's governmental and judicial organs have witnessed significant improvements in general observance of the rule of law over the last two decades. But insolvency law and practice remain underdeveloped. The insolvency law currently in force, often criticized as being obsolete, is 13 years old and is due to be replaced by a totally new statute—the Law of Georgia on Rehabilitation and Collective Satisfaction of Creditors starting from 1 April 2021, which is more voluminous and detailed (but as of yet untested). Moreover, the bench lacks experience in applying insolvency concepts, and the insolvency office holder profession requires strengthening. The law does include judicial restructurings, but due to lack of experience in the courts, whenever possible lenders aim to achieve consensual restructurings |
| | Based on the above, a workout would be highly preferred. There have been a number of successful workouts in Georgia (using overlays). English law is regularly used in cross-border financial transactions |
| | World Bank Resolving Insolvency rank/score/recovery rate: 64/56.2/40.5 |
| | CPI 2020 Rank: 45 |
| | Contributor(s): Avto Svanidze, Partner, Dentons Tbilisi |
| Hungary | The Principles are generally understood amongst insolvency practitioners and lenders, though international lenders seem more ready to apply them. The National Bank of Hungary has promoted workouts by issuance of non-binding recommendation to Hungarian banks (No. 6/2017 (V/ 30)). Although the Principles are not commonly referred to by name, they mirror a shared approach amongst many lenders in the country |
| | Hungary's insolvency law (dating from 1991, Act XLIX of 1991 on Restructuring and Liquidation Proceedings) has seen numerous amendments. The market's view is it should be updated to be more in step with best international practice. The law includes judicial restructurings, but these are not widely used. Unpredictability of courts, non-commerciality of the bench, and lack of unified and business-minded approach of many insolvency office holders favor a consensual approach |
| | A number of workouts have been achieved in Hungary (via overlays). Both German and English law are regularly used in cross-border financial transactions |
| | World Bank Resolving Insolvency rank/score/recovery rate: 66/55.0/44.2 |
| | CPI 2020 Rank: 69 |
| | Contributor(s): Dr. Gabriella Pataki, Senior Associate, Dentons Budapest |

(continued)

(continued)

| Region/Country | |
| --- | --- |
| Kazakhstan | The Principles are not well known in Kazakhstan. There is to date limited workout experience in the country. The regulator has not actively promoted the Principles |
| | Kazakhstan's insolvency law provisions are not included in a single insolvency law but rather in various isolated legislative acts (Civil Code, Laws on Bankruptcy, Banks and Banking Activities, Insurance Activities, Grain Law, etc.). Insolvency legislation thus needs a major overhaul. It includes judicial restructurings, but these are not widely used. Most distressed borrowers go into insolvent liquidation. That said, several banks have been successfully liquidated with practically full repayment of creditor claims. Accordingly, experience with judicial restructurings is limited. Rule of law and lack of transparency unfortunately remain issues in Kazakhstan (particularly in regional courts). The insolvency office holder profession requires strengthening |
| | Workouts are not yet widely used in Kazakhstan. Nonetheless, due to the above factors, a consensual approach (if achievable) should result in better and more predictable recoveries. English law is widely accepted for cross-border financial transactions |
| | World Bank Resolving Insolvency rank/score/recovery rate: 42/66.7/39.8 |
| | CPI 2020 Rank: 94 |
| | Contributor(s): Abai Shaikenov, Partner, Dentons Almaty; Victoria Simonova, Partner, Dentons Almaty |
| Poland | The Principles are generally understood amongst practitioners and lenders, though not always known by their formal name. The regulator has not actively promoted the Principles. However, the Polish Bank Association has promoted best practices for workouts (2019) |
| | Polish insolvency law is generally viewed as viable, though in certain respects poorly drafted. The law leaves some legal uncertainty, meaning that gaps must be bridged by judicial interpretation. The law is gradually being amended to remove those gaps and to adapt to market standards and needs. Polish insolvency law includes judicial restructurings. Still, certain factors drive a strong lender preference for workouts. These include substantial court backlog/delays, perceived limited commerciality of the bench and/or of insolvency office holders, undeveloped provisions for group restructurings, and lender perception of unfair bias favoring borrowers. That said, judicial restructurings are used. In some cases, they may present advantages (e.g., no imputed income on waived claims for tax purposes). No significant perennial issues with rule of law or transparency arise. The insolvency office holder profession is also generally viewed as adequate |

(continued)

(continued)

| Region/Country | |
|---|---|
| | Given the above, workouts are generally preferred (unless a cramdown is needed). They are also common in practice (via overlays and/or coordinated bilateral amendments). Polish law is used in domestic restructuring transactions. English law is usually used in cross-border consensual restructurings |
| | World Bank Resolving Insolvency rank/score/recovery rate: 25/76.5/60.9 |
| | CPI 2020 Rank: 45 |
| | Contributor(s): Tomasz Trocki, Partner, Dentons Warsaw; Stanislaw Soltysik, Counsel, Dentons Warsaw |
| Romania | The Principles are known and accepted by professionals and international and local lenders (though not always by name and are less known by local borrowers). Local lenders have a slightly less favorable attitude toward consensual workouts (given negative regulatory impact), whilst international lenders are more sanguine. The regulator has not actively promoted the Principles |
| | The Insolvency Law 85/2014 includes judicial restructurings, but certain aspects (e.g., no pre-pack, long observation period) make these impractical. The bench can also be overly formalistic, displaying a paternal attitude favoring borrowers. Borrower attitudes against financial transparency are also often unhelpful. Rule of law has become much less of a concern in Romania over the last decade. The insolvency office holder profession is still developing, though improving |
| | Due to the lack of a workable judicial restructuring regime, workouts carry a premium (where achievable). A number of large restructurings have taken place (via overlays or, where there was only one syndicated facility, by its amendment and restatement). English law is widely used in cross-border finance documents in Romania |
| | World Bank Resolving Insolvency rank/score/recovery rate: 56/59.1/34.4 |
| | CPI 2020 Rank: 69 |
| | Contributor(s): Simon Dayes, Partner, Dentons Bucharest; Tiberiu Csaki, Partner, Dentons Bucharest; Simona Marin, Partner, Dentons Bucharest |

(continued)

(continued)

| Region/Country | |
|---|---|
| Russia | The Principles are not widely known in Russia. Some professionals, as well as international banks and their subsidiaries, are aware of the Principles. Local lenders (including state banks) tend to be less familiar and typically pursue individual agendas. The regulator has not actively promoted the Principles |
| | Russia's insolvency law (the Law on Insolvency [Bankruptcy] of 2002) has undergone a number of reforms. It includes judicial restructurings, but these are not widely used (and are complicated by a lengthy observation period, no cramdown, no pre-pack). The lion's share of insolvencies goes into liquidation. The rule of law still struggles in Russia, especially where adverse parties are state-owned, a case attracts interest of the state, or a party precipitates state intervention. The insolvency office holder profession is self-regulated though not yet independent |
| | Workouts thus carry a premium, to enhance predictability and recoveries. A sizeable number of these have been successfully completed (via overlay or, when a single syndicate is involved, via amendment and restatement of the facility). English law is frequently used in cross-border finance documents |
| | World Bank Resolving Insolvency rank/score/recovery rate: 57/59.1/43.0 |
| | CPI 2020 Rank: 129 |
| | Contributor(s): Timothy Stubbs, Partner and Head of Banking Russia, Dentons Moscow |
| Slovak Republic | The Principles are not used as an official guide in distress situations, though professionals and lenders (particularly international lenders and/or their Slovak subsidiaries) follow them in practice. The regulator has not actively promoted the Principles |
| | Slovakia's insolvency law (Act No. 7/2005 Coll. on Bankruptcy and Restructuring) and its judicial restructuring procedures remain relatively under-utilized. Insolvent liquidations are still the trend (often because it is too late to restructure and/or due to lack of trust in the judicial restructuring process). The insolvency office holder profession has also been viewed by some as in need of a higher level of professionalism |
| | Due to the above issues, there is a preference for a workout (where achievable). English law is commonly used for cross-border financial transactions in Slovakia |
| | World Bank Resolving Insolvency rank/score/recovery rate: 46/65.5/46.1 |
| | CPI 2020 Rank: 60 |
| | Contributor(s): Stanislava Valientová, Partner, Dentons Bratislava; Soňa Kurillová, Associate, Dentons Bratislava |

(continued)

(continued)

| Region/Country | |
|---|---|
| Turkey | The Principles are not well known by name in practice in Turkey. That said, many international banks follow the concepts embedded in the Principles. Local banks have historically been less amenable to them. The regulator has introduced framework restructuring legislation as guidelines for local banks to restructure certain types of debt |
| | Turkey's insolvency law (the Code of Execution and Bankruptcy numbered 2004) was recently amended to include a restructuring procedure (*konkordato*) similar to the 2019 EU Directive. However, its courts are perceived as not yet sufficiently experienced and somewhat unpredictable. Moreover, the law includes a 1-year initial observation period (which may be extended to 2 years), which impedes restructurings. The local insolvency office holder profession is still underdeveloped. That said, some practitioners note improvement in rule of law (despite legacy pessimism) |
| | To overcome the above, a workout is highly desirable in Turkey. And indeed in practice, a number of large workouts have been successfully completed. English law is regularly used for cross-border finance documents |
| | World Bank Resolving Insolvency rank/score/recovery rate: 120/38.5/10.5 |
| | CPI 2020 Rank: 86 |
| | Contributor(s): Semih Sander, Partner, Dentons Istanbul; Tamsyn Mileham, Partner, Dentons Istanbul |

(continued)

(continued)

| Region/Country | |
|---|---|
| Ukraine | The Principles are not widely known but attract attention and observation by name in the larger workouts, particularly where international advisers (investment banks, major law, and accountancy firms) are involved. The Principles are more readily accepted by international banks and less so by local banks. The regulator has not actively endeavored to promote the Principles |
| | Ukraine continues to suffer a poor reputation for general observance of the rule of law and for a non-independent, non-transparent, unpredictable judiciary. The country recently (in 2018) adopted a new Insolvency Code which is seen as a major improvement on the prior law. The law itself is not seen as the main impediment to judicial restructurings—rather, it is the judiciary. The insolvency office holder profession requires strengthening |
| | It is thus highly preferable to pursue consensual restructurings (where achievable). There have been a relative handful of successful ones (by a single overlay, supplemented by implementing bilateral amendments for local-law compliance). English law is widely used for cross-border finance documents |
| | World Bank Resolving Insolvency rank/score/recovery rate: 146/31.4/9.0 |
| | CPI 2020 Rank: 117 |
| | Contributor(s): Natalia Selyakova, Partner, Dentons Kyiv |
| Uzbekistan | The Principles are not widely known in Uzbekistan. The regulator has not actively endeavored to promote them |
| | Uzbekistan's insolvency law was updated in 2003 (the Law on Bankruptcy No. 474–11) and has a separate chapter devoted to workouts [*dosudebnaya sanatsia*]). The law also includes judicial restructurings, though these are not widely used. Rule of law issues tends to be less prevalent when the parties are purely private (not state-owned). The insolvency office holder profession remains perceived as underdeveloped and lacking independence |
| | Workouts are not yet widely used in Uzbekistan. But as the insolvency law expressly sanctions them, they will likely be welcomed by local borrowers and lenders. English law is generally accepted for cross-border finance documents |
| | World Bank Resolving Insolvency rank/score/recovery rate: 100/43.5/34.4 |
| | CPI 2020 Rank: 146 |
| | Contributor(s): Shukhrat Yunusov, Partner, Dentons Tashkent |

(continued)

(continued)

| Region/Country |
| --- |

*Latin America and Caribbean Region*

| | |
| --- | --- |
| Argentina | The Principles are not often referred to by name but nonetheless have driven legislative promotion of workouts. In 2002 Argentina reformed its insolvency system to promote workouts (*Acuerdo Preventivo Extrajudicial* or "APE"). Workouts then became increasingly common, especially with larger corporate borrowers who suffered from the 2001 financial crisis and resultant peso devaluation. The Principles are now more frequently used as a roadmap in APE negotiations. That said, no Argentine public authorities have actively promoted the Principles |
| | Argentina's insolvency law N°24,522 (as amended) includes modern judicial restructuring provisions. Likely due to its recurrent historical macroeconomic difficulties (eliciting reforms), Argentina may be considered one of the more progressive emerging markets in its law on the books (which has US Chapter 11 type provisions). There is a relatively high rule of law for the region and an experienced insolvency office holder network. That said, there are cases of influence in politically sensitive cases (e.g., to keep large employers functioning or intervene in the insolvency of companies in sectors considered strategic). Workouts are becoming more common in Argentina, and are far preferred to judicial restructurings for being more flexible, less intrusive, and speedier. New York law is widely accepted for cross-border financial documents |
| | World Bank Resolving Insolvency rank/score/recovery rate: 111/40.0/19.2 |
| | CPI 2020 Rank: 78 |
| | Contributor(s): Roberto P. Bauzá, Partner, Dentons Buenos Aires; Maximo Capón, Associate, Dentons Buenos Aires |

(continued)

(continued)

| Region/Country |
| --- |

| Bolivia | The Principles are not well known in Bolivia, and Bolivian authorities have neither promoted nor publicized their implementation thus far |
| --- | --- |
| | Bolivia's insolvency laws are contained in its Commercial Code and in sectoral laws related to the financial sector. Insolvencies are handled by ordinary civil judges, who many observers perceive are insufficiently qualified to handle complex insolvencies. Judges also lack the resources to hire qualified staff versed in insolvency concepts. Entrepreneurs are perceived negatively in the business community when they file for insolvencies. Consequently, in recent decades bankruptcies in Bolivia are extremely rare. Often, the cases filed are dismissed rather than administered (as they can take years to be resolved). In an attempt to bypass these hurdles, the Bolivian government enacted law no. 1055 in 2018, allowing employees to safeguard their workplace in insolvent companies by converting them into "social companies." But so far no company has been successfully converted. Based on the complexities of both insolvency and conversion, businesses in Bolivia prefer to liquidate rather than undergo formal insolvency. Moreover, some commentators flag unreliability of the courts and inconsistent application of rule of law |
| | The strong preference for a restructuring in Bolivia is likely to be on a consensual basis. New York law is sometimes used for cross-border financial transactions, but enforcement in Bolivia of such choice of law can be problematic (Art. 804 of the Bolivian Commercial Code requires contracts performed in Bolivia to be governed by Bolivian law, and the point remains unsettled under local jurisprudence) |
| | World Bank Resolving Insolvency rank/score/recover rate: 103/42.3/40.8 |
| | CPI 2020 Rank: 124 |
| | Contributor(s): Alejandra Guevara, Senior Associate, Guevara & Gutierrez S.C., Bolivia |

(continued)

(continued)

| Region/Country | |
| --- | --- |
| Brazil | The Principles are not well known in Brazil, apart from the academic community and professionals in global consultancy firms. The regulator has not actively promoted the Principles. International lenders display positive attitudes toward workouts, whilst local lenders tend to be more litigious. Workouts are rare in Brazil, and hence judicial restructurings are more the norm |

Brazil's insolvency law (Federal Law No. 11.101/2005 as amended by Federal Law No. 14.112/2020) includes developed judicial restructuring provisions. They are widely used. Brazil has a relatively high level of rule of law and transparency. At the same time, the bench experiences frequent shortages, and its docket is often overloaded (hence causing large delays). Another challenge is the high level of appellate practice (often used tactically, to delay implementation of court decisions). There is a large range of regional differences in the courts due to the country's size. Larger cities (e.g., Sao Paulo, Rio de Janeiro) display a quicker, more effective judiciary. They also have specialized branches for insolvencies, creating more predicable outcomes. Generally, there is a high level of respect for the insolvency office holder profession

Accordingly, a distress situation is likely to be resolved by judicial (rather than consensual) restructuring, unless the bulk of lenders are international and decide (with the borrower) that a workout is appropriate. This would indeed be highly desirable given the above-described systemic issues. A quicker solution (with higher returns) would probably be achievable. Due to its location in the Americas, New York law is widely accepted for cross-border financial transactions. The provision of an arbitration clause is the norm in cross-border transactions as the Brazilian judicial system is not reliable on the application of foreign law. The possibility of cross-border insolvencies (both for proceedings started under Brazilian jurisdiction reaching international lenders and vice versa) was incorporated into law only very recently. Some struggles on the implementation of cross-border insolvencies are to be expected

World Bank Resolving Insolvency rank/score/recovery rate: 77/50.4/18.2

CPI 2020 Rank: 94

Contributor(s): Carolina Mansur de Grandis, Partner, Dentons Sao Paulo

(continued)

(continued)

| Region/Country | |
|---|---|
| Cayman Islands | Cayman Islands' financial community is generally familiar with the Principles (if not always by name). That said, local lenders tend to be secured creditors, thus not reliant on restructurings for recovery. Workouts are rarer than elsewhere for this reason. The regulator has not actively promoted the Principles |
| | Cayman Islands' insolvency law (the Companies Act and Winding Up Rules made under the Act) is reliable and predictable (though probably in need of some updating). There is a high level of rule of law. The bench is experienced and independent (with a separate division for financial services matters, including insolvencies). The highest court of appeals is the Judicial Committee of the Privy Council in London, which draws its judges from the same pool as the UK Supreme Court. Litigants thus have the reassurance of final appeal in London. The islands' insolvency office holder community is highly experienced and independent. Creditor foreclosure on collateral (followed by liquidation) tends to be most prevalent, although applications for winding up on a just and equitable basis are also common |
| | The island's status as a self-governing British Overseas Territory makes English law prevalent in cross-border finance documents |
| | World Bank Resolving Insolvency rank/score/recovery rate: no data published |
| | CPI 2020 Rank: no data published |
| | Contributor(s): Michael Wingrave, Partner, Dentons Cayman Islands |
| Chile | The Principles are not well known in Chile. Workouts are relatively rare at least amongst local lenders, though lenders do regularly engage in bilateral discussions with borrowers to avert or address distress as it arises. The regulator has not actively promoted the Principles |
| | Chile's insolvency law (Insolvency and Re-Entrepreneurship Law) was relatively recently overhauled, including to promote judicial restructurings. These are now commonly used. Chile has its own branch of specialized insolvency courts. The country enjoys a comparatively high degree of rule of law in the region. Chile's insolvency office holder profession is generally seen as satisfactory |
| | Thus, a judicial restructuring would be a likely outcome of distress unless a workout were achievable (e.g., by a group of international lenders). Given its location in the Americas, New York law is regularly used in cross-border finance transactions |
| | World Bank Resolving Insolvency rank/score/recovery rate: 53/60.1/41.9 |
| | CPI 2020 Rank: 25 |
| | Contributor(s): Jose Manuel Larrain, Partner, Dentons Santiago |

(continued)

(continued)

| Region/Country | |
| --- | --- |
| Colombia | The Principles are not well known in Colombia, nor has the regulator actively promoted them<br>However, Colombia's insolvency laws are well written in line with international standards (Law 1116/2006). Its insolvency system is showcased as one of the best in the region. The law provides for judicial restructurings, which (unlike many other emerging markets jurisdictions) are commonly used. That said, proceedings can be lengthy, and the court system experiences delays. Colombia has made improvements with the rule of law in the courts, and its insolvency office holders are generally well-regarded<br>Consensual restructurings are relatively rare in Colombia, with more reliance on judicial restructurings. Accordingly, it could be expected that a distress situation would most likely be resolved in this manner. Given its location in the Americas, New York law is regularly used in cross-border finance transactions<br>World Bank Resolving Insolvency rank/score/recovery rate: 32/71.4/68.7<br>CPI 2020 Rank: 92<br>Contributor(s): Bernardo Cardenas, Managing Partner, Dentons Bogota |

(continued)

(continued)

| Region/Country | |
|---|---|
| Costa Rica | The Principles are not well known in Costa Rica, nor has the regulator actively promoted them. Most distress situations are resolved through formal insolvency proceedings. Where private arrangements are made, these often arise after commencement of proceedings. Accordingly, a workout culture has not yet solidified |
| | Costa Rica has no standalone insolvency law. Rather, its insolvency regime is included in various legislative acts, including the Commercial Code, the Civil Code, and the Civil Procedure Code. There are no formal judicial restructuring provisions as such (but a judicial restructuring may be approved by the court). There can be long delays, including a long initial observation period. The law is in need of substantial reform. The country's legislature is currently considering a reform. Its judicial system experiences no significant perennial issues with rule of law. At the same time, the insolvency office holder profession is not seen as uniformly competent or efficient, and office holders have been known to create delays |
| | Based on the above, whilst a distress situation would in the ordinary course likely be resolved judicially, nonetheless, where a workout is achievable, this would be beneficial (e.g., in avoiding long delays and maximizing recoveries). Due to its location in the Americas, New York law is often seen in cross-order financial transactions |
| | World Bank Resolving Insolvency rank/score/recovery rate: 137/34.6/29.5 |
| | CPI 2020 Rank: 42 |
| | Contributor(s): Roy de Jesus Herrera, Partner, Dentons San Jose |

(continued)

(continued)

| Region/Country | |
|---|---|
| Ecuador | The Principles are not well known in Ecuador, and the authorities have neither promoted nor publicized their implementation |
| | Ecuador's insolvency laws are contained in various legal acts (Civil Code, Code of Commerce, and Codifications of the Superintendent of Banks, and others). Nevertheless, Ecuador has adopted several types of preventive insolvency proceedings to permit debtors to obtain more favorable conditions and terms for payment to creditors and restructuring of their businesses. The debtor must generally demonstrate that it has assets or income to cover its obligations |
| | In 2006 the government introduced preventive insolvency proceedings, addressed only to companies (*Ley de Concurso Preventivo*). Moreover, in 2015 a specific process for individuals and corporations was incorporated in the COGEP (General Organic Code of Proceedings—COGEP). In 2020, provisions were created focused on the restructuring of new companies or businesses five years old or less (Organic Law of Entrepreneurship and Innovation). Finally, in connection with the global COVID-19 pandemic, the Organic Law of Humanitarian Support was enacted for negotiation of pre-insolvency agreements to assist debtors to fulfil their obligations to creditors. Practitioners hope for some harmonization of these different acts, to eliminate confusion and contradictions |
| | Given the above, it is likely that a workout would provide a rational solution for a distress situation in Ecuador. New York law is often used for cross-border financial transactions |
| | World Bank Resolving Insolvency rank/score/recover rate: 160/25.5/18.3 |
| | CPI 2020 Rank: 92 |
| | Contributor(s): Rocío Córdova, Partner, Dentons Ecuador |

(continued)

(continued)

| Region/Country | |
|---|---|
| El Salvador | The Principles are not well known, nor has the regulator actively endeavored to promote them. There is a difference in attitudes toward distress as between international and local lenders. Local lenders' individualistic behavior often impedes workouts |
| | El Salvador's insolvency provisions are not contained in a single law but rather found in various legislative acts (Code of Commerce, Law of Commercial Procedure, and Code of Civil Procedure). The law unfortunately does not include special provisions on judicial restructuring per se but includes a so-called "deferral of payment" procedure (which does not provide protection of an automatic stay). The law requires a major overhaul. The country has witnessed a strong public fight to tackle rule of law issues, but how successful these will be remains to be seen. The insolvency officer holder profession remains relatively undeveloped |
| | Given the above, it is preferable to aim for a workout where achievable. Due to its location in the Americas, New York law is sometimes used in cross-border finance transactions |
| | World Bank Resolving Insolvency rank/score/recovery rate: 92/45.6/32.4 |
| | CPI 2020 Rank: 104 |
| | Contributor(s): Benjamin Rodriguez, Managing Partner, Dentons San Salvador |

(continued)

(continued)

| Region/Country | |
|---|---|
| Honduras | The Principles are not well-known in Honduras, nor has the local regulator actively endeavored to promote or implement them |
| | Honduras's insolvency law does not include express judicial restructuring provisions. Moreover, insolvency proceedings are not very common in Honduras generally. Thus, a workout would be a valuable tool (when compared to an insolvency proceeding, which would likely be unpredictable and high-risk for lenders). The insolvency law is extremely outdated (the Honduran Commercial Code of 1950) and is in need of an overhaul to bring it in line with international insolvency practice. The Honduran courts are viewed as slow and underfunded. International observers do not consider the judicial system to have a high level of observance of the rule of law. Moreover, the insolvency office holder profession remains undeveloped (due primarily to the infrequency of insolvency cases) |
| | Given the above, a workout would certainly present the best possible solution for lenders and would likely also be welcomed by local lenders |
| | The Honduran Promotion and Protection of Investments Law permits the application of foreign law for cross-border transactions. Due to the country's location in the Americas, New York law is seen in cross-border financial transactions |
| | World Bank Resolving Insolvency rank/score/recovery rate: 143/32.6/19.9 |
| | CPI 2020 Rank: 157 |
| | Contributor(s): Nadia Arriaga, Senior Associate, Dentons Tegucigalpa |
| Mexico | The Principles are well known in Mexico by insolvency experts and sometimes used as a guide, particularly when international lenders are involved. However, the regulator has not actively promoted them |
| | Mexico's insolvency law (Commercial Bankruptcy Law) is relatively well-developed and includes judicial restructurings (including pre-packs, which are highly preferred, to avoid the delays and other negative aspects of ordinary judicial restructurings). The insolvency office holder profession is generally considered to be knowledgeable (if not uniformly efficient) |
| | Workouts are relatively common in Mexico (with use of overlays). At the same time, a judicial restructuring in Mexico probably would not be a bad outcome given its well-developed law. In cross-border financial transactions, both New York and Mexican law are common (with the choice depending on party composition and other factors) |

(continued)

(continued)

| Region/Country | |
| --- | --- |
| | World Bank Resolving Insolvency rank/score/recovery rate: 33/70.3/63.9 |
| | CPI 2020 Rank: 124 |
| | Contributor(s): Amanda Valdez, Partner, Dentons Mexico City |
| Nicaragua | The Principles are not well known in Nicaragua, nor has the regulator actively promoted them |
| | Nicaragua's insolvency law includes judicial restructuring procedures, but these are not commonly used (the Civil Code and the Commercial Code). The law is in need of an overhaul. A strong perception unfortunately persists of rule of law issues in the Nicaraguan courts. The courts are also seen as inefficient. The insolvency office holder profession is not yet viewed as having established strong independence and efficiency |
| | Based on the above, it is preferable to aim for a workout in a distress situation. A number of successful workouts have been achieved (via overlays, sometimes with parallel bilateral amendments, and in other cases merely via a series of bilateral amendments). But a judicial restructuring would also not be a bad second choice. Due to its location in the Americas, New York law is often used in cross-order financial transactions |
| | World Bank Resolving Insolvency rank/score/recovery rate: 33/70.3/63.9 |
| | CPI 2020 Rank: 159 |
| | Contributor(s): Edgard Torres, Managing Partner, Dentons Managua |

(continued)

(continued)

| Region/Country | |
|---|---|
| Panama | The Principles, as such, are not widely known in Panama, nor has the regulator actively promoted them. This said, it could be stated that in practice, the Principles are generally reflected in the reorganization (restructuring) rules of Panama's insolvency law |
| | Panama's insolvency law (Law 12 of May 19, 2016 effective as of January 2, 2017) includes judicial restructuring proceedings, though these were introduced only relatively recently. That said, the proceedings are not yet commonly used (although as a result of the Covid-19 pandemic, certain local companies have opted to seek the protection granted by the restructuring process). The insolvency courts are heavily underfunded, lack a specialized insolvency bench, and are prone to backlogs. Insolvency cases are heard by ordinary civil courts. Panama still struggles with a perennial negative perception of rule of law, lack of transparency, and unpredictability of court practice. That said, the insolvency office holder community is generally viewed favorably |
| | Due to the above, a workout is preferable in Panama. Given its location in the Americas, New York law is generally accepted in Panama for cross-border finance documentation |
| | World Bank Resolving Insolvency rank/score/recovery rate: 113/39.5/27.0 |
| | CPI 2020 Rank: 111 |
| | Contributor(s): Fernando Aued, Partner, Dentons Panama City |
| Peru | The Principles are not well known in Peru, nor has the regulator actively endeavored to promote them. Insolvency proceedings are far more common in Peru than workouts |
| | Peru's insolvency law (the 2002 Bankruptcy Law No. 27809) is frequently used. Local borrowers and lenders unfortunately tend to wait until it is too late to work things out privately. The law provides for two separate types of non-judicial restructuring proceedings: ordinary bankruptcy and a so-called preventative bankruptcy. The country's courts are not perceived as having significant persistent issues with rule of law, and the insolvency office holders are generally positively viewed |
| | Due to the strong culture of reliance on insolvency proceedings in Peru, a distress situation would likely be resolved through formal proceedings, rather than a workout. Given its location in the Americas, New York law is often seen in cross-border financial transactions |
| | World Bank Resolving Insolvency rank/score/recovery rate: 90/46.6/31.3 |
| | CPI 2020 Rank: 94 |
| | Contributor(s): Manuel Barrios, Managing Partner, Dentons Lima |

(continued)

(continued)

| Region/Country | |
|---|---|
| Trinidad and Tobago | The Principles are not widely known, nor has the regulator actively promoted them. Trinidad and Tobago's insolvency law was recently updated (Bankruptcy and Insolvency Act 2007 [the BIA]). Prior to the BIA, insolvency was governed by the provisions of the Companies Act, Chapter 81:01, which only made provision for traditional receiverships and liquidations. The introduction of the BIA now allows debtors to use it for recovery/rehabilitation purposes. The bench is experienced and independent. The highest court of appeals is the Judicial Committee of the Privy Council in London, which draws its judges from the same pool as the UK Supreme Court. Litigants thus have the reassurance of final appeal in London. The insolvency office holder profession is generally seen as effective |
| | Given the above, a distress situation can be resolved through the courts. However, under the provisions of the BIA, a company facing insolvency is granted a moratorium from enforcement, so that it can make proposals to the creditors for a workout. English law is often seen in cross-border financial transactions |
| | World Bank Resolving Insolvency rank/score/recovery rate: 83/48.4/26.1 |
| | CPI 2020 Rank: 86 |
| | Contributor(s): Shalini R. Campbell, Partner, Dentons Trinidad and Tobago |
| Uruguay | The Principles are not widely used in Uruguay. The local regulator has not actively endeavored to promote them. Nonetheless, significant workouts do happen in practice, particularly when large international lenders are present |
| | Uruguay's insolvency law (18.387) includes judicial restructurings, though these are under-utilized. Uruguay has witnessed significant improvement in the last decade in the rule of law and suffers no major transparency issues. Its insolvency office holder profession is generally independent and professional (if not uniformly effective) |
| | Given difficulties in judicial restructurings, if achievable workouts are desirable. Uruguay's law saw a major liberalization in choice of law, with the long-awaited Private International Law Act of November 2020. As from 2021, the parties to cross-border transactions are free to choose the law governing their contract (including financial transactions). Given Uruguay's location in the Americas, New York law is probably a good choice for cross-border finance documents |
| | World Bank Resolving Insolvency rank/score/recovery rate: 70/53.6/44.4 |
| | CPI 2020 Rank: 21 |
| | Contributor(s): Bruno Steneri, Senior Associate, Dentons Montevideo |

(continued)

(continued)

| Region/Country | |
| --- | --- |
| Venezuela | The Principles are not well known in Venezuela. The regulator has not actively promoted them. Consensual multi-creditor restructurings unfortunately remain relatively rare. Lenders and borrowers tend to agree on individual (uncoordinated) ad hoc bilateral arrangements |
| | Venezuela's insolvency laws (which are contained in its Commercial Code) do not include judicial restructuring provisions as a separate type of insolvency proceeding. Courts can grant judicial restructuring, in the context of approval of the manner in which a formal insolvency proceeding advances, but this is rare. The typical outcome of insolvency is liquidation. Insolvency laws are generally perceived as poorly drafted and outdated (dating back to 1955), significantly out of step with best international insolvency practice. This leaves a high level of unworkability and unpredictability in the laws' application. Furthermore, the rule of law in Venezuela is seen to have suffered in recent years. The insolvency office holder profession requires strengthening |
| | Given this, it is highly desirable, where achievable, to aim for a workout. Given Venezuela's location in the Americas, it is common to see cross-border finance documents governed by New York law |
| | World Bank Resolving Insolvency rank/score/recovery rate: 165/18.5/5.3 |
| | CPI 2020 Rank: 176 |
| | Contributor(s): Ruben Eduardo Luján, Partner, Dentons Caracas |

(continued)

(continued)

| Region/Country |
| --- |

*Asian Region*

China     The Principles are not well known in China. Rather, market participants follow the judicial insolvency rules expressly prescribed by the bankruptcy law in distress situations. The regulator has not actively promoted the Principles. Consensual multi-creditor restructurings are effectively non-existent—instead, lenders virtually always rely on judicial insolvency proceedings. International lenders' access to the domestic lending market has also been historically limited by tight foreign debt quotas, though these quotas have been relaxed in recent years

China's Bankruptcy Law includes judicial restructurings (applied in ca. 30% of cases). The country's observance of rule of law in purely commercial matters has improved in recent years. The insolvency office holder profession has also improved over the last decade

Absent special circumstances, the most likely path forward for the parties in a distress situation will be a judicial restructuring. Cross-border financial transactions in China are often governed by English or Hong Kong law or any other laws of which the predominant creditors in the transaction decide to apply

World Bank Resolving Insolvency rank/score/recovery rate: 51/62.1/36.9

CPI 2020 Rank: 78

Contributor(s): Chunyang Wang, Partner, Dentons Beijing

(continued)

(continued)

| Region/Country | |
|---|---|
| Hong Kong | The Principles are known and understood in Hong Kong, if not always by name. Whilst the regulator itself has not endeavored to promote the Principles, the Hong Kong Institute of Certified Public Accountants (in collaboration with INSOL International) has done so |
| | Hong Kong's law includes effective judicial restructuring procedures (schemes of arrangement). Companies (Winding Up and Miscellaneous Provisions) Ordinance (Cap. 32) (the "C(WUMP)O") and the Companies (Winding Up) Rules (Cap. 32H). The C(WUMP)O also cross-refers to and incorporates certain provisions of the Bankruptcy Ordinance (Cap. 6). That said, the insolvency law is in need of updating to introduce a US Chapter 11 style proceeding. Being one of the (if not the) most highly developed emerging market financial capitals, Hong Kong's rule of law is extremely high (thanks also to its historic connection with the British Empire). The insolvency office holder profession is perceived as competent and independent |
| | Workouts are commonly used in Hong Kong (often by overlays). But if necessary, a judicial restructuring presents an excellent alternative. Cross-border financial transactions are usually governed by Hong Kong law or by English law |
| | World Bank Resolving Insolvency rank/score/recovery rate: 45/65.7/87.2 |
| | CPI 2020 Rank: 11 |
| | Contributor(s): Keith Brandt, Managing Partner, Dentons Hong Kong |

(continued)

(continued)

| Region/Country | |
|---|---|
| Indonesia | The Principles are not widely known, nor has the regulator actively promoted them. However, some of the concepts embedded in the Principles are reflected in the bankruptcy law |
| | Indonesia's bankruptcy law (the 2004 Law No. 37 on Bankruptcy and Suspension of Payments) includes two distinct types of restructurings: a longer judicial restructuring procedure, and a shorter, expedited proceeding known as suspension of debt payment obligations (or PKPU). Although the PKPU proceedings are more user-friendly and allow quicker reorganizations, many PKPU cases unfortunately later fall into insolvent liquidation. There has been some discussion in recent years of further reform of the law. The country's courts have improved in their observance of rule of law (though some observers remain doubtful). There is relatively high regard for the insolvency office holder profession (subject to some discrete cases where creditor-appointed office holders appear not to have acted independently) |
| | Given the system of judicial restructurings discussed above, the most likely path forward in a distress situation would be judicial restructuring or PKPU (not a workout). That said, where achievable, a workout would certainly present benefits. It is common to see English law used for significant financial transactions if there is a foreign entity as the party, however, for the security documents especially for the assets located and registered in Indonesia, the security documents usually be governed by the Indonesian law |
| | World Bank Resolving Insolvency rank/score/recovery rate: 38/68.1/65.5 |
| | CPI 2020 Rank: 102 |
| | Contributor(s): Erwin K. Winenda, Partner, Dentons Jakarta |
| Malaysia | The Principles are familiar and regularly referred to by the financial community in distress situations. Whilst the regulator has not formally promoted them by name, a key NGO—the Insolvency Practitioners of Malaysia (aka iPAM), as a member of INSOL International seems to have been established with a view of achieving such objective whereby one of its key aims is to impact legislative reform specifically in the areas of insolvency. Critically, the Central Bank of Malaysia (Bank Negara Malaysia) has formed the Corporate Debt Restructuring Committee (or CDRC) whereby companies in financial difficulties may opt to seek the CDRC's assistance on a voluntary basis to act as a mediator in distress situations. In that regard, Bank Negara Malaysia and the CDRC have created a voluntary Code of Conduct for creditors and debtors in distress situations. Thus, there is a strong foundation for workouts |

(continued)

(continued)

| Region/Country | |
|---|---|
| | Malaysia's laws notably include three different restructuring options that require judicial involvement to different degrees: schemes of arrangement, judicial management, and corporate voluntary arrangement, under the recently amended Malaysian Companies Act 2016 (the latter two procedures being introduced in 2016). All three procedures work well. There are no significant perennial issues with rule of law in Malaysia. The insolvency office holder profession is generally viewed as satisfactory |
| | Due to the broad range of restructuring options, either a consensual or a judicial management restructuring would probably work well. Given Malaysia's historic connection with the United Kingdom, cross-border financial transactions may be governed by English law |
| | World Bank Resolving Insolvency rank/score/recovery rate: 40/67.0/81.0 |
| | CPI 2020 Rank: 57 |
| | Contributor(s): Zain Azrin Zain Azahari, Senior Partner, Dentons Kuala Lumpur; Su Ann Kok, Senior Partner, Dentons Kuala Lumpur; Pauline Ngiam, Partner, Dentons Kuala Lumpur |
| Papua New Guinea | The Principles are not well known or used in PNG. International lending into PNG by international lenders is relatively limited and usually only at the sovereign level; accordingly, most PNG borrowers will borrow locally from PNG lenders. The regulator has not actively promoted the Principles |
| | PNG's insolvency regime does not include judicial restructuring and is in need of updating (PNG's insolvency law is contained within the Companies Act 1997). That said, the rule of law in PNG is not viewed as overly problematic, given its legacy connections with Australia and the British Empire and adoption of English common law as it was in England on the date of PNG's independence on 16 September 1975. The insolvency office holder profession is generally well regarded, albeit limited. However, the court system in PNG is usually regarded as inefficient and consequently expensive |
| | Due to the above, a workout where achievable is likely to be the much preferred option in distress. English law is often used in cross-border financial transactions |
| | World Bank Resolving Insolvency rank/score/recovery rate: 144/32.2/24.9 |
| | CPI 2020 Rank: 142 |
| | Contributor(s): Stephen Massa, Partner, Dentons Sydney and Port Moresby |

(continued)

(continued)

| Region/Country | |
|---|---|
| Singapore | The Principles are well known and understood in Singapore, if not always by name. The regulator has not actively promoted the Principles. That said, there is a strong understanding by the financial community of the merits of workouts |
| | As discussed in the book, Singapore's insolvency regime is one of the most highly developed amongst emerging markets. It includes both schemes of arrangement and judicial management now found in the omnibus legislation for both personal bankruptcies and corporate insolvencies, i.e., the Insolvency, Restructuring and Dissolution Act 2018. Singapore has since 2017 ramped up its efforts to be a regional hub for restructurings involving borrowers and obligors from other countries in the region. The insolvency office holder profession is generally well-regarded |
| | Workouts are common in Singapore (by both overlays and sets of parallel bilateral amendments). But if necessary a court-supervised restructuring can be a good alternative, especially if a moratorium (automatic stay) is required. English law is frequently used in cross-border financial transactions in Singapore |
| | World Bank Resolving Insolvency rank/score/recovery rate: 27/74.3/88.7 |
| | CPI 2020 Rank: 3 |
| | Contributor(s): Koh Kia Jeng, Senior Partner, Dentons Singapore |

(continued)

(continued)

| Region/Country | |
|---|---|
| South Korea | The Principles are not widely known in Korea (by name). However, the first seven of the Principles are reflected in Korea's laws on private workouts. The regulator has not endeavored directly to promote the principles as such, but again, the concepts embedded in the Principles are incorporated into laws on private workouts |
| | Both private workouts and judicial restructurings are common in South Korea (with a preference for workouts). Judicial restructurings are effectuated under the Debtor Rehabilitation and Bankruptcy Act. The law works quite well, placing South Korea high in the rankings of emerging markets. There is a high level of observance of the rule of law in South Korea. The insolvency office holder profession is well regarded, with a high level of independence and effectiveness |
| | Workouts are common in South Korea (often by a single overlay restructuring agreement which involves the company and its lenders). But if necessary a judicial restructuring presents a good alternative. Cross-border financial transactions often occur, and the governing law can be that of a foreign country; for example, an overlay restructuring agreement may set the New York or English law as the governing law |
| | World Bank Resolving Insolvency rank/score/recovery rate: 11/82.9/84.3 |
| | CPI 2020 Rank: 33 |
| | Contributor(s): Ghil-Won Jo, Senior Managing Attorney, Dentons Seoul; Kurt Gerstner, Senior Attorney, Dentons Seoul |

(continued)

(continued)

| Region/Country |
| --- |

*Middle East Region*

Egypt — The Principles are generally not well-known on the Egyptian domestic market, though they are known by international lenders and consultants. The regulator has not actively promoted them

Egypt recently adopted a new bankruptcy law in 2018 aimed at meeting international standards (Bankruptcy Law No. 11 of 2018). It includes judicial restructurings. As these provisions are novel, they remain largely untested. Insolvency proceedings in general are extremely time-consuming in Egypt. They can drag on for years. Rule of law issues within the judiciary present a moderate risk. The insolvency office holder profession requires strengthening

Although not common, workouts do occur (e.g., using a single overlay). Due to likely delays in the courts and novelty of the new judicial restructuring procedures, it is highly desirable to aim for a workout wherever possible in a distress situation. English law is frequently used in Egypt for cross-border financial transactions

World Bank Resolving Insolvency rank/score/recovery rate: 104/42.2/23.3

CPI 2020 Rank: 117

Contributor(s): Frederique Leger, Legal Consultant, Dentons Cairo

Qatar — The Principles are generally not well-known on the Qatar domestic market, though they are known by some international lenders and consultants. The regulator has not actively promoted them

The Qatar domestic insolvency regime unfortunately is not in a standalone insolvency law, it was adopted only recently (2006) and remains untested to date (Commerce Law, Sh. 6). It has no express judicial restructuring provisions. The Qatar Financial Center (QFC) insolvency regime is touted as more modern. The observance of rule of law in Qatar in the courts is favorably viewed, and the country scores highly in its region. The insolvency office holder profession requires strengthening

Due to the above issues, if achievable a workout is highly desirable in Qatar. In practice, cross-border financial transactions may be governed by English law

World Bank Resolving Insolvency rank/score/recovery rate: 123/38.0/30.0

CPI 2020 Rank: 30

Contributor(s): Safwan Moubaydeen, Managing Partner, Dentons Doha and Dentons Amman

(continued)

(continued)

| Region/Country | |
| --- | --- |
| Jordan | The Principles are generally not well-known on the Jordanian domestic market, though they are known by some international lenders and consultants. The regulator has not actively endeavored to promote them |
| | Jordan's insolvency regime is not in a standalone insolvency law, and its provisions in the commercial code on insolvency remain quite outdated (Law on Insolvency). It has no express judicial restructuring provisions. The observance of rule of law in Jordan in the courts is generally viewed favorably. The insolvency office holder profession requires strengthening |
| | Due to the above, if achievable a workout is highly desirable in Jordan. In practice, cross-border financial transactions may be governed by English law |
| | World Bank Resolving Insolvency rank/score/recovery rate: 112/39.7/27.3 |
| | CPI 2020 Rank: 60 |
| | Contributor(s): Safwan Moubaydeen, Managing Partner, Dentons Doha and Dentons Amman |
| Saudi Arabia | The principles are not well known in the Kingdom of Saudi Arabia, nor has the regulator actively sought to promote them. Some major successful workouts have been achieved (via overlays) |
| | Formal insolvency proceedings can be extremely difficult to navigate. The new insolvency law's provisions have not been tested extensively, and the bankruptcy courts have not been applying the black letter of the law, thus leaving unpredictability (Bankruptcy Law). It can be difficult and time-consuming to resolve distress situations by judicial proceedings. Furthermore, the Kingdom's courts are viewed by many observers as not being independent. Confidence in the insolvency officer profession is lacking |
| | Given this, wherever possible, achieving a successful workout will carry a high premium for lenders. Cross-border finance documents are often Shari'ah or English law |
| | World Bank Resolving Insolvency rank/score/recovery rate: 168/0.0/No Practice |
| | CPI 2020 Rank: 52 |
| | Contributor(s): Mahmoud Abdel-Baky, Partner, Dentons Riyadh |

(continued)

(continued)

| Region/Country | |
|---|---|
| UAE | The Principles are well known in the professional community, though perhaps less so amongst local lenders and corporates UAE has three separate insolvency regimes: (1) the onshore UAE, governed by the federal law no 9 of 2016 in relation to bankruptcy (as amended) (the UAE Bankruptcy Law); (2) the DIFC, governed by DIFC law no 1 of 2019 (the DIFC Insolvency Law) (which includes traditional UK law concepts [although in less detail than UK legislation] as well as more recent additions to the restructuring tool kit such as a DIP rehabilitation regime, the appointment of an administrator in cases of mismanagement and the adoption if the UNCITRAL model law to assist with cross-border insolvencies) and (3) the ADGM, which is covered by the ADGM Insolvency Regulations 2015 (as amended) (the ADGM Insolvency Regulations) (and broadly follows English law). The 2016 UAE Bankruptcy Law is relatively new and untested in major insolvencies. Previously, high-profile distress situations (e.g., Dubai World and Nakheel) were resolved consensually due to the lack of legislative support. More recently, the UAE Bankruptcy Law has been used to restructure Drake & Scull PJSC, a listed company, under the control of the "Financial Restructuring Committee," which is responsible for the restructuring and insolvency matters in relation to UAE listed companies and banks and regulated FIs. The professional community awaits to see whether the UAE Bankruptcy Law is further amended to address perceived disadvantages. Rule of law is generally not perceived to be overly problematic in commercial litigation (including insolvency). The insolvency office holder profession requires strengthening. Evidence suggests UAE authorities are taking action to address this (as done in other recent amendments)<br>For now, consensual restructuring (especially of subsidiaries owned by government-related entities) remains the preferred option. Cross-border (and often domestic) financial transactions are regularly governed by English law<br>World Bank Resolving Insolvency rank/score/recovery rate: 80/49.3/27.7<br>CPI 2020 Rank: 21<br>Contributor(s): Stephen Knight, Partner, Dentons Abu Dhabi |

(continued)

(continued)

| Region/Country |
| --- |

*African Region*

| Kenya | The Principles are not particularly well-known, nor has the regulator actively endeavored to promote them |
| --- | --- |
| | Kenya recently adopted a new insolvency act in 2016 (the Kenyan Insolvency Act of 2016). Practice in large insolvencies remains relatively limited. Kenya has to date seen major judicial restructurings in the form of either administration or schemes of arrangement. Practitioners note the rule of law in commercial matters including insolvency is generally satisfactory. The insolvency office holder profession is generally seen as satisfactory |
| | Workouts have been successfully implemented in Kenya. Cross-border financial transactions are often governed by English law |
| | World Bank Resolving Insolvency rank/score/recovery rate: 50/62.4/31.8 |
| | CPI 2020 Rank: 124 |
| | Contributor(s): Adil Khawaja, Managing Partner, Dentons Nairobi; Nafysa Adam Abdalla, Partner, Dentons Nairobi |
| Mauritius | The Principles are well known in Mauritius. The regulator has endorsed a formal Guideline on the Principles. Accordingly, a workout would probably be positively received at the local level |
| | Mauritius has a modern insolvency law aligned with international standards, together with a good set of precedent insolvency case law (Insolvency Act of 2009). It includes judicial restructuring provisions, though these are not commonly used. The companies act also allows restructurings in the form of compromises with creditors or schemes of arrangement approved by the court. There is no persistent significant rule of law issues in the courts. The insolvency office holder profession is generally regarded as effective |
| | Workouts have been successfully achieved (via overlays) and are generally perceived as adding value through speed. At the same time, a judicial restructuring might be a reasonable second choice (but would likely face some unpredictability, given the limited use of these) French and English law are often used in cross-border financial transactions |
| | World Bank Resolving Insolvency rank/score/recovery rate: 28/73.8/67.4 |
| | CPI 2020 Rank: 52 |
| | Contributor(s): Priscilla Balgobin, Partner, Dentons Mauritius |

(continued)

(continued)

| Region/Country | |
|---|---|
| South Africa | The Principles are not particularly well-known in South Africa. That said, the concepts embedded in them are to some extent reflected in the country's corporate legislation on business rescues and compromises with creditors. The regulator has not actively endeavored to promote the Principles |
| | South Africa's insolvency law needs some modernization (Law of Insolvency). The previous judicial restructuring process was abandoned for more modern insolvency structures such as business rescues or compromises under corporate legislation (subject to sanction by the court). As a general matter, the observance of rule of law in South Africa within courts is high. That said, administration of the courts is often under-resourced or lacking in experience to handle a heavy docket. This can result in time-consuming and costly delays. The insolvency officeholder profession is generally regarded as independent and competent |
| | Workouts are thus achievable, though if necessary a business rescue or compromise procedure may be a reasonable alternative (subject to the caveat re delay). Cross-border financial transactions in South Africa often use English law |
| | World Bank Resolving Insolvency rank/score/recovery rate: 68/54.6/34.7 |
| | CPI 2020 Rank: 69 |
| | Contributor(s): Vanessa Jacklin-Levin, Managing Partner, Dentons Johannesburg; Kirith Haria, Senior Associate, Dentons Johannesburg |
| Uganda | The Principles are not well known in Uganda, nor has the regulator actively sought to promote them |
| | Uganda's companies and insolvency laws were relatively recently amended to bring them in line with international standards (2012 Companies Act, 2011 Insolvency Act, 2013 Insolvency Regulations). The laws provide for judicial restructurings in the form of arrangements or compromises with creditors (under the companies act) or administration (under the insolvency act). There is no significant perennial rule of law issues in Uganda's courts, given its legacy connection with the British Empire. There is also high esteem for the well-regulated insolvency office holder profession |
| | Consensual restructurings are not widely used, though the law expressly provides for them. They do indeed occur when achievable (via overlays supplemented by bilateral amendments). In cross-border financial transactions, English law is often seen |
| | World Bank Resolving Insolvency rank/score/recovery rate: 99/43.6/40.3 |
| | CPI 2020 Rank: 142 |
| | Contributor(s): David Mpanga, Senior Partner, Dentons Kampala |

(continued)

(continued)

| Region/Country | |
| --- | --- |
| Zambia | The Principles are not well known in Zambia, nor has the regulator actively sought to promote them |
| | Zambia recently substantially overhauled its insolvency law (Corporate Insolvency Act 2017). The law provides for judicial restructurings (in the form of schemes of arrangement and business rescue proceedings), but due to its novelty, it remains largely untested. Distress still frequently results in insolvent liquidation, though the new law provides hope this will change. There is some perception of problems with the rule of law. At the same time, Zambia's courts (in particular at the appellate level) have demonstrated independence and a desire to protect the rule of law. The country's legal system is based on English law. The insolvency office holder profession requires strengthening |
| | Some successful workouts have occurred in Zambia (using overlays). Whilst a judicial restructuring might be considered, given the law's novelty and low usage of these types of proceedings, there would be some unpredictability and learning curve. Thus, the workout option would be far preferable. In cross-border financial transactions, English law is often seen |
| | World Bank Resolving Insolvency rank/score/recovery rate: 79/49.3/51.0 |
| | CPI 2020 Rank: 117 |
| | Contributor(s): Joseph Alexander Jalasi, Partner, Dentons Lusaka |

# Annex 2: Selected Bibliography

## Legal

1. ACT Borrower's Guide to the LMA Facilities Agreement for Leveraged Transactions, September 2008, Association of Corporate Treasurers (ACT), at www.treasurers.org
2. A Toolkit for Out-of-Court Workouts, The World Bank, 2016
3. Chehi, M/Contributing Editor, Insolvency, Chambers Global Practice Guide, 2018
4. Collier International Business Insolvency Guide, LexisNexis, 2020
5. EBRD Core Principles of an Effective Insolvency System, www.ebrd.com, September 2020
6. Garrido, J., Out-of-Court Debt Restructuring, A World Bank Study, The World Bank, 2012

7. Godfrey, Newcombe, Burke, Chen, Schmidt, Stadler, Coucouni, Johnston and Boss, Bank Confidentiality—A Dying Duty But Not Dead Yet? *Business Law International* Vol. 17, No. 3. September 2016

8. Gruson, M., Restructuring Syndicated Loans: The Effect of Restructuring Negotiations on the Rights of the Parties to the Loan Agreement (summarizing the position under New York law), *International Law Revista Colombiana de Derecho Internacional*, num. 3, junio 2004, pp. 322–342, Pontificia Universidad Javeriana, Bogota, Colombia

9. INSOL II Principles: www.insol.org/_files/Publications/StatementOfP rinciples/Statement%20of%20Principles%20II%2018%20April%202 017%20BML.pdf

10. Jaglom, A.R., and Galligan, M.W., "New York Law as the Gold Standard Choice for Global Business Contracts," New York State Bar Association www.nysba.org, 2019

11. McKnight, A., *The Law of International Finance*, Oxford University Press, 2008

12. McKnight and Zakrzewski, *On the Law of Loan Agreements and Syndicated Lending*, Oxford University Press, 2019

13. Newcomb, D., Recent Trends in Senior Loan Negotiation, A Practitioner's Guide to European Leveraged Finance, at www.lw.com/though tLeadership/recent-trends-in-senior-loan-negotiation

14. Wood, P.R., *Principles of International Insolvency*, Thomson Sweet & Maxwell, 2nd Ed., 2007

15. Wood, P.R. "Ten Points for Choosing the Governing Law of an International Business Contract," www.ibanet.org, 2020

## Macroeconomics

1. Allen, William A., *International Liquidity and the Financial Crisis*, Cambridge, 2013

2. Allen, Frankin and Gale, Douglas, *Understanding Financial Crises*, Oxford, 2007

3. Blanchard, Olivier, et al., *In the Wake of the Crisis: Leading Economists Reassess Economic Policy*, The MIT Press, Cambridge, 2012

4. Blanchard, Olivier, et al., *What Have We Learned*, The MIT Press, Cambridge, 2014

5. Calvo, Guillermo, *Emerging Capital Markets in Turmoil*, MIT, Cambridge MA, 2005

6. Calvo, Guillermo A., *Macroeconomics in Times of Liquidity Crises*, MIT, Cambridge MA, 2016

7. Charpe, Mathieu, et al., *Financial Assets, Debt and Liquidity Crises*, Cambridge University Press, New York, 2011

8. Daniels, Joseph, *International Monetary and Financial Economics*, South-Western, Nashville, 2001

9. Eichengreen, Barry, *Hall of Mirrors*, Oxford University Press, Oxford, 2015

10. Godely, Wynne and Lavoie, Marc, *Monetary Economics*, Palgrave-Macmillan, London, 2012

11. Joyce, Joseph, *The IMF and Global Financial Crises*, Cambridge University Press, New York, 2013

12. Kindleberger, Charles and Aliber, Robert Z., *Manias, Panics and Crashes* (6th Edition), Palgrave-Macmillan, 2011

13. Montiel, Peter J., *Macroeconomics in Emerging Markets*, Cambridge, 2011

14. Montiel, Peter J., *Ten Crises*, Routledge, London, 2014

15. Minsky, Hyman P., *Stabilizing an Unstable Economy*, McGraw Hill, New York, 1986

16. Sarno, Lucio and Taylor, Mark P., *The Economics of Exchange Rates*, Cambridge, 2002

17. Schiller, Robert J., *Irrational Exuberance*, Broadway Books, New York, 2005

18. Sheng, Andrew, *From Asian to Global Financial Crisis*, Cambridge, 2009

19. Uribe, Martin and Schmitt-Grohe, Stephanie, *Open Market Economics*, Princeton, 2017

20. Wolfe, Martin, *The Shifts and the Shocks*, Penguin, New York 2014

## Risk Management and Markets

1. Brunnermeier, Markus et al. (Editors), *Risk Topography: Systemic Risk and Macro Modelling*, University of Chicago Press, Chicago, 2014

2. Bychuk, Oleg, and Haughey, Brian, *Hedging Market Exposures: Identifying and Managing Market Risks*, Wiley, Hoboken, 2011

3. Castagna, Antonio and Fede, Francesco, *Measuring and Managing Liquidity Risk*, Wiley, West Sussex, UK, 2013

4. Choudhry, Moorad, *The Principles of Banking*, Wiley, Singapore, 2012

5. Dermine, Jean, *Bank Valuation and Value-Based Management*, McGraw Hill, New York, 2015

6. Fouque, Jean Pierre and Langgsam, Joseph A., *Handbook on Systemic Risk*, Cambridge, 2012

7. Fraser, John, *Enterprise Risk Management*, Wiley, Hoboken, 2010

8. Freixas, Xavier and Rochet, Jean-Charles, *Microeconomics of Banking*, MIT, Cambridge MA, 1997

9. Fridson, Martin and Alvarez, Fernando, *Financial Statement Analysis*, Wiley, Hoboken, 2011

10. Fridson, Martin and Alvarez, Fernando, *Financial Statement Analysis Workbook*, Wiley, Hoboken, 2011

11. Ganguin, Blaise and Bilardello, John, *Fundamentals of Corporate Credit Analysis*, McGraw Hill, New York, 2005

12. Gilson, Stuart, *Creating Value Through Corporate Restructuring*, Wiley, 2010

13. Golin, Jonathan and Delhaise, Philippe, *The Bank Credit Analysis Handbook*, Wiley, Singapore, 2013

14. Gray, Dale and Malone, Samuel W., *Macro-Financial Risk Analysis*, Wiley, Hoboken, 2008

15. Guthner, Mark, *Quantitative Analytics in Debt Valuation and Management*, McGraw, New York, 2012

16. Hull, John C., *Risk Management and Financial Institutions*, Wiley, Hoboken, 2012

17. Jha, S., *Interest Rate Markets*, Wiley, Hoboken, 2011

18. Kocis, J.M., et al., *Inside Private Equity: The Professional Investor's Handbook*, Wiley, Hoboken, 2011

19. Matz, Leonard, *Liquidity Risk Measurement and Management*, Matz—Xlibris, USA, 2011

20. Ong, L.L. (Editor), *A Guide to IMF Stress Testing*, IMF, Washington, DC, 2014

## Annex 3: Bank of Commerce—Financial Analysis

In this Annex, we do not give answers but rather address salient issues to assist the reader in validating (or not) the concerns Kristi raised in the Pre-Restructuring Phase. The approach here is a more high-level and narrow focus on the critical risks confronting the Bank of Commerce. We do not present a full financial analysis.

1. Economic growth has slowed, with the impact that non-performing loans may well increase. Lenders are cutting back on loan growth, both to limit portfolio risk and limit leverage.

2. The resulting rise in provisions will have a negative impact on profitability and eventually could pressure solvency. Besides limiting the growth in risk

assets, banks are raising new capital, both Tier 1 and Tier 2, in order to increase equity buffers.

3. With the deterioration in the external accounts, foreign capital providers may have begun to reassess their exposure and hence curtail supply. With pressures building on the exchange rate peg in the form of capital outflows, there is likely to be an upward trend in market interest rates. Institutions with short open currency positions are increasingly moving to mitigate this risk. Additionally, there is a general move in the market to extend funding maturities to protect against future pressures. Overall, the industry's cost of funding is rising.

4. In the case of the Bank of Commerce:

   • What has been driving profitability?

| Income Statement | (Millions - Local Currency) | | | |
|---|---|---|---|---|
| | Year "T-3" | Year "T-2" | Year "T-1" | Year "T" |
| Grosa Interest Income | 180 | 330 | 368 | 400 |
| Cost of Funds | 100 | 203 | 206 | 215 |
| Net Interest Margin | 80 | 127 | 162 | 185 |
| (%) | 44% | 38% | 44% | 46% |
| Fees and Others | 30 | 40 | 50 | 90 |
| OPEX | 75 | 85 | 95 | 120 |
| Provisions | 5 | 10 | 10 | 35 |
| Net Operating Income | 30 | 72 | 107 | 120 |
| (%) | 17% | 22% | 29% | 30% |
| Taxes | 5 | 11 | 16 | 18 |
| Net Income | 25 | 61 | 91 | 102 |
| (%) | 14% | 18% | 25% | 26% |
| Dividends | 24 | 59 | 85 | 100 |
| Dividend Payout Ratio | 96% | 97% | 93% | 98% |
| ROA | 3.3% | 4.1% | 5.3% | 5.3% |
| ROE | 13.2% | 20.9% | 26.9% | 30.0% |

   • How does the evolution of the cost of funding differ from the industry?

| Calculation of NIM | (Millions - Local Currency) | | | |
|---|---|---|---|---|
| | Year "T-3" | Year "T-2" | Year "T-1" | Year "T" |
| GLP | 750 | 1,500 | 1,750 | 2,000 |
| Portfolio Yield | 24% | 22% | 21% | 20% |
| Interest Income | 180 | 330 | 368 | 400 |
| | | | | |
| Debt & Deposit Funding | 625 | 1,356 | 1,584 | 1,790 |
| Cost of Funding | 16% | 15% | 13% | 12% |
| Interest Expense | 100 | 203 | 206 | 215 |
| | | | | |
| Net Interest Income | 80 | 127 | 162 | 185 |
| % | 44% | 38% | 44% | 46% |
| | | | | |
| Industry Averages: | | | | |
| Portfolio Yield | 21% | 21% | 20% | 20% |
| Cost of Funding | 9% | 11% | 12% | 13% |
| NIM | 12% | 10% | 8% | 7% |

- What might this tell one about the funding strategy and hence the risks relative to the industry?
- What has been happening to "capital adequacy" over the period (the "CAR")?
- Why?
- How does the current level compare to the industry?
- Where does the current level sit in relation to the regulatory minimum?
- Overall, how would you characterize the Bank's solvency?

| Balance Sheet | (Millions - Local Currency) | | | |
|---|---|---|---|---|
| | Year "T-3" | Year "T-2" | Year "T-1" | Year "T" |
| Cash and Marketable Securities | 35 | 28 | 22 | 15 |
| Gross Loan Portfolio | 750 | 1,500 | 1,750 | 2,000 |
| Loan Loss Reserve | (20) | (30) | (40) | (75) |
| Net Loan Portfolio | 730 | 1,470 | 1,710 | 1,925 |
| Total Assets | 765 | 1,498 | 1,732 | 1,940 |
| | | | | |
| Deposits | 300 | 350 | 375 | 400 |
| Senior Debt | 275 | 856 | 1,019 | 1,200 |
| Total Liabilities | 575 | 1,206 | 1,394 | 1,600 |
| | | | | |
| Sub Debt (Tier 2) | 50 | 150 | 190 | 190 |
| Paid-in Capital | 100 | 100 | 100 | 100 |
| Retained Earnings | 40 | 42 | 48 | 50 |
| Total Equity | 190 | 292 | 338 | 340 |
| | | | | |
| Total Liabilities and Equity | 765 | 1,498 | 1,732 | 1,940 |

- Using the Duration Gap Schedule below:
  - How would you characterize the funding situation of the Bank?
  - Given market conditions, what vulnerabilities exist?

**Liquidity - Duration Gap Analysis   (Millions - Local Currency)**

| Contractual Maturity Gap (in mm) | O/N | ≤ 1 mo | > 1 mo ≤ 3 mo | > 3 mo ≤ 6 mo | > 6 mo ≤ 12 mo | > 1 yr ≤ 3 yrs | > 3 yrs | Perp | Total |
|---|---|---|---|---|---|---|---|---|---|
| Cash | 8 | 5 | - | - | - | - | - | - | 13 |
| Unrestricted at CB | 2 | - | - | - | - | - | - | - | 2 |
| Banks | - | - | - | - | - | - | - | - | - |
| Financial Investments | - | - | - | - | - | - | - | - | - |
| Net Loans | - | 50 | 150 | 100 | 300 | 900 | 425 | - | 1,925 |
| Fixed and Other assets | - | - | - | - | - | - | - | - | - |
| Total Assets | 10 | 55 | 150 | 100 | 300 | 900 | 425 | - | 1,940 |
| Deposits (retail) | - | - | - | - | - | - | - | - | - |
| Deposits (Wholesale) | - | 100 | 100 | 200 | - | - | - | - | 400 |
| Senior Secured Debts | - | - | 200 | 400 | 400 | 200 | - | - | 1,200 |
| Senior Unsecured Debts | - | - | - | - | - | - | - | - | - |
| Senior Bonds | - | - | - | - | - | - | - | - | - |
| Sub debts & bonds | - | - | - | - | - | 190 | - | - | 190 |
| Other Liabilities | - | - | - | - | - | - | - | - | - |
| Equity | - | - | - | - | - | - | - | 150 | 150 |
| Total Liabilities and Equity | - | 100 | 300 | 600 | 400 | 390 | - | 150 | 1,940 |
| Liquidity Gap | 10 | (45) | (150) | (500) | (100) | 510 | 425 | (150) | |
| Cumulative Gap | 10 | (35) | (185) | (685) | (785) | (275) | 150 | - | |

- Evaluate the open currency position?

**FX Position    (Millions - Local Currency)**

| | Year "T-3" | Year "T-2" | Year "T-1" | Year "T" |
|---|---|---|---|---|
| FX Assets | 173 | 345 | 403 | 450 |
| FX Liabilities: | 423 | 1,018 | 1,203 | 1,290 |
| Desposits | 150 | 175 | 188 | 200 |
| Senior Debt | 223 | 693 | 825 | 900 |
| Sub Debt | 50 | 150 | 190 | 190 |
| Net Position | (250) | (673) | (800) | (840) |
| Net Open Position to Equity | -132% | -230% | -237% | -247% |
| FC:LC | 1.00 | 1.00 | 1.00 | 1.00 |

5. What happens if the crisis arrives as Kristi has warned? How might it appear? We'll assume here two developments occur: (i) the peg is broken and the currency depreciates by 45%; and (ii) there is a significant increase in non-performing loans. Below, we present such a scenario and its pro-forma impact on capitalization:

| | Current Balance Sheet | Pro-Forma Balance Sheet |
|---|---|---|
| Cash | 15 | 15 |
| GLP | 2,000 | 2,203 |
| Loan Loss Reserve | (75) | (225) |
| NLP | 1,925 | 1,978 |
| **Total Assets** | **1,940** | **1,993** |
| Deposits | 400 | 490 |
| Senior Debt | 1,200 | 1,605 |
| **Total Liabiities** | **1,600** | **2,095** |
| Sub Debt | 190 | 276 |
| Common Equity | 100 | 100 |
| Retained Earings | 50 | (478) |
| **Total Equity (incl T-II)** | **340** | **(103)** |
| **Total L & E** | **1,940** | **1,993** |
| CAR | 17.5% | -5% |

**(1) FX Effect**

| | Start | Change |
|---|---|---|
| FX Assets (GLP) | 450 | 203 |
| FX Liabiliities | 1,290 | 581 |
| Deposits | 200 | 90 |
| Senior Debt | 900 | 405 |
| Sub-Debt | 190 | 86 |
| **Net** | **(840)** | **(378)** |
| **Net Open Position to Equity** | -247% | |
| FX/LC (change - depreciation ) | | 45% |
| FX:LC | 1.00 | 1.45 |

**(2) Provision Effect**

| | |
|---|---|
| Loan Loss Reserve (begin) | 75 |
| Increase Non-Performing Loans | 150 |
| (New) Provisions | 150 |
| Loan Loss Reserve (end) | 225 |

**(3) Impact of (1) and (2) on Retained Earnings (ex-tax effect)**

**Retained Earnings**

| | |
|---|---|
| Begin | 50 |
| Change in Provision | (150) |
| FX Translation | (378) |
| **End** | **(478)** |

**In Million LC**

On liquidity, we do not depict a specific scenario. We suggest to the reader to consider the natural reaction of lenders and depositors to the threat of the insolvency and how the duration mismatch risk of the Bank may play out.

# Annex 4: Country Telecom

This Annex consists of two sections: (1) The Complete Case Study and (2) Synopsis of Model Answers

## Section 1—Complete Case Study

*Introduction*

We begin here another (albeit briefer) restructuring narrative similar to the Bank of Commerce. However, the approach differs in two respects. *First*, the story will be broken into four parts, presented in Sect. 1 of this Annex. *Second*, the narrative forms the basis for a series of exercises. These will be in both short answer and essay form. The exercises appear at the end of each respective part, with a synopsis of model answers in Sect. 2 of the Annex.

Our narrative deals with a 1990s dotcom era-telecom company in an emerging market economy. The local government has liberalized markets, including telecommunications, consistent with the wisdom of the Washington Consensus.[3] For the telecom sector, the envisioned liberalization coincided with two complementary developments. *First*, there was the coming of age of the internet, supported by a unique historical explosion of innovation in wireless and fiber-based media/telecom technologies and applications. Legacy fixed-line and international gateway monopolies were broken up, and the new or rapidly changing sectors of the market (such as mobile cellular and broadband operations) opened up to new entrants. *Second*, in many emerging and frontier market economies, a period of renewed capital inflows took place, after the long hangover of the developing world's 1980s version of the Lost Decade. Significant amounts of foreign debt and equity capital became available to the start-ups in the telecom space. Into these propitious conditions stepped the syndicate of investors behind the star of our narrative: Country Telecom.

---

[3] The Washington Consensus is a set of economic policy recommendations for developing countries, and Latin America in particular, that became popular during the 1980s. The term Washington Consensus usually refers to the level of agreement between the IMF, the World Bank, and the U.S. Department of Treasury on those policy recommendations. All shared the view, typically labelled "neoliberal," that the operation of the free market and the reduction of state involvement were crucial to development in the global South. *See* https://www.britannica.com/topic/Washington-consensus.

Country Telecom secured a 2G GSM bandwidth license and a second set of authorizations that would provide the basis of broadband data transmission operation. In the mobile cellular sector, Country Telecom became part of duopoly along with the privatized mobile business of the former state-owned monopoly. With a more dynamic and well-funded business strategy, Country Telecom moved quickly to rival and ultimately to surpass its rival in terms of subscribers and revenue, but had still not arrived at cash-flow breakeven. In the broadband space, their foreign investors had seen the potential for fiber-based, high-speed internet well before the competition did. They were years ahead of the market in laying fiber and had succeeded in monopolizing building access rights to much of the capital city's business district, the university, and the upscale residential areas. However, today, most of the fiber remained dark. Even in their upside business cases, the substantial investments would take years to pay off. Meanwhile, leverage kept building up.

The core mobile cellular business had been expected to help carry this financial burden. Yet, at the end of the last fiscal year, they were further away from cash flow breakeven than a year before. An unexpected election result had intervened. To lower costs for the public, the new, left-of-center government had opened the previous duopoly to unlimited virtual network operators and required the two incumbent operators, including Country Telecom, to lease capacity on their radio access networks. Three had entered the market. Subscriber numbers and unit revenues were declining. Country Telecom's attempt to buy and kill one or two of these operators to arrest the slide had unfortunately failed.

Meanwhile, their construction crews continued to dig up the streets. Country Telecom's insatiable appetite for debt grew apace.

*Players*

| | |
|---|---|
| Peter | Managing Director—Investment Banking: Thompson Dale and Partners |
| Sandy | Chief Financial Officer: Country Telecom |
| Carlos | Chief Risk Office: Thompson Dale and Partners |
| Yves | Head of Credit Audit: Thompson Dale and Partners |
| Nina | Head of Restructuring: Thompson Dale and Partners |
| Jenifer | Managing Director—Mergers and Acquisitions: Thompson Dale and Partners |

Narrative—Part 1

Peter recalled the conversation as if it were yesterday.

"Sandy, this a risky approach, don't you think?" He had asked Country Telecom's CFO. "Your leverage is sky-high, cash flow break-even is receding further into the distance, and someday funders, including my house – Thompson Dale – may not be there. Pay a bit more now to get longer-duration paper. It's a cheap insurance policy."

"Dammit, Peter. We've been over this a dozen times. With today's steep yield curve, we save 250 basis points a year over your longer-term alternative. By year three, we'll be an even more attractive issuer and can refinance at even better terms." Sandy's voice rose, "And no more lectures about my leverage!" Sandy's intercom buzzed. There was mumbling on the line. At length, she spoke again, "Peter, I don't have time to debate this with you anymore. If you don't want the bloody deal, I have lots of other banks ready to step into your role."

"We do. My debt capital markets team stands behind our bid. It's just… it's just that I thought you might want to take advantage of the markets today, go a bit farther out on the curve and buy yourself some flexibility, just in case your business doesn't roll out as quickly as planned. Our risk guy, Carlos, would even approve a larger ticket, if you stretch out the tenor…"

"Sure. And make yourselves some more money!"

Peter began to respond, but Sandy had cut him off as only she could. Peter's DCM colleagues had later enjoyed a good laugh at his expense when he related the conversation. They all had been on the receiving end of one of Sandy's dressing downs. None really cared about the treatment, including Peter. A big pay day was more than worth it.

Now, almost two years later, Peter had a problem—Country Telecom may have run out of time. The threat was coming from within.

Surprisingly in his opinion, money had kept flowing. They had needed to go farther afield to rustle up new lenders and investors, as the first generation of funders was full up. If anything, the work became easier. Being part of the success story of the new economy in a fast-growing emerging market was a seductive lure to second-tier banks, provincial insurance companies, and pension funds. Even the analyst community still couldn't see through the hype of the new telecom/internet story to the simple truth that, with each passing month, their performance slipped further, and the company depended increasingly on fresh funds to keep current on debt service. Maybe they did see the truth, but honesty didn't sell bonds.

Sandy's manner had mellowed, but she was no less manipulative. She had succeeded in positioning Country Telecom as an exciting internet growth story, for which negative EBITDA was a badge of honor, proof positive of its long-term potential. Even Peter's own risk management colleagues had bought into the story line, into the official suspension of the law of gravity. Carlos' support kept the dream alive, however improbable.

To support the company's ever-growing expansion plans and facilitate his market maker role for the bonds, Peter had needed to double-down on his bet. Hell, quintuple down, more like it. Another even larger bond issue to refinance existing debt, an MTN facility, three syndications and a hefty bilateral line of credit to feed the company's insatiable demand for debt. He and Sandy had been successful in perpetuating this near Ponzi scheme. Until now.

Until today's unexpected "credit-audit meeting." Credit-audit was a newly formed function, a kind of grand jury inside Peter's house. The activity reported directly to the risk and audit committee of the board. Its head a former European central banker named Yves, terrified Peter. A variation on the internal audit concept, Yve's team focused on people like Peter and how he did what he did. Business staff, even risk management, were overly subjected to greed, the Thompson Dale's newly promoted CEO had believed. Credit-audit was his answer. This was the first time Peter was being put under their spotlight, and he didn't like it. Looking across the corridor outside the board room, he spied the region's chief risk officer, Carlos. His expression belied the same worry Peter felt. This was not going to end well.

Peter's eyes focused on the consolidated Country Telecom financial projections prepared by Yves' team that rested on his lap. He shook his head and thought to himself, "The true story is even worse."

Cash Flow

| | 1996 | 1997 | 1998 | 1999-Forecast | 2000-Projected |
|---|---|---|---|---|---|
| Net Income | 75 | 40 | 0 | -30 | -70 |
| Non-Cash Charges | 125 | 160 | 200 | 240 | 290 |
| Interest | 48 | 50 | 79 | 112 | 142 |
| **FCF before Investments** | **152** | **150** | **121** | **98** | **78** |
| Capex | 300 | 350 | 375 | 300 | 200 |
| Working Capital | 50 | 60 | 70 | 80 | 90 |
| **FCF** | **-198** | **-260** | **-324** | **-282** | **-212** |
| Debt Amortization | 200 | 250 | 300 | 400 | 450 |
| New Debt | 350 | 465 | 625 | 675 | 665 |
| New Equity | 50 | 50 | 0 | 0 | 0 |
| **Change in Cash** | **2** | **5** | **1** | **-7** | **3** |
| **Begin Cash** | **4** | **6** | **11** | **12** | **5** |
| **End Cash** | **6** | **11** | **12** | **5** | **8** |
| **Debt** | | | | | |
| Begin | 800 | 950 | 1,165 | 1,490 | 1,765 |
| Amortization | 200 | 250 | 300 | 400 | 450 |
| New | 350 | 465 | 625 | 675 | 665 |
| End | 950 | 1,165 | 1,490 | 1,765 | 1,980 |
| **Common Equity** | | | | | |
| Begin | 200 | 250 | 300 | 300 | 300 |
| New | 50 | 50 | - | - | - |
| End | 250 | 300 | 300 | 300 | 300 |

*Figures in Millions (USD)*

*Exercise*

You sit in mid-1999. The operations of Country Telecom have been affected by the fallout of the 1997–1998 Asian Financial Crisis. The economy has slowed and revenue growth with it. The overall cost of funding and the currency risk has risen. As evidenced by the numbers, the operations and financial results of the company are weakening.

1. Based on the limited background and financial data available, how would you describe Country Telecom's current financial posture?
2. Assuming Yves' projections are generally accurate, is Country's Telecom's future trajectory sustainable? Explain your answer.
3. What do you reckon Yves will say to Peter and Carlos? How should Peter and Carlos respond?

Part 2

The door opened, and an alert young administrative assistant stuck her head out.

"Gentlemen, the committee is ready to discuss Country Telecom."

Peter and Carlos entered the room to see a dozen or so staff seated at the conference table. Most were largely unknown to Peter, save for Yves.

"Where is Nina?" asked Yves.

"Here I am," responded a mature woman just entering the room, flanked by two associates.

Peter's heart stopped. Nina was the head of restructuring, based in New York. "Why has she flown 15 hours to come to this meeting?" He thought to himself. Deep down, he knew.

Yves waited for Nina and her team to settle in. He then spoke.

"Peter and Carlos, I have asked Nina to join us. Two weeks ago, the pre-committee reached the conclusion that this company is on an unsustainable path. The evidence is inconvertible. Given the capex requirements of the business, new debt is necessary to pay interest on the old. The hole is getting bigger by the day. For our bank, we face not just a financial, but also a grave reputational risk."

Glaring at Carlos, he continued. "That Risk Management did not see this or, worse, saw it but was complicit with the business presents us with equally serious failures of governance and operational risk…"

Peter raised his hand, indicating his intention to speak, but Yves waved him off.

"… controls. With the agreement of New York, we asked Nina to take over the case. We will use the rest of this meeting to review a presentation which Nina and her team prepared, on their recommended next steps."

Nina flashed the following slides on the screen:

**Consolidated Free Cash Flow**

| | 1996 | 1997 | 1998 | 1999-Forecast | 2000-Projected |
|---|---|---|---|---|---|
| Net Income | 75 | 40 | 0 | (30) | (70) |
| Non-Cash Charges | 125 | 160 | 200 | 240 | 290 |
| Interest | 48 | 50 | 79 | 112 | 142 |
| **FCF before Investment** | 152 | 150 | 121 | 98 | 78 |
| Capex | 300 | 350 | 375 | 300 | 200 |
| Working Capital | 50 | 60 | 70 | 80 | 90 |
| **FCF** | (198) | (260) | (324) | (282) | (212) |
| Debt Amortization | 200 | 250 | 300 | 400 | 450 |
| New Debt | 350 | 465 | 625 | 675 | 665 |
| New Equity (ex- RE) | 50 | 50 | 0 | 0 | 0 |
| **Change in Cash** | 2 | 5 | 1 | (7) | 3 |
| Begin Cash | 4 | 6 | 11 | 12 | 5 |
| End Cash | 6 | 11 | 12 | 5 | 8 |

*USD (Millions)*

**Mobile Cellular Free Cash Flow**

| | 1996 | 1997 | 1998 | 1999-Forecast | 2000-Projected |
|---|---|---|---|---|---|
| Net Income | 150 | 190 | 160 | 135 | 125 |
| Non-Cash Charges | 40 | 50 | 50 | 60 | 60 |
| Interest | 15 | 15 | 20 | 20 | 30 |
| FCF before Investment | 175 | 225 | 190 | 175 | 155 |
| Capex | 60 | 40 | 40 | 40 | 40 |
| Working Capital | 40 | 40 | 45 | 50 | 50 |
| FCF | 75 | 145 | 105 | 85 | 65 |
| Debt Amortization | 50 | 50 | 50 | 50 | 50 |
| New Debt | 0 | 0 | 0 | 0 | 0 |
| New Equity (ex-RE) | 0 | 0 | 0 | 0 | 0 |
| Change in Cash | 25 | 95 | 55 | 35 | 15 |

*USD (Millions)*

**Broadband Free Cash Flow**

| | 1996 | 1997 | 1998 | 1999-Forecast | 2000-Projected |
|---|---|---|---|---|---|
| Net Income | (75) | (150) | (160) | (165) | (195) |
| Non-Cash Charges | 85 | 110 | 150 | 180 | 230 |
| Interest | 33 | 35 | 59 | 92 | 112 |
| FCF before Investment | (23) | (75) | (69) | (77) | (77) |
| Capex | 240 | 310 | 335 | 260 | 160 |
| Working Capital | 10 | 20 | 25 | 30 | 40 |
| FCF | (273) | (405) | (429) | (367) | (277) |
| Debt Amortization | 150 | 200 | 250 | 350 | 400 |
| New Debt | 350 | 465 | 625 | 675 | 665 |
| New Equity (ex-RE) | 50 | 50 | 0 | 0 | 0 |
| Change in Cash | (23) | (90) | (54) | (42) | (12) |

*Figures in Millions (USD)*

| | 1996 | 1997 | 1998 | 1999-Forecast | 2000-Projected |
|---|---|---|---|---|---|
| | | **Leverage** | | | |
| **Consolidated Debt** | | | | | |
| Begin | 800 | 950 | 1,165 | 1,490 | 1,765 |
| Amortization | 200 | 250 | 300 | 400 | 450 |
| New | 350 | 465 | 625 | 675 | 665 |
| End | 950 | 1,165 | 1,490 | 1,765 | 1,980 |
| | | | | | |
| **Equity** | | | | | |
| Begin | 200 | 325 | 415 | 415 | 385 |
| New | 50 | 50 | - | - | - |
| Net Income | 75 | 40 | - | (30) | (70) |
| End | 325 | 415 | 415 | 385 | 315 |
| | | | | | |
| **Debt to Equity** | 2.9 | 2.8 | 3.6 | 4.6 | 6.3 |
| | | | | | |
| **Mobile Cellular Debt** | | | | | |
| Begin | 350 | 300 | 250 | 200 | 150 |
| Amortization | 50 | 50 | 50 | 50 | 50 |
| New | - | - | - | - | - |
| End | 300 | 250 | 200 | 150 | 100 |
| | | | | | |
| **Equity** | | | | | |
| Begin | 125 | 125 | 125 | 125 | 125 |
| New | - | - | - | - | - |
| Net Income | 150 | 190 | 160 | 135 | 125 |
| End | 125 | 125 | 125 | 125 | 125 |
| | | | | | |
| **Debt to Equity** | 2.4 | 2.0 | 1.6 | 1.2 | 0.8 |
| | | | | | |
| **Broadband Debt** | | | | | |
| Begin | 450 | 650 | 915 | 1,290 | 1,615 |
| Amortization | 150 | 200 | 250 | 350 | 400 |
| New | 350 | 465 | 625 | 675 | 665 |
| End | 650 | 915 | 1,290 | 1,615 | 1,880 |
| | | | | | |
| **Equity** | | | | | |
| Begin | 75 | 50 | (50) | (210) | (375) |
| New | 50 | 50 | - | - | - |
| Net Income | (75) | (150) | (160) | (165) | (195) |
| End | 50 | (50) | (210) | (375) | (570) |
| | | | | | |
| **Debt to Equity** | 13 | NM | NM | NM | NM |

Three hours later, the meeting broke up.

Nina went into a side office and made three phone calls. One to Thompson Dale's telecom M&A head Jenifer, a second to Country Telecom's CFO Sandy, and a third to her husband, warning him she would be away for a while.

*Exercise*

1. What do you think Nina and her team concluded, and why?
2. What do you think Nina's and her team's plan will be going forward? If helpful, please feel free to make up your own assumptions to support your view.

## Part 3

A month later, Nina and Jenifer sat in Sandy's office.

Nina spoke out. "Let's review where we are. Given your current business plan, you need to raise roughly $1.3 to 1.4 billion in debt. Agreed?"

Sandy nodded in agreement.

"Your free cash flow was over 300 million in the red last year, and by slowing down your broadband build out to the minimum allowed under your agreements with local government you can bring this down to 200 million next year. Still the '99 – 00 total is half a billion."

"We have some flexibility there," Sandy interjected, "We can cut it by half to two thirds, without contractual problems."

"Does this affect the revenue?" Asked Jenifer

"Not materially."

Nina walked over to the whiteboard and sketched out some figures, talking all the while.

"For purposes of illustration, let's keep everything constant in the current numbers save for capex and debt. With that, we should have this." She pointed to the new tables:

**Consolidated Free Cash Flow**

| | Existing | | New | |
| --- | --- | --- | --- | --- |
| | 1999 | 2000 | 1999 | 2000 |
| FCF before Investments | 98 | 78 | 98 | 78 |
| | | | | |
| Capex | 300 | 200 | 100 | 0 |
| Working Capital | 80 | 90 | 80 | 90 |
| | | | | |
| FCF | (282) | (212) | (82) | (12) |
| | | | | |
| Debt Amortization | 400 | 450 | 400 | 450 |
| New Debt | 675 | 665 | 480 | 460 |
| New Equity | 0 | 0 | 0 | 0 |
| | | | | |
| Change in Cash | (7) | 3 | (2) | (2) |
| | | | | |
| Begin Cash | 12 | 5 | 8 | 5 |
| End Cash | 5 | 8 | 5 | 3 |

**Consolidated Debt**

| | Existing | | New | | Difference |
| --- | --- | --- | --- | --- | --- |
| | 1999 | 2000 | 1999 | 2000 | |
| Begin | 1,490 | 1,765 | 1,490 | 1,570 | (195) |
| Amortization | 400 | 450 | 400 | 450 | - |
| New | 675 | 665 | 480 | 460 | (205) |
| End | 1,765 | 1,980 | 1,570 | 1,580 | (400) |

(USD Millions)

"So this cuts your end of 2000 debt by 400 million. And of the 1.6 billion, all but 100 million odd is in the broadband business. Assuming equity is roughly 300 million, this makes a debt-to-equity ratio of five. Follow me?"

Both ladies acknowledged the comment.

"Now, at this level, given the overall projections, you can't service this debt going forward without new borrowings. As your lead bank, I have to be frank: this isn't going to be possible much longer. Our DCM team's soundings were not positive. The market has come back a little since the depths following the floating of the Thai Baht, but folks are waking up to the size of the hole in the broadband business. Global Connections' default[4] has dampened demand for this sector. Even if we succeed in plugging the gap in 1999 – 2000, we can't

---

[4] A global fiber optic network.

assume so, thereafter. In fact, despite Peter's optimism, I am not sure 2000 is safe, even at these reduced levels."

Jenifer jumped in. "Sandy, listen, we have to be frank. Unless you divest the broadband business, you won't survive."

Silence followed for several minutes. When Sandy did not respond, Jenifer continued.

"Even with the increased competition from the virtual mobile operators, your mobile business is generating 50 to 100 million in free cash flow. Given the expectation the economy will rebound from the recent financial turbulence, the market's turn to higher value-added services, and the new entrants' financial constraints, we believe Country Telecom's operations will strengthen, and our projections call for you to get the cash flow number back into the 150 – 175 million range over the next couple years. At this level, we think you can service 500–600 million of debt, assuming you can stretch out the amortizations. So, roughly a third of what you have now. The debt burden of the broadband business will only grow. I checked with our San Francisco office, and their analysis says you'll not get this business to cash flow positive for another 7 or 8 years, if then. A downside case says 10 years. There is simply not enough broadband demand in the country for now. New equity will not come into the consolidated business at any valuation that leaves your current shareholders in control."

"Which leads us to the house view," Nina continued, "that your only viable way forward is to find someone to take the broadband business off your hands and assume the debt."

"But Nina! We all know no one will do that," cried Sandy.

"I have two thoughts. One is we find a buyer, transfer some debt to the mobile business and then effectively give the operation away for a dollar. The moving number is how much debt you need to strip away. Then, we restructure the debt in the mobile business. If as Jenifer feels this is not possible, then…"

"Not after Global Connections," Jenifer agreed.

"… then we approach the government and give them an early Christmas present. Again, some debt assumption by the mobile business will be necessary, but certainly less than in the case of commercial transaction. Our county manager here is related to the Minister of Telecommunications, and he feels a deal should be possible. If so, then I'd say we move in this direction and use the first alternative as a fall back."

"I have to consult with my CEO and the board first."

"Understood. Make the assumptions that the maximum debt the mobile business can carry is 500 million and that the run rate cash flow is 150.

Once a deal is set, we will refinance the mobile operations' debt, say, for five to seven years. At the same time, the government will have gotten a couple billion worth of network for assuming roughly half that in debt. We will offer to help the Ministry deal with the lenders."

"Ok."

"But we need to do this all quickly before the sky comes tumbling down." Nina closed.

*Exercise*

Put yourself into Sandy's shoes. She is presenting the case to her board. Prepare a half a dozen or so bullet points summarizing the situation, the alternative courses of action and her recommendation.

## Part 4

The subsequent board consultations were rocky for Sandy and her CEO. The board and the investors argued that Thompson Dale was overreacting. They ordered Sandy to research the major assumptions further.

Meanwhile, telecom market conditions globally were mixed. 3G license auctions hit record valuation levels. But the fallout of the Global Connections default continued. Several competing global and regional fiber-optic network companies had to pull financings due to insufficient market demand. Mobile was in, pure broadband plays were out. For Country Telecom, even Sandy now agreed, their only road forward was as a pure mobile play. Still, the board balked.

When several banks exercised their option to withdraw from Country Telecom's revolving credit and their bonds traded down over several weeks, Sandy called Nina and Jenifer to advise that the board had finally reconsidered. They wanted to engage Thompson Dale to work on their "plan."

*Exercise*

Using the numbers provided in the previous chapters as the basis:

1. Create the overall restructuring plan. Where figures are missing, make your own assumptions.
2. Consider the restructuring process and identify the major challenges to Nina to implement her plan.

## Section 2: Synopsis of Model Answers

1. The overall restructuring plan.

- The broadband business is to be transferred to the Ministry of Telecommunications (a "NewCo" to be created) for a nominal sum, along with roughly USD 1.1 billion of debt. This leaves a total of USD 500 million of debt on the books of Country Telecom, post-transaction. We assume that each lender transfers an equal, pro-rata amount of their debt to the NewCo. The transaction requires lender approval for the transfer and assumes the transferred debt is supported with a government guarantee, and is to be amortized on a schedule equal to that of the debt remaining on the books of Country Telecom.
- Country Telecom will work with the government to provide technical and operational services for a period up to 24 months post-transaction.
- Sandy works with Nina on a set of projections. They want to prove to the lenders that the residual debt amount can be serviced without new debt. This approach produces the following numbers:

**Consolidated Free Cash Flow**

|  | 2000 | 2001 | 2002 | 2003 | 2004 | 2005 | 2006 | 2007 |
|---|---|---|---|---|---|---|---|---|
| FCF before Investments | 78 | 86 | 94 | 104 | 114 | 126 | 138 | 152 |
| Capex | 5 | 10 | 11 | 12 | 13 | 14 | 15 | 16 |
| Working Capital | 10 | 11 | 11 | 12 | 12 | 13 | 13 | 14 |
| FCF | 63 | 65 | 73 | 81 | 89 | 99 | 110 | 122 |
| Debt Amortization | 63 | 63 | 63 | 63 | 63 | 63 | 63 | 63 |
| New Debt | 0 | 0 | 0 | 0 | 0 | 0 | 0 | 0 |
| New Equity (ex- RE) | 0 | 0 | 0 | 0 | 0 | 0 | 0 | 0 |
| Change in Cash | 1 | 3 | 10 | 18 | 27 | 37 | 48 | 60 |
| Begin Cash | 3 | 4 | 6 | 16 | 34 | 61 | 98 | 146 |
| End Cash | 4 | 6 | 16 | 34 | 61 | 98 | 146 | 205 |

**Consolidated Debt**

|  | 2000 | 2001 | 2002 | 2003 | 2004 | 2005 | 2006 | 2007 |
|---|---|---|---|---|---|---|---|---|
| Begin | 500 | 438 | 375 | 313 | 250 | 188 | 125 | 63 |
| Amortization | 63 | 63 | 63 | 63 | 63 | 63 | 63 | 63 |
| New | 0 | 0 | 0 | 0 | 0 | 0 | 0 | 0 |
| End | 438 | 375 | 313 | 250 | 188 | 125 | 63 | - |

( USD Millions )

- At the Country Telecom level, a set of financial covenants and limitations on new indebtedness debt and investments, amongst other provisions are to be agreed. Additionally, a cash sweep arrangement is to be established for defined excess cash flow.

2. Process

At a *very high* level, there are two sets of negotiations:

- Stage 1: Negotiate terms of transfer of the broadband business to the Ministry of Telecommunications' NewCo.
- Stage 2: Based on the outcome of Stage 1 discussions, negotiate the terms of debt restructuring with the lenders for both batches of debt (Country Telecom and Ministry of Telecommunications' NewCo).

The first stage with the government will entail discussions with a variety of stakeholders within the executive branch and, should any incremental budgetary or other approvals be required, the legislative branch. Let's assume here only the former is necessary. Even in this case, this stage can be time-consuming and therefore arrangements must be put in place with the lenders. The ideal is to continue interest payments, whilst establishing a standstill on principal payments. In these conversations, "friends" help convince the government that the transaction is in the public interest both financially (the assets can generate commensurate direct financial returns over time) and more-broadly stated, economically (the benefits of broadband connectivity).

In the second stage, we move into a more traditional restructuring process, albeit with the complication of having to coordinate two borrowers (Country Telecom and the NewCo), one of which is the government where staffing and approval processes are less nimble. In our case, we assume the government engages an experienced advisor and that Nina and her team work closely and cooperatively with the government's team. The usual speed bumps are present. However, the deal is an alternative to bankruptcy and roughly two-thirds of each lenders' debt moves from private to government risk, and therefore lenders see the benefit of cooperation.

*Post-script*: In the real world, this is not a simple solution. The arrangement with the government has a very high degree of difficulty. The actual financial terms of the transfer from Country Telecom to the NewCo could well be less attractive. Further, the price to be paid by the equity in Country Telecom would likely be more onerous than we assume.

## Annex 5: Discussion Questions—Thoughts

In this Annex 5, we provide suggested thoughts for consideration in response to the Discussion Questions we posed in our initial narrative of the Bank of

Commerce. These are intended to assist the reader in reaching his or her own conclusions and not to represent definitive responses as such.

## Number 1

1. *What explains the difference in temperament amongst our three financiers—personalities or institutional pressures?*

   A combination (see below).

2. *Edinburgh Partners (EP) is the least financially exposed, yet Todd is clearly the most agitated. Why? How does the answer affect how Kristi and Maya will approach managing Todd's house?*

   - Todd is new to EP. His hiring was in response to his aggressive sales pitch where he sold the firm on taking a chance on a non-traditional asset class. He has had just a couple of years to show his results. A loss the size of his Bank of Commerce exposure would blow a hole in his profits.
   - EP is well-known for being a well-paying but an "unforgiving" employer, where missed profit numbers translate often and quickly to an early end to a career. Todd's job is thus on the line.
   - Kristi and Maya must consider that Todd will be desperate to redeem himself and will adopt an assertive position, even to the point of endangering a group solution.

3. What is the significance of Kristi and Maya coming from the risk or restructuring versus the business origination side of the house? How might this influence how they operate on the deal? And Todd?

   - Kristi and Maya come from the restructuring side of the house. They were not involved in the origination or approval of the investments. Their role is to pick up the pieces when something goes wrong. In contrast, Todd is the investment officer who originated the investment and was its proponent during the approval process. Whilst others signed off alongside Todd and hence share some collective responsibility, Todd will be ultimately the accountable party.
   - As a result, Kristi and Maya may be less emotionally involved in the relationship and hence the transaction's outcome than Todd. How this difference plays could be either be a positive or negative influence on the outcome. Overall, Todd is unlikely to be a constructive force.

# Number 2

1. *How practical is Kristi's macro-focused approach? Is she correct in believing that investors should have seen this coming?*

   - Adverse macroeconomic or market shocks can create destabilizing pressures on the creditworthiness of investment counterparties. The severity of impact of a specific, potential, or actual episode varies according to the financial condition of a particular counterparty and can be roughly estimated. However, the likelihood and hence the timing of occurrence defies precise prediction.
   - Despite this uncertainty, when the likelihood of occurrence rises above a certain moderate level, being prepared and adapting the credit structure to mitigate against the risk is warranted. In the case of the Bank of Commerce, in a country whose economy is dependent on a single cyclical commodity like copper, this level was arguably always surpassed. At a minimum, the impact on the exchange rate of a severe fall in export revenue, and the knock-on effects on the broader economy should have been factored into the credit structure (e.g., open currency position covenant, etc.).

2. *On the question of shareholder support, who is at fault? New West or Todd? How should the lenders' group play the angle of an implied support, if at all?*

   - Todd made a mistake to assume that he had a guarantee, just because JK verbally said so on a call. You cannot ordinarily take a person's verbal word into court. A legal document is usually necessary (in the form of an appropriately drafted and executed guarantee and indemnity, suretyship, or other credit support document). Many legal systems (both developing and emerging) establish a strict written requirement for one party's suretyship or guarantee of another party's obligations (often called a "statute of frauds").

     For example, under English law, the general position is that a guarantee must always be in writing (or evidenced in writing) and signed by the guarantor or a person authorized by it (Section 4, Statute of Frauds 1677).

     Under New York law, a similar statute of fraud applies (NY GEN OBLIG § 5-701). However, there may be an exception to this rule where new consideration flows to the promisor, the latter benefits, and the parties intend the promisor to become a principle debtor primarily liable (Martin Roofing v. Goldstein, 60 N.Y.2d 262, 265, 469 N.Y.S.2d

595, 457 N.E.2d 700, cert. denied 466 U.S. 905, 104 S.Ct. 1681, 80 L.Ed.2d 156).

This is not to say however that a parent or majority shareholder will never be free from liability for its subsidiary's obligations. Other issues may arise, e.g., where the parent/shareholder has engaged in fraud or misrepresentation (e.g., as to the subsidiary's financial condition, off-balance sheet obligations, etc.), where the corporate veil may be pierced (or corporate form disregarded) under relevant companies laws and/or where vicarious liability applies under relevant insolvency rules. Where such potential exposure exists, lenders may well have the leverage to force the parent/shareholder to "come to the table to talk."

- Lenders probably will have no legal grounds to argue that New West is obligated to guarantee the debt.

## Number 3

1. *How would you characterize the board's approach?*

   - The stance assumed by JK and his board appears harsh. It could be just a negotiating ploy—play hardball at the outset to set the tone and establish some initial boundaries—or a reflection of JK's view that the lenders have to adopt his design.
   - Whatever the case, the approach carries risk, as lenders could harden their positions and, in the case of rogues like EP, call a default and accelerate.

2. *What are the underlying considerations driving Martin and Ursula's opposition?*

   - For Martin, the mission of his organization (a DFI) is developmental in nature. A disorderly end to the Bank of Commerce is not consistent with its mission.
   - Ursula recognizes that New West's behavior in this case will be watched by the broader market. If New West comes across as having acted in a rash and irresponsible manner, as Stephen and JK's approach risks, there could be negative impact on its market perception, at a time when, for example, it is struggling to refinance the New Perspectives Energy acquisition debt (of which the reader will learn at the narrative unfolds).

3. *Who should be leading the New West contingent, Ursula or Stephen? Why?*

   - Between the two, clearly Ursula.

- This is due to Ursula being known and respected by many of the institutions, and her personality is less acerbic than Stephen's. Hence, she is a better messenger.

4. *What might explain the absence of the management of the Bank in this pre-meeting?*

- Good question. This was a big mistake.
- The lenders' relationship is more with the Bank of Commerce than with New West. Having New West lead also focused attention on the shareholder and potential support, the last thing the borrower side should have wanted.

## Number 4

1. *How would you critique the evaluation of the Bank's financial position, as discussed above?*

See Annex 3. Once the reader has studied this, consider the pre-crisis situation:

i. liquidity: (a) a declining level of cash and marketable securities; (b) the duration gap analysis, which identifies a significant deficit over the near-term; and (c) both Basel III liquidity related ratios below prudent levels;
ii. solvency—above the regulatory minimum but exhibiting a downward trajectory, which differs from the industry average's increasing level; and
iii. the level of the open currency position (c. 250%).

Overall, it is fair to conclude that the Bank exhibits liquidity and solvency characteristics that make the institution vulnerable to the events that Kristi feels will likely occur as copper prices fall.

2. *What steps could be taken at this time to address the inherent risks?*

- Hedge the short FX position
- Build up a pro-cyclical capital buffer
- Stretch out the maturities of the funding to reduce the near-term duration gap and consider a variety of actions (e.g., shorten credit terms, arrange lines of credit, etc.) to strengthen liquidity coverage.

3. Should this have been the point at which a discussion of restructuring alternatives began?

Not necessarily. If the three steps in (2) above could be taken quickly, then there could be adequate protection for a mild shock.

## Number 5

1. *How serious is the threat? Is Kristi overstating matters?*
   - If the FX peg is broken, then the threat is serious.
   - Kristi could be mildly criticized for characterizing the outcome as certain, versus a high probability call, but overall, her forecast was spot on.

2. *How would you characterize the situation?*

Please note your response here. To the extent relevant, reference economic and financial data.

3. *If you were advising Ursula, what would you say to her?*

   Please note your response here.

4. *After Ursula's brush-off, what should Kristi have done?*

In framing your response, make an assumption on the question of whether her loan agreement has a broadly drafted MAC clause and circumstances warrant an acceleration under it (see Chapter 11 in this respect). If not, then she must wait for a covenant breach. Our omission of her invoking a MAC is intentional, given the practical consideration that lenders are typically hesitant to do so.

## Number 6

1. *What should be done before the two sides "start talking?"*
   - Informal contacts between the two sides should proceed in order to ascertain the "temperature," scope out a broad-brush set of deal parameters, and agree a process.

- The Bank and New West should prepare the data room with all relevant financial and operational data and information necessary to allow the lender-side fully to understand the situation.

2. *Who should be involved?*

- To prepare for the "informal contacts" in (1), Kristi should convene a small group of trusted lenders to discuss the situation and the coming process.
- At a minimum, Ursula and Kristi should talk privately to exchange views. Ideally, this pre-meeting discussion would have a broader audience. Given the role of JK in New West, he should be engaged in direct conversations with the lenders. Irrespective, the objectives of the pre-meeting dialogue should be to agree on process and, to establish a common vision of the problems to be addressed and the means to resolve them.

## Number 7

1. *What could Ursula have done at this point?*

- The sin had already been committed. No pre-meeting dialogue between the parties had been initiated. The message (a stuff-down of a one-sided solution) and the messenger (Stephen) created the worst-possible beginning to what will be a challenging workout.
- Given the shareholder's crucial role in the solution and the politics at the board level, Ursula's flexibility is limited. Had Kristi not acted to stop the meeting, then Ursula would have needed to have done so.

2. *Did Kristi handle the situation correctly?*

- Pre-meeting, she should have mobilized a few key lenders to insist on a planning discussion before agreeing to attend the meeting.
- At the meeting, she did the right thing in recessing the meeting and organizing a direct and forceful lender response.

## Number 8

1. *Critique the roles and interactions of Kristi, Maya, Martin, and Ursula.*

- Kristi: She has taken control of the process, as someone had to do or risk a breakdown. There must always be a leader or a leadership cohort.

- Maya: She provides support to Kristi, validating in part, broader lender support. One lender, no matter their size and/or influence, should not act alone.
- Martin: His role may appear unrealistic to some. We disagree. As the DFI representative, he represents the actor who straddles the divide between the two sides, by facilitating discussions, troubleshooting around potential pitfalls, and helping to keep all focused on the need to arrive at a workable outcome for all stakeholders.
- Ursula: She has performed badly up until now. She cannot be too heavily criticized for defending her sides' legitimate interests. But she can be for having not contributed to better process management.

2. *Is it realistic that Ursula can break with her board like this? If not at present, what does she have to do to neutralize Stephen and coax the board to adopt a more constructive posture?*

- It is not clear how far she is prepared to go. She has accepted the need to resuscitate the process by finding a common way forward, which clearly requires each side "giving." That she would act as she has in this forum is understandable. What happens later? That's key.
- She will need to rely on Martin and any allies she has on the board. Dumping Stephen should prove easy, given the breakdown in the meeting. As regards the substance of the restructuring, this will require much more work and will depend on the flexibility of all the involved stakeholders in the deal.

3. *Look for examples of when and how a cooperative partnership amongst parties straddling the multiple sides of a transaction proves itself to be an essential element in a successful outcome.*

In responding here, think about your experiences, not just in business, but in other aspects of your life. How important has a trusted party, even on the "opposing team," ever been in resolving an argument or solving a situational challenge?

## Number 9

1. *Consider the significance of the shareholder situation in this case. Does it act for or against a constructive role in the Bank of Commerce Restructuring?*

- The lenders all believed the market hype about New West. There was never any doubt about the capacity of the shareholder to support the Bank. Indeed, Todd can be excused to a slight degree for having allowed himself to be duped by JK. Then again, he should have known better. People make and break promises all the time. He needed proper credit support (a guarantee, suretyship, etc.) if he was reasonably going to rely on a promise of shareholder support. The immediate reaction in the kick-off meeting was the capacity is there but the willingness to act is absent.
- Now, there is a recognition that New West just writing a check is not so easy. Still, not all will believe that the shareholder is unable to step in, should they really want to.
- The impact of the news is therefore mixed. For some (e.g., Todd) nothing will change. For others (e.g., Kristi and likely Maya), there is the growing recognition that no "white knight" is likely to "ride to the rescue."

2. *Why might Ursula's view differ from that of JK and the majority of the board?*

- We only know JK's and Martin's views.
- JK is a product of Wall Street. He is highly transactional. He will push hard to maximize his interests with little (or no) concern about the impact on the other side.
- Martin comes from the development finance world, where the longer term impact of actions often enters more into the thinking. Martin is an example of forward-thinking and the avoidance of setting negative precedents to gain immediate advantage (something that is known to happen).

3. *What do you think is going through Kristi's mind? How might it affect her attitude and approach?*

- She is likely to be saying to herself, "we need to monitor the outcome of the New Perspectives Energy refinancing," seeing the successful completion as a necessary, but not sufficient condition to meaningful financial support from New West.
- Therefore, she is operating on the assumption that the solution may not include significant shareholder support, if any.

4. *Given the sensitive nature of the New Perspectives Energy information, how do the parties incorporate it into the discussions?*

Firstly, each participant in the conversation should be familiar with obligations of confidentiality and/or bank secrecy binding his or her respective institution (see Chapter 11). For Kristi, she should make a quick review of her loan document, for Martin, any shareholders agreement, NDA, and/or other documents. The disclosure of such information to third parties could well be a breach of these obligations. Hence the information must be treated with great discretion. At the same time, it appears Ursula has (verbally) implicitly approved the disclosure of the information to Maya and Horizon Bank. Let's also not forget, New Perspectives Energy is a public company. Information received in respect of it may well be price sensitive (that is, capable of affecting prices of its securities or an investor's decision to purchase, sell, or hold securities). Each institution will have an internal policy on insider trading. The participants should discuss the information received on New Perspectives with their respective compliance officers to determine which actions should (or should not) be taken with respect to such information.

## Number 10

1. *Interpret and critique Stephen's call to Reggie. What was the purpose? Did it help or hurt?*

   - His purpose was to undercut the lender who appeared to be the de facto leader of the lender group, and hence best positioned to direct a counter-proposal.
   - A Machiavellian ploy that can backfire all too easily. Kristi's natural reaction will not be positive, and his call will harden her attitude. Unless Reggie is prepared to support Stephen and succeeds in convincing Robert to force a more accommodative posture or even replacing Kristi, Stephen's call will likely have made matters worse. Robert was not swayed.

2. *Why did Kristi ask for a legal audit of their debt documents?*

   This follows from Number 10 (3), above. Kristi is planning for the contingency that a going-concern solution and/or orderly wind-down solution becomes unviable. A proper internal legal audit of loan documentation should be made immediately whenever a borrower is in distress and a risk of formal insolvency proceedings arises. It is not uncommon for defects in legal documents (e.g., missing signatures, lost original wet-ink execution copies) to be unearthed and which can weaken or undermine a lender's claim in a local insolvency court. See Chapters 5 and 11.

# Number 11

Note how Maya and Kristi have handled the preliminary "approval" of the term sheet. In each case, their institution has effectively delegated to them the authority to negotiate the best possible deal in their opinion without requiring a committee approval at this point.

1. *What are the pros and cons of such an approach?*

   - The core strength is negotiating efficiency/effectiveness. This approach allows those closer to the deal and involved in the negotiations to make these decisions within the lenders' group without having to consult with distant committees.
   - The weakness or risk is the obvious danger that the deal team negotiates a deal, which is then turned down in committee.

2. *Should institutions allow even these experienced individuals to operate this way?*

   - It is important to stress that the usual and customary approval authorities remain. Thinking ahead in the Bank of Commerce case, Kristi will still have to take the final deal to committee for approval.
   - From the point of view of the restructuring practice, the answer is yes. However, a more centralized risk management governance environment may see there being too much risk in this approach, no matter the track record of the individuals involved.
   - Her experience here manifests itself not just in a generic structuring sense, but also to know what will fly within her organization. She may well consult informally with her colleagues inside the firm from time to time to test her view on a particular element.

# Number 12

1. *Does Kristi's approach of polling a limited group in this way make sense to you?*

   In considering your response, weigh the same set of pros and cons as discussed in Number 11, above.

2. *Why do you think she chose to do it in this way?*

   Same suggestion as in (1) above.

## Number 13

1.  *What are the possible explanations for Kristi and Maya having applied pressure on the lenders for the rest of the deal before knowing whether the new money was forthcoming?*

    -   A fair question. Two possibilities exist. One could be they were highly confident New West would come through with the cash and simply got it wrong. Another could be they wanted to force out a position from the lenders with the new money involved to use as a starting point for other alternative structures.
    -   What do you think?

2.  *Martin undoubtedly knew of the difficulty in advance. What should he have done?*

    Same suggestions as in (1) above.

3.  *Where do they go from here?*

    -   It's time for Plan B. This will most likely mean that the going-concern outcome is not possible, given past lender reactions.
    -   If you haven't already read on, what do you think they will do? If you have, what do you think about their reaction?

## Number 14

1.  *Why the resistance to a bankruptcy procedure?*

As discussed in Chapter 11, insolvency systems in emerging markets vary greatly. Many such markets' insolvency laws are outdated and function poorly. Many such markets have systemic problems with the judiciary's efficiency and the rule of law. Often, the recoveries in the judicial insolvency are far less than they would be in a successful workout (whether as a going concern or orderly wind-down).

2.  *For an orderly wind-down, why would the shareholders' committing a modest amount of capital be helpful?*

The impact is more related to politics within the lending institutions. Despite the fact the shareholder could well lose all their equity, the lenders would naturally want to see some gesture from the shareholders.

### 3. *Why do you think they are prepared to consider it in this case?*

In the context of our tale: (i) New West—to show the market (their current and future investors) they are acting responsibly; (ii) International Development Fund—an investment in market stability.

### 4. *What underlies the concerns of the Bank of Commerce CEO?*

Many countries' insolvency laws oblige an officer or director to file for voluntary insolvency where indicia of insolvency arise (cash flow or balance sheet). The failure to file (referred to as "wrongful trading") can result in personal liability for the officer or director. Other laws (e.g., corporate and/or financial regulatory) may also create personal liability. See Chapter 11. Even where a formal violation has not occurred, perception by the local regulator that an officer or director has been remiss can impact on his or her future career and obtaining regulatory approvals for new appointments. At the same time, a properly drafted orderly wind-down agreement should mitigate against this risk, and counsel will need to work with local management to ensure they understand and accept this.

## Number 15

### 1. *What are the issues with the local financial authorities? Why the need for secrecy?*

- In their supervisory role, the local financial authority has a responsibility to ensure systemic stability and protect the interests of the public. Were the local authority to have been aware of all the potential problems, they may have felt obligated to act.
- All the parties in the transaction understood and accepted their obligations under local law and regulations. For example, were the circumstances actually to require a declaration of insolvency, no one in the deal would have objected to taking this step.
- What the parties wanted to avoid are unnecessary disclosures that might result in having public opinion or other factors forcing the supervisor to act pre-emptively, even if the institution is still in compliance with all

relevant laws and regulations. In our case, keeping the institution liquid and solvent was imperative, and the parties ensured this.

2. *What should the lenders be thinking about around the problem of Edinburgh Partners?*

- Are they just negotiating for a sweeter deal, or are they prepared to take drastic action (liquidation)?

# Number 16

1. *Is it realistic that the Lenders did not consider acting earlier to force a sale of the Bank of Commerce with the limited goal of maximizing their debt recovery? Why or why not?*

- The idea must have come in some quarters.
- The lack of progress in pursuing such an alternative likely reflected the view that New West would step up and recapitalize the Bank.

2. *Consider when later New West discloses they will not be able to recapitalize the Bank. Is your answer the same?*

- No, the failure of the players in our tale to consider such an alternative is open to questions.

3. *What might such a deal have looked like?*

- The lenders force New West to agree to work constructively to achieve a sale that maximizes recoveries for the lenders, with the surplus, if any, going to the shareholders.
- The lenders engage a financial advisor or create a team from their midst to run a sales process and take steps to ensure regulatory compliance during the process.
- Following a short listing, a final buyer is identified in the bidding process and given a period of exclusivity.
- Legal counsel is engaged in connection with the above.
- Pre-clearance with the local financial supervisory authority is completed.
- Transaction closure occurs with, for example, a price that conforms to 96% of book value, divided between the lenders (95%) and the shareholders (1%), with the latter being to cover expenses, etc., for the shareholders.

4. *What would likely be the reaction of the local financial supervisory authority to such a solution to the Bank of Commerce case?*

  - As an alternative to a liquidation and assuming regulatory compliance, the local authorities would be expected to be supportive.

# Glossary of Terms

**Act of God** A naturally occurring exogenous phenomenon (not created by human beings) which is extraordinary, unforeseeable, and uncontrollable, such as hurricanes, tropical cyclones, tsunamis, earthquakes, volcano eruptions, fires, pandemics, and the like. These are also sometimes referred to in common parlance as "force majeure" (the latter is a legal doctrine to excuse liability for failure to perform, and which may or may not apply in such cases depending on the agreed contractual terms and applicable law).

**ALM or Asset Liability Management** The practice of managing financial risks that arise due to mismatches between the assets and liabilities.

**Antecedent transaction** A transaction which may be challenged (and invalidated, sometimes also resulting in a claw-back) in an insolvency proceeding, often due to its being concluded during de facto insolvency of the borrower, or due to its being undervalue (e.g., non-market and/or without sufficient consideration) and/or creating a preference in the settlement of one creditor's claim over other creditors' claims.

**Automatic stay** The moratorium (i.e., statutory prohibition) on enforcement of creditors' rights against a debtor and/or its assets, which arises under applicable insolvency law upon initiation of insolvency proceedings.

**Balance of Payments** The sum of the country's exports, imports, financial transfers, capital flows, and changes in FX reserves.

**Capital Flows** Inward or outward, consisting of foreign direct investment, portfolio investment, debt securities, and other forms of cross-border movements of capital.

**Capitalization of Interest** When accrued but unpaid interest is added to the outstanding principal amount of a loan or other credit instrument.

R. Marney and T. Stubbs, *Corporate Debt Restructuring in Emerging Markets*, https://doi.org/10.1007/978-3-030-81306-2

**Cash Flow**  Cash Flow is the increase or decrease cash held by a business, institution, or individual has. Operating cash flow or OCF is the amount of cash generated by the regular operating activities of a business within a specific time period. OCF consists of net income adjusted for non-cash items and changes in networking capital.

**Central bank swap facility**  A central bank liquidity swap is a type of swap used by a country's central bank to provide liquidity of its currency to another country's central bank. In a liquidity swap, the lending central bank uses its currency to buy the currency of another borrowing central bank at the market exchange rate and agrees to sell the borrower's currency back at a rate that reflects the interest accrued on the loan. The borrower's currency serves as collateral.

**Currency Peg**  The establishment of a specific fixed exchange rate of a local currency in terms of second currency.

**Current Account**  A country's trade balance plus net earnings on cross-border investments, and its net transfer payments. A current account deficit is a useful form of shorthand representing its operating deficit for which external funding must be arranged.

**Debt Service Coverage**  The relationship between cash available for debt service and the amount of these obligations. In corporate finance, an example is EBITDA (earnings before interest, taxes, depreciation, and amortization) to principal and interest due in a given period. In macroeconomics, this concept can be expressed in a number of ways, including for example liquid FX reserves to external interest and principal obligations due in a period.

**Debt to Equity Conversion**  The conversion of a senior or subordinated loan into equity of the borrower, at an agreed upon conversion ratio. A debt to equity conversion will significantly benefit the borrower's balance sheet, as it eliminates debt service requirements and helps the debtor to achieve statutory solvency.

**Devaluation v. depreciation**  A devaluation occurs when a country makes a conscious decision to lower its exchange rate in a fixed or semi-fixed exchange rate. A depreciation is when there is a fall in the value of a currency in a floating exchange rate. A depreciating exchange rate helps exports but causes imports and financial obligations to become more costly.

**Development finance institution (or DFI)**  A specialized (usually majority) governmentally owned institution which uses lending and investing in the private sector of low- and middle-income countries to promote its respective development mandate, which is often economic, social, political, and environmental. DFIs can be owned by a national government (for example, FMO of the Netherlands) or multilaterally by multiple governments. Examples of the latter include EBRD, BSTDB, AFIB, AIB, EIB, AIIB, IFC, and others. In the opening narrative of this book (on the Bank of Commerce), Martin's institution, the International Development Fund, is a fictional DFI.

**DIP financing**  New moneys (in the form of debt) advanced by a party to the debtor in insolvency proceedings. Some insolvency systems will give DIP financing a statutory priority in repayment over other existing claims against the debtor (including other existing unpaid loans). In a workout, where liquidity is problematic and must be resolved by the advance of new moneys by one or more lenders as part of the restructuring, the parties may try to replicate DIP financing contractually through subordination of the non-advancing lender(s) to the advancing lender(s).

**Dollarization** When the U.S. dollar is used in addition to or instead of the domestic currency of the local country. Dollarization provides benefits in the form of stabilizing elements of the macroeconomy, but takes away or limits the government's monetary policy and lender-of-last-resort capabilities.

**Early Exit** When a lender leaves a creditor group by selling and/or (partially) forgiving its debt. Where the exit is in the form of a repayment with partial forgiveness, clearly funding such repayment can be an issue, but because of the forgiveness (discount) element, the step often helps the debtor to achieve statutory solvency.

**Equity creditors** Creditors affiliated with the borrower, e.g., parent companies, subsidiaries, and/or sister companies (i.e., other group companies) who have some form of contractual or other claims against the borrower (and hence compete with other creditors generally in their claims against the borrower's estate).

**Export Credit Agency, or ECA** A public agency or entity (usually from an industrialized nation) providing government-backed loans, guarantees, and insurance cover to exporters from its home country for the export of goods and services to emerging markets. Collectively, ECAs are one of the largest categories of funders of private-sector projects in emerging markets.

**EWS or Early Warning System** A system for detecting early warning signals of a borrower's potential financial distress. There are many different approaches, but in their most simple form, the approach is to monitor the causes of insufficient cash flow to cover debt service obligations with the objective of detecting the threat of payment default early enough to undertake meaningful remedial actions.

**Foreign v. local currency lending** The currency in which the loan is denominated: foreign denotes when in a currency other than that of the country in which the borrower is domiciled, whilst local pertains to when the loan is dominated in the host country currency.

**FX reserves** Cash (foreign currencies) and other reserve assets such as gold held by a central bank or other monetary authority.

**FX Reserve Adequacy** A measure of a country's potential FX liquidity needs in adverse circumstances against which reserves could be held as a precautionary buffer. Its size relative to reserves could be a measure of a country's vulnerabilities and hence provide an indication of adequacy.

**Glass–Steagall** A U.S. law named for its congressional sponsors (also known as the Banking Act of 1933). It separated commercial and investment banking. It prohibited securities firms and investment banks from taking deposits, and commercial banks from dealing in non-governmental securities for customers, investing in non-investment grade securities for themselves, under-writing or distributing non-governmental securities, and affiliating (or sharing employees) with companies engaged in these activities. In 1999, the law was effectively repealed by the U.S. Gramm-Leach-Bliley Act.

**Global Financial Crisis** A period of extreme stress in global financial markets and banking systems between mid-2007 and early 2009.

**High, upper-middle, middle, and low income countries** The World Bank classifies the world's economies into four income groups—high, upper-middle, lower-middle, and low. We base this assignment on Gross National Income per capita (current US$).

**Holdout, or rogue** A lender unwilling to support a workout and hence posing the risk that it may call a default, accelerate and/or enforce rights against the borrower and/or its assets (in a multi-lender scenario, this often creates a domino effect of cross-defaults, leading to formal insolvency proceedings).

**INSOL II Principles** The voluntary principles for multi-creditor workouts developed by INSOL International in 2016–2017 (the Principles are set forth in full in Chapter 11).

**Insolvency** A state of insolvency (also known as bankruptcy), i.e., cash flow or asset insolvency, of a business entity, and/or formal insolvency proceedings related to such entity under applicable insolvency laws, as the context may imply. In this book, the authors generally use the term insolvency (rather than bankruptcy, though the terms are generally synonymous).

**Liquidity** The ease with which an asset, or security, can be converted into ready cash without affecting its market price.

**LMA** The London-based Loan Market Association at http://www.lma.eu.com. The LMA is an industry association based in London, UK formed to improve liquidity, efficiency, and transparency in the primary and secondary syndicated loan markets in Europe, the Middle East, and Africa. Its membership includes banks, institutional investors, law firms, service providers, and rating agencies.

**Loan covenants** The overall package of contractual obligations which a borrower undertakes under a loan document. These are generally categorized as "finan-cial covenants" (by which the borrower agrees to abide by key financial ratios, such as LTC, LTV, DSCR, ISCR, etc.), "information covenants" (requiring the borrower regularly to disclose certain financial information to the lender), "change of control covenants" (which may oblige the borrower's owners not to lose control over it, e.g., by selling shares in it), "affirmative covenants" (by which the borrower agrees to do certain things) and "negative covenants" (by which the borrower agrees not to do certain things).

**Non-performing loans (NPLs)** A classification used by financial institutions for loans and advances on which the principal is past due and on which no interest payments have been made for a period of time.

**Open currency position** An excess of assets (including off-balance sheet forward purchase contracts) over liabilities (including off-balance sheet forward sales contracts) (a "long position") held by a financial institution denominated a foreign currency, or an excess of liabilities (including off-balance sheet forward sales contracts) over assets (including off-balance sheet forward purchase contracts) (a "short position") held by a financial institution denominated a foreign currency.

**Orderly wind-down agreement** A restructuring agreement which implements an orderly wind-down of a borrower to prevent it from insolvent liquidation. Often in the form of an overlay agreement (i.e., signed by multiple participating lenders together with the borrower (and often with its major shareholder(s) and/or equity creditors)). (Other parties, such as a liquidation monitor, may also be party to the agreement.) Orderly wind-down agreements are discussed in more detail in Chapter 11.

**Orderly Wind-down v. Bankruptcyor Liquidation** An orderly wind-down is an arrangement contractually agreed between a borrower with its creditors allowing the borrower to continue to do business, but with the goal of ultimately winding the borrower's business down and achieving a solvent liquidation. This will ordinarily involve some form of (often substantial) debt forgiveness in the process. Although the debt forgiveness may trigger tax liability for the borrower (as imputed income), the payment of such liability is accounted for. An orderly wind-down keeps the borrower out of insolvency proceedings and often achieves a greater return for the lenders than a formal insolvency proceeding.

**Overlay restructuring agreement** A single restructuring agreement signed by multiple participating lenders together with the borrower (and often with its major shareholder(s) and/or equity creditors) in a workout inter alia amending the lenders' respective loans, waiving any prior defaults and otherwise implementing the workout, which may involve balance sheet and/or business restructuring. (Other parties, such as a project monitor, may also be party to the agreement.) Overlay restructuring agreements are discussed in more detail in Chapter 11.

**Pre-negotiation letter** A formal letter from a lender to a borrower (as a rule, countersigned by the borrower) confirming that the parties are discussing the terms of a possible future workout, designed to preserve the status quo between them and to disclaim any actual or implied waiver of rights or remedies or amendment of existing loan documents. A pre-negotiation letter reserves rights and remedies. It confirms the continued legal force and effect of the loan documents. It may contain confidentiality provisions. It is not a standstill agreement, nor does it create a standstill. It expressly confirms that the parties may terminate their discussion at any time and that their discussions are settlement discussions (and hence inadmissible before a tribunal). It has the legal force and effect of a contract.

**Provisions and Reserves (Loan Loss)** A provision is an income statement expense set aside as an allowance for uncollected loans and loan payments, whilst a reserve is the corresponding balance sheet entry. When loans are written off, the amount is deducted from the balance sheet reserve.

**Regulatory Capital** The amount of capital which a bank or other financial institution has to have as required by its respective financial regulator.

**Reservation of rights letter** A formal letter issued by a lender to a borrower (often unilateral and not required to be countersigned, but if circumstances dictate it, the lender may require that the borrower countersign it in order for it to enter into force). Such a letter is usually issued inter alia to reserve rights (as the name implies) and to disclaim any waiver of rights which might be inferred under applicable law from the lender's delay in enforcing its rights (e.g., waiver of the right to call a default and to accelerate).

**Secured debt** Often (but not always) synonymous with senior debt. Secured loans will generally be entitled to receive the proceeds from their respective security (e.g., pledges and other security interests, mortgages, assignments by way of security, etc.) in insolvency proceedings, subject to any waterfalls and procedures for security enforcement in such proceedings. The legal effectiveness of security may be attacked in an insolvency proceeding as preferential, undervalue, and/or otherwise invalid.

**Senior debt** Generally, secured loans with greater priority in an insolvency proceeding than other creditors (e.g., unsecured or subordinated), excluding so-called "super-priority" creditors, e.g., costs and expenses of the insolvency proceedings, DIP lenders (if any), employee payroll, (often but not always) tax obligations, and (for licensed banks or other FIs) depositors. Each country's own insolvency laws will determine the extent of "seniority" for a debtor.

**Set off** The legal right of a party to set off its own legal obligations to a counterparty against the legal obligations of that counterparty to it. Countries vary widely in their approach to set off in insolvency. Some permit it, whilst others do not, linked primarily to the historical development of their legal system. *See* P.R. Wood, op. cit., Chapter 15.

**Small and medium enterprises and lending** Lending to businesses whose assets, employees, and/or revenue, fall below a certain level. These companies are referred to as SMEs. The threshold will vary by country.

**Solvency** The capacity of a borrower to meet its long-term debts and financial obligations.

**Special Purpose Vehicle (SPV)** A separate legal entity created by an organization, often for the purpose of isolating assets and liabilities to isolate financial risk, to share risks, to transfer assets, and/or for other special business purposes..

**Standstill agreement** A formal legal agreement a borrower by its creditors (usually lenders or other financial creditors) implementing a standstill.

**Standstill, or standstill period** An agreed limited period of time given to a borrower in financial difficulties by its creditors (usually lenders or other financial creditors) during which inter alia the creditors agree not to call a default and accelerate and the borrower agrees not to take actions allowing leakage of value or change of creditor priorities, consistent with the INSOL II Principles, either on the basis of a formal standstill agreement or on a less formal basis (e.g., a gentleman's agreement or handshake).

**Subordination** A legal arrangement imposed by contract or statute by which a creditor (often referred to as a junior creditor) is given lower priority in repayment than other (more senior) creditors. Many emerging markets' insolvency and other laws do not expressly mention subordination per se as an enforceable arrangement in insolvency. By contrast, emerging markets' laws on regulated financial institutions(FIs) generally recognize subordinated loans for purposes of formation and maintenance of regulatory capital.

**Syndication** The practice of groups of lenders lending to one or more borrowers under a single loan facility (document), often using precedent facility forms developed by the LMA or other analogous associations of lenders. A syndicated loan is not a single loan but rather a collection of loans. The practice is described in more detail in Chapter 11, as relevant to workouts.

**Systemic risk** The risk of collapse of an entire financial system or entire market, as opposed to the risk associated with any one individual entity.

**Term sheet** Sometimes also called a heads of terms, memorandum of understanding, protocol of intent, etc., this is a summary of terms and conditions which the parties confirm they are prepared to agree, usually in a later, more detailed definitive agreement. The body (or operative terms) of a term sheet is usually non-legally binding (hence effectively a "gentleman's agreement" or "agreement to agree"), whilst it is common to see other, more technical terms (such as confidentiality, applicable law, and dispute resolution) as binding.

**Wrongful trading** The violation by a borrower's officers or directors (and/or sometimes shareholders and/or other controlling persons) of their statutory obligation to file for insolvency under the relevant insolvency law during the statutorily prescribed period, which period usually commences once indicia of the borrower's insolvency become apparent to them. Where such a violation occurs, these persons may become personally liable for further debts of the borrower, as they accrue. Each country's relevant insolvency law(s) will determine whether such a duty exists.

# Index

Printed by Printforce, the Netherlands